LETTERS OF FRANZ LISZT.

VOL. II.

1.

We welcome thee, from southern sunnier clime,
To England's shore,
And stretch glad hands across the lapse of [time
To thee once more.

11.

Full twice two decades swiftly have rolled by
Since thou wast here;
A meteor flashing through our northern sky
Thou didst appear.

111.

Thy coming now we greet with pleasure keen,
And loyal heart,
Adding tradition of what thou hast been
To what thou art.

1b.

No laurel can we weave into the crown
Long years entwine,
Nor add one honour unto the renown
Already thine:

b.

Yet might these roses waft to thee a breath
Of memory,
Recalling thy fair Saint Elizabeth
Of Hungary.

b1.

We welcome her, from out those days of old,
In song divine,
But thee we greet a thousand thousand fold,
The song is thine!

C. B.

LETTERS

OF

FRANZ LISZT.

COLLECTED AND EDITED

BY

LA MARA.

TRANSLATED BY

CONSTANCE BACHE.

VOL. II.

FROM ROME TO THE END.

WITH A FRONTISPIECE

GREENWOOD PRESS, PUBLISHERS
NEW YORK

ML
410
.L7
A31
Vol 2

36,523

Originally published in 1894
by Charles Scribners Sons

First Greenwood Reprinting, 1969

Library of Congress Catalogue Card Number 69-13973

PRINTED IN UNITED STATES OF AMERICA

CONTENTS.

CONTENTS. ix

SUPPLEMENT.

ROME.

1. To Dr. Franz Brendel.

[ROME,] *December 20th*, 1861.

DEAR FRIEND,

For the New Year I bring you nothing new; my soon ageing attachment and friendship remain unalterably yours. Let me hope that it will be granted to me to give you more proof of it from year to year.

Since the beginning of October I have remained without news from Germany. How are my friends Bronsart, Dräseke, Damrosch, Weissheimer? Give them my heartiest greetings, and let me see some notices of the onward endeavours and experiences of these my young friends, as also of the doings of the *Redactions-Höhle* * and the details of the Euterpe concerts.

Please send the numbers of the paper, from October onwards, to me at the address of the library Spithöver-Monaldini, Piazza di Spagna, Rome. Address your letter "*Herrn Commandeur Liszt*," Via Felice 113. "*Signor Commendatore*" is my title here; but don't be afraid that any Don Juan will stab me—still less that on my return to Germany I shall appear in your *Redactions-Höhle* as a guest turned to stone!—

Of myself I have really little to tell you. Although my acquaintance here is tolerably extensive and of an

---

* Editorial den.

3

attractive kind (if not *exactly* musical !), I live on the whole more retired than was possible to me in Germany. The morning hours are devoted to my work, and often a couple of hours in the evening also. I hope to have entirely finished the Elizabeth in three months. Until then I can undertake nothing else, as this work completely absorbs me. Very soon I will decide whether I come to Germany next summer or not. Possibly I shall go to Athens in April—without thereby forgetting the Athens of the elms ! . — .

First send me the paper, that I may not run quite wild in musical matters. At Spithöver's, where I regularly read the papers, there are only the *Augsburger Allgemeine*, the Berlin *Stern-Zeitung*,[1] and several French and English papers, which contain as good as nothing of what I care about in the domain of music.

Julius Schuberth wrote a most friendly letter to me lately, and asks me which of Dräseke's works I could recommend to him next for publication. To tell the truth it is very difficult for me in Rome to put myself in any publisher's shoes, even in so genial a man's as Julius Schuberth. In spite of this I shall gladly take an opportunity of answering him, and shall advise him to consult with Dräseke himself as to the most advisable opportunity of publishing this or that Opus of his, if a doubt should actually come over our Julius as to whether his publisher's omniscience were sufficiently enlightened on the matter !—

Remember me most kindly to your wife.

Yours most sincerely,

F. Liszt.

[1] Doubtless the *Kreuzzeitung.*

Please give my best greetings to Kahnt. Later on
I shall beg him for a copy of my songs for a very
charming Roman lady.

2. To A. W. Gottschalg, Cantor and Organist in Tieffurt.[1]

Dear Friend,

Although I cannot think otherwise than that
you remain ever equally true to me, yet the living
expression of your kindly feelings towards me is
always a pleasure and a comfort. First of all then
accept my warmest thanks for your two letters, which
bring back to me the best impressions of your morning
and evening visits to me in my blue room on the
Altenburg.

It goes without saying that I have no objection to
make to the publication of the Andante from the
Berg Symphony in the Jubilee Album in honour of
Johann Schneider. I only beg, dear friend, that you
will look the proof over accurately, and carefully correct
any omissions or mistakes in the manuscript.

I should be very glad if I could send you a new
Organ work, but unfortunately all incentive to that
sort of work is wanting to me here ; and until the

---

[1] "*Der legendarische Cantor*" [the legendary Cantor] the Master
jokingly named this faithful friend of his. "I value him as a
thoroughly honest, able, earnestly striving and meritorious comrade
in Art, and interest myself in the further progress—which is his due,"
wrote Liszt to the late Schuberth. Meanwhile Gottschalg was long
ago advanced to the post of Court organist in Weimar. He is widely
known as the editor of the "*Chorgesang*" [chorus singing] and of the
"Urania."

Tieffurt Cantor makes a pilgrimage to Rome all my
organ wares will certainly remain on the shelf.

Ad vocem of the Tieffurt Cantor, I will tell you that
I have been thinking of him very particularly these
last few days, whilst I was composing St. Francis's
Hymn of Praise (" *Cantico di San Francesco* "). The
song is a development, an offspring as it were, a
blossom of the Chorale " in dulci jubilo," for which of
course I had to employ Organ. But how could I be
writing an Organ work without immediately flying to
Tieffurt in imagination ?—And lo, at the entrance to
the church our excellent Grosse [1] met me with his
trombone, and I recollected an old promise—namely, to
compose a " pièce " for his use on Sundays. I immediately set to work at it, and out of my " *Cantico* " has
now arisen a *Concertante* piece for Trombone and Organ.
I will send you the piece as an *Easter egg* by the
middle of April. [2] Meanwhile here are the opening
chords :—

[1] The trombonist of the Weimar orchestra (died 1874), who was
so faithfully devoted to Liszt, and whom the latter remembered in
his will.

[2] Published by Kahnt in Leipzig.

and on a lovely evening in May will you play the whole with Grosse in your church at Tieffurt, and perpetuate me with Organ and Trombone!—

It has struck me that your name is not mentioned among the fellow-workers in the Johann Schneider Jubilee Album. If there is still time and space you might perhaps contribute your arrangement of the Fugue from the Dante Symphony (with the ending which I composed to it for you). This proposal is open to amendment, on the supposition that Härtels are willing to agree to it—and, above all, that it suits you.

.—. N.B.—I beg you most particularly to make *no* further use of the two Psalms "By the waters of Babylon," of which you have a copy, because I have undertaken to make two or three *essential* alterations in them, and I wish them only to be made known and published in their present form. I send the new manuscript at the same time as the *Cantico di San Francesco*.

My best greetings to your wife, and rest assured always of my sincere thanks, and of the complete harmony of my ideas with your own.

F. LISZT.

ROME, *March 11th, 1862.*

When I am sending several manuscripts at Easter, I will write a couple of letters to Weimar and thank Jungmann [1] for his letter. I feel the want of time almost as much in Rome as in Weimar, and I have observed a strict Fast in correspondence as a rule, so

---

[1] A pupil of Liszt's in Weimar; died there in September 1892.

that for three months past I have hardly sent as many as three to four letters to Germany.

Remember me most particularly to Herr *Regierungsrath* Müller.[1]

3. To Dr. Franz Brendel.[*]

DEAR FRIEND,

Your friendly letter has again brought me a whiff of German air, which is all the more welcome to me here as I have not too much of it. One sees extremely few German papers in Rome—also I read them very irregularly—and my correspondents from Germany are limited to two, of whom friend Gottschalg, my *legendary* Tieffurt Cantor, is the most zealous. His letters flow from his heart—and are therefore always welcome to me.

For all of good news that you tell me I give you twofold thanks. Firstly, because you have for the most part brought it about, prefaced it, and seen it through. And then, because you tell it me in so friendly a fashion. Although I have long been prepared to bear the *fiasco* of my works quietly and unmoved, yet still it is pleasant to me to learn that the *Faust* Symphony in Leipzig did not have such a very bad fate.[2] Do not fail, dear friend, to give Herr Schnorr my best thanks—and if perchance my songs would be a little pleasure to him will Kahnt

---

[1] A friend of Liszt's, a multifarious writer on music; died 1876.

[*] Autograph in the possession of Herr Alexander Meyer Cohn in Berlin.

[2] In one of the "Euterpe" concerts, under Bronsart's conducting, at which Schnorr of Carolsfeld sang the tenor solo.

be so good as to send Schnorr a copy (*bound*) at my order ?

With regard to the Bronsart affair, I sincerely regret that I had not the opportunity of smoothing matters down sooner. Between people of one mind dissension and variance should never appear—much less lead to an outbreak. As you ask me for my opinion, I openly confess that *in the main* Bronsart appears to me perfectly justified in vindicating his choice of new compositions for the musical directors, in spite of the fact that the two or three experiments he has made do not show in favour of the principle (as seen by the consequences). But between ourselves we must not conceal the fact that a great part of the laxity and corruption of our musical condition in Germany (as also elsewhere) is to be attributed to the too great—or too petty—yielding and pliancy of conductors and music-directors. I well know that the Euterpe Committee nourishes and cherishes quite another idea than that of the company X. Y. Z., or of the Court Theatre directors A. B. C. D. Yet the question constantly arises—Shall the cook cook ? Shall the coachman drive ?—Ergo let the musician also have his own way. The harm that may spring from that is not so very terrible.

On the other side, I consider a change of persons in the management of a *new* institution is not desirable. In intellectual movements in particular the leaders of them are especially recommended to keep themselves *conservative* as regards their people. The public requires *definiteness* before all else—and just this is endangered by a change of persons. The substitute for B., whom you mention to me (his name also begins with B.), is

certainly highly to be recommended in all that concerns
talent, position, and I think also worthy character;
none the less do I vote very *decidedly* that Bronsart be
retained—*if possible.*

I do not need to add, dear friend, that this opinion
of mine is a purely *objective* one. I have not heard a
word from Bronsart since last September, and, as I
said to you before, my musical news from Germany
is limited to two, or at most three letters which Gottschalg wrote me.

With the wish that all difficulties may be smoothed
in the best way by your intelligent gentleness and forbearance, I remain your warmly devoted

F. Liszt.

[Rome,] *April 12th,* 1862.

P.S.—More next time (though little of interest to
you, as absolutely nothing occurs here that could touch
you closely).—I am preparing to stay here for the
summer, and somewhat longer.—In order not to lose
the post I only send you to-day these few lines.

4. To Madame Jessie Laussot in Florence.[1]

Your charming lines, Madame, reached me at
the beginning of Holy Week. At that moment one
no longer belongs to oneself in Rome; and I have felt

---

[1] Madame Laussot, an English lady, became later the wife of Dr.
Carl Hillebrand, the celebrated writer. She was the intimate friend
of Liszt, Von Bülow, etc., and is herself a musician of great repute, to
whom many artists of note, Sgambati, Bache, Buonamici, etc., owe
much of the success of their career. She started a musical society in
Florence, the "*Società Cherubini,*" which she conducted for many
years, and introduced there much of the best music of Germany
(Liszt's included).

this more than others, for the services and ceremonies of the Sistine Chapel and of St. Peter's, to which I attached a special musical interest, have absorbed all my time during the last fortnight. Pray excuse me therefore for not having thanked you sooner for your kind remembrance, which touches me much.

Some one has made a mistake in telling you that I am coming to Florence. I have no longer any taste for moving about from one place to another, and, unless something very unforeseen happens, I shall not stir from here so soon. Rome is a more convenient place than others for those who ask nothing better than to work in their own fashion. Now, although I have become very indifferent as to the fate of what I write, *work* none the less continues to be the first need of my nature. I write therefore simply to write—without any other pretensions or care—and for this it suits me best to remain in one place.

Will you be so kind, Madame, as to give my very affectionate respects to Madame Ritter,[1] to which please add my best remembrances to her family, and pray accept also the expression of my very sincere and affectionate regards.

F. LISZT.

May 3rd, 1862. (VIA FELICE, 113—ROME.)

5. TO DR. FRANZ BRENDEL.

ROME, *June 12th*, 1862.

Grand, sublime, immeasurably great things have come to pass here lately. The Episcopate of the whole

---

[1] Mother of Carl Ritter—Wagner's friend—and of Alexander Ritter, the composer of *Der faule Hans*.

world assembled here round the Holy Father, who performed the ceremony of the canonisation of the Japanese
martyrs at Whitsuntide in the presence of more than
300 bishops, archbishops, patriarchs, and cardinals.
I must abstain, dear friend, from giving you any
picture of the overpowering moment in which the
Pope intoned the Te Deum ; for in Protestant lands
that which I might call the spiritual illumination is
wanting. Let us therefore, without any other transition, return to our everyday musical matters !

I am convinced that your determination to make a
change in the choice of conductors of the Euterpe has
been made only after mature consideration. . — . In
my last letter I pointed out, as the chief thing, that in
concert societies the principle of stability in the matter
of the Musical Direction is the most important thing,
whereby I did not in the least mean to say that one
must on that account agree to extreme consequences—
or rather inconsequences. Well, as your decision is
made, any further discussion is useless. Blassmann [1]
has now to approve himself, and actively to fulfil the
favourable expectations which his talent and good name
justify. So be it, and as Schuberth says, *Punktum* [a
full stop].

As regards the place of meeting for the next *Tonkünstler-Versammlung* I am quite of your opinion. First
of all I advise you to consult Bülow. Owing to his long
connection with the Court at Carlsruhe he is best
qualified to take the preliminary measures ("to pave
the way"!). If the Grand Duke and Grand Duchess
take up the matter favourably, then without doubt all

---

[1] He moved to Dresden some years later, and there he died.

that is requisite and necessary will be done in the most desirable manner. The most essential things are :

(*a*) Letting us have the theatre free of charge for two to three evenings—(as at *Weimar*—would not it perhaps be best to mention this in the 1st letter ?).

(*b*) Official preparatory measures by the Intendant to ensure the co-operation of the Carlsruhe orchestra and chorus, also free of charge.

You will have to consult more fully with Dr. Devrient and Kalliwoda as to the best time for it. But the thing to be done before all else is to gain the Grand Duke's interest—and if you think it would be practicable for me to write a few lines to H.R.H. later on I will do so with pleasure. I only beg that you will give me exact particulars of the steps already made and their results.

For my part I think that to Bülow, *a priori*, ought to be entrusted the conducting of the Musical Festival, and this point should be at once mentioned as settled in the introductory letter to the Grand Duke. Otherwise Bülow's position in the affair would not be sufficiently supported.

To sum up briefly : Request Bülow to undertake the conductorship of the Musical Festival ; and address the Grand Duke of Baden, either by letter or by word of mouth (as opportunity may warrant), with the request that H.R.H. would graciously support the proposed Musical Festival of the third *Tonkünstler-Versammlung*, by giving it his patronage, as the Grand Duke of Weimar did last year, etc., etc.

. — . That excellent Pohl has quite forgotten me. I asked him, through Gottschalg, to send me my *Gesam-*

melte Lieder [complete songs], the Dante Symphony (in score and arrangement for 2 Pianos), the 4-hand Symphonic Poems, and a couple of copies of my Catalogue (published by Härtel).

I have been waiting in vain for these for two months. A few days ago I wrote to Frau von Bülow to send Pohl an execution; perhaps this may help matters at length !

The Berlioz parts have remained at Weimar. Grosse knows about them—and possibly they have also gone to Pohl with the rest of the scores. As soon as they are found I shall be happy to make a present of them to the library of the *Musikverein* for their use, as well as the scores, and I *authorise* you with pleasure, dear friend, to do the same with the score and parts of the Gran Mass.

The newspaper has not reached me from Pohl any more than the parcel.

Hearty greetings to your wife from yours in all friendship,

F. L.

6. To Dr. Franz Brendel.

DEAR FRIEND,

Well, as the parcel has come at last, Pohl shall not be scolded any more, and his "innocence" shall shine out in full splendour ! . — .

I have just received a few lines from Berlioz; Schuberth, whom I commissioned, before I left, to send the dedication-copy of the Faust score to Berlioz, has again in his incompetent *good nature* forgotten it, and perhaps even from motives of economy has not had

the *dedication-plate* engraved at all ! !—Forgive me, dear
friend, if I trouble you once more with this affair, and
beg you to put an *execution* on Schuberth in order to
force a copy with the *dedication-page* from him. The
dedication shall be just as simple as that of the Dante
Symphony, containing only the name of the dedicatee,
as follows,

"To Hector Berlioz."

After this indispensable matter has been arranged
I beg that you will be so kind as to have a tasteful
copy, *bound in red or dark green*, sent, perhaps through
Pohl (?), to Berlioz at Baden (where he will be at the
beginning of August). In case neither Pohl nor his
wife should go to Baden this summer (which however
I scarcely expect will be the case), send the copy to
Fräulein Genast (who, as I learn from the *"Zeitschrift"*
[periodical], is at present in Carlsruhe) with the request
that she will give it to Berlioz.

Is there not any talk of bringing out an arrangement
of the Faust Symphony for 2 Pianofortes?—Schuberth
is sure to have far greater things in contemplation, and
I almost regret having incommoded him by giving up
the manuscripts !—

None the less please take him to task about it, or,
better, bully him into *action* with *"Faust-Recht"* [Faust
rights or Faust justice]. In truth the final chorus of
Part III. of the Faust tragedy, "faithful to the spirit
of Part II. as composed by Deutobold-Symbolizetti-
Allegoriowitsch-Mystifizinsky"—

"Das Abgeschmackteste
Hier ward es geschmeckt,

Das Allvertrackteste
Hier war es bezweckt " *—

can often be applied to matters of publishing. And
while I am touching on this, to me, very disagreeable
chapter, may I also take the opportunity of inquiring
how long our amiable friend and patron Julius Schuberth is intending to ignore the 2 Episodes from Lenau's
Faust (*Nächtlicher Zug*—and "*Mephisto Walzer*"), which
I recommended to his good graces more than a year
ago, and gave him in manuscript ?

Must the pages perchance become quite mouldy, or
will he bring them out as an *œuvre posthume* [posthumous
work] ? I am tired of doing silent homage to this
noble mode of proceedings, and intend next time to help
the publisher out of all his perplexities † by putting the
manuscripts back in their place again.—

"O Freunde, nicht diese Töne, sondern lasst uns
angenehmere anstimmen ! " ‡ (I am perhaps not quoting
exactly, although the *sense* of the apostrophe remains
clearly present, especially in musical *enjoyments* and
experiences !)

* A parody on the concluding lines of Goethe's *Faust*. The parody
may be freely translated as follows :—

> " The most insipid
> Here was tasted ;
> In queerest nonsense
> Here all was wasted."

† Untranslatable pun on "Verleger" and "Verlegenheiten."

‡ A quotation from Schiller's "Ode to Joy " in Beethoven's Choral
Symphony : "O friends, not tones like these, but brighter ones let
us sing."

Amongst the "more pleasant" things I at once place much information given in your letter and the newspaper (which reached me at the same time in some 16 numbers with Pohl's parcel). My most earnest wishes are, first and foremost, bound up in the complete prospering, upspringing, and blossoming of the "grain of mustard-seed" of our *Allgemeine Deutsche Musik-Verein*. With God's help I will also support this in other fashion than mere "wishes." According to my opinion the third *Tonkünstler-Versammlung* will be the chief factor in strengthening and extending the *Allgemeine Deutsche Musik-Verein*, which comprises in itself the entire development and advancement of Art.

Various reasons led me to recommend Carlsruhe to you in my last letter as the most suitable place for the third *Tonkünstler-Versammlung*, that is, supposing that H.R.H. the Grand Duke gives his countenance to the matter, and grants us favourable conditions with regard to the disposal of the theatre, orchestra, and chorus. It behoves Bülow, as conductor of the musical performances, to undertake to "pave the way" towards a favourable promise on the Grand Duke's side. Within two to three months the necessary preliminaries can be fixed, and I shall then expect fuller tidings from you about the further plans and measures.

Without wishing to make any valid objection to Prague—rather with all due acknowledgment of what Prague has already accomplished and may still accomplish—yet it seems to me that the present political relations of the Austrian monarchy would make it inopportune to hold the *Tonkünstler-Versammlung* in

Prague just now. On the other hand I am of opinion that a more direct influence than has yet been possible on South Germany, which is for the most part in a stagnating condition, would be of service. Stuttgart in particular, through Pruckner, Singer, Stark, etc., might behave at it differently from what it did at a previous Musical Festival in Carlsruhe!

Dr. Gille's interest in the statutes and deliberations of the M.V. [Musik-Verein] is very advantageous, as also Pohl's previous removal to Leipzig. . —. The constant intercourse with you, together with the Leipzig acids and gases, will be sure to suit him well.

From Weimar I have received a good deal of news lately from Count Beust, Dingelstedt, Gille, and Stör. To the latter my answer will be little satisfactory ; but I cannot continue with him on any other road, and let the overpowering *Dominant* of his spasmodic vanity serve as the *Fundamental note* of our relations.

I am writing to Gille by the next post, and also to Müller, who rejoiced me lately by his *Erinnerungs-Blatt* [remembrance] from Weimar, (in the 8th November issue of the " *Zeitschrift,*" which I have only now received). Will you, dear friend, when you have an opportunity, give my best thanks to Kulke for his article upon Symphony and Symphonic Poem— and also the enclosed lines to Fräulein Nikolas, from whom I have received a charming little note ?

Already more than 140 pages of the score of my *Elizabeth* are written out complete (in my own little cramped scrawl). But the final chorus—about 40 pages—and the piano-arrangement have still to be done. By the middle of August I shall send the entire work to Carl Götze at Weimar to copy, together with the Canticus of St. Francis, which I composed in the spring.[1] It would certainly be pleasanter for me if I could bring the things with me—but, *between ourselves*, I cannot entertain the idea of a speedy return to Germany. If later there seems a likelihood of a termination to my stay in Rome, you, dear friend, shall be the first to hear of it.

With hearty greetings to your wife, I remain

Yours in sincere and friendly attachment,

F. Liszt.

Rome, *July 12th*, 1862.

Your little commission about Löwenberg shall be attended to. Let me soon have news of you and of my intimate friends again. There is absolutely nothing to tell you from here that could interest you. In spite of the heat I shall spend the summer months in Rome.

7. To Dr. Franz Brendel.*

What a delightful bunch of surprises your letter brings me, dear friend ! So Pohl has really set to work on the Faust brochure—and Schuberth is actually not going to let the piano-arrangement of the Faust Symphony lie in a box till it is out of date. How curious it all sounds, just because it is so exactly the right thing and what I desired !—If you are back in Leipzig please send me soon a couple of copies of

---

[1] "Cantico del Sole," for baritone solo, men's chorus, and organ. Kahnt.

* Letters 7, 8, 9, 18, and 24 to Brendel have been partially published in La Mara's "*Musikerbriefe*" (Letters of Musicians), Vol. II.

the Faust brochure (those numbers of the journal
containing Pohl's articles have not reached me), and
also send me the 2-pianoforte arrangement of the
Faust Symphony (a few copies when convenient).
I have as yet received nothing of the parcel which
Kahnt announced as having sent me with some of my
4-hand things; and as I have fished out here a very
talented young pianist, Sgambati [1] by name, who makes
a first-rate partner in duets, and who, for example,
plays the Dante Symphony boldly and correctly, it
would be a pleasure to me to be able to go through the
whole cycle of the Symphonic Poems with him. Will
you be so good therefore, dear friend, as to ask Härtel
for the whole lot in the 2-pianoforte arrangement (a
double copy of each Symphonic Poem, for with *one
copy alone* I can do nothing, as I myself can only play
the thing from notes!), and also the 4-hand arrangement, with the exception of the *Festklänge*, which
Härtels have already sent me?

Besides these, I expect in the same parcel the
Marches which Schuberth has published (the " *Goethe
Marsch* " and the Duke of Coburg) and the *Künstler
Festzug* [Artists' procession] (for 4 hands), which I
ordered previously.—

The *Legend of St. Elizabeth* is written out to the very
last note of the score; I have now only to finish a part
of the piano arrangement, and the 4-hand arrangement
of the Introduction, the Crusaders' March, and the final
procession—which shall be done by the end of this

---

[1] A pupil of Liszt's, and now one of the first pianoforte players and
composers of Italy; has been, since 1871, Professor at the *Accademia
Sta. Cecilia* in Rome.

month at latest. Then I send the whole to Weimar to be copied, together with a couple of other smaller manuscripts. What will be its ultimate fate will appear according as . . . Meanwhile I will try one or two little excursions into the country (to Albano, Frascati, Rocca di Papa—and a little farther still, to the "Macchia serena" near Corneto, where in earlier times much robbery and violence took place!), and before the end of September I hope to be able to set steadily to work again, and to continue my musical deeds of "robbery and murder"! Would that I only could hear, like you, the Sondershausen orchestra, and were able to conjure friend Stein and his brave phalanx into the *Colosseum*! The locality would assuredly be no less attractive than the " Loh," [1] and Berlioz's Harold Symphony, or *Ce que l'on entend sur la montagne*,[2] would sound there quite "sondershäuslich " [curious].* I often imagine the orchestra set up there, with the execrated instruments of percussion in an arcade—our well-wishers Rietz, Taubert, and other braggarts of criticism close by (or in the Aquarium!)—the directors of the *Deutsche Musik-Verein* resting on the " Pulvinare," and the members all around resting on soft cushions, and making a show in the reserved seats of the Subsellia, as senators and ambassadors used to do!—

Tell Stein of this idea, and give him my most friendly thanks for all the intelligent care and pains that he so

---

[1] The Sondershausen concerts are, as is well known, given in the "Lohgarten."

[2] One of Liszt's Symphonic Poems.

* Play of words on Sondershausen and "sonderbar" or "sonderlich."

very kindly gives to my excommunicated compositions. As regards the performances of the Sondershausen orchestra I am quite of your opinion, and I repeat that they are not only not outdone, but are even not often equalled in their sustained richness, their judicious and liberal choice of works, as well as in their precision, drilling, and refinement.—It is only a shame that no suitable concert-hall has been built in Sondershausen. The orchestra has long deserved such an attention; should such a thing ever fall to their lot, pray urge upon Stein to spread out the Podium of the orchestra as far as possible, and not to submit to the usual *limited space*, as they made the mistake of doing in the *Gewandhaus*, the *Odeonsaal* in Munich, etc., etc., and also, alas, in Löwenberg. The concert-hall of the Paris Conservatoire offers in this respect the right proportions, and a good part of the effect produced by the performances there is to be ascribed to this favourable condition.—

According to what I hear Bülow is not disposed to mix himself up in the preliminaries of the next *Tonkünstler-Versammlung*. Accordingly some one else must be entrusted with the afore-mentioned task in Carlsruhe, although Bülow was the best suited for it. If you do not care to enter at once into direct communication with Devrient, Pohl would be the best man to "pioneer" the way. It would not be any particular trouble to him to go from Baden to Carlsruhe, and to persuade Devrient to favour the matter. This is before all else needful, for without Devrient's co-operation nothing of the sort can be undertaken in Carlsruhe. If the *Tonkünstler-Versammlung* takes place not out of the theatre season, then one or more theatrical performances can be given in conjunction with it, especially of Gluck's Operas; as also an ultra-classical Oratorio of Händel's might well be given over to the Carlsruhe Vocal Unions. . — .

What "*astonishing* things" are you planning, dear friend? This word excites my curiosity; but, on the other hand, I share your superstition to speak only of actions accomplished ("faits accomplis"). In Schelle you will gain a really valuable colleague. Has his "History of the Sistine Chapel" come out yet? If so, please be so good as to send me the book with the other musical things.—

My daughter, Frau von Bülow, writes to me that Wagner's new work *Die Meistersinger* is a marvel, and amongst other things she says :—

"These 'Meistersinger' are, to Wagner's other conceptions, much the same as the *Winter's Tale* is to Shakespeare's other works. Its phantasy is found in gaiety and drollery, and it has called up the Nuremberg of the Middle Ages, with its guilds, its poet-artisans, its pedants, its cavaliers, to draw forth the most fresh laughter in the midst of the highest, the most ideal, poetry. Exclusive of its sense and the destination of the work, one might compare the artistic work of it with that of the *Sacraments-Häuschen* of St. Lawrence (at Nuremberg). Equally with the sculptor, has the composer lighted upon the most graceful, most fantastic, most pure form,—boldness in perfection; and as at the bottom of the *Sacraments-Häuschen* there is Adam Kraft, holding it up with a grave and collected air, so in the *Meistersinger* there is Hans Sachs, calm, profound, serene, who sustains and directs the action," etc.

This description pleased me so much that, when once I was started on the subject, I could not help sending you the long quotation. The Bülows, as you know, are with Wagner at Biebrich—at the end of this month there is to be a performance of *Lohengrin* at Frankfort under Wagner's direction. There must not fail to be a full account of this in the *Neue Zeitschrift*, and for this I could recommend my daughter as the best person. The letters in which she has written to me here and there of musical events in Berlin and elsewhere are really charming, and full of the finest understanding and striking wit.—

Berlioz was so good as to send me the printed pianoforte edition of his Opera *Les Troyens*. Although for Berlioz's works pianoforte editions are plainly a deception, yet a cursory reading through of *Les Troyens* has nevertheless made an uncommonly powerful impression on me. One cannot deny that there is enormous power in it, and it certainly is not wanting in delicacy —I might almost say *subtilty*—of feeling.

Pohl will let you know about the performance of Berlioz's comic Opera *Beatrice and Benedict* in Baden, and I venture to say that this Opera, which demands but little outside aids, and borrows its subject from a well-known Shakespeare play, will meet with a favourable reception. Berlin, or any other of the larger theatres of Germany, would certainly risk nothing of its reputation by including an Opera of Berlioz in its *répertoire*.[1] It is no good to try to excuse oneself, or

[1] This took place a quarter of a century later.

to make it a reason, by saying that Paris has committed a similar sin of omission—for things in which other people fail we should not imitate. Moreover Paris has been for years past developing a dramatic activity and initiative which Germany is far from attaining—and if special, regrettable personal circumstances prevent Berlioz from performing his works in Paris, the Germans have nothing to do with that.

Hoping soon for news of you (even if not about the "*astonishing things*"), I remain, dear friend, with faithful devotion,

F. LISZT.

ROME, *August 10th*, 1862. VIA FELICE, 113.

Who has corrected the proofs of the Faust Symphony? Please impress upon Schuberth not to send out into the world any unworthy editions of my works. Bülow is so good as to undertake the final revision, if only Schuberth will take the trouble to ask him to do so.

8. TO DR. FRANZ BRENDEL.

VIA FELICE, 113 [ROME], *August 29th* [1862].

DEAR FRIEND,

In explanation of the main point of your last letter (which crossed mine), namely, the question as to *where* the next *Tonkünstler-Versammlung* is to be held, let me add the following in colloquial form.

I should not, without further proof, exactly like to consider Carlsruhe as a town altogether unsuitable for the purpose—although Pohl and Bülow are afraid it is, and have various reasons for assuming it to be so. As regards Bülow, I have already asked you not to trouble him with any of the preliminary details. When the time comes, he is certain to do *his* part—that is, more than could be expected or demanded of him. Only he must not be tormented with secondary considerations, not even where, owing to his position and antecedents, he is best known (for instance, in Carlsruhe, as already said). His individuality is such an exceptional one that its singularities must be allowed scope. Hence let us meanwhile leave him out of the question, he being what he is, with this *reservation*—that he undertakes to conduct the musical performances—as I hope and trust he will finally arrange to do. But again as to Carlsruhe, I would propose that unless you have important, positive objections to the place, you should write to the Grand Duke yourself and beg him in my name to take the *Musik-Verein* under his patronage, etc.—The worst that could happen to me in return would be to receive a courteously worded refusal ; this, it is true, is not a kind of thing I cultivate as a rule, but as a favour to such an honourable association I would gladly face the danger, in the hope that it might prove of some use and advantage.

Write and tell me, therefore, in what spirit Seifriz has answered you, and what information Riedel has gathered in Prague. Prague, for *certain* (yet rather uncertain ?) considerations, is indeed much to be recommended ; only one would need, in some measure, to have the support of the musical authorities and notabilities of the place, as well as that of the civic corporation (because of municipal approbation and *human* patronage). In short, if the *Tonkünstler-Versammlung* were taken up and set in a *good light* there by a few active and influential persons, everything else would be easy to arrange, whereas otherwise all further steps would be so much trouble thrown away. I cannot altogether agree with your opinion, dear friend, that "the difficulties would in no way be greater in Prague than in Leipzig"—you forget that *you* yourself, in the capacity of a Leipzig citizen, removed most of the difficulties by your unswerving perseverance and your personal influence, whereas in Prague you could act only through the intervention of others. The question, therefore, is whether you can confidently reckon upon reliable friends there.

Until I receive further news from you, it seems to me that Bülow's idea of *preferring Löwenberg to all other places* is one very well worth consideration. Our amiable Prince would certainly not fail to give his earnest support to the *Tonkünstler-Versammlung*, and the small *miseries* of the little town of Löwenberg might be put up with or put down, for a few days at all events. Think this plan over again carefully, and do not look at Löwenberg through the glasses of our excellent friend Frau von Bonsart!—Of course a date would have to be fixed when the orchestra is assembled there, and the whole programme arranged with Seifriz and drawn up with his friendly co-operation. In my opinion many things might be possible in Löwenberg that could scarcely be broached elsewhere; and as, in fact, Bülow conceived the idea I expressly recommend it you as a means for "paving the way" to a happy issue.—

Together with your last letter I received three of the Faust essays by Pohl. I shall send him my warm thanks

for them by next post, and shall add, for his biblio-
graphical and statistical edification, the little remark that
Mademoiselle Bertin had an *Italian* opera performed in
Paris before the Revolution of July, entitled *Faust* or
Fausto. Before Pohl's articles appear in pamphlet form
I should like to have read them all through—but if he
is in a hurry about them, do not mention this to him ;
perhaps, however, if it did not make the pamphlet too
thick, it might be well to include Pohl's essay on the
Dante Symphony (as it appeared in Härtel's edition of
the score).

In spite of the unsatisfactory performance of the
Dante Symphony in Dresden (partly, moreover, the
fault of the bad, incorrectly written orchestral parts,
and my careless conducting), and without regard to
the *rapture* of the *spiritual* substance (a matter which
the general public tolerates only when demanded by
the higher authority of *tradition*, and then immediately
gapes at it upside down !)—in spite, therefore, of this
grievous Dresden performance, which brought me only
the one satisfaction of directly setting to work at some
not unessential improvements, simplifications, and
eliminations in the score—that had taken hold of me
during the rehearsals and the performance, and which
I felt at once, without troubling myself about the
audience present . . .—Now, what was I about to say,
after all these parentheses and digressions ? Yes, I
remember now :—the Dante Symphony is a work that
does not need to be ashamed of its title,—and what
you tell me of the impression produced by the *Berg-
symphonie* (in Sondershausen) strengthens me in my
presumption. Hence I should be glad to see the

preface by Pohl printed again, and placed at the end
of the Faust pamphlet; for, considering what most
people are, they require to *read* first, before attaining
the capacity for *learning, understanding, feeling,* and
appreciating.— —

The edition of the Faust Symphony (arranged for
two pianofortes) is worthy of all praise, and, in the
language of music-sellers, elegant. The printer has
done well in so arranging the type that a number of
lines are brought on to one page and a number of bars
on to every line. Schuberth shall ere long receive a
complimentary note from me, together with a few
" proof " indications for the Faust Symphony. But, in
fact, I have come across only a few and unimportant
errors as yet.

The publication of Lenau's two *Faust Episodes* (a
point Pohl touches upon in his essay with fine dis-
crimination) Schuberth might undertake according as
he sees fit. I am pretty well indifferent as to whether
the pianoforte arrangement or the score appears first ;
only, the *two pieces* must appear simultaneously, the
" *Nächtlicher Zug* " as No. 1 and " *Mephisto's Walzer* "
as No. 2. There is no thematic connection between
the two pieces, it is true ; but nevertheless they *belong
together,* owing to the contrast of ideas. A *Mephisto* of
that species could proceed only from a *poodle* of that
species !— . — .

With the *Elizabeth* (of which I have now to write
only the pianoforte score, which will take about a
fortnight's time) I am also sending to Weimar the
three Psalms in their new definitive form. It would
please me if, some day, a performance of the 13th

Psalm, "How long wilt Thou forget me, O Lord?"
could be given. The tenor part is a very important
one;—I have made *myself* sing it, and thus had King
David's feelings poured into me in flesh and blood!—

It is to be hoped that Schnorr will be kind enough
to adapt himself to the tenor part (the only solo voice
in the Psalm, but which affects everything, and pene-
trates and sways chorus and orchestra). Theodor
Formes sang the part very well eight years ago in
Berlin; but that performance at Stern's Concert was
to me only a *first trial* performance!—

With notes alone nothing can be accomplished; one
thirsts for soul, spirit, and actual life. Ah! composing
is a misery, and the pitiful children of my Muse appear
to me often like foundlings in a hospital, wandering
about only as Nos. so and so!—

Please give my best thanks to Schnorr for having
so kindly interested himself in my orphaned *Songs*.
His better self-consciousness—the God we carry in
our breasts—requite him for it!—My daughter, Frau
von Bülow, writes and tells me marvels about Schnorr
and his wife, and of the performance of *Tristan* at
Wagner's in Biebrich. If only we possessed electric
telegraphs in favour of musical ubiquity! Assuredly
I would not make any misuse of them, and only rarely
put myself in correspondence with the music-mongers;
but Tristan and Isolde are my "soul's longing"!

The French journals contain nothing but praise and
exclamations of delight at the success of *Benedict and
Beatrice*, Berlioz's new opera, which was performed in
Baden. Pohl is sure to give you a full report of it.
To judge from his essay, the tenor solo at the end

of the Faust Symphony caused less offence in Leipzig (it was the stumbling-block in the Weimar performance, so much so that influential and well-disposed friends have urgently advised me to strike out the solo and chorus and to end the Symphony with the C major common chord of the orchestra). It was really my intention at first to have the whole Chorus mysticus sung *invisibly*—which, however, would be possible only at performances given in theatres, by having the curtain lowered. Besides which, I felt doubtful whether the sound would not have thus become too indistinct. . . .

However it may be with this and other things, I will not fail to exercise patience and goodwill—but neither will I make too great a demand upon yours. Enough, therefore, for to-day from your heartily devoted

F. Liszt.

P.S.—N.B.—With the next sending of music please enclose the choruses from Schumann's *Manfred* (*Songs* and pianoforte accompaniment). I shall probably this autumn be engaged with the same subject, which, in my opinion, Schumann has not exhausted.

9. To Dr. Franz Brendel.

Dear Friend,

You will have heard of the grievous shock I received in the middle of September.[1] Shortly afterwards Monsieur Ollivier came to Rome, and during his stay here, which lasted till the 22nd October, I could not calculate upon being able to take any interest in

[1] Liszt's eldest daughter, Mme. Blandine Ollivier, had died.

other outward matters. This last week I have had to spend in bed. Hence my long delay in answering you.

So far as I understand the position of affairs with regard to the *Tonkünstler-Versammlung*, it seems difficult to give any definite advice. The question here is not one of theoretical, but of absolutely practical considerations, with regard to which unfortunately my influence is very limited. In my last letter I believe I told you that I am prepared, in case you decide upon Prague, to subscribe my name to the petition addressed to the Austrian ministry in behalf of state support. At the same time I intimated to you that my cousin Dr. Eduard Liszt would be the best one to draw up the said petition (in accordance with a draft sent to him), and in fact might aid the undertaking with good advice, and otherwise promote its interests. I, on my side, will not spare myself any trouble in order to obtain from the Austrian government a favourable result for the objects of the *Tonkünstler-Versammlung*. I cannot, of course, guarantee success beforehand; still I consider it not impossible, and when the time comes I will communicate all further details to you.

In the first place, however, comes the question whether I can take any personal part in the meeting of the *Tonkünstler-Versammlung* in the year '63?[1] And unfortunately this question I am forced to answer decidedly in the *negative*. Owing to its being my custom not to enlighten others by giving an account of my own affairs, I avoid, even in this case, entering further into particulars. Of this much you may meanwhile

---

[1] This meeting did not take place in 1863, but in 1864.

be assured with tolerable certainty : I have neither the intention nor the inclination to make any lengthened stay in Germany. Probably, however, during the course of next summer I may go to Weimar for perhaps a three weeks' visit to my gracious Master the Grand Duke. From Weimar I should go to Leipzig, and then return here by way of Trieste or Marseilles.

Requests for concert performances of my works under my direction have been addressed to me from several quarters of late. Yesterday again I received a letter on this same subject from London, to which, as in the case of the others, I shall reply with grateful thanks and excuses.—

I am firmly resolved for some length of time to continue working on here undisturbed, unremittingly and with an object. After having, as far as I could, solved the greater part of the *Symphonic* problem set me in Germany, I mean now to undertake the *Oratorio* problem (together with some other works connected with this). The *Legend of Saint Elizabeth*, which was altogether finished a couple of months ago, must not remain an isolated work, and I must see to it that the society it needs is forthcoming ! To other people this anxiety on my part may appear trifling, useless, at all events thankless, and but little profitable ; to me it is the one object in art which I have to strive after, and to which I must sacrifice everything else. At my age (51 years !) it is advisable to remain at home ; what there is to seek, is to be found within oneself, not without ; and, let me add, I am as much wanting in inclination to wander about as I am in the necessary means for doing so.

But enough of my insignificant self. Let us pass over at once to the subject of those two brave fellows who, in your opinion, ought to play a chief part in the next *Tonkünstler-Versammlung* : Berlioz—and Wagner.

To class them together thus seemed strange to me at first, considering the present state of affairs. And, so far as their two-headed personality is drawn in, I hold it to be impossible even. So let us take each apart.

A) Berlioz. Considering what has occurred, and what has appeared in print, it strikes me as more than doubtful whether Berlioz would make up his mind to undertake the musical conductorship of the *Tonkünstler-Versammlung*, even though Benazet should come forward *en personne* as mediator. Besides which his moral influence at the Festival and the negotiations would be hindering and disturbing. Hence let us leave Berlioz in Paris or in Baden-Baden, and be content in being consistent and in giving him a proof of our admiration by getting up a performance of one of his larger works. (Perhaps the *Te Deum* ?—if I am not mistaken it lasts a good hour. For Prague this choice would be appropriate—unless the Requiem might be preferred. We might even consider whether the *two* might not be given *together*; this would abundantly fill one concert. Discuss the requisite means, etc., for giving these, with Riedel.)

B) Wagner. What am I to say to you of Wagner ? Have you had any talk with him lately in Leipzig ? On what terms are you with him at present ? . . . Ah, it is a pity that we cannot procure a stream of gold for him, or have some palaces of gold built for him !

What can he do with admiration, enthusiasm, devotion, and all such non-essential things ?

Nevertheless it is our indebtedness and duty to remain faithful and devoted to him. The whole German *Musik-Verein* shall raise up a brazen wall in his honour !—He is verily worthy of it !

Hence, dear friend, see what can be arranged with Wagner. Since I left Berlin we have not corresponded. But I am surprised almost that I did not receive a line from him after Blandine's death ! . — .

Au revoir, therefore, dear friend. In Weimar or in Leipzig only can I tell you what I may be able to accomplish later. I must, however, most urgently beg to be exempted from undertaking to direct the German *Musik-Verein* for the year '63 !—

With cordial and most friendly greetings,

Yours sincerely,

November 8th [1862].   F. Liszt.

P.S.—Best thanks for your Sondershausen essays.

10. To A. W. Gottschalg.

Dear Friend,

Your kind letter reached me on October 22nd, and this day, which could not pass without sorrow, has this year been brightened by many loving and solemn remembrances. Accept my thanks, and present my best remembrances to all those whose names you mention, and who have so kindly thought of me. Unfortunately there is no prospect of my soon being able to celebrate the 22nd October with Weimar friends ; but I may tell you that I intend paying H.R.H. the

Grand Duke a visit during the course of the summer.
And we two shall then also have a bright and happy
day in Tieffurt—and look through a couple of new
Organ pieces together.   Grosse must not fail to be there
likewise, nor his *trombone box*, which I have specially
had in my mind ever since the journey to Paris.[1]
Meanwhile, however, tell dear, good Grosse not to be
vexed about the delay in connection with the promised
despatch of his " *Sonntags-Posaunenstück*." *   It is
long since finished, also some three or four Organ pieces,
which, dear friend, I wrote for you last spring.   But
the postal arrangements are so little safe, under present
circumstances, that I do not care to send manuscripts
by this means.   In despatching parcels to Vienna or
Paris I could, of course, make use of the courtesy of
the embassies ; but it is more difficult with Weimar
. . . and so the parcel with the *Legend of Saint Elizabeth*, the three Psalms instrumented (and essentially
remodelled), several Pianoforte and Organ pieces,
together with Grosse's "Sunday-piece," must remain
in my box till some perfectly reliable opportunity presents itself.   If the worst comes to the worst I shall
bring the whole lot myself.

The Schneider-Organ-Album, and the one to appear
later—the Arnstädter-Bach-Organ-Album (which is to
contain the magnificent fugal subject from Bach's Cantata
that I arranged for the Organ—and not without difficulty), I beg you to keep in your library till my return.

I am very unpleasantly affected by the hyper-mer-

---

[1] Grosse took his instrument with him on the journey, in order that
it might be at hand in case Liszt should want it.

* Sunday piece for trombone.

cantile craftiness of one of my publishers whom you mention in your letter. It would truly be unjust if *you* were not to receive the usual discount, and indeed an exceptional amount, when purchasing the Faust Symphony. But who would ever succeed in washing a negro white ? And, in addition, one has generally to put up with the inky blackness of his bills !—I could tell many a tale of such doings, and indeed of persons who are afterwards not ashamed to talk braggingly of their friendship for me ! " O friends, not these tones, rather let us strike up *pleasanter* ones," sings Beethoven.

The *Elizabeth*, it is to be hoped, contains something of the sort. At least, as far as possible, I have laboured carefully at the work, and, so to say, *lived it through* for more than a year. In No. 3 of the score— the *Crusaders*—you will come across the old pilgrim song from the days of the Crusades which you had the kindness to communicate to me. It has rendered me good service for the second subject of the Crusaders' March. In the concluding notice of the score I acknowledge my thanks to you for it and give the whole song from your copy.

Among the pleasant bits of news (exceptions to the rule !) which reach me from our quarters is that about the improvement of your pecuniary position, which is probably accompanied by your appointment as teacher at the newly established *Seminary classes*. In the way of merit you lack nothing, and nothing in zeal and energetic perseverance. Let me hope, dear friend, that you may more and more meet with your due reward !

With kindest greetings,

ROME, *November* 15*th*, 1862.   F. LISZT.

11. To Eduard Liszt.

Dearest Eduard,

The feeling of our double relationship is to me always an elevating and comforting one. Truly you abide with me, as I do with you—*cum sanguine, corde et mente.*

Accept my thanks for your kind lines, and excuse my not having written to you long ago. I might indeed have told you many a thing of more or less interest; but all seemed to me tiresome and insufficient in writing to you. I needed more than ever, and above all things, ample time to compose myself, to gather my thoughts, and to bestir myself. During the first year of my stay here I secured this. It is to be hoped that you would not be dissatisfied with the state of mind which my 50th year brought me; at all events I feel it to be in perfect harmony with the better, higher aspirations of my childhood, where heaven lies so near the soul of every one of us and illuminates it! I may also say that, owing to my possessing a more definite and clearer consciousness, a state of greater peacefulness has come over me.

Blandine has her place in my heart beside Daniel. Both abide with me bringing atonement and purification, mediators with the cry of " Sursum corda !"—When the day comes for Death to approach, he shall not find me unprepared or faint-hearted. *Our* faith hopes for and awaits the deliverance to which it leads us. Yet as long as we are upon earth we must attend to our daily task. And mine shall not lie unproductive.

However trifling it may seem to others, to me it is indispensable. My soul's tears must, as it were, have lacrymatoria made for them ; I must set fires alight for those of my dear ones that are alive, and keep my dear dead in *spiritual and corporeal* urns. This is the aim and object of the *Art task* to me.

You know that I have finished the *Legend of Saint Elizabeth* (200 pages of score—2½ hours' duration in performance). In addition to this some other compositions have been produced, such as : the Sun-Canticus ("Cantico del Sole") of Saint Franciscus —an instrumental *Evocatio* in the Sistine Chapel —two Psalms, etc. I trust you may again find *us* in these, in mind and feeling.

I am now about to set myself the great task of an Oratorio on Christ. By the 22nd October, '63, I hope to have solved the difficulty as far as my weakness and strength will permit.

As you see, dearest Eduard, it is impossible to get out of my head the idea of writing notes.* In spite of all good precepts and *friendly* counsellors (who mean it much better by me than I can ever understand !) I go so far as to maintain that for several years past and in many yet to come I have not done and shall not do anything more ingenuous than cheerfully to go on composing. And what more harmless occupation could there be ? especially as I never force my little works upon any one, nay, have frequently begged persons to refrain from giving certain too unconscientious† renderings of them,—and that I ask for no further

* Notenköpfe.
† Play on words "gewissen" and "ungewissenhaft"

appreciation or approval than can, in fact, be granted according to taste and disposition.

From Pest I have lately received through Baron Pronay, in the name of the Council of the Conservatoire, an invitation to establish my domicile there, and to promote the interests of Hungarian music. Probably you will hear of my *excusatory* reply.

Between ourselves, and frankly said in plain German, it would be of no advantage to me again to take up any outward musical activity (such as my conductorship in Weimar which came to an end a few years ago, and after September 1861 became a *locked door* to me through my Chamberlain's key). But possibly I may later find a fitting opportunity for composing something for Hungary. After the precedent of the *Gran Mass* I might, for instance, on some extraordinary occasion, be entrusted, say, with a *Te Deum* or something of the kind. I would gladly do my best, and only on some such terms could I regard my return to Hungary as becoming.

Meanwhile remains quietly in Rome, honestly striving to do his duty as a Christian and an artist,

Thine from his heart,

F. LISZT.

ROME, *November* 19*th* (*St. Elizabeth's Day*), 1862.

12. TO DR. FRANZ BRENDEL.

DEAR FRIEND,

The difficulties and troubles of the musical situation of which you speak in your last letter but one, I can, unfortunately, only too well understand. No one is better acquainted with such matters than I am, and hence no one is better able to appreciate and recognise the value of your unselfish, persevering work and efforts, which also show you so sincere in your convictions. And one of the dark sides in my present position, dear friend, is that I can be of so little use to you, that I am compelled to remain in a state of passivity and forbearance that does not at all agree with me. However, you may rely upon my readiness to render any assistance wherever I may still be able to help.—In accordance with your wish I shall take an early opportunity of writing to Prince H [ohenzollern] concerning the *Tonkünstler-Verein*. It is to be hoped that our amiable, noble-minded patron will show himself no less disposed in our favour than he has done on former occasions. And you, on your part, do not fail to discuss with Seifriz by letter the points and *modals* of the support expected. It is a pity that Bülow's proposal to hold the next meeting of the *T. K. Verein* in Löwenberg has not proved feasible. Were it likely to be broached again I should not make any objections to it, because, in fact, the place seems to be precisely a favourable centre at present. But, as already said, it is not my place to express any definite opinion on the subject, and I am entirely satisfied in leaving all that has to be done to your judgment and foresight.

I am delighted to hear of Bülow's extraordinary success in Leipzig, and still more so to hear of your renewed and intimate relations with him. He is the born *prototype* of progress, and noble-minded to a degree! Without his active co-operation as director and standard-bearer a *Tonkünstler-Versammlung* at the present time would at least be an anachronism.

From Wagner I lately received a letter in which he informed me of a performance of his *Tristan* in Vienna towards the end of January. Afterwards he intends arranging some concerts in Berlin—and, it seems, in St. Petersburg also. My endeavours to secure him comfortable quarters in Weimar seem for the time being to be useless, because of his dislike to an insignificant appointment, and the adverse circumstances of life in a small town. Certainly his project of drawing annually 3,000 thalers (£450), by some agreement between the Grand Dukes of Weimar and Baden, is much more to the point. The question is only whether their Highnesses will consent to it ? . — .

With heartiest greetings, most sincerely yours,

December 30th, 1862.   F. LISZT.

13. TO BREITKOPF AND HÄRTEL.

DEAR HERR DOCTOR,

The four scores of the Beethoven Symphonies, of which you advised me in your friendly letter, reached me yesterday. My eyes are meanwhile revelling and delighting in all the glories of the splendid edition, and after Easter I shall set to work. Nothing shall be wanting on my part, in the way of goodwill and industry, to fulfil your commission to the best of my power. A pianoforte arrangement of these creations must, indeed, expect to remain a very poor and far-off *approximation.* How instil into the transitory hammers of the Piano breath and soul, resonance and

power, fulness and inspiration, colour and accent?—
However I will, at least, endeavour to overcome the
worst difficulties and to furnish the pianoforte-playing
world with as faithful as possible an illustration of
Beethoven's genius.

And I must ask you, dear Herr Doctor, in order
that the statement on all the title pages—" critically
revised edition "—may be complied with, to send me—
together with your new edition of the scores of the
Pastoral, the C minor, and A major Symphonies—a
copy of my own transcriptions of them. Probably
I may alter, simplify, and correct passages—and add
some fingerings. The more intimately acquainted one
becomes with Beethoven, the more one clings to certain
singularities and finds that even insignificant details
are not without their value. Mendelssohn, at whose
recommendation you formerly published my pianoforte
scores of the Pastoral and C minor Symphonies, took
great delight in these minutiæ and niceties!—

With regard to the agreement about the A major
Symphony I mean shortly to write to Carl Haslinger,
and expect that he will be quite willing to meet my
wish.[1]

With grateful thanks, dear Herr Doctor, I remain
yours in readiness and sincerity,

F. LISZT.

ROME, *March 26th,* 1863.

P.S.—The four Symphonies shall be finished before
the end of summer and sent to Leipzig. If you are
satisfied with my work would you entrust the arrange-

---

[1] A pianoforte transcription of this Symphony by Liszt had been
published by Haslinger.

ment of the Overtures to me when I have finished the Symphonies—provided, of course, that you have not made any agreement with any one else?

14. To A. W. GOTTSCHALG IN WEIMAR.

DEAR FRIEND,

This year my name-day fell in the middle of Easter week, on Maundy Thursday. Your hearty letter again brought what to me is the pleasantest news in the world. Thank you for it, and let those know of it who share your sincere, friendly, and faithful sentiments! First let me mention Carl Götze,[1] whose kindly words I should so gladly like to answer in accordance with his wish, and then my dear *Kammer*-virtuoso, Grosse. *Grosse's trombone* no doubt officiated brilliantly at Bülow's concert and at the performance of Berlioz's opera! An echo of the former reached me, thanks to your inspired notice in Brendel's paper, where I accidentally came across a little remark which you had addressed to one of the most estimable and graceful of German lady-singers anent my little-heeded songs. I certainly cannot find fault with you for showing some interest in the songs and for thus frankly expressing your opinion. On the contrary, your sympathetic appreciation is always welcome, amid the direct and indirect disparagement which falls to my lot. Unfortunately, however, I must make up my mind that only by way of an exception can I expect to find friends for my compositions. The blame is

---

[1] A chorister in Weimar (a favourite copyist of the Master's) became a musical conductor in Magdeburg and died in 1886.

mine; why should one presume to feel independently, and set the comfortable complacency of other folks at defiance?—Everything that I have written for several years past shows something of a pristine delinquency which is as little to be pardoned as I am unable to alter it. This fault, it is true, is the life-nerve of my compositions, which, in fact, can only be what they are and nothing else.—

In the Psalms I have made some important alterations, and shall shortly send Kahnt the manuscript. A few passages (especially the verse "Sing us one of the songs of Zion") which had always appeared awkward to me in the earlier version, I have now managed to improve. At least they now pretty well satisfy my soul's ear.

The *Christus* Oratorio is progressing but slowly, owing to the many interruptions which I have to put up with this winter. It is to be hoped I may obtain some entire months of work during the summer. I thirst for it.

Of the musical undertakings here you will learn the more noteworthy events from a paper I sent to Brendel last week. Further and fuller news about myself is meanwhile uncertain. Probably I shall in the end not find myself able to do anything better than to put my whole story in the musical notes that I am incessantly writing down, but which need not either be printed or heard.

However that may be, I remain, dear friend, in sincere affection, yours gratefully and in all friendship,

F. LISZT.

ROME, *April 14th,* 1863.

P.S.—The Bach-Album and other music which you say you had to send me (*e.g.*, your arrangement of the Dante fugue if it has been printed) please let me have through Kahnt. Enclose also a copy of the Ave Maria for Organ.

15. To Dr. Franz Brendel.

DEAR FRIEND,

    The last months brought so many interruptions in my work that I still feel quite vexed about it. Easter week I had determined should, at last, see me regularly at work again; but a variety of duties and engagements have prevented my accomplishing this. I must, therefore, to be true to myself and carry out my former intention, shut myself up entirely. To find myself in a net of social civilities is vexatious to me ; my mental activity requires absolutely to be free, without which I cannot accomplish anything.

    How things will turn out later about my proposed journey to Germany I do not yet know. Probably my weary bones will be buried in Rome. Till then their immovability will serve you better than my wandering about on railways and steamboats. On the other hand, there is but little for me to do in Germany. War is at the door ; drums and cannon will come to the fore ; God protect the faith of heroes and give victory to the righteous among humanity ! . —.

    Where is Wagner, and what about the performances of *Tristan*, the *Nibelungen*, and the *Meistersinger* in

Weimar or elsewhere? Tell me of this. I have not written to Weimar for long, and have also not had any news from there. My only German correspondent (Frau von Bülow) is suffering from some eye-trouble, which has interrupted our exchange of letters . . . so I am absolutely ignorant of what is going on. The February numbers of the *Neue Zeitschrift* are the last I have received. Your articles on Criticism are excellent, and, indeed, nothing else was to be expected. Give Louis Köhler my most friendly thanks for his kind perseverance in "*paving the way* for my scores to receive more kindly appreciation." The more thankless the task the more heartily grateful do I feel to my friends.

Most sincerely yours,

F. LISZT.

ROME, *May 8th*, 1863.

16. TO EDUARD LISZT.

DEAREST EDUARD,

Weariness or something of the sort carried my thoughts back to my "*Berceuse.*" Various other *Berceuses* rose up in my dreams. Do you care to join my dreams? It shall not cost you any trouble; without touching the keyboard yourself, you will only need to rock yourself in the sentiments that hover over them. A really amiable and variously gifted lady will see to this. She plays the little piece delightfully, and has promised me to let it *exercise its charms* upon you. I shall, therefore, ere long send you a copy of the new version of the *Berceuse* addressed "to the Princess

Marcelline Czartoryska, Klostergasse 4." [1] Wend your
way thither—and, in case you do not find the Princess
at home, leave the manuscript with your card. I have
already told her of your contemplated visit, and have
spoken of you as my heart's kinsman and friend. You
will find the Princess Cz. possessed of a rare and fine
understanding, the most charming figure in society,
and a kindly and enthusiastic worshipper of *Mozart,
Beethoven, and Chopin*, and, above all this, the illumi-
nating faith of the Catholic Church reflected in Polish
blood.

Patria in Religione et Religio in patria might be the
motto of Poland. God protect the oppressed!

One other commission for the Princess Cz. please
undertake for me. During her residence here she
on several occasions expressed the wish to become
acquainted with some of my compositions (to which,
whether intentionally or not, she had hitherto not paid
much attention). I played with her my arrangement
of the Symphonic Poems for 2 pianofortes—the
Héroïde funèbre, *Tasso*, and the *Préludes*—which she
received with kindly and courteous tolerance. Without
desiring more—for ample experience has taught me
that my compositions more readily rouse estrangement
than attraction—I should, nevertheless, like the musical
threads of our pleasant relations not to be entirely
dropped, and wish therefore to present her, first of all,
with various pieces of music by way of making amends.
In the badly stocked music shops of Rome I could not
find anything suited to her talent, and promised to ask
your help in the matter. I beg you, therefore, dearest

[1] A pupil of Chopin's.

Eduard, to get the following works simply and neatly bound in one volume (in the following order), and to present them soon to the Princess Cz.:—

1. Glanes de Woronice (Leipzig, Kistner).
2. Mélodies de Chopin, transcrites par Liszt (Berlin, Schlesinger).
3. Mazurka (Senff, Leipzig).
4. 2 Polonaises (idem).
5. 2 Ballades (1 and 2. Kistner, Leipzig).
6. Consolations (Härtel, Leipzig).

If the volume is not too thick with the above you might add the "Valse mélancolique" and "Romanesca" (second edition of Haslinger). Of course let all this, contents and binding, be put down to my account, and given to the Princess-artist as a present from me. If the pieces cannot be procured in Vienna, order them speedily from Leipzig through Haslinger or Spina.

A propos of Spina: has the arrangement for 2 piano-fortes of my orchestral setting of Schubert's magnificent C major Fantasia not yet been published? This delay, or, more properly, this remissness, is by no means a pleasant matter to me. With all my heart, thine,

F. LISZT.

ROME, *May 22nd*, 1863.

17. TO DR. FRANZ BRENDEL.

DEAR FRIEND,

I had to remain in bed all last week—and am still pretty weak on my legs. But there is nothing further wrong: my head is free again; the rest can be imagined. The day after to-morrow I quit my rooms in the Via Felice and move to Monte Mario (an hour's distance from the city). Father Theimer is kind enough to allow me to occupy his apartments in the almost uninhabited house of the Oratorian. The view is indescribably grand. I mean now, at last, to try and lead a *natural* kind of life. I hope I may succeed in approaching more closely to my monastico-artistic ideal. . . . Meanwhile you may laugh at me about it. In my next letter I will tell you where to address me.

Pastor Landmesser will bring you further news about me to Leipzig, before the end of July, on his way back to Dantzig. I shall get him to take you the manuscript of the Psalms (of which I spoke to you). They are now ready for publication, and will not disgrace Kahnt's house of business.

The corrected copy of the Faust Symphony, too, I will send you by this opportunity, for Schuberth.

With regard to performances of my works generally, my disposition and inclination are more than ever completely in the *negative*. My friends, and you more especially, dearest friend, have done their part in this respect fully and in the kindest manner. It seems to me now high time that I should be somewhat forgotten, or, at least, placed very much in the background. My name has been too frequently spoken of; many have taken umbrage at this, and been uselessly annoyed at it. While "paving the way for a better appreciation," it might be advisable to regard my things as a reserve corps, and to introduce new works by other composers.

This will sufficiently intimate that the *Legend of St. Elizabeth* may quietly go on slumbering in my paper-box. As may also the work upon which I am now engaged, and which to my regret is making but very slow progress, owing to the many interruptions which perpetually plague me.

Should any one of the programmes be filled with one of my compositions, it would be best to select one of those already published, in order that, at all events, the publisher's approval may, in some measure, be held up to view.

In my opinion you have made a good choice in Porges. The young man is reliable, intelligent, and capable of inspiration, and what he may still lack in skilfulness he will easily acquire. The essential point in a task of this kind is a modest, honest, and not too dry effort. What I have heard and know of Porges makes me feel assured that he will best fulfil the various demands made by the editorial office.

What is one to think of the marvels which Pohl has brought back from Löwenberg? I haven't sufficient imagination to form any clear idea about them from the preliminary hints you communicated to me. Let me have a fuller report, therefore, if you think that, under certain conditions, I should mix myself up with the matter. And also tell me frankly, without periphrase, *what* the *Musik-Verein* wishes and expects from the patronage of the Grand Duke of Weimar?—One ought not to shoot about at random with Royal Highnesses! It would only lead to a vexatious loss of powder.

How is Kap[ellmeister] Wehner? Is he still in his King's good graces?[1] Kapellmeister Bernhard Scholz

---

[1] He was in the service of the King of Hanover; and is long since dead.

was here last month—but he did not honour me with a visit.

To-day's post has brought me some very friendly lines from my worthy precentor Gottschalg in Tieffurt. He tells me of a concert in *Denstedt*, where several pieces of mine were performed—among others one of the Psalms (which I shall shortly send to Kahnt by Landmesser, an *essentially improved* version); they were sung by Fräulein Genast. This lady, so Gottschalg writes, is to be married to-day. Do you know to whom ? I am so entirely cut off from all my Weimar connection that I had not heard anything about this. But as I still retain a very friendly recollection of this excellent lady-exponent of my songs, I beg you, dear friend, to let me have her new name and to tell me whether her husband resides in Weimar or elsewhere.

I am perfectly satisfied with my new abode at Monte Mario.—Pastor Landmesser will give you a description of it—and perhaps I may find a photograph of the place—if not I shall order one for you later.

Your sincerely devoted

F. Liszt.

Rome, *June 18th*, 1863.

18. To Dr. Franz Brendel.

Dear Friend,

You will receive these lines in the lovely Sondershausen Park. One gladly accustoms oneself to the place, and the admirable performances of the *Loh*-concerts—I derive the word from "Lohe" [flame] —give the atmosphere a certain spiritual stimulus. My friendly greetings to Stein—and present my warm thanks to the courageous orchestra, which has not been scandalised by the "Symphonic Poems"! . . .

The parcel from Kahnt reached me safely a few days after your letter (of 26th June). Mililotti [1] intends writing to Riedel to thank him for his kindness in forwarding his programmes. When Mililotti's concerts prove more of a success he may, by way of a return, send his Roman programmes to Leipzig. But at present the musical doings here are of but small interest to other countries.

By sending me the score edition of *Mignon* and *Loreley* Kahnt has given me peculiar pleasure. It seems to me correct, and I am foolish enough to find the instrumentation pretty. By the way, other instrumental settings occur to me : those of several of Schubert's songs ("Erlking," "Gretchen," "The Young Nun," and a few others) that I wrote for Fräulein Genast. They are not mere manufactured arrangements, and might not altogether displease musicians of fine feeling. The manuscript of the scores was left with Seifriz in Löwenberg. If any publisher should feel inclined to accept them they are at his disposal. . — .

In answer to an important point in your letter, I quite agree about presenting the Grand Duke of Weimar with a *Report* describing the object and aims of the *Allgemeine Deutsche Musik-Verein*. And on this occasion H.R.H. should be respectfully and graciously invited to address an appeal to his illustrious relatives

---

[1] Director of the Classical Music Association in Rome; he had requested Professor Riedel to send him the programmes of his concerts.

to take some interest in the progress and success of
the Association: in plain language, to strengthen his
protectorship by letters of recommendation, or in some
other way. In presenting the *Report* (which might
most appropriately be undertaken by Pohl and
Regierungsrath Müller) the Grand Duke or His
Excellency Count Beust might be addressed directly
by word of mouth, and be distinctly given to understand the desirability of obtaining the sympathy of
the Grand Duchess, the Queen of Prussia, the King
of Holland, T.R.H. the Grand Duchesses Helene and
Marie (of Russia), the Grand Duke Peter of Oldenburg
(in St. Petersburg), the Grand Duke and Grand Duchess
of Baden, the Hereditary Prince of Meiningen, the
Dukes of Altenburg and Coburg, etc. I give these
names because, owing to their near relationship with
the Grand Duke and their own personal fondness for
music, they should stand first as patrons and supporters
of the *Allgemeine Deutsche Musik-Verein*.

Gladly would I have undertaken the duties of diplomatist to the Association in Weimar, and endeavoured
to obtain the Grand Duke's active intervention. . . .
But at this distance I cannot, for the time being, accomplish anything. My gracious Master has no leisure for
lectures on artistic subjects that I might concoct in the
Eternal City; and if I tried to enlighten him in any
such way his first and only word in reply would be :
" Why does not Liszt come back, in place of writing
such allotria * ? "—A short time ago I received from him
a very kind, monitory letter, calling upon me to return
to Weimar for the *Künstler-Versammlung* in August. . — .

* Observations beside the mark.

I would advise you to make use of your stay at
Sondershausen by getting an introduction to the Prince,
and by obtaining his support as regards the *Musik-
Verein*. Discuss this matter with Stein, for he is best
able to attend to it. Possibly a larger performance in
the Loh might be got up for the benefit of the
Association. . — .

This letter is so filled up with Royal Highnesses,
Majesties, and illustrious personages, that it offers me
a natural transition to tell you of an extraordinary,
nay, incomparable honour I received last Saturday
evening, the 11th of July. His Holiness Pope Pius IX.
visited the Church of the Madonna del Rosario, and
hallowed my apartments with his presence. After
having given His Holiness a small proof of my skill
on the harmonium and on my work-a-day pianino, he
addressed a few very significant words to me in the
most gracious manner possible, admonishing me to
strive after heavenly things in things earthly, and by
means of my harmonies that reverberated and then
passed away to prepare myself for those harmonies
that would reverberate everlastingly.—His Holiness
remained a short half-hour ; Monsign. de Merode and
Hohenlohe were among his suite—and the day before
yesterday I was granted an audience in the Vatican
(the first since I came here), and the Pope presented
me with a beautiful cameo of the Madonna.—

I must add one other princely personage to this
letter, and with this I am obliged to close. A visit at
this very moment is announced from the Principe della
Rocca, who has driven up with his photographic appara-
tus. You shall, therefore, ere long have a little picture

of the Madonna del Rosario which, since the Pope's visit here, has been the talk of Rome.

A thousand hearty greetings.

F. L.

July 18th, 1863.

19. To Breitkopf and Härtel.

Rome, *August 28th,* 1863.

My dear Sir,

The work that you were good enough to entrust to me is almost finished, and by the same post you will receive the *Piano* score of 8 Symphonies of Beethoven, whilst awaiting the 9th, which I propose to send you with the proofs of the preceding ones. Nos. 1, 2, 3, 4, and 8 are bound in one volume ; there is only the Funeral March from the Eroica Symphony wanting, which is published in the Beethoven-Album by Mechetti, Vienna. I shall require to see this arrangement again (which you will oblige me by sending with the next proofs), for probably I shall make numerous corrections and modifications in it, as I have done in the Symphonies in *C* minor, in *A*, and the *Pastoral*, which were edited some twenty years ago. The copies of these are returned to you to-day with a great many alterations, *errata* and *addenda*, inasmuch as—in order to satisfy my own criticism—I have been obliged to apply to them the torture of red pencil and gum, and to submit them to a very considerable alteration.

Whilst initiating myself further in the genius of Beethoven, I trust I have also made some little progress in the manner of adapting his inspirations to the piano, as far as this instrument admits of it ; and I have tried not to neglect to take into account the relative facility of execution while maintaining an exact fidelity to the original. Such as this arrangement of Beethoven's Symphonies actually is, the pupils of the first class in the Conservatoires will be able to play them off fairly well on *reading them at sight*, save and except that they will succeed better in them by working at them, which is always advisable. What study is deserving of more care and assiduity than that of these *chefs d'œuvre*? The more one gives oneself to them the more one will profit by them, firstly in relation to the sense and æsthetic intelligence, and then also in relation to the technical skill and the attaining of perfection in virtuosity—of which one should only despise the bad use that is sometimes made.

By the title of *Pianoforte score* (which must be kept, and translated into German by *Clavier-Partitur* or *Pianoforte-Partitur?*) I wish to indicate my intention of associating the spirit of the performer with the orchestral effects, and to render apparent, in the narrow limits of the piano, sonorous sounds and different *nuances*. With this in view I have frequently noted down the names of the instruments : oboe, clarinet, kettle-drums, etc., as well as the contrasts of strings and wind instruments. It would certainly be highly ridiculous to pretend that these designations suffice to transplant the magic of the orchestra to the piano ; nevertheless I don't consider them superfluous. Apart from some little use they have as instruction, pianists of some intelligence may make them a help in accentuating and grouping the subjects, bringing out the

chief ones, keeping the secondary ones in the background, and—in a word—regulating themselves by the
standard of the orchestra.

In order to be perfectly satisfied with regard to my
work allow me, my dear sir, to beg you to let Mr.
Ferdinand David and Monsieur Moscheles see it before
it is printed. The minute familiarity they have acquired
with the Symphonies of Beethoven will show them in
a moment any errors, oversights, faults and misdeeds
of which I, very unwittingly, may have been guilty.
Will you please assure them that any information from
them in these respects will be most valuable to me,
and that I shall not fail to profit by it for the honour
of your edition. In particular I should like to know
from Mr. David whether the *N.B.* placed on page 78
of the manuscript (Finale of the 8th Symphony—
"*the execution of the principal figure,* etc.") is authorised,
—and I should be very grateful to him for any other
particulars he is kind enough to give me. As to Mr.
Moscheles, I hope he will not disapprove of my having
followed his example in putting a profuse fingering
for the greater ease of the mass of performers ; but
perhaps he would be so kind as to suggest a better
fingering himself, and to let me know his observations
upon such and such an artifice of " piano arrangement"
of which he is a consummate master. There is only
one point on which I would venture even to an act
of rebellion—it is that of the pedals, a *bass* [*base*]
passion of which I cannot correct myself, no matter
how annoying the reproaches it may draw upon me !— [1]

[1] " Even if one may presuppose," he writes on another occasion
(27th August, 1861) to Breitkopf and Härtel, " a correct use of the

If, as I venture to flatter myself, my arrangement of the Symphonies satisfies you, I should be tempted to propose to you, for next year, a similar work on the Quartets, those magnificent jewels in Beethoven's crown which the piano-playing public has not yet appropriated in a measure suitable to its musical culture.

But I really fear to exhaust your patience by giving you proofs of mine . . . . consider therefore this project of the Quartets as not having been proposed if it seems to you inopportune, and pray accept, my dear sir, the expression of my very sincere and devoted sentiments.

F. LISZT.

(MONTE MARIO, MADONNA DEL ROSARIO.)

P.S.—As it has been impossible for me to hunt out here a copyist who will fulfil the conditions that may reasonably be exacted (the one whom I employed pretty much last year divides his time between the prison and the public-house!), I am compelled to send you the manuscript such as it is, with many apologies for its badly written appearance. To make a fair copy of it some one with plenty of experience is needed ; and I can safely recommend you such an one in Mr. Carl Götze ("Member or Vice-director of the theatre chorus") at Weimar. He is accustomed of old to my writing, and would make the copy of the Symphonies with intelligence and care.

N.B.—A copy of the *Orchestral Score* of the Symphonies will be a great help to the work of the copyist

pedal on the part of piano-players, I am nevertheless, through manifold unpleasant experiences to my ears, brought back to giving the most minute indications of it."

of my manuscript, for exactness in *nuances*, division of parts and indication of the instruments.

In any case it will be necessary for me to revise the final proofs. . — .

Let me add, in conclusion, that I shall be glad to receive, with the proofs or even sooner, a copy of my *Etudes d'execution transcendante*, and also those *d'après Paganini* (Breitkopf and Härtel edition), which I have promised to give to an excellent pianist here, Mr. Sgambati, who is most capable of playing them well in public;—and, besides these, a copy/of my *Ave Maria* (for chorus with Organ accompaniment) which is shortly to be performed here.

20. To Dr. Franz Brendel.

Dear Friend,

This morning I sent off manuscripts and corrections to Härtel and Schuberth—and thus had to write the word Leipzig several times. It struck me as a reproach as regards yourself, and I mean forthwith to get rid of it. You shall not hear of me through *others* without having the trouble of reading my own bad handwriting yourself. I have not, however, anything very special to relate. The summer has passed quietly and I have not wandered abroad much ; have, in fact, been pretty constantly sitting at my work. My abode continues to suit me more and more, so I intend to spend the winter here. You no doubt received with my last letter the photograph of the " Madonna del Rosario." Unfortunately I cannot send you a picture of the grand, truly sublime view that can be enjoyed from every window. So you must imagine it to embrace all Rome, the wondrous *Campagna*, and all the past and present glories of the district.

For some time past I have had no other news of you than your excellent articles on "artistic individuality," etc., in which, among many other right and fine observations, I was specially pleased with the axiom : "The artistic temperament, when genuine, corrects itself in consequence of the change of contrasts." May it prove so in my case ;—this much is certain,—that in the tiresome business of self-correction few have to labour as I have, as the process of my mental development, if not checked, is at all events rendered peculiarly difficult by a variety of coincidences and contingencies. A clever man, some twenty years ago, made the not inapplicable remark to me : "You have in reality three individuals to deal with in yourself, and they all run one against the other ; the sociable *salon*-individual, the virtuoso and the thoughtfully-creative composer. If you manage one of them properly, you may congratulate yourself."—*Vedremo* !*

Weitzmann's "Carnival in Rome towards the Middle of the Seventeenth Century," I read with great pleasure in the *Neue Zeitschrift*. It is a pleasant, lively sketch, spiced with learning but without pedantic lead. Did a very remarkable "History of the Pianoforte," etc., by the same author, appear in your paper ? Frau von Bülow wrote to me lately that Hans is busy with some essays for the *N. Z.* Probably he is writing a review of Weitzmann's "History of the

* We shall see !

Pianoforte," which would be most appropriate; if this is not the case I would advise you to get one of your staff to undertake the work and to give several quotations from it. The confounded pianoforte has its unmistakable significance, were it only because of the general abuse to which it is put!—In honour of Härtel's edition of Beethoven I have been occupying myself again with studies and experiments in pianoforte pieces. The arrangements of the 8 Beethoven Symphonies which I am about to send to Leipzig are, I trust, successful. They cost me more trouble, in attempts of various sorts, in corrections, eliminations and additions, than I had anticipated. As we grow old we deliberate more and are less readily satisfied. . . .

To Schuberth I have sent the corrections of the 2-pianoforte arrangement of the Faust Symphony, together with a pretty, tuneful arrangement of the *Préludes* by Herr Klauser (of New York), and was thus induced to play the hackneyed piece through again, to touch up the closing movement and give it new figuration. In the hands of a skilful player it will prove brilliantly effective.

But enough of all this pianoforte stuff! I feel forced to set to work again in blackening score-sheets —and first of all the Christus Oratorio shall be proceeded with.—Write and tell me whether Kahnt is publishing the two Psalms which Pastor Landmesser took him, and advise him to request Herr von Bülow to revise the last proofs. There is nothing more vexatious to me than careless editions, full of errors, such as Schuberth would like to have if one gave free reins to his *good nature*!

From the Committee of the Association for the Completion of Cologne Cathedral I have received an invitation to the Festival arranged for the 14th and 15th October. The letter reminds me, in the most courteous terms, that in the year '42 I had the honour of being a member of the *Council*. I had not forgotten this peculiar distinction ; but the worthy gentlemen seem absolutely not to have considered how my activity could now appropriately be of service, and they wisely guard against mentioning any of my ecclesiastical compositions, although it might have occurred to them that I could manage something in that species of music. However, the worthy Committee find the old story of the "period of my brilliancy," and the "bewitching strains I drew from the keys," etc., more voluble and convenient. Besides which some *small sum* would have to be forthcoming were I to agree in considering myself *what* the good folks would like to consider me. Fortunately the determination of my work does not lie in their hands, and on account of this very evident conviction I answered their communication most courteously, modestly referring to my present occupation in Rome, and enclosing an extract from one of the Hymns of St. Ambrosius, from the Liturgy of the *Three Holy Kings*, an incident intimately connected with Cologne Cathedral. At the same time I feel satisfied that I have not shown any intention to give annoyance, and declared myself as perfectly content to fulfil my duties as an honorary member of the Council, *in quietude*, by composing a work specially for the Cathedral (which I shall not fail to do), but without laying the slightest

claim to the sympathy—much less to the patronage—
of the worthy gentlemen of Cologne.—I flatter myself
that I am not in the bad graces of the Three Holy
Kings, consequently do not need to trouble myself
about the rest of the Cologne folk !

Now my Leipzig parcels can be despatched with an
easy mind.

With heartiest greetings,

Yours devotedly,

F. Liszt.

September 7th, 1863.
Monte Mario (Madonna del Rosario).

P.S.—Sgambati, an excellent Roman pianist, wishes
to study my A major Concerto. Schott has as yet
omitted to send me the complimentary-copy of this
piece, to which I am entitled, so I beg you to enclose
in Kahnt's next sending a *duplicate copy* (*arranged for
2 pianofortes*, as there can be no thought of an
orchestral performance of it here). From Härtel I
have also ordered for Sgambati and Bach [1] my Etudes,
the Paganini ones, and *my Ave Maria* (*chorus-score and
voice parts,* for a performance at the Classical Concerts
conducted by Mililotti). It would be advisable, owing
to the expense of forwarding music, to send the things
all in one parcel ; please be kind enough to suggest
this to Härtel, and to get the 3 opus from him, and
I do not wish to have to wait beyond the end of
October for them. Gottschalg will soon have some
copy to send me which might come at the same time.

[1] This is no doubt meant for Bache.

21. To Justizrath Dr. Gille of Jena.

DEAR FRIEND,

I trust you will forgive my long silence. I could not excuse myself in any other way than by a worse lamentation about the variety of circumstances, moods and occupations that have more and more encouraged my habitual dislike to letter-writing. Unless some definite object demands it of me, I do not write to any one in Germany, with the exception of Bülow, my cousin Eduard in Vienna, and Brendel, to whom I am very grateful for the kindness with which he looks after the more important details connected with my musical affairs. As regards my Weimar friends, my inclination to communicate with them is spoilt by my imagining that they would as gladly see me among them as I should feel at home among them. And as I cannot write to them and say: "I am coming to remain with you," I get more and more silent.

My stay in Rome is not an accidental one; it denotes, as it were, the third part—(probably the close) of my life, which is often troubled, but ever industrious and striving upwards. Hence I require ample time to bring various long works and myself to a *good ending*. This requisite I find in my retirement here, which will probably become even more emphatic; and my present monastic abode provides me not only with the most glorious view over all Rome, the Campagna and the mountains, but also what I had longed for; quiet from without and peacefulness.—Enclosed is a photograph of the "Madonna del Rosario," as an illustration to the notices that have lately appeared in the newspapers in connection with the Holy Father's visit here.

Your friendly lines came strangely in conjunction with the *Dettingen Te Deum* to which you refer, and which I was playing through at the very moment your letter was handed to me. A very amiable English lady delighted me a little while ago by presenting me with the praiseworthy London edition—"Novello's Centenary Edition"—of the Oratorios of Händel, Haydn, Mendelssohn, etc. (and all sold at from 1 to 3 shillings each); these works are always welcome society to me. The number containing the Dettingen Te Deum also contains the "Coronation Anthem" (composed in 1741). "Zadok the priest, and Nathan the prophet, anointed Solomon King." *

The commencement is wonderfully grand and powerful, like the Bible itself.—

However notwithstanding all my admiration for Händel, my preference for Bach still holds good, and when I have edified myself sufficiently with Händel's common chords, I long for the precious dissonances of the Passion, the B minor Mass, and other of Bach's polyphonic wares.

Remember me kindly to your wife, and with heartiest greetings to M. Gille, *junior*, I am

Your sincerely attached
F. LISZT.

ROME, *September* 10*th* [1863].
(MONTE MARIO, MADONNA DEL ROSARIO.)

Do not omit in your next letter to tell me something about *your* musical Jubilee in Jena.

* This sentence is written in English by Liszt.

22. To Dr. Franz Brendel.

DEAR FRIEND,

I am deep in my work. The more we sow a field the more it spreads. One would need to live to the age of a Methuselah to accomplish anything plentiful!

Your letters, unlike so many others, are always so welcome, and I thank you most sincerely for all the goodness, kindness, honesty and warmth of feeling that the continuance of our friendship brings with it. For even though you may not always be able to communicate pleasant or enjoyable news, still things disagreeable I can tolerate more readily from you, because of your ever moderate and characteristically steadfast interpretation. The experience you had lately to make with Y. Z. I regret sincerely, and would gladly make you some compensation for a loss that is as unexpected as it is unfortunate. But I am sorry to say I do not know of any one who would exactly suit you. There is truly a great dearth of *men* [*Menschen*] in this world! When they are put to the test they prove themselves useless. My ten years' service in Weimar gave me abundant proof of this!

Probably you will just have to drag on with your contributors, till we finally get into smoother water again. It is more than three months since I received any numbers of the *Neue Zeitschr.*; do not forget to enclose the numbers in the next sending (together with the music I want from Härtel), and address always to "*Madonna del Rosario* (of which a photograph herewith), *Monte Mario*—Rome."

Kahnt's willingness to publish the score of the two Psalms is very flattering to me. He shall have the manuscript soon, and I should like to enclose the instrumentation of the Songs from Wilhelm Tell. Should a convenient opportunity occur some kindly-disposed singer might be found to bring them into notice (perhaps Schnorr?). The instrumental-fabric is not plain or ordinary, and enhances the effect of the vocal part. My critical ex-colleague Stör praised it formerly when performed at one of the Court-Concerts at which Caspari sang the songs,—and since then I have added some dainty little bits. One must praise oneself, especially when others too often fail in doing so !—

With regard to the *Tonkünstler-Versammlung*, it seems to me that the choice of Leipzig is *most advantageous* for the purpose at present, and I would advise you to adhere to this. In the course of the winter we will have an "exchange of thoughts" ("un échange d'idées," as Prince Gortschakoff is ever saying) about the programme and arrangements, and this will assuredly lead to more harmonious results than the Russian notes. Fortunately we do not need to quarrel about the extent of the treaties of 1815 !

Hearty greetings from your sincerely devoted

F. Liszt.

October 10th, 1863.

P.S.—About six weeks ago there appeared in the Leipzig *Illustrirte Zeitung* a biographical notice of F. Liszt, together with a portrait. Let me have the number, and tell me *who* wrote the article.

. — . Has anything new in the way of scores or

pianoforte pieces been published that is likely to
interest me? Here people speak of Mendelssohn and
even Weber *as novelties*!

23. To Madame Jessie Laussot.

Herewith, dear Madame, are a few lines that
I beg you to forward to Madame Ritter (*mère*), as I
do not know where to address to her.[1]

The melancholy familiarity with death that I have
perforce acquired during these latter years does not
in the least weaken the grief which we feel when our
dear ones leave this earth. If at the sight of the
opening graves I thrust back despair and blasphemy,
it is that I may weep more freely, and that neither
life nor death shall be able to separate me from the
communion of love.—

She whom we are mourning was especially dear to
me. Her bodily weakness had perfected the intuitive
faculties in her. She took her revenge inwardly and
lived in the beyond. . . . At our first meeting I thought
I should meet her again. It was at Zürich at Wagner's,
whose powerful and splendid genius she so deeply
felt. During several weeks she always took my arm
to go into the *salle à manger* at the hour of dinner and
supper,—and she spread a singular charm of amenity,
of sweet and conciliatory affection in that home to
which a certain exquisite degree of intimacy was
wanting. She possessed in a rare degree the secret
of making her presence agreeable and harmonious.

---

[1] She had lost her daughter Emilie, the sister of Carl and Alexander
Ritter.

Everything in her, even to her very silence, was comprehensive, for she seemed to *understand*, or rather to determine the thoughts which words render in only an unformed manner, and worked them out in her noble heart.

May her soul live for ever in the fulness of the light and peace of God!—

Very cordially yours,
F. Liszt.

October 15*th*, 1863.
(Madonna del Rosario, Monte Mario.)

Pray excuse my delay in these few lines. It was only yesterday that I learned your address through Mr. Sgambati.

24. To Dr. Franz Brendel.

Dear Friend,

Kahnt's last sending that reached me last week brought me much that I found pleasant and encouraging in the numbers of the *Neue Zeitschrift.* I could verily not have imagined that so mild and kindly a ray of light could have been shed over my compositions discussed there, as is given under cipher 8. Let me know who writes under cipher 8—I promise not to divulge the secret—and meanwhile present my as yet unknown reviewer with my sincerest thanks for his appreciation of my nature, which he manifests in so kind and sympathetic a manner in his commentary to the "*Seligkeiten*" [Beatitudes] and the instrumentation of "Mignon's Song."[1]

---

[1] The review was written by Heinrich Porges.

He has formed the most correct estimate of my endeavours by pointing to the result, namely, to throw life into the truly Catholic, universal and immortal spirit—hence to develop it—and to raise the "culture that has been handed down to us from the remote Middle Ages, out of the heavy atmosphere of the monasteries and, as it were, to weave it into the life-giving ether of the free spirit pervading the universe."

I also perfectly agree with the extremely applicable close of the same article: "Our age has not yielded its right to feel itself connected with the Infinite," and I intend to set to work in earnest to comply, as far as possible, with the kindly expectations of my reviewer. His reference to my Psalms leads me to wish that I might soon see the four Psalms published in score (they are very diverse, both as regards feeling and musical form). Kahnt's willingness to publish them is, therefore, welcome news to me, and I beg he will give me a proof of his goodwill by kindly having them ready for next Easter's sale.

He can settle everything about the form and equipment "al suo commodo" (as people say here).

Still the Psalms should be published in the same form, and should Kahnt decide upon retaining the form of the Prometheus score (as he writes to me) I shall be quite content and satisfied. The day after to-morrow I shall send him the instrumentation of the 23rd and 137th Psalms together with the score of the 13th. The latter is one of those I have worked out most fully, and contains two fugue movements and a couple of passages which were written with tears of blood. Were any one of my more recent works likely to be performed at a concert with orchestra and chorus, I would recommend this Psalm. Its poetic subject welled up plenteously out of my soul; and besides I feel as if the musical form did not roam about beyond the given tradition. It requires a lyrical tenor; while singing he must be able to pray, to sigh and lament, to become exalted, pacified and biblically inspired.— Orchestra and chorus, too, have great demands made upon them. Superficial or ordinarily careful study would not suffice. . . .

Pardon me, dear friend, for having troubled you to such an extent with marginal comments to my manuscripts. I will only add that I should be glad to see the short Choral Psalm for men's voices (" The Heavens declare the glory of God ") printed in time for the Easter's sale, in score-form from the copy I left Kahnt before I went away ;—and now to return to the Articles in the *Neue Zeitschrift*, I feel specially grateful, in the first place, for the communications concerning the Hungarian orchestra in Breslau.

To hear again of my Ex-Chamber-Virtuoso Josy [1] in so friendly a way pleased me extremely, and I beg you to send my sincerest thanks to the author of the article for having so carefully studied my Rhapsodies and the less well-known book (not to speak of the erroneous interpretation it has had to endure at other hands !) on " Hungarian Gipsy Music "; at the same time will you

---

[1] An extremely musical gipsy boy of this name was presented to Liszt in Paris in 1844 by Count Sandor Teleki. Liszt's endeavours to train the boy as an artist failed, however, owing to the impossibility of accustoming the child of nature to engage in earnest study, as Liszt himself relates in " Die Zigeuner und ihre Musik in Ungarn " [The Gipsies and their Music in Hungary] (Ges. Schriften, Bd. vi.).

beg him to accept the enclosed photograph of my humble self, in return for the one he gave Josy? In your next let me have some account of the position and work of this worthy Breslau correspondent, for I have not before met with anything from his pen in the *Neue Zeitschrift.* I herewith send you a second photograph of my present abode, " Madonna del Rosario," as the first one went astray, but to prevent a like accident in the post I shall register this letter.

Bülow's searches into and out of the subject are splendid, and his farewell words in memory of Fischl show the noblest beat of heart. When are the articles on Offenbach, etc., from the same intellectual region, to appear? . . . I am curious also to see what news there will be of the Berlin Orchestral concerts, instituted and conducted by Bülow.

You mention cursorily some new programme-form concerning which " you rather flatter yourself." Tell me more about this and send me a few of the programmes.

From Pohl I lately received a very cordial letter which I answered forthwith. His *Vorschlag zur Güte,* etc., in the N. Z. I have not yet read, and this is the case with many other articles in the last numbers, which, however, I mean ere long to overtake. In spite of my retirement and seclusion I am still very much disturbed by visitors, duties of politeness, musical *protégés*—and wearisome, mostly useless correspondence and obligations. Among other things the St. Petersburg Philharmonic Society has invited me, during the Lent season, to direct two of their concerts, giving performances of my own compositions. The letter certainly reads somewhat more rationally than that of the Cologne Cathedral Committee (of which I told you); but the good folks can nevertheless not refrain from referring to the trash about " my former triumphs, unrivalled mastery as a pianist," etc., and this is utterly sickening to me—like so much stale, luke-warm champagne. Committee gentlemen and others should verily feel somewhat ashamed of their inane platitudes, in thus unwarrantably speaking to my discredit by reminding me of a standpoint I occupied years ago and have long since passed.—Only one Musical Association can boast of forming an honour-able exception to this since my departure from Germany, namely the Society "Zelus pro Domo Dei," in Amsterdam, which, in consequence of the approval and performance of my Gran Mass last week, has conferred on me their diploma by appointing me an honorary member, in addition to a very kind letter written in a becoming tone.

The diploma is headed: " Roomsch Catholiek Kerk-musiek Collegie," and the Society was founded in 1691.

For your wife's amusement and as a piece of French reading I send a copy of my answers to the letters from St. Petersburg and Amsterdam. When you have read them please send both copies to my daughter in Berlin, as an addition to her small collection of my miscellaneous correspondence.

Most cordial greetings.—Yours in all friendship,

F. Liszt.

November 11*th*, 1863.

25. To Breitkopf and Härtel.

DEAR SIRS,

. — . Pray present my kindest thanks to Conzertmeister David for his consent to the *N.B.* in the Finale of the 8th Symphony. The method of execution, as indicated, was the one important question to me ; by the satisfactory solution of this I am now perfectly content, and it is pleasant to me, therefore, to be able to agree to your wish to undertake the publication of the 9 piano-scores forthwith, without asking advice *elsewhere.* My former request on this subject was meant only to serve as a proof of my sincerest conscientiousness ; as soon as you consider it superfluous let it be so.

Your letter also settles the copyist-difficulty. Still, notwithstanding all the model-works that issue from the House of Breitkopf and Härtel, I could scarcely expect that the printers would worry over my bad musical writing, that is rendered even more indistinct by my numerous erasures and corrections—and for this reason I recommended Herr Carl Götze of Weimar by way of help; he is very quick at deciphering my untidy manuscripts. But of the best copyists it may be said "Better none," to use Beethoven's words in pronouncing his verdict upon Mälzel's metronome.

Permit me therefore, dear sirs, to reduce all these preliminaries and details to the simplest form, by giving you *absolute power* concerning the publication of the 9 Symphonies—provided that the last proofs are sent to me for revision.

While awaiting the Beethoven scores (Quartets,

Egmont, and Christ on the Mount of Olives) I send you my best thanks in advance, and shall hope to send you later a specimen of my small *savoir-faire* in the matter of Quartet arrangements to look at. If it should meet with your approval I would gladly, next summer, proceed in working out a former pet idea of mine ; to make pianoforte transcriptions of Beethoven's Quartets " for the home circle," and, as it were, to make them a link in the Master's *catena aurea*, between his Sonatas and Symphonies.—No considerations in the way of honorarium need form any hindrance to this project, especially as in such matters not the smallest difficulty has ever arisen in our relations with one another, which have now lasted over 20 years. Besides, the way and manner you accept my proposal offers the best prospect for its realisation, to our mutual satisfaction in *tempore opportuno*.

. — . I beg you, dear sirs, to accept my sincere thanks as well as the assurance of my respectful attachment.

F. Liszt.

Rome, *November 16th,* 1863.
(Monte Mario, Madonna del Rosario.)

26. To Dr. Franz Brendel.

Dear Friend,

By way of excusing my delay in writing I must tell you at once of an indisposition, which during Christmas week prevented my undertaking any other occupation or amusement than that of keeping in bed. For several weeks after that there were other things, entirely unconnected with musical doings and affairs, which, however, urgently demanded attention.

Your admirable New Year's letter I received yesterday. It perfectly confirms my opinion of the state of
affairs (as became clear to me long since), and my
agreement with you as regards our " Debit and Credit."
The latter, unfortunately, does not show the right
equilibrium—but must be made to do so. In the first
place *three* points have to be secured ; and to save
useless explanations between us, I shall describe these
in geographical style, under the names of Weimar,
Löwenberg, Carlsruhe. They at present embrace and
solve all the essential questions : division of work,
appointment of suitable persons, procuring adequate
means, active organisation of the *Musik-Verein*, etc.,
etc. And, granted that you are not deceiving yourself
about my very limited influence, my personal presence
and intervention would seem indispensable. Still I
will not conceal the fact that it is, at least, *inconvenient*
for me to leave Rome even for a short time, and people
should not object to my finding more satisfaction in my
retirement here than in the barren unpleasantries of
a so-called " circle of activity." But if, as you assure
me, the question affects the good cause, and I could
really be of service to a few dear friends,—well in that
case every other consideration shall give way and my
willingness be put to the proof. Although it will be
very difficult for me to make up my mind to start, I
will towards the beginning of June have my passport
visé'd for Carlsruhe, in order that I may attend the
Musical Festival there, *provided that Bülow conducts.*
In the intervals between the rehearsals and performances we should discuss with active friends the *Whys*
and *Wherefores* connected with the *Musik-Verein*

which, first of all, requires to be placed on a firm footing. And so far as I can assist in doing this (especially by advocating its cause with our patron and the Hohenzollern princes) it certainly shall be done.

Pohl seems to have put on wrong spectacles if he reads in my letter that I have no greater wish than to return to unique Germany! People may think about it what they please; the *positive* truth is that I do not bother myself about fools of any species, whether German, French, English, Russian or Italian, but am peacefully industrious in my seclusion here. " Let me rest, let me dream," not indeed beneath blossoming almond trees, as Hoffmann sings,[1] but comforted and at peace under the protection of the *Madonna del Rosario* who has provided me with this cell. My German friends would certainly be acting much more reasonably were they to come and visit me here, instead of tempting me abroad. However you may assure the rest of my acquaintances that I will not inconvenience them with my presence for any length of time, and that my interference at the Musical Festival in Carlsruhe is only a temporary one and altogether harmless. By the middle of July, at latest, I intend to be back here again, or earlier if possible.

The *Pro memoria* of the A. D. *Musik-Verein*, addressed to the Grand Duke, together with the protocol of the audience on the 17th of November, I received through Gille. My thanks and reply I shall send shortly. Likewise also the programme of a very *exceptional* solemnity which takes place on the 5th February,

---

[1] A song which Liszt set to music.

and which is already engaging my attention in a variety
of ways.

In all friendliness,

Your cordially devoted

F. LISZT.

January 22nd, 1864.

To Kahnt my best thanks for having sent the last
parcel of music correctly.   Postage and dues cost over
13 Prussian thalers.   By the way, do not offend me
any longer by *franking* your letters.   I on my part
frank my letters only when I send you a *letter-parcel*
containing copies, etc.

Last postscript. . — .   Do me the one other favour of
seeing that my enclosed answer safely reaches Herr B.
I do not know his address—and, although we may have
met in Weimar, as he once wrote to me, I have
scarcely any recollection of the fact.

Do not be vexed at the apparent presumption and
vain-glory of this *last* communication for to-day. . . .
My modesty will sufficiently come to my rescue to
prevent my putting too many feathers in my cap !*
Besides, thank God, I am too honest and truth-loving
to fall a victim to vanity.

27. TO DR. FRANZ BRENDEL.

DEAR FRIEND,

Excuse an intermezzo on music-publishers to-
day.   I have received from Julius Schuberth and from
Peters' *Bureau de Musique* contradictory letters about

---

* The German proverb of which Liszt makes use is "allzugrosse
Rosinen im Kopfe tragen."

some *right* or *un*righteous edition of my arrangement
of Beethoven's Septet.   Schuberth's communication is
many-sided, the other very one-sided, but neither of
them enlightens me in the least, for it is a question
of long since, and I scarcely remember where and
for whom I arranged the Septet, now more than 20
years ago.   And although Schuberth has given me but
little cause to be satisfied with his editions, still I
should not wish to do him any injury by this piece of
business,* and hence I have not sent him any reply.
For the same reason I shall leave Peters' communication unanswered, and must get you, dear friend, to
make these two gentlemen understand that I cannot
mix myself up with any of their disputes as publishers.
And in order that you may obtain an insight into the
matter I send you, herewith, Peters' letter, with
regard to which I can only say that I have no recollection of having made a duet arrangement of Beethoven's
Septet. . . . Yet this is precisely what I do *not* wish to
say.   Let the two gentlemen settle the matter amicably
between themselves and ignore my existence altogether.

As Bülow is happily back, the programmes of the
Carlsruhe Musical Festival will now soon be finally
drawn up.   Reményi, who has played here some half-
dozen times in the Teatro Argentina with *extraordinary*
success, has a decided inclination to appear at the
Musical Festival; I told him, however, that Conzert-
meister Singer had probably already been engaged.
Should Singer not be able to come, I would recommend
Reményi with absolute confidence.   Of all the violinists
I know, I could scarcely name three who could equal

* An untranslatable pun on the words *Handel* and *Händel*.

him as regards effect. Tell Bülow of Reményi's friendly offer, and let me know at your convenience whether it is accepted.—

As soon as I hear more definitely about the programme I shall answer Gille's friendly note. Meanwhile (after 4 months' incessant interruptions) I have again set to work, and cannot now leave it till the time comes for my journey.

What a royal and marvellous act is Ludwig of Bavaria's letter to Wagner! It ought verily to be engraved in the Walhalla in letters of gold. Oh that some other Princes would adopt a similar style!—

In all friendship, yours sincerely,

F. LISZT.

ROME, *May 28th*, 1864.

28. TO DR. FRANZ BRENDEL.

DEAR FRIEND,

Shortly after sending off my letter anent the Peters-Schuberth squabble, I received the programme-sketch of your last letter but one. Exceedingly important and indispensable are the Wagner-numbers. Let me hope he has already given you a favourable reply. Bülow will be the best one to arrange things and to conduct. I wrote to him the day before yesterday to advise him again to be strictly moderate with regard to the number of my compositions. *The half* of what is given in your sketch of the programme would be amply sufficient. People do not want to hear so much of my things, and I do not care to force them upon them. . . . On this occasion, especially, my wish is only to *see* some of my friends *again*—in no way to seek appreciative approval from the public. Such misleading abuses have long since and entirely ceased for me. Hence, dear friend, do not have me playing the braggart on your programme! If a place is to be retained for Reményi he will fill it brilliantly. For both as a soloist and a quartet player his accomplishments are extraordinary.

You ask me about "definite news of my journey." As already said, I am determined to attend the *Tonkünstler-Versammlung*, and afterwards to go to Weimar for a few days. My departure from here depends upon the date of the Carlsruhe concerts. I shall arrange to be there a few days previously, and shall ask Bülow to secure apartments for me. A variety of considerations (among which are economical ones too) compel me not to extend my absence from Rome beyond a month, and before returning I am in duty bound to pay my mother a visit in Paris. Hence I shall have but little time for strolls on the banks of the Ilm or elsewhere. . . . But let me hope that my journey will not prove pure idling, and I shall do my best "to pave the way" to meeting *all your wishes* in as satisfactory a manner as possible. Further details on this subject I shall give you by word of mouth towards the end of August. All mere reports about my remaining in Germany for some length of time I beg of you to contradict most emphatically. Some newspapers seem anxious that it should be known that I am about to settle in Hungary. There is nothing whatever in this report beyond the anticipated order for my composing a second *Gran Mass*, and perhaps publishing an Hungarian translation of the *Elizabeth*. These two tasks may,

during the course of next year, lead to my revisiting
Hungary (?).

Kindly present my excuses to Riedel, who wishes
me to attend his concert in the St. Thomas Church
(at the beginning of July). I am delighted that the
"*Seligkeiten*" find a place in his programme, and I am
sincerely grateful to H. von Milde for having contributed so much to their success by his fine interpretation and inspired delivery. Whether the Psalm ("By
the waters of Babylon") is not somewhat too low for
Frau v. Milde's voice, I should not like to say. I
remember, however, that she sang it on one occasion
at the Altenburg *gloriously*. Of course I can consider
it only a very flattering mark of attention and amiability
on the part of Frau von Milde to venture anywhere
to introduce any one of my compositions under her
vocal protection, but especially in Leipzig.

With hearty thanks and kindest greetings yours,

F. LISZT.

ROME, *June* 13*th*, 1864.

29. TO THE COMMITTEE OF THE SOCIETY FOR THE
SUPPORT OF NEEDY HUNGARIAN MUSICIANS IN
PEST.

GENTLEMEN,

You are good enough to invite me in a very
flattering manner to take part in the Association that
you are starting, with the object of helping needy and
infirm musicians in Hungary. Every tie which unites
me to our noble country is dear to me. I cordially
accept to be *entirely yours*, and am pleased to hope

that the esteem in which you are held, added to your intelligent solicitude for this good work, will secure it speedily and lastingly excellent results.

The good that you propose to realise is not liable to controversy, but is so plainly evident that you will receive on all sides nothing but approbation, encouragement, help and support. Nevertheless, as you do me the honour to ask my explicit opinion with regard to the statutes of your Society, I will venture to observe that it seems to me desirable not to limit oneself exclusively and for ever to helping sick and infirm musicians—and their needy heirs. Those who are in health, when they are at the same time well-deserving, have a claim also on your sympathy. . . Without enlarging on this point here, I only recommend to your attention, gentlemen, the statutes (published at Leipzig) of the Association which was formed at Weimar in August 1861, under the name of "Allgemeiner Deutscher Musik-Verein," in which the needs of *music* and of *musicians* of our day have been taken into consideration simultaneously.

If I had not the sad honour of being poor I should hasten to put a considerable sum at your disposal. Pray pardon me, then, the moderate offering of *a hundred florins* which you will shortly receive (through my cousin Dr. Eduard Liszt, of Vienna), and I beg you to accept, gentlemen, the assurance of my sincere desire to render in future the best service to your work, as also the expression of my very distinguished and devoted sentiments.

F. LISZT.

ROME, *June 18th*, 1864.   (MADONNA DEL ROSARIO.)

30. To Eduard Liszt.

Very dear Eduard,

Assuredly I have not been *"complaining"* of you to Count Gallenberg nor to anybody else in the world. Quite the contrary, and on every occasion I *boast* of my beloved cousin, and am happy and proud of his loyal, delicate and noble friendship, which is one of the sweetest kindnesses of Providence to me. Nevertheless I am much obliged to Count Gallenberg for having somewhat driven you to write to me, *extra*, so good and tender a letter, for which I thank you from my heart and soul.

The electoral circular you added to it gives me real satisfaction, and I am pleased at the public evidence that has been attained of your "honourableness, firmness of character and great capability." It seems to me that it was not possible, under the actual circumstances, to have obtained a more complete success in the competition with Schuselka ; [1] but I hope that your turn will come soon. The waiting is painful for you, without doubt, and is also too prolonged as regards your deserts . . . still one must be resigned to it, and that as simply as possible, by abstaining from useless words and taking useless steps. To be ever deserving, though only occasionally obtaining—much or little— is still the wisest thing to do in this world, where " he who endures little will not endure long ! "—

. — . Shall I see you at Carlsruhe at the end of

---

[1] Eduard Liszt was at that time standing against Schuselka as a andidate for the *Reichstag* (Parliament), but without success.

August? I hope so most truly. Before returning here (at the beginning of October) I shall spend a few days with my mother in Paris. You will not be vexed with me for beginning with her first, and for postponing till another year my transient visit to you at Vienna, which I accept in the same manner as you offer it, and for which the occasion will be found when I return to Hungary, supposing that they are inclined (as appears likely) to give me an order similar to that of the " *Graner Messe.*" Otherwise, and unless there be any determining circumstance for me, I am resolved not to tire people with my presence, as also to withdraw myself from the idle fatigue that people cause me. Thank God I have something to work at without disturbing myself at my work further than is necessary for the good conscience I hope always to keep. For this Rome is peculiarly adapted to me, and I shall not go away for the smallest thing without *well knowing* what it is for.

I send herewith my answer to the Committee of the Association in aid of poor musicians in Hungary,[1] to which I beg the Princess to authorise you to add the sum of 100 florins. Let them be sent at once to the Committee, begging for an acknowledgment, which you will send to me.

Reményi will come and see you shortly. He has spent nearly two months here, and has been heard very often at the Argentina Theatre with extraordinary success. I have invited him to come to Carlsruhe, as I am persuaded that he will succeed no less well there

---

[1] See the foregoing letter of 18th June.

than in Rome.   Meanwhile I beg you to give him a
cordial reception.

Yours ever affectionately,

F. LISZT.

June 22nd, 1864 [ROME].

Greetings and love to your dear ones.

It goes without saying also that I think most
affectionately of Cornelius and Tausig, which you will
tell them.

31. To Dr. Franz Brendel.

DEAR FRIEND,

. — . *I can assure you of* Reményi's co-operation.
By the middle of July I expect a letter from him with
his fuller address. It will be superfluous to mention
him in the preliminary programme of the concert-
performances. But what about Wagner ?—Frau von
Bülow sends me very sad news of him. . . . If he
definitely refuses to attend the *Tonkünstler-Vers.*
all we can do is to obtain his consent to give the
extracts—previously enumerated in the programme—
from his *Meistersänger* and other of his works (together
with the scores and voice parts).   In my opinion these
pieces are *indispensable* for the principal day of the
Carlsruhe programme.   It would be best if Bülow
alone brought the matter to the desired issue.   It seems
to me impossible that Wagner could give him and all
of us the pain of an absolute refusal! At all events
everything must be done to avoid such a misfortune—
nay, I may even say, such a *scandal.*

For the future, dear friend, you shall be totally

relieved of the trouble of sending me these detailed communications. Frau von Bülow is going to report to me of the further progress of the preliminary arrangements concerning the *Tonk.-Vers.* ; you yourself have more than enough to do with writing, negotiating, deciding, preparing, weighing to and fro, and in thinking things out, etc., etc.

It is settled, therefore, that I am coming, and you will have to look after me during my couple of weeks' stay in Germany, as it is mainly your fault that I am coming. Between ourselves I may tell you that, had it not been for your pressing letters, I should probably have confined myself to giving the Bülows a *rendez-vous* in Marseilles, and to paying my mother a few days' visit in Paris. Of other roads there are extremely few for me nowadays—and those that I have still to tread are not to be found in journeys, but only indeed at my quiet writing-table !

With hearty greetings and in all friendship, yours,

F. LISZT.

July 1st, 1864.

Yesterday I received a friendly letter from Séroff. Could not some fragment from his " Judith " be fitted into your Carlsruhe programme ?

32. To WALTER BACHE IN LONDON.[1]

I reply to your letter, dear Mr. Bache, by assuring you once more of my very sincere and affec-

---

[1] The addressee (1842—1888), a pupil of Liszt's, settled in London as teacher, pianist and conductor, devoted his whole life there to making Liszt's music known in England. His annual Recitals and Orchestral concerts were devoted mainly to this object.

tionate interest. You will never find me wanting or behindhand when it is a question of proving this to you ; be very sure of that.

The good news you give me of Madame Laussot is very welcome to me. I hope she will give me the pleasure of coming again to Rome, for I see no chance of my coming to Florence. Towards the middle of August I shall start for Carlsruhe, where I have promised to be present at the third *Tonkünstler-Versammlung*. Thence I shall go to Weimar, and shall take Paris on the way in order to see my mother again before returning here at the beginning of October.

Please tell Madame Laussot that she would wrong me if she did not count me amongst her most truly affectionate and devoted adherents. I especially preserve a grateful remembrance of her in connection with the " *Ideale*," and all that attaches to it. She is of the very small number of noble and intelligent exceptions in the too great number of my friends and acquaintances. I was speaking to this purpose the day before yesterday to a young person of Grecian origin who lives in Florence at the Count de Sartiges' house (and who frequents Madame Laussot's concerts). The Athenian plays the piano marvellously and charmingly.

You will bring me Ehlert's Scherzo with other of his compositions.

Meanwhile I commission you to give my best compliments to Ehlert.

A thousand cordial and affectionate things, and *à revoir* next winter.

July 2nd, 1864. MADONNA DEL ROSARIO.   F. LISZT.

Thanks for the triple photograph,[1] which is thrice welcome.

33. To ?*

DEAR FRIEND,

  The parcel of music you kindly announce has not yet come; but I will not delay in sending you my thanks, as I am about to leave here for six or seven weeks.

The day after to-morrow I travel to Carlsruhe to attend the *Tonkünstler-Versammlung,* the concerts there (conducted by Bülow) being given between August 22nd and 26th. Thence I go to Weimar on a visit. By the end of September I shall be with my dear mother in Paris, and back here by the middle of October. You must not be surprised if in newspaper-fashion I leave it undecided whether or not I change my abode and remain in Rome for ever.

The words *for ever* remind me of the 22nd Psalm (according to the usual Protestant numbering the 23rd) which, in reality, I composed for a tenor, whereas the 137th is meant for a mezzo-soprano (Fräulein Genast, now married to Herr Merian, in Basle).

I am therefore surprised that you should have proposed the latter Psalm and not the 22nd for Herr Erl, and I fear the effect of it will not be good sung by a tenor. The violin accompaniment which on several

[1] Probably of Mme. Laussot, Pinelli and Bache, who were taken together.

* Autograph letter (without address) in the possession of Monsieur Etienne Charavay in Paris. The letter appears to be addressed to a friend in Vienna.

occasions is in unison, as well as the concluding chorus, "Jerusalem, Jerusalem," are written exclusively for women's (or boys') voices, and thus demand a female soloist. Besides which it seems to me that the sentiment and spiritual tonality of the Psalm do not move in the masculinum. Israelitish gentlemen must not be called upon to sigh, to dream and to abandon themselves to their grief in any such way.

I shall be much pleased to become fully acquainted with the new works by Kremser, Hasel and Ziehrer, which you promise me, on my return.

Meanwhile with best thanks and kind greetings, yours in all friendship,

F. LISZT.

ROME, *August 7th*, 1864. (MADONNA DEL ROSARIO.)

34. TO EDUARD LISZT.

WEIMAR, *September 7th*, 1864.
(IN THE BLUE ROOM OF THE ALTENBURG.)

It grieved me to have to do without your presence at the *Tonkünstler-Versammlung* in Carlsruhe, dearest Eduard. Your letter, however, speaks of your having made some advance in your career, and this greatly delights me. I hope you will soon have more definite news to communicate to me on the subject. You know that to see you prosperous is one of the satisfactions I most desire in life!—

As regards the *Tonkünstler-Versammlung* you will find a kindly and satisfactory *résumé* of the proceedings in the supplement of the *Allgemeine Augsburger Zeitung*—31st August, 1st to 3rd September. Bülow was unfortunately prevented by serious illness from conducting. From a personal as well as an artistic point of view I felt his absence very keenly—however no complaint whatever can be made about the performance, and the reception accorded by the audience, especially to my Psalms, was extremely favourable. I assuredly never expected to meet with such sympathetic appreciation, after my experiences of former years. Friend Löwy had, on this occasion, no reason to hide himself in a seat at the back! In the Chamber-music soirées three of my Songs ("Es muss ein Wunderbares sein," "Ich liebe Dich," and "Mignon") were sung by Herr and Frau Hauser, and an encore was demanded. Reményi played magnificently, and Fräulein Topp[1] is a marvel.

At the conclusion of the *Tonkünstler-Versammlung* I started early on Sunday morning for Munich with Cosima (who remained with me the whole week of the concerts). Hans was confined to bed at the Bairischer Hof; his nervous rheumatic complaint has now settled in his left arm, which he will probably be unable to move for several weeks to come. In addition to the physical pain he suffers most grievously from this enforced state of inactivity. To endure things patiently is to some natures an absolute impossibility. He travelled back to Berlin, ill as he was, last Saturday, accompanied by his wife, and I have promised to go and spend a couple of days with him after my visit to Prince Hohenzollern in Löwenberg, where I go in a day or so.

Of Wagner's wondrous fortune you are sure to have

[1] Alida Topp, a pupil of Liszt's.

heard. No such star has ever before beamed upon a tone- or a word-poet. N.B.—H.M. the King of Bavaria addresses his communication, " To the Word- and Tone-Poet, Richard Wagner." More by-and-by about this remarkable affair of Wagner's. I saw him in Munich on several occasions, and spent one day alone with him in his villa on the Starnberger See.

I have been here since the day before yesterday. . — .

Continue to love me—as I do you.

With all my heart your
F. LISZT.

Address me to *Weimar* (at the Altenburg). I must return here from Löwenberg (between the 15th and 18th September) in order to await the Grand Duke at the Wartburg.

35. To BREITKOPF AND HÄRTEL.

DEAR HERR DOCTOR,

Together with the corrected proofs of the Pastoral and the C minor Symphonies (in which I found one or two errors) I sent you (from Weimar) my pianoforte arrangement of the 3rd instrumental movements of the 9th Symphony. After various endeavours one way and another, I became inevitably and distinctly convinced of the impossibility of making any pianoforte arrangement of the 4th movement for *two hands*, that could in any way be even approximately effective or satisfactory. I trust you will not bear me any ill-will for failing in this, and that you will consider my work with the Beethoven Symphonies as concluded with the 3rd movement of the 9th, for it was not a part of my

task to provide a simple *pianoforte score* of this over-
whelming 4th movement for the use of chorus directors.
Arrangements of this kind have already been made,
and I maintain that I am *not* able to furnish a better or
a more satisfactory one for helpless pianofortes and
pianists, and believe that there is no one nowadays
who could manage it.

In my edition of the 9th Symphony for *two pianos*,
prepared for Schott, the possibility was offered to me
of reducing the most essential parts of the *orchestra-
polyphony* to ten fingers, and of *handing over* the chorus
part to the second piano. But to screw both parts,
the instrumental and vocal, into two hands cannot be
done either *à peu près* or *à beaucoup près* !

In case other proofs of the remaining Beethoven
Symphonies are ready, you might send me them to
Weimar before Tuesday, 20th September. I should
be glad at the same time to receive the splendid 6
Mottets of Bach in eight-voice parts (among which
is " Sing unto the Lord a new song "). I am all the
more in need of reading such works, as I am at present unable to hear a performance of them.

Next week I shall again spend a few days in
Weimar (or Wilhelmsthal) ; thence I go to pay my
mother a visit in Paris, and by 18th October, at
latest, I shall be back in Rome.

Yours respectfully and sincerely,

F. Liszt.

Schloss Löwenberg, *September 14th,* 1864.

I requested Herr Kahnt to return to you with my
best thanks the copy of the Symphonic Poems which
was kindly forwarded to me in Carlsruhe.

36. To Breitkopf and Härtel.

Dear Herr Stadtrath,*

In compliance with the wish you so kindly express, I will again make an attempt to " adapt " the 4th movement of the 9th Symphony to the piano, and soon after my return to Rome will set to work upon the required *tentative*. Let us hope that the variation of the proverb : " Tant va la cruche à l'eau qu'à la fin . . . *elle s'emplit*"—may prove true.†

While talking of *various readings* allow me to draw your attention to an exceptionally valuable collection. A very carefully and well-trained musician with whom I have been acquainted for many years past—Herr Franz Kroll (in Berlin)—has, with industrious and unceasing perseverance, been collecting, copying and arranging for publication the noteworthy *various readings* of Bach's manuscripts of the " *Wohltemperirtes Clavier*." ‡ Last week he showed me several of them, and I became convinced of the substantial interest of the collection and encouraged friend Kroll to send you a full account of them. In now enclosing his letter to you—written at my instigation—I take upon myself, with pleasure and the fullest conviction, the musical duty of advocating the publication of ⸲these various Bach readings, and of heartily recommending Kroll's work as an essentially useful, complementary addition to your admirable edition of the " *Bach-Gesellschaft*." §

* Town Councillor.
† So often goes the pitcher to the water that at last it is filled.
‡ The well-tempered Piano.
§ The Bach Society.

Pray accept, dear Herr Stadtrath, the assurance of my sincere esteem and devotion.

F. LISZT.

WILHELMSTHAL, *October 1st,* 1864.

37. TO MADAME JESSIE LAUSSOT.

You will be good enough to excuse me, dear Madame, for having delayed replying to your kind letter. Amongst your many rare qualities there is one that I particularly admire; it is the prowess of your musical sympathies. Nevertheless I must scruple to expose you to too harsh trials, and, knowing by experience with how little favour my works meet, I have been obliged to force a sort of systematic heedlessness on to myself with regard to them, and a resigned passiveness. Thus during the years of my foreign activity in Germany I constantly observed the rule of never asking any one whatsoever to have any of my works performed; more than that, I plainly dissuaded many persons from doing so who showed some intention of this kind—and I shall do the same elsewhere. There is neither modesty nor pride in this, as it seems to me, for I simply take into consideration this fact—that Mr. Litz * is, as it were, always welcome when he appears *at the Piano* (— especially since he has made a profession of the contrary—) but that it is not permitted to him to have anything to do with thinking and writing according to his own fancy.

---

* Liszt quotes the very common misspelling of his name which has frequently been seen since he was " *le petit Litz* " in Paris.

The result is that, for some fifteen years, so-called friends, as well as indifferent and ill-disposed people on all sides, sing, enough to split your head, to this unhappy Mr. Litz, who has nothing to do with it, "Be a pianist, and nothing but that. *How is it possible not to be a pianist* when, etc., etc."

Possibly they are right—but it would be too much to expect me to sign my own condemnation. Far from that, I confess that contradiction ends by tempting me seriously, and that I am resolved to pursue it to the end, without any illusion or approbation whatever. Only at certain moments I fancy that that judicious maxim of Champfort is somewhat applicable to me: "Celebrity is the punishment of talent and the chastisement of merit."

Our friend Sgambati is happily in a fair way to incur this *punishment* and *chastisement*—and certainly with very good reason. He has done wonders this winter at his four concerts, which have had a success both of fashion and of real good taste. I, for my part, have gained a *thorough* affection for Sgambati, and the remarkable development of his talent of so fine and noble a quality interests me keenly.

A thousand very cordially affectionate and devoted things.

F. LISZT.

ROME, *March 6th*, 1865.

38. TO DR. FRANZ BRENDEL.

DEAR FRIEND,

While awaiting from you definite word about the next *Tonkünstler-Versammlung* in Dessau, let me,

meanwhile, thank you for your last communication.
The main interest of the musical performances is, of
course, on this occasion centred in Riedel and his
Verein. In the programme-sketch I notice my Psalm
137 at the very beginning. What lady takes the solo ?
—mind and soul are indispensable in it.

Bronsart wrote to me at the beginning of March that
he entertained the idea of a concert-tour to the Russian
provinces on the Baltic. I should be glad to hear that
the Euterpe squabble and quarrel in connection with
the T.K.V. in Dessau were at an end, and that Bronsart
was to undertake the conductorship.

As a supplement to this I send you herewith the
programme of the concert held in the hall of the Capitol,
where for some years past no special festivities have
been given, and probably never anything of this kind
before. For the first time the different orchestras in
Rome (the Sistine, St. Peter's, Lateran and Liberian)
all united to give a performance which upon the whole
may be said to have been as successful as it was well
received.

The concert was proposed to the Holy Father, and
approved of by him. Owing to the exceptional character
of the undertaking, which, like that of last year, was
made to fit in with the plan of the detailed arrangements—(some ladies belonging to the aristocracy, and
commissionaires distributed the tickets which were sold
at a *minimum*, no advertising, etc.), I determined to
give my co-operation. I played the *Cantique* (the last
number of the "*Harmonies poétiques et religieuses*"
published by Kistner), and, as there was no end to
the applause, I added my transcription of Rossini's

"*Charité*" (published by Schott). Everybody in Rome with any claim to culture was present, and the hall was more than full.

With friendliest greetings, your sincerely devoted

F. LISZT.

April 3rd, 1865.

P.S.—Please get Kahnt to inquire of Härtel as soon as possible, how far the printing of my arrangement of the Beethoven Symphonies has progressed, and whether I may rely upon his sending—during Easter week as already settled—the orchestral parts (autographed) of several of my Symphonic Poems,—more especially of the Dante Symphony ? It is possible that the Dante Symphony may be performed here towards the end of April. But you shall have further news of me before that.

Bote and Bock will shortly publish a very simple Hymn of mine (for pianoforte) entitled " The Pope's Hymn."

39. TO PRINCE CONSTANTINE OF HOHENZOLLERN-HECHINGEN.

MONSEIGNEUR,

Your Highness will understand that it is a necessity of my heart to speak to you of a very happy juncture that assures me henceforth, in full degree, the stability of feeling and of conduct to which I aspired. It seems to me that I should be guilty of ingratitude and wanting in respect to the condescending friendship with which you are good enough to honour me, did I not let you know of the determination I have taken.

On Tuesday the 25th April, the festival of St. Mark the Evangelist, I entered into the ecclesiastical state on receiving minor orders in the chapel of H.S.H. Monseigneur Hohenlohe at the Vatican. Convinced as I was that this act would strengthen me in the right road, I accomplished it without effort, in all simplicity and uprightness of intention. Moreover it agrees with the antecedents of my youth, as well as with the development that my work of musical composition has taken during these last four years,—a work which I propose to pursue with fresh vigour, as I consider it the least defective form of my nature.—

To speak familiarly ; if "the cloak does not make the monk" it also does not prevent him from being one ; and, in certain cases, when the monk is already formed within, why not appropriate the outer garment of one ?—

But I am forgetting that I do not in the least intend to become a monk, in the severe sense of the word. For this I have no vocation, and it is enough for me to belong to the hierarchy of the Church to such a degree as the minor orders allow me to do. It is therefore not the frock, but the cassock that I have donned. And on this subject Your Highness will pardon me the small vanity of mentioning to you that they pay me the compliment of saying that I wear my cassock as though I had worn it all my life.

I am now living at the Vatican with Monseigneur Hohenlohe, whose apartment is on the same floor as the *Stanze* of Raphael. My lodging is not at all like a prison cell, and the kind hospitality that Monseigneur H. shows me exempts me from all painful constraints.

So I shall leave it but rarely and for a short time only, as removals and especially journeys have become very burdensome to me for many reasons. . . . It is better to work in peace at home than to go abroad into the world,—except in important cases. One of these is awaiting me in the month of August, and I shall fulfil my promise of going to Pest at the time of the celebration of the musical fêtes that are being got up for the 25th anniversary of the establishment of the Conservatoire. My Oratorio of *Saint Elizabeth* and the Symphony of the "Divina Commedia" form part of the programme.

Next year, if Your Highness still thinks of realising your noble project of a musical congress at Löwenberg, I should be very happy to take part in it, and place myself entirely at your orders and service.

Permit me, Monseigneur, to express anew to you my most grateful thanks for the evidences of sympathy you have so generously accorded to myself and to my works ; and graciously accept the homage of unchanging sentiments of most respectful devotion with which I have the honour to be

Your Highness's most humble and affectionate servant, F. LISZT.

VATICAN, *May 11th,* 1865.

40. TO BREITKOPF AND HÄRTEL.

DEAR HERR DOCTOR,

My old musical weaknesses have not left me ! The weakest and worst thing about them is perhaps that I never cease composing ; but such wondrous things go wandering about in my head that I cannot help putting them down on paper.   And I have wanted to hear something about the fate of the manuscripts I sent you for printing.   Have the pianoforte scores of the Beethoven Symphonies been published?   How has the printing of the *Concerto* for 2 pianos (in E minor)[1] progressed?   Would you kindly let me have a few copies soon?

With regard to the autographed orchestral parts of my Symphonic Poems, I should be glad if they could be out by the end of July.   Probably at the beginning of August I go to Pest, where several of my compositions (more especially the *Dante Symphony*) are to be performed in connection with the festivities at the Conservatoire.   If the parts should be ready, please, dear Herr Doctor, forward them to me to Pest.   At present I do not require them here; but should the *Préludes* be ready you would greatly oblige me by sending all the orchestral parts, with four copies of the quartet, *if possible by the beginning of next month*, to Dr. R. Pohl (571, Hirschgasse, *Baden-Baden*).   I have been asked for the loan of them for some festival in Baden conducted by Monsieur Reyer.

Pray kindly excuse all the trouble I am giving you, and receive the expression of my most sincere esteem.

F. LISZT.

THE VATICAN, *May 27th,* 1865.

41. TO DR. FRANZ BRENDEL.

DEAR FRIEND,

Your favourable accounts of the *Tonkünstler-Versammlung* in Dessau delighted me greatly.   Owing

---

[1] Concerto pathétique.

to the *crooked* way in which my works have been listened to in past years, I have felt oppressed; and in order that my freedom in my work might remain unaffected, I was obliged wholly to disregard their outward success. Hence my absolute distrust of performances of my own compositions, and this was not to be accounted for by any exaggerated modesty on my part. As to the *Battle of the Huns* I was specially doubtful; the Christian significance of Kaulbach's picture—as represented in the *Chorale*—seemed to me a stumbling-block in the way of favourable criticism. Kaulbach had indeed suggested this interpretation by having *thrown a special light upon the cross* . . . yet there are neither mendicant friars nor bishops in the picture . . . and, besides, at the time of the *Battle of the Huns* the organ was *not* yet invented! This last sweeping argument was triumphantly hurled at me in Weimar by the infallible censors. Since then I have hesitated to allow the work to be performed, and have remained satisfied with sending Kaulbach the arrangement for 2 pianofortes. And in that form it was *executed** in his *salon*, whereupon, of course, there were loud lamentations about my squandering my time upon such an abominable jumble of sounds, when I might be charming people in a more agreeable fashion with my piano-playing! . . . . So if the Dessau Meeting really derived some pleasure from the *Battle of the Huns* I feel richly rewarded for my small amount of suffering.

I beg you to present my best thanks to Fräulein

* Executirt.

Wigand.[1] It is a good deed of hers to have obtained willing ears for my Psalm—and if I am in Germany again next year I shall want to hear it.

I will with pleasure take Weitzmann's place as examiner of the manuscripts sent in. Send them to me in *parcel form* to Rome ; I promise to look through them quickly and to let you have my good or bad opinion of them. For such work I am always inclined, and am, perhaps, not an awkward hand at it.

. — . From the Committee in Pest I have not had any news for some time past. I shall, however, hold myself in readiness to start from here by the beginning of August. Meanwhile let nothing be sent to me *to Rome*. As soon as I know anything definite about my stay in Hungary I will let you know.

With all friendly greetings to your wife, I am your sincerely attached

F. Liszt.

July 21st (Villa d'Este-Tivoli), 1865.

Any probable performance of the *Elizabeth* in Coburg we can discuss later. I should consider it advisable to have my name but little mentioned in the programme of the next Meeting of the *Tonkünstler-Versammlung*. As regards a larger work (one to occupy a whole concert) it would be well for Gille to leave the choice of it to the Duke. The local taste would be a very important point in the matter, and, for my own part, I know only too well that people do not want to know or to hear too much of me—in Coburg as well as in many other places !—

[1] Emilie Wigand, studied under Prof. Götze in Leipzig.

42. To Abbé Schwendtner in Buda-Pest.*

RIGHT REVEREND SIR AND FRIEND,

Having returned to my abode here, I cannot refrain from again thanking you most heartily for all the goodness and kindness you showed me in so unusually abundant a measure, during my stay in the town-vicarage of Pest. The five weeks I spent there in the pleasantest way—owing to your considerate care and attention—will remain an unextinguishable point of light in my life. You admonish, and at the same time encourage and strengthen me, to carry out further the artistic task that is set me. In the hope that your Reverence will in the future continue to show me the sympathy so kindly and generously expressed, I pray you to implore God's blessing to keep me ever a *good child of the State and Church.*

May I add another request? On the 22nd October (my birthday) for some years past a Mass has been read in the Franciscan Church in Pest, and at the words: "Memento Domini" I [am] held in remembrance. . . . I would ask your Reverence to remember my wish that this may be done also on the same day in the parish church.

In sincere veneration and gratitude, I remain cordially and faithfully

Your Reverence's devoted

F. LISZT.

THE VATICAN, *September 20th,* 1865.

* Autograph in the possession of Frl. Therese v. Lavner in Pest. —Liszt became acquainted with the Abbé in 1865, and frequently enjoyed his hospitality when visiting Pest, up to the time when he himself became connected with the Musik-Academie there.

My respectful compliments to the amiable lady
president of the morning coffee—Fräulein Resi[1]—who
conducts and beautifies the real Magyar hospitality
at the Vicarage in an incomparably graceful manner.
I shall take the liberty one day of sending Fräulein
Resi a few Roman trifles. Bülow has undertaken to
send you the medallion of my humble self, a masterly
piece of work by Rietschel. As you will know,
Rietschel is the sculptor who made the Lessing statue
in Brunswick, the Goethe and Schiller group in Weimar,
etc.—

43. To Dr. Franz Brendel.

Dear Friend,

Accept my best thanks for having admitted into
your *Neue Zeitschrift* Bülow's account of the Musical
Festival in Pest. These three articles are a masterly
piece of work, and, as your paper has for several years
past followed the difficult process of my development
as a composer in so kind and careful a manner, I wished
specially that the very successful performances of the
Elizabeth and of the Dante Symphony in Pest should
receive confirmation in the *Neue Zeitschrift*.

With regard to the *Elizabeth* I have received
offers from Vienna and a few other places; but it is
in no way my intention to wage war in a hurry with
this work. I shall, therefore, decline the invitations
with thanks, and await an opportunity more convenient
to myself for the next performance. Whether this
may be at the *Tonkünstler-Versammlung* in Coburg I

---

[1] A niece of the Abbé's.

do not know, and, frankly said, this will depend upon the Duke's *bon plaisir*.[1] For my own part I am in no great hurry, as I have heard enough of the work in Pest, and found no alterations to make in it. Then also there is no hurry with regard to its publication, and my reply a short time ago to a willing publisher (who, curiously enough, offered me a respectable honorarium for it!) was, that only by next summer could I decide whether to have it published or not.

Gille has the kind intention of arranging a performance of the *Elizabeth* in Jena as soon as possible. I don't want to enter into a fuller correspondence with him on the subject; but please tell him, in all friendliness, that I regret to be obliged somewhat to check his admirable zeal. Apart from certain considerations of propriety (which I will never disregard in the slightest degree) there is an irremovable difficulty in the matter of the performance itself. It cannot be given in Jena without the co-operation of the Weimar performers. And why plague our dear and excellent Weimar singers and artists, and how—with their many theatrical engagements—could they find the necessary time for studying the parts, for rehearsals ?—etc., etc.—

Hence let us give a simple *no* as regards Jena, and put a sign of interrogation ? nay, even two or more ? ? ? as regards the *Tonkünstler-Versammlung* in Coburg, for (as I told you in my last letter but one) we shall there have entirely to submit to the Duke's opinion concerning the larger (or longer) work which is to fill the first day's programme.

(N.B.—*Elizabeth* lasts about three hours, including

[1] It was not performed at a *Tonkünstler-Versammlung* in Coburg.

the intervals.   Bülow's conductorship would be *indispensable.*)

For ten days past I have again been back in the Vatican, and think of remaining here over the winter. At the present moment I am engaged in arranging the *Pope's Hymnus*, published last month by Bote and Bock for pianoforte as a solo and in duet-form, for chorus (with Italian words).   I think something of this piece, for which Kaulbach has made a splendid drawing.   If it is performed here you shall hear about it.   As soon as possible I mean to set to work with my *Christus Oratorio.*   Unfortunately I have had to set it aside for a year, as the *Vocal Mass* and other smaller works prevented my doing anything to it.   I shall require from six to eight months before I get the Christus finished, for I am scarcely half-way through yet.

My health is good, and I can unconcernedly allow people the pleasure of referring to me as "physically broken down" and a "decayed wreck" (as I have been described in the *Augsburger Allegemeine Zeitung*).

One favour do me at once, dear friend.   Request Kahnt to purchase for me the steel-plates (or wood-cuts) of Schwind's *Elisabeth-Galerie* in the Wartburg, published in Leipzig by Weigel or Brockhaus, and let them be sent safely, quickly and correctly, addressed to "Herr Baron Anton von Augusz — *Szegzard*" (Tolnaer Comitat—Hungary).   If I am not mistaken, the drawings are published in *two* parts.   The first part contains the pictures of St. Elisabeth's arrival at the Wartburg, the miracle of Roses—up to her death. The second part gives the medallions depicting her *works of charity.* I wish to send the *complete Elisabeth-Galerie* to Baron Augusz. The price is not high, and the money shall be refunded to Kahnt as soon as I get the bill.

By the way Kahnt would be doing me a favour by presenting *Reményi*, through Roszavögli (Pest), with a copy of Pflughaupt's arrangement for pianoforte and violin of my "Cantique d'amour" and "Ave Maria" —and by granting my humble self a copy also, at his convenience. Reményi will be glad to play the pieces with Plotenyi and thus make them known, and I would get Sgambati and Pinelli[1] to do the same here.

With hearty greetings to your wife,

Your unchangeably sincere and devoted

THE VATICAN, *September 28th,* 1865. F. LISZT.

Let me know of the despatch of the *Elisabeth-Galerie*, and also send me a few copies of Bülow's three articles.

Why have my organ-pieces (from Körner, Erfurt) not yet reached me? Please remind Kahnt or Gottschalg of this.

44. TO EDUARD LISZT.

DEAREST EDUARD,

My heartiest thanks to you for remembering the 22nd October. The day was celebrated quietly and happily like last year in my former residence (Madonna del Rosario)—and you were present with me in my inmost heart.

Before I received your lines I had already answered

---

[1] A Roman violin virtuoso (born 1843), was appointed in 1872 Director of the "*Società musicale romana,*" in Rome.

Dunkl's and Herbeck's letters relating to the *Elizabeth* Oratorio. You know how much against my wish it is to put this work into *circulation*. And, however flattering it may be to me (perhorrescised composer!) to receive offers from various places about it, still I think it advisable to avoid precipitancy, and not to expose my friends so soon again to unpleasantnesses such as my earlier works brought upon them. Löwy's empty stalls (with the *Préludes*) are significant . . . and, considering the various kinds of abuse which my works have had to endure, silence would seem to be most becoming.

Therefore be good enough, dearest Eduard, to tell those kindly disposed "*Musical Friends*," *emphatically* that I cannot make up my mind to the proposed performance of the *Elizabeth*, and beg them to pardon this small-mindedness in me. Besides the score is no longer at my disposal, as I have sent it to Bülow, who requires it for a performance desired by H.M. the King, for which I have already invited Herbeck. Bülow is giving some concerts this month and next in Berlin, Dresden, Prague, etc. Hence he cannot begin rehearsing the *Elizabeth* till later. Of the Munich performance you shall hear details when the time comes.

With regard to your communication to the Princess, I assure you again that *as soon as* and *as often as* it is possible for me to do you a service, as certainly shall it be done.

Kindest greetings to your wife from

Your truly devoted

[ROME,] *November 1st*, 1865.   F. LISZT.

45. To Dr. Franz Brendel.

DEAR FRIEND,

My answer to you has been delayed in order that I might at the same time tell you of a variety of things.

A) At the beginning of March I intend going to Paris. The Gran Mass is to be given on March 15th in the Church of St. Eustache at the anniversary "*de l'œuvre des écoles*" to which the *Maire* of the 2nd Arrondissement, M. Dufour, sent me an official invitation the other day.

B) The report spread in various newspapers about the Hungarian Coronation-Mass which I am to compose, is for the present only officiously correct. Probably it may become true shortly.[1]

C) At the opening of the *Dante Gallery* here at the end of the month my *Dante Symphony is to be performed*. I enclose the article from the *Osservatore Romano* in which this extraordinary event is discussed in detail—also another number of the same paper containing a short notice on the "*Stabat mater speciosa*" (a very simple chorus from my *Christus Oratorio*), that was sung last Thursday in the Franciscan Church *Ara Coeli* (on the Capitol).

D) I am quite determined to attend the *Tonkünstler-Versammlung* in Coburg, and expect to hear from you shortly more about it. It is to be hoped that Bülow will conduct. If there should be any thought of giving the *Elizabeth*, Bülow will be *indispensable.*—

As regards the *Elizabeth*, pray make my best excuses

[1] This did occur, as is well known.

to Kahnt. I did not reply to his friendly request, because I have made up my mind *not* to have this work published meanwhile, and hold fast to this negative determination. Do not let Kahnt take this ill of me, and let him be assured of my sincere willingness to meet his wishes in all other matters.

. — . I am in want of a great many things, but most of all in want of more time !—

With friendliest greetings, sincerely and devotedly yours,

F. LISZT.

THE VATICAN, *January 14th*, 1866.

46. TO DR. FRANZ BRENDEL.

DEAR FRIEND,

So there is to be no *Tonkünstler-Versammlung* this year; in place of it war-cries, and symphonies of bayonets and cannon ! Here, probably, we shall remain in peaceful quietude under the protection of France.—As regards my humble self, I mean to try, during the second half of this 66th year, to overtake what I was compelled to neglect during the first half of it. My Christus Oratorio shall be finished by Christmas.—Prince Hohenlohe, with whom I have been residing since April 1865, has been made Cardinal and shortly leaves the Vatican. Last Sunday I returned to my old quarters at *Monte Mario, Madonna del Rosario*, where I am as comfortable as possible. Next year I think of going to Germany, first to Munich. As you know, the King of Bavaria has conferred upon me the title of Knight of the Grand Cross of the Order of

St. Michael. And the Emperor Maximilian that of the Guadeloup order. —

My stay in Paris will not prove unfruitful. People may say of it what they like.—I must mention to you the name of Camille Saint-Saëns in Paris, as specially deserving of notice in the *Neue Zeitschrift* as a distinguished artist, virtuoso and composer. Last year he was in Leipzig, so he told me, and played his Concerto at the Gewandhaus there. But people could not make anything out of him, and in dignified ignorance allowed him to pass. Langhans [1] sees him frequently and could give you fuller information about him for the *Zeitschrift*.

Give Kahnt my grateful thanks for carefully carrying out the orders from Paris. I mean to wait another year before publishing the *Elizabeth*. I also want several illustrations for it, for, as the work is dedicated to the King of Bavaria, I wish it to present the choicest and noblest appearance.

If Kahnt should be disposed to take it next year, I shall be glad to come to some arrangement with him about it. Still I am determined not to have the *Elizabeth* published till then ; to several publishers who have offered to undertake the publication I have already replied,—may every kind of printing long be held at a distance from this score. —

Allow me to recommend to your friendly interest a few other things I have at heart.

Ask Kahnt, in my name, not to be sparing in supplying Bülow with copies of the Liszt-compositions he has published. I should more especially like my Quartets for male voices circulated, and a few complimentary

[1] A Berlin musical composer and critic who died in 1892.

copies from Kahnt would be useful in this respect. No fear need be entertained of Bülow's making indiscreet demands, and one may confidently grant him all he wishes.

. — . Härtel will shortly be sending me some music. Please enclose the last numbers of the *Neue Zeitschrift* in the parcel in order that my ignorance on matters musical may be relieved.

In sincere attachment I remain in unalterable friendship,

Yours,

ROME, *June 19th*, 1866.   F. LISZT.

The score of the Gran Mass presumably reached Riedel safely (6 weeks ago). The vocal parts I have meanwhile left with Giacomelli. Later an edition of the choral and orchestral parts will become a necessity.

47. TO DR. FRANZ BRENDEL.

DEAR FRIEND,

Your last letter but one, the registered one, has reached me safely. As it contained more in the way of answers than was wanted I hesitated to write to you. As already said, I have made up my mind to wait another year before publishing the *Elizabeth*. In the first place it is necessary that I should correct the frequent errors in the copy of the score—a piece of work that will take a couple of weeks.—Then, before its appearance, I should like an opportunity of quietly hearing the work once in Germany, and this perhaps might occur next year. Meanwhile give Kahnt my best thanks for his ready consent, of which, however, I cannot make use till later, provided that an honorarium of a couple of thousand francs (which has been offered me elsewhere) does not frighten him. . — . So far as one can plan a journey nowadays, I intend to be in Germany again for a few weeks during the summer of 1867.— To-morrow I shall write to Dr. Härtel and tell him that you have kindly expressed yourself ready to discuss with him the small matter about the Dräseke *brochure*. It would please me greatly to hear that some amicable arrangement had been made.

With regard to the publications of the *Allgemeine Deutsche Musikverein*, I would vote for the Overture by Seifriz. Likewise for the continuation of the Chamber music performances in Leipzig—and, of course, for the compensation from the Society's purse due to you.

Stade's article on the Faust Symphony I have not yet received. My last number of the *Zeitschrift* is that of July 6th. I am glad that Stade does not disapprove of these *Faust-things*.—Schondorf's Polonaise, Impromptu, etc., which Kahnt has sent me, I have read through with pleasure and interest. With the next sending to Rome please enclose the *Petrus* Oratorio by Meinardus (the pianoforte score). In case the pianoforte score has not appeared, then let me have the full score. And together with the Petrus Oratorio please also send me the fragment of the Christus Oratorio by Mendelssohn (published by *Härtel*).

My Christus Oratorio has, at last, since yesterday got so far finished that I have now only got the revising, the copying and the pianoforte score to do. Altogether it contains 12 musical numbers (of which the *Seligkeiten* and the *Pater Noster* have been published by Kahnt), and takes about three hours to perform. I have composed the work throughout to the Latin text from the Scriptures and the Liturgy. After a time I shall ask Riedel for his assistance and advice with regard to the German wording.

Please give Alex. Ritter my cordial thanks for his Amsterdam report.

I cannot, at present, promise you any literary contributions for the proposed Annual of the D. M. If the instrumental Introduction to the *Elizabeth* (for pianoforte) would suit you I would gladly place it at your disposal, reserving the copyright for the subsequent publisher of the score, that is, his right to publish the same Introduction again.

As far as I can foresee I shall remain here the whole winter. My address is simply : To Commandeur Abbé Liszt—Rome. Fuller performances of the Beethoven Symphonies and of the Dante Symphony are to be given next Advent in the Dante Gallery. Sgambati is to conduct them, and I have promised to attend the rehearsals.

Heugel of Paris (Director of the *Ménestrel*) is shortly to publish a new edition of my Franciscus-legends.

With friendliest greetings, your attached

F. LISZT.

October 2nd, 1866.

48. TO BREITKOPF AND HÄRTEL.

MUCH ESTEEMED HERR DOCTOR,

It is very mortifying to me to have to confess that I have most awkwardly come to a standstill with the transcription of the Beethoven Quartets. After several attempts the result was either absolutely *unplay-able*—or insipid stuff.   Nevertheless I shall not give up my project, and shall make another trial to solve this problem of pianoforte arrangement.   If I succeed I will at once inform you of my " Heureka." *   Meanwhile I am occupied exclusively with the Christus Oratorio, which has, at last, advanced so far that all I have now to do is to put the marks of expression in the score and the pianoforte score.

Pray kindly excuse me if a small piece of vanity leads me to address you with a wish.   My Symphonic Poems have, as you know, had a regular deluge of halberds hurled at them by the critics.   After all these murderous and deadly blows that have been aimed at them, it would be very gratifying to me if the analyses of these Symphonic Poems in which, a few years ago, Felix Dräseke discussed them severally in the *Anre-gungen* † could now be published by you all together in the form of a *brochure,* for they are written with a thorough knowledge of the subject, yet in a kindly spirit.

On this account I begged Dr. Brendel to discuss the matter with you, and now take the liberty of addressing you personally on the subject of my wish.

With much esteem, yours sincerely,

F. LISZT.

ROME, *October 4th,* 1866.

Will you kindly send *Cantor* Gottschalg in Tieffurt a good copy of my pianoforte scores of the nine Beethoven Symphonies ?

* Discovery (from a Greek word).—TRANS.
† Notices.

49. To Dr. Franz Brendel.

DEAR FRIEND,

My heartfelt sympathy in the grievous loss which you have sustained.[1] It is an immeasurable sorrow on which one can only be silent !—

Let us pass over to the business part of your letter. Our Grand Duke informs me that there is to be a Wartburg Festival this summer (a Jubilee in celebration of the 800th year of the Wartburg's existence). And for this fête he wishes a performance of the *Elizabeth*-Legend under my personal direction. I have agreed to this, for, as the occasion is· an exceptional one, I too am enabled to make an exception to meet his commands. Now as the Duke is Patron of the *Tonkünstler-Verein*, it seems to me appropriate that this year's *T. K. Versammlung* should be brought into some connection with the Wartburg Jubilee. Think the matter over and discuss it with Gille. The date of the Wartb. Festival has not been announced to me, and will probably not be settled till later. As for myself I could not promise to remain more than one month in Germany. Hence it would be agreeable to me personally if the *T. K. Versammlung* were not kept apart from the Wartburg Jubilee, and were arranged for about the same date ; I could then attend both. In case Bülow cannot undertake to act as conductor, those to be mentioned as substitutes would be, no doubt, Seifriz, Riedel, Damrosch, Lassen.—

[1] On November 15th, 1866, Dr. Brendel lost his wife, Elizabeth *née* Trautmann (born in St. Petersburg 1814). She was a pianist and a pupil of Field and Berger. Dr. Brendel survived her only two years.

Seifriz's hesitation with regard to the publication of his Overture I consider to be scrupulous *beyond measure*, and am of the opinion that he should not hold to it any longer. Gille's circular (of December 9th) I, of course, agree with, only the compensation of 50 thalers [about £71 0s. 0d.] is somewhat too modest. I should like to see an o added to the 50.—

The full score and pianoforte score of the *Elizabeth* contain a mass of errors. The revising will take me a couple of weeks. At the beginning of February I will send you the manuscript for Kahnt's disposal, that is, if he is willing to comply with my conditions about the publication (which I will write out carefully for you). You know that I should have preferred to postpone the publication of the *Elizabeth* for some time longer—still I understand Kahnt's difference of opinion, and desire to prove myself willing, provided that you approve of my willingness.

. — . Kindly, when you have an opportunity, remind Härtel about sending the dedication-copy of my pianoforte scores of the Beethoven Symphonies to Bülow. The copy ought to be properly bound (in three volumes —3 Symphonies in every volume), and addressed to Bülow, *Johannis-Vorstadt* 31, *Basel.*

With sincere thanks and hearty good wishes for the year 1867, I remain in unchanging friendship, yours,

F. LISZT.

ROME, *January 6th*, 1867.

The *Neue Zeitschrift* has not come for more than six months.

50. To Doctor Cuturi, Pisa.*

Sir,

I am told that you would be good enough to take into consideration my recommendation of Mr. Alexander Ritter. I hasten therefore to assure you of the sincere esteem in which I hold his remarkable talent as a violinist and his capability as an orchestral conductor. His very extensive musical knowledge, his frequent and close connection with *virtuosi* and celebrated composers, and his practical experience of the best-known works and orchestras qualify him in a high degree for the post that would be offered to him at Pisa. The best judges discern in Mr. Ritter not merely a brilliant *virtuoso*, able to obtain everywhere applause and approbation, but also—which is more rare—a consummate musician, endowed with the most noble feeling for Art, and possessing the most perfect understanding of the works of the great masters.

Besides this, sir, I am sure that you will find much pleasure in your personal relations with him. All who know him bear testimony to his honourable character as well as to his gentlemanly manners; and I will merely add that amongst all my German friends there are few of whom I preserve so affectionate a remembrance.

Pray accept, *Monsieur le Docteur*, the expression of my esteem and distinguished consideration.

F. Liszt.

Rome, *January 22nd*, 1867.

* From a rough copy of Liszt's in possession of Herr Alexander Ritter in Munich.

51. To Julius von Beliczay in Vienna.[1]

Dear Sir,

Accept my sincere thanks for your very friendly letter and for the dedication of the Beethoven Cadenza. It sounds well and is pleasant to play. Of course somewhat more might have been made of *the thing*, and a different key taken at the outset than *C minor*. But it is easier for me to play the critic than to do things myself, and so to-day I will merely thank you and assure you of my interest in your efforts and your success.

Very truly yours,

Rome, *April 29th*, 1867.   F. Liszt.

52. To Madame Jessie Laussot.

Dear Madame,

I cannot tell you how your generosity of mind and heart touches me. The favourable reception you have obtained at Florence for the *Beatitudes* and the *Pater noster* is a link the more in the chain of my musical obligations to you, dear and valliant *Maëstra*. Will you kindly convey my best thanks to your co-operators. . — .

As a slight musical indication observe that in the *Pater noster* I simply modulate and develop somewhat, —in the somewhat confined limits of a sentiment of trusting and pious submission,—the Gregorian intonation as sung in all our churches—

Pa - ter nos - ter qui es in cœ - **lis**

[1] Hungarian composer, living in Budapest since 1871.

following the traditional intonations for each verse. This framework was naturally adapted to the arranging of my Oratorio—*Christ*,—in which I employed two or three other intonations of the plain-song, without considering myself guilty of a theft by such a use.

You know that the rehearsals of the *Christ* have begun. With the help of our dear and admirable Sgambati it will be able to be given here at the end of June. I shall invite you to come and hear it, and shall send you shortly the programme of the whole work, which is going to be published previously.

But since you interest yourself with so rare a zeal in my poor works and in making them known, I am tempted to propose to you the 23rd and 137th Psalms for your Florence programmes. The latter has been sung here this winter with some success. It is not very troublesome to study ; provided that the singer understands what she has to say the rest goes of itself. The accompaniment is limited to four instruments,—Harp, Violin, Harmonium and Piano ; and, as in the Magnificat of the Dante Symphony, the chorus is written for Soprano and Alto voices (without Tenors or Basses). The text is excessively simple, and is reduced to the one word, Jerusalem !

Perhaps you may also meet with a kind soul who is willing to translate into Italian the Chorus of Reapers (" Schnitterchor ") from the Prometheus, which could be performed quite simply with piano accompaniment.

I will permit myself to send you the two Psalms next week by Mrs. Pearsoll (of New York), to whom I have sung your praises, a matter in which I yield to no one.   Happily the opportunity for practising this recurs often : Mme. d'Usedom (whom I met the other evening at Bn. Arnim's) will speak to you of it.   . — .

As soon as I receive positive tidings about the coronation at Pest you shall know.   I shall certainly not stir from Rome this time without coming to spend some hours with you at Florence.

Continue your friendship to me, and believe in mine, very cordial and grateful.

F. Liszt.

Rome, *May 24th*, 1867.

The success of Bronsart's Trio delights me.   You will give him great pleasure if you will write him a couple of lines, which you must address simply " *H. v. B.   Intendant des Hoftheaters.   Hannover.*" Tell him about Sgambati and his Trio at Rome and Florence. I, on my side, will write to Bronsart as soon as my summer plans are fixed.

53. To Eduard Liszt.

Very dear Eduard,

You know that the Coronation Mass has met with the most kind reception.[1]   None of my works up to the present time had been so favourably accepted. I have begged Franz Doppler in particular to let you know about it, knowing that you would like to hear me praised, even with some exaggeration, by a friend as competent as he is affectionate.   Since the performance of the Gran Mass Doppler has always shown the kindest feelings towards me.   Tell him that I am very sincerely grateful to him.

[1] At its performance at Ofen (Budapest).

I am anxious to thank Schelle[1] for his excellent
article in the *Presse*, and send you herewith a few
lines which you will be good enough to give him. . . .

The rehearsals of my Oratorio "*Le Christ*" are progressing. It will probably be performed in the early
part of July, and I will have the programme sent to
you.

Towards the end of July I shall go to Weimar.
The "*Wartburg Festival*" is fixed for the 28th August.
On that day the *Elizabeth* will be heard in the hall
of the *Minnesingers*. A fortnight before that the
concerts of the *Tonkünstler-Versammlung* will take
place at Meiningen. Possibly you may be able to
come and look me up in the course of this same
month of August.

Yours ever from heart and soul,

F. LISZT.

ROME, *June 20th*, 1867.

54. TO WILLIAM MASON IN NEW YORK.

DEAR MR. MASON,

Your kind letter gives me a very cordial pleasure,
and I beg you to be assured of the continuance of my
very affectionate feelings. I frequently hear your
success in America spoken of. You deserve it, and
I rejoice to know that your talent is justly appreciated
and applauded. Your compositions have not yet
reached me, but I am fully disposed to give them a
good reception.

---

[1] Musical critic of the Vienna *Presse*, since dead.

In about a fortnight I shall start for Weimar. The *Tonkünstler-Versammlung* is to take place at Meiningen this year from the 22nd to the 25th August. I shall be present at it, as also at the Jubilee Festival at the *Wartburg*, at which my Oratorio *Saint Elizabeth* will be performed on the 28th August. Perhaps I shall meet there Mr. Theodore Thomas and Mr. S. B. Mills, of whom you speak. I have heard the highest praises of the capability of Mr. Thomas, whom I have to thank particularly for the interest he takes in my Symphonic Poems. Artists who are willing to take the trouble to understand and to interpret my works cut themselves off from the generality of their fraternity. I, more than any one, have to thank them for this, therefore I shall not fail to show my thanks to Messrs. Thomas and Mills when I have the pleasure of making their acquaintance.

The news which reaches me from time to time about musical matters in America is generally favourable to the cause of the progress of contemporaneous Art which I hold it an honour to serve and to sustain. It seems that, among you, the cavillings and blunders and stupidities of a criticism adulterated by ignorance, envy and venality exercise less influence than in the old continent. I congratulate you on this, and give you my best wishes that you may happily pursue this noble career of an artist,—with work, perseverance, resignation, modesty, and the imperturbable faith in the *Ideal*, such as was indicated to you at Weimar, dear Mr. Mason, by your very sincerely affectionate and attached

F. LISZT.

ROME, *July 8th*, 1867.

55. To E. Repos, Director of the "Revue de Musique sacrée" in Paris.*

Dear Sir,

I am very much obliged to you for the kind feelings you express to me, and beg to assure you of my desire to correspond to them. By your activity and the character of your publications our interests are naturally similar; I will take care to make them as agreeable as possible to you.

The day after to-morrow I will send you four or five small pages which, if I mistake not, will suit you,—and which may be propagated. It is a simple and easy version for Organ of the hymn "Tu es Petrus," lately performed here on the eighteen-hundredth anniversary of St. Peter. I hope you will find an organist in Paris who is willing to appropriate this piece and by his talent to make it worth hearing.

As I am anxious that your edition should be perfectly correct I beg that you will send me the proofs. Address them to me, from the 10th to the 30th August, at *Weimar, Grand Duke of Saxe-Weimar, Germany.* The performance of my Oratorio *Saint Elizabeth,* at the Jubilee Festival of the Wartburg on the 28th August, calls me into those parts of Thuringia which *Saint Elizabeth* has illustrated.

I shall start from here in about a week. Will you therefore defer what you are so kindly intending to send me until my return to Rome (end of October)?

Accept, dear sir, my best thanks, together with the

* Autograph of all the letters to Repos in the possession of Herr Dr. Oscar von Hase in Leipzig.

assurance of my very distinguished and devoted
sentiments.

                                        F. Liszt.
Rome, *July 12th*, 1867.

Here, as in Germany, my name is enough without
any more detailed address.

56. To Prince Constantine Czartoryski.*

My Prince,

The two letters which you have done me the
honour to address to me at Rome and Munich have
reached me at the same time.   I cannot but feel myself
highly flattered at your kind proposition with regard
to the performance of my Oratorio "Saint Elizabeth"
at one of the concerts of the musical society over
which you preside.   The great renown of these concerts, the rare capability of their conductor Mr.
Herbeck, the talent of the artists who take part in
them, and the care that is taken to maintain the
traditions of the musical glory of Vienna, make it very
desirable for every serious composer to take a place in
their programme.   Thus I am most sincerely grateful
to you, my Prince, for procuring me this honour, which
however, much to my regret, I should not be able to
accept without some delay.

It would be wearisome to enter into many details ;
one fact alone will suffice : the score of the *Elizabeth*
is to be sent back to be engraved, and I promised the

* From a rough copy in Liszt's own handwriting enclosed in the
following letter. The addressee, President of the Society of the
Friends of Music, died in 1891 in Vienna, where he was Vice-President
of the *Herrenhaus*.

editor not to let it go anywhere else before its publication. Besides this the voice and orchestral parts which were used at the Wartburg are no longer available.

Kindly pardon me therefore that I cannot in this matter satisfy your favourable intentions as I should like. " What is deferred is not lost," says a proverb to which I prefer to attach myself to-day, while begging you to accept, my Prince, the expression of the sentiments of high esteem and consideration with which I have the honour to be

Your Highness's very humble and devoted servant,

F. LISZT.

MUNICH, *October* 14*th*, 1867.

57. TO EDUARD LISZT.

DEAREST EDUARD,

My hearty thanks to you for your letter. It almost made me determine to send Prince Czartoryski an answer in the affirmative ; but when I came to think the matter over more fully it did not seem suitable, considering my peculiar position. Enclosed is a copy of my letter to Czartoryski ; I hope you may not disapprove of it ; let me give you a few more reasons.

1st. I really cannot at present send off the only existing copy of the score of the *Elizabeth,* for it is required for printing. Nor should I care to have the orchestra and chorus parts from Munich used, and this I wrote to Prince Cz. It was for this very same reason that I declined offers respecting performances of the *Elizabeth* from Düsseldorf, Leipzig, Dresden, etc.

2nd. I do not share your rosy hopes of this work proving a success in towns where my earlier works not only met with little appreciation, but even received unseemly rebuffs. In Vienna, Leipzig, Berlin and even larger cities, the hisses of half a dozen stupid boys or evil-disposed persons were always sufficient to delude the public, and to frustrate the best intentions of my somewhat disheartened friends. In the newspaper criticisms these hissing critics are sure to find numerous supporters and pleasant re-echoes as long as the one object of the majority of my judges of this species is to get me out of their way. The improvement, which is said of late to have shown itself in regard to my position, may be interpreted somewhat thus : " For years in his Symphonic Poems, his Masses, Pianoforte works, Songs, etc., Liszt has written mere bewildering and objectionable stuff; in his *Elizabeth* he appears to have acted somewhat more rationally— still, etc., etc."—Now as I am in no way inclined to cry *peccavi* for all my compositions, or to assume that the castigations they received were just and justifiable, I do not consider it advisable to subscribe to the supposed *extenuating circumstances* of the *Elizabeth*. I well know the proverb : " Non enim qui se ipsum commendat, ille probatus est," and do not think I am sinning against it. However it is possible that my resolute friends may, in the end, be right in asserting that my things are not so bad as they are made out to be !—Meanwhile what I have to do is to go on working quietly and undismayed, without in the smallest degree

urging the performance of my works—nay in restrain-
ing some friendly disposed conductors from undertaking them.

3rd. After having two years ago excused myself to
Herbeck about allowing a performance of the *Elizabeth*
in Vienna, I cannot now immediately accept the friendly
offer of Prince Czartoryski. It might be somewhat
different had Herbeck attended the Wartburg performance, as I invited him to do through Schelle. But
much as I appreciate and admire Herbeck's talent as
a conductor, still I cannot know in advance whether
he likes my work or not, or how far he agrees with my
intentions. At all events I should have to come to
some personal understanding with him on the subject
before a performance is given in Vienna, just because
this is a matter of importance to me, and the performance ought not to be a *dementi* of the preceding ones.
It is much more to my advantage not to have my
works performed at all, than to allow them to be
performed in a half-and-half or unsatisfactory manner.
—I may say quite frankly that it would certainly
be very agreeable to me to stand in a somewhat
better light in Vienna as a composer than I have
hitherto done. But the time has not come for that—
and if it should ever come, half a dozen of my compositions, for instance the 13th Psalm, the Faust and Dante
Symphonies, some of the Symphonic Poems, and even,
horribile dictu ! the Prometheus Chorus, would have
to be introduced to the public in *proper style*. Three
concerts would be necessary for this, and would have
to be announced beforehand, arranged and rehearsed,
and there the *Elizabeth* might also then find a place among

them. Herbeck would be an excellent one to arrange and conduct these concerts, provided he were not too much afraid of the obligations due to criticism. My personal position will not permit of my taking any part in them as a conductor; nevertheless I should not care to be altogether idle on the occasion, and hence should like, first of all, to have a careful discussion with Herbeck about various points that must absolutely be given *thus* and *in no other way*. It was in this sense that I wrote to Czartoryski that: "Ce qui est différé n'est pas perdu" ("Aufgeschoben ist nicht aufgehoben") *—and so I may possibly come to Vienna—in the winter of '69.

First of all, however, I need several quiet months in Rome in order again to take up the work that has been interrupted for so long. The Bülows have persuaded me to spend my birthday with them. The Munich *Musik-Schule* is in full activity and seems as if it were likely to outstrip the other Conservatoires. Bülow is assuredly justified in saying, "Go and do likewise"!—

Before the end of the month I shall be back in Rome. All hearty good wishes to you and yours, from your faithfully attached,

F. LISZT.

MUNICH, *October 16th*, 1867.

P.S.—Before long you will receive a visit from August Röckel. This name will probably call up to your imagination—as it has done in many other cases—an ultra-revolutionary agitator; in place of which you will find a gentle, refined, kindly and excellent man.

* Put off is not given up.

I should like you to cultivate his acquaintance, and can cordially recommend him to you. His daughter (at the Burg Theatre) you are sure to know—and you will also know of his old friendship with Wagner and Bülow. It was not till I came here that I became acquainted with Röckel and learned to value him.

Have you read in the *Augsburger Allgem. Zeitung* the extremely kind notice of my stay in Stuttgart? Best thanks also for sending me your article on the Wanderer.

58. To Eduard von Liszt.

DEAREST EDUARD,

By some mistake I did not receive your letter of the 16th till to-day. From my last you will have clearly seen that I do not wish any further performance of the *Elizabeth before the score is published*. As I told you, I have declined the offers from Düsseldorf, Dresden and other towns. Even as regards Leipzig, where I am under special obligations to Riedel (for he has on several occasions got his Society to give excellent performances of the Gran Mass, the Prometheus choruses, the *Seligkeiten*, etc.), I shall endeavour to defer the promised performance of the *Elizabeth*. The matter would be one of special importance to me as regards Vienna,—and for this very reason I am anxious not to be in too great a hurry. Hence I most gratefully accept your mediation with Prince Czartoryski. Be my kind mediator and point out to him my peculiar position, so that there may not be any sort of vexation—and let the *Elizabeth* remain *unperformed*.

I think I have clearly stated my reasons for this *passive*, or, if you prefer it, this *expectative* mode of action.

It would interest me to know how the Coronation Mass was performed and received in Vienna. Ask Herbeck in my name not to drag the *tempi*; the *Gloria*, more especially, must be taken the more rapidly as it proceeds—the time to be beaten throughout *alla breve*. Send me word about this to Rome.

To please the Bülows I shall remain here till October 24th,—and be back in Rome, at latest, on the 30th.

If Bülow goes on working here for a couple of years, Munich will become the musical capital of Germany. In addition to my interest in all musical matters here, my stay has offered many other points of interest and pleasure by my intercourse with Kaulbach, Liebig, Heyse, Geibel, Redwitz, etc.—

Cordially yours,

MUNICH, *October 20th*, 1867.　　　　　　　F. LISZT.

Enclosed is a tolerably good photograph of my humble self.

59. To PETER CORNELIUS IN MUNICH.

DEAREST CORNELIUS,

I am grieved not to have met you yesterday, so as to have thanked you at once for the indescribable pleasure your poem gave me. The little interpreter Lulu[1] recited it twice admirably without the smallest error or stumbling. I most sincerely wish that all your works may find such interpreters as Lulu, so

---

[1] Daniela, the eldest daughter of H. v. Bülow, now married to Prof. Dr. Thode.

fully able to grasp your sentiments that your audience has nothing to do but to weep—as was our feeling yesterday with Cosima, when we both wept like children !

With all my heart, your

Wednesday, October 23rd, 1867 [MUNICH].

F. LISZT.

60. TO EDUARD VON LISZT.

DEAREST EDUARD,

The enclosed letter from *Chordirector* Kumenecker[1] I received only on my return to Rome (November 6th). Be so good as to pay the writer of it a visit in my name, and ask him kindly to excuse my not complying with his request. Also tell him that I have not got either the chorus or the orchestral parts of the Coronation Mass. The only existing copies are those belonging to the Court orchestra of Vienna ; hence these parts would have either to be obtained or to be copied if a performance of the work is to be given elsewhere, and this I should not care either to advise or disadvise.

The Mass fulfilled its object in Pest on the Coronation Day. If it should be given on any future occasion, I would recommend the conductor to take the *tempi* solemnly always, but *never dragging*, and to beat the time throughout *alla Breve*. And the *Gloria*, more especially towards the middle and before the commencement of the *Agnus Dei* up to the Prestissimo, must be worked up brilliantly and majestically.

---

[1] The Director of the *Altlerchenfelder Kirchenmusik-Verein*, in Vienna, had requested Liszt to grant him permission to give a performance of the Coronation Mass.

Whether and when the Coronation Mass is to appear in print I do not know. Dunkl (Roszavöglyi) in Pest had intended to publish it, but the honorarium of 100 ducats seems to make him hesitate, and I will not accept any smaller sum. Two movements from it (the Offertorium and Benedictus) I have transcribed for the piano, and these may be bought separately, which will be an advantage to the publisher. And the pianoforte arrangements for one or two performers are to appear simultaneously with the score.—It is of no importance to me to have the work published immediately. If you should meet Carl Haslinger and have an opportunity, ask him whether he would risk 100 ducats upon it. As he has already published a number of Masses, this one might suit him as well. If not, it is all the same to me. Only I cannot make any alteration about the honorarium I have now fixed upon.[1]

Yours,
F. LISZT.

ROME, *November 6th*, 1867.

61. TO E. REPOS.

DEAR SIR,

Pray excuse me for replying so late to your kind and cordial letter. Various matters detained me in Germany longer than I expected, and I have only been back three days at my house at "Santa Francesca Romana," where I shall spend the winter. Your publications will be excellent company to me here. I

---

[1] The Coronation Mass, like the Gran Mass, was published by Schuberth, Leipzig.

accept with gratitude the Gradual and Vesperal*
(in–12) that you are kind enough to offer me, and beg
you to let me have them shortly. What can I on my
side send you that will be agreeable to you? Something will be found, I hope, for I sincerely desire to
satisfy you.

It seems to me that it would not be of any use for
you to undertake to publish now one or two large
works of my composition. In order to be somewhat
accredited, they must first of all be performed and
heard, not *en passant*, but seriously and several times.
For this I have no support in France, and should even
expose myself to unpleasant dispositions and interpretations if I in the least endeavoured to bring myself
forward there. It is only in Germany, Hungary, and
Holland that, in spite of frequent and lively opposition,
my name as a composer has acquired a certain weight.
In those countries they continue performing my music
by inclination, curiosity, and interest, without my
asking anybody to do so. You have probably heard
of the favourable reception that the *Legend of
St. Elizabeth* met with at the Festival of the Wartburg
at the end of August. For two years past this work
has been performed several times at Pest, Prague,
Munich, and I have recently been asked for it from
Vienna, Dresden, Leipzig, Aix-la-Chapelle, etc., but as
the score has to be sent to be engraved I have not
been able to lend it further. I shall give myself the
pleasure of sending you a cópy towards Easter.—It
is also in Germany (probably at Munich) that my

* Gradual = a portion of the Mass. Vesperal = book of evening
prayer.

Oratorio *Le Christ* will be first given : now, as it is important to me that the first *complete* performance (for the one in Rome on the occasion of the centenary of St. Peter was only a tentative and partial one) should be as satisfactory as possible, I must be present at it. Consequently it will not take place till the winter of '69—if I am still in this world then,— it being my intention not to leave Rome for a year.

Pardon me these details, dear sir. As the cordiality of your letter assures me that we shall have long business relations with one another, it is better to put you at once in possession of the facts of my musical situation. It prescribes to me duties attached to many restrictions which my ecclesiastical capacity increases still more. " Providemus enim bona non solum coram Deo sed etiam coram hominibus."—

To return to your publications. Palestrina, Lassus, the masters of the 16th and 17th centuries, are your models *par excellence.* You have plenty of work for years to come to edit their admirable works, and to put yourself on a par with the collection published (cheap) at Ratisbon under the title of " *Musica divina.*" Moreover there is nothing to prevent you from adding many a composition more or less modern. Dispose of my few, as you are pleased to admit them. You might begin with the *Credo* (from the Coronation Mass), and the *Te Deum* in plain song [*cantus planus*] of which you speak. Later on a tolerably simple Mass, with organ accompaniment only, might perhaps find a place. Then, two excerpts from the Oratorio *Christ,* —" *the Beatitudes* " and the " *Pater noster* "—which have already appeared at *Leipzig*, might reappear in Paris, especially if there were any favourable opportunity of getting them heard. As to the Oratorio entire, it will be better still to wait awhile longer.

" Expectans expectavi " . . . . and let my biographical notice which you have in view also wait. In order to make it exact and comprehensive, it would be necessary for me to give some data to the writer who would undertake the task of representing me to-day to the public. Many things have been printed about me in a transient way. Amongst the most remarkable articles that of Mr. Fétis, in his *Biographie universelle des Musiciens* (second edition), of which you tell me, takes the foremost place. Nevertheless, however much disposed I am to acknowledge the conscientious and kind intentions towards myself of the illustrious and learned man, and even whilst really thanking him for raising the importance of my works which he connects with " one of the transformations of Art," I shall not have the false humility of accepting some of his valuations as definitive judgments. Of all the theorists whom I know, Mr. Fétis is the one who has best ascertained and defined the progress of harmony and rhythm in music ; on such chief points as these I flatter myself that I am in perfect accord with him. For the rest he must excuse me for escaping in different ways from the critical school whose ways he extols. According to his theory Art ought to progress, develop, be enriched, and clothed in new forms ; but in practice he hesitates, and kicks against the pricks,—and, for all that, would insist that the "transformation" should take place without in the least disturbing existing customs, and so as to *charm* everybody with the greatest ease. Would to Heaven that it might be so ! Between this and them, pray accept, dear sir, my best thanks, together with the expressions of my very distinguished and devoted sentiments.

F. Liszt.

Rome, *November 8th*, 1867.—Santa Francesca Romana.

P.S.—My sincere congratulations for the cross of St. Sylvestre. People outside are quite mistaken in thinking that they are lavish with decorations here.

I have informed the Princess W. of your kind arrangements relative to the edition of the work that Monseigneur de Montault mentioned to you.

62. To Madame Jessie Laussot.

Dear Maëstra,

No one knows better than you how to relieve the virtue of obligingness by the most cordial kindness. You make a point of persuading your friends that you are in their debt for the services you render them. In so far as they give you the opportunity of exercising your fine qualities you are perfectly right, but further than that you are not ; and for my part I beg you to be as fully assured of my sincere *gratitude* as of my entire devotion.

I am not going to set about pitying you much for the difficulties and contradictions that your artistic zeal encounters. The world is so formed that the practice of the Good and the search for the Better is not made agreeable to any one ; not in the things of Art, which appear the most inoffensive, any more than in other things. In order to deserve well one must learn to endure well. The best specific for the prejudice, malice, imbroglios and injustice of others is not to trouble oneself about them. It seems that such and such people find their pleasure where we should not in the least look for it : so be it, reserving to ourselves to find ours in nobler sources. Besides, how could we dare to lament over difficulties that run counter to our good pleasure ? Have not the worthiest and most illustrious servants of Art had to suffer far more than we ? . . . This consolation has its melancholy side, I know ; nevertheless it confirms the active conscience in the right road.

This *à propos* of the *prélude extra muros* of your last concerts. Let us pass on to the programmes of them, dear and victorious Maëstra.

The Panis Angelicus,[1] the Schumann Quintet and the sublime Prelude to Lohengrin are works which a well-brought-up public ought to know by heart. You will do well therefore to reproduce them often. There is no criticism admissible on this subject ; and, if you absolutely exact it that I should make one at all, it would only be on the adjective "celebrated," appended to the Schumann Quintet, which would do without it without disadvantage. Pardon me this hair-splitting.—

As to the "*Beatitudes*" I *entirely* approve of your not having exhibited them a second time. You know, moreover, that I usually dissuade my friends from encumbering concert programmes with my compositions. For the little they have to lose they will

[1] By Palestrina.

not lose it by waiting. Let us then administer them in homœopathic doses—and rarely.

I am delighted with what you tell me of Wilhelmj. Please assure him of my best regard and of the pleasure I shall have in showing it to him with more consequence. The Concerto for which he asks has already been begged for several times from me by Sivori and Reményi. I don't know when I shall find time to write it. There is not the least hurry for it, as long as criticism constrains violin-virtuosi to limit themselves to a *répertoire* of four or five pieces, very beautiful doubtless, and no less well known. Joachim naïvely confessed to me that after he had played the Beethoven and Mendelssohn Concertos and the Bach Chaconne he did not know what to do with himself in a town unless it were to go on playing indefinitely the same two Concertos and the same Chaconne.

Sgambati and Pinelli announce six *matinées* of Chamber Music every Wednesday, beginning the day after to-morrow. The audience will be more numerous this year than formerly. People are beginning to talk about these *matinées* in the aristocratic *salons* in which it is often *de bon ton* not to listen to good music.— Towards spring Sgambati will bring you his new laurels, and will also tell you about his future prospects. The deciding of his marriage will influence all the rest : it might almost be regretted that our friend should abandon himself to an excess of honourable feeling !

Without offending any one, the famous saying about the Chassepot rifle may be applied to the Chickering

Piano ; *it is doing wonders* at Rome.   Everybody talks
to me of it, and wants to see and hear it.   One of
my archæological friends calls it " the Coliseum of
Pianos " !

My affectionate respects to your mother ;—*sympathetic* remembrances to Miss Williams ; a friendly
shake of the hand to Callander ;—admiring chirps to
Bocage ;—warmest compliments to the Pearsolls, and

Very cordially yours,

F. Liszt.

Rome, *January* 13*th*, 1868.

63. To Dr. Franz Brendel.

Dear Friend,

My hearty congratulations upon our Falcon-
colleagueship [1]—and henceforth always, " *Vigilando
ascendimus.*"

As I was expecting parcels and news from Leipzig
I delayed answering your friendly letter.   I have not
yet received either the Almanack, or the corrected
proofs of the *Elizabeth.*   How did the performance in
the Pauliner Church [2] go off?   Ask Kahnt to let me
have one or two of the notices of it—especially the
unfavourable ones.   Remind him also to write to Otto
Roquette about the translation of the Latin chorus
at the end, to which I referred in my last letter to
him.

Berlioz's Requiem is the corner-stone of the programme for the Altenburg *Tonkünstler-Versammlung.*

---

[1] Brendel had received the Weimar Order of the Falcon of
Watchfulness [Falkenorden der Wachsamkeit].

[2] Riedel had arranged a performance of the *Elizabeth* in Leipzig.

I have often speculated about the possibility of having this colossal work produced. Unfortunately the Weimar churches were not sufficiently spacious, and in Brunswick, where the Egidien church would be a magnificent place for musical festivals of any kind, other difficulties stood in the way. Probably Altenburg also does not possess any building sufficiently large to hold an orchestra for the *Dies irae*, and Riedel will have to reduce the 16 drums, 12 horns, 8 trumpets and 8 trombones to a minimum. But, even though it should not be possible to give a performance of the whole work, still there are portions of it—such as the " Requiem æternam," the " Lacrymosa and Sanctus " —that are extremely well worth hearing and appreciating.

The sketch of the programme furnishes an excellent antidote to Berlioz's Requiem, in Händel's *Acis and Galatea* ; and some smaller things of Dräseke, Lassen and my humble self might be introduced in between.

Sgambati's co-operation will depend upon my journey. I am unable as yet to say anything definite about it. Not till June can I decide whether I can come or not. To speak frankly it will be difficult for me to leave Rome at all this year.

With regard to your personal affairs I can but again assure you that I take the liveliest interest in them. The modesty of your claims, dear friend, is very much out of proportion with the importance of the services you have rendered. One rarely meets with demands that are as just and as unpretending as yours. Be assured of my sincere readiness to promote your interest in higher quarters, and to do what I can to satisfy you.

With warmest thanks and kindest greetings yours,

F. LISZT.

ROME, *January* 26*th*, 1868.

Sgambati's *matinées* for Chamber-music are better attended than ever this winter.   They include all that is musically interesting as regards Rome.

64. TO WALTER BACHE.

DEAR MR. BACHE,

I thank you cordially for your kind letter, and beg you to rely always on my feelings of sincere affection and esteem.

It would certainly be a great pleasure to me to see you again in London this summer, yet I could not venture to promise or to keep my promise, and must abstain from either.

Please therefore to make my excuses to the Secretary of the Philharmonic Society, and to thank him for his kind intentions towards me.   If an opportunity of realising them should occur later on,—without disappointment or disagreeableness to any one,—I should be much pleased.   As regards the present time it is superfluous to give any thought to the proposition you transmit to me, in view of the obligations which will retain me elsewhere.   I am even doubtful whether it will be possible for me to accept the invitation of my German friends to the *Tonkünstler-Versammlung* at Altenburg in July.—

The good news you give me of Klindworth is very

pleasant to me. May he remember me sufficiently well to know how much I appreciate him and what an affection I have for him.

Sgambati is very much in fashion this winter, and the fashion is perfectly right in this. He sends you a thousand affectionate greetings, and Lippi,[1] Mdlle. Giuli[2] and the other *patients* of the " Scuola" [School] hold you in warm remembrance.

Accept also, dear Mr. Bache, the assurance of my very sincere devotion.

F. LISZT.

ROME, *January 30th*, 1868.

The performance of my symphonic works in London must, like the concert of the Phil. Society, be postponed. Your zeal in this matter touches me much. I would not wish to suppress it, and only beg you to moderate it so that it may be all the more fruitful.

65. TO DR. FRANZ BRENDEL.

DEAR FRIEND,

I have nothing to find fault with in the sketch of the Altenburg programme except that my name occurs too often in it. I am afraid of appearing obtrusive if several works of mine are produced at every *Tonkünstler-Versammlung*. Certainly the repetition of the 13th Psalm might be permissible and even advantageous to myself, as you kindly remark ; also I should not care to raise any protest against the chorus " *An die Künstler*," and simply because it has hitherto been

---

[1] A Roman pupil of Liszt's.
[2] Liszt's best lady-pupil in Rome.

more *screamed at* than heard, for it has been accounted one of my most culpable heresies to have set these words of Schiller's to music after Mendelssohn, and indeed without copying Mendelssohn and without humouring the customary taste of Vocal Societies. Parenthetically be it said that Schiller and "Manhood's dignity" forbade me to make this composition any pleasanter. I dreamt a temple and not a kiosk !—

If you run the risk of giving this Artists' Chorus in Altenburg I must beg the conductor to take all possible care in rehearsing it—and to aim at the most dignified *composure* in the performance. Like reverberating marble-pillars must be the effect of the singing !—

Please thank Stade[1] most warmly for his friendly intention to play one of my Organ pieces. He will probably choose either the Variations on the *Basso continuo* of Bach's Cantata "*Weinen, sorgen, seufzen, klagen*" [Weeping, grieving, sighing, lamenting]—or the BACH-Fugue.

Discuss the matter again with Riedel and Stade, as to whether 3 items by Liszt on the programme are not too much. I will gladly yield to your decision, and wish only there were more prospect of my being able to attend this *Tonkünstler-Versammlung.* However I cannot say anything definite about it till June.

Sgambati gives a concert next week in Florence. On his return at the end of April it will be decided whether he can undertake the journey to Altenburg or will have to remain here all summer.

Sgambati is decidedly not an artist for a *watering-*

---

[1] Director of the Court orchestra, and Court organist in Altenburg (born 1817) ; he was a friend of Liszt's for many years.

place, although as a virtuoso his talent is extraordinary and undoubtedly effective. He plays Bach, Beethoven, Chopin, Schumann, and my most troublesome things with perfect independence and in a masterly style. His artistic tendencies and sympathies are altogether "*new-German*." This winter we heard two of his larger works : a *Pianoforte-Quintet* and a *Nonet* for strings. Both of these deserve to be brought out by our *Musik-Verein*.

Ad vocem of the dedication of Seifritz's Overture, you have come to the right resolution in dedicating the 2nd year's issue of the Almanack to Prince Hohenzollern. I likewise approve of the following numbers being dedicated to the Princes in whose capitals the *Tonkünstler-Versammlungen* are held.

The first number of the Almanack seems to me very successful. But the *historical Calendar* might gain in interest by omissions and additions. Mediocre local celebrities such as "H.S. in E., T.D. in B., L.A. in L.," etc., etc., do not need to figure as *historical*. As little do a couple of first performances that were given in Weimar under my conductorship. See to it, dear friend, that more important data are collected in good time, and that superfluous data are rejected.

As I told you in Leipzig, the Grand Duke has determined to have me in Weimar for a couple of months during the winter (towards the beginning of '69). Perhaps I may go somewhat sooner.

With the next sending of proofs please ask Kahnt to enclose the *manuscript* of the 18th Psalm ("The Heavens declare the glory of God") for male voices. It is written on very large sheets of music-paper and bound in boards. But in order that the parcel may be made a more convenient size let the boards be removed and the manuscript paper doubled up. Kahnt will remember that I left him this manuscript seven years ago.

With hearty greetings, yours most sincerely,

F. LISZT.

March 31st, 1868.

66. TO JOHANN VON HERBECK.

DEAR FRIEND,

My cousin Eduard will bring you the score of the 18th Psalm intended for the *Männergesang-Verein** in Vienna. Allow me at this opportunity again to offer you my sincerest thanks for the kindly feelings you have always entertained for me. The further fate of the Psalm forwarded to you I leave wholly in your hands. You will have to decide whether it is suitable for being performed at the Jubilee Festival of the *Männergesang-Verein.* If you think it is I shall be glad ; still I beg you not to make it any special consideration, and if you think it more advisable not to burden the Festival-programme with it, I shall be quite content, feeling convinced, dear friend, that you will know best what is most to my advantage.

Otherwise the study of it would give no trouble. The Psalm is very simple and massive—like a *monolith.* And, as in the case of other works of mine, the conductor has the chief part to play. He, as the chief *virtuoso* and *artifex,* is called upon to see that the whole is harmoniously articulated and that it receives a living

---

* Vocal Society for Men's Voices.

form.   In the rhythmical and dynamical climax, from letters B to E (repeated from H to L), as also in some of the *ritenuti*, especially in the passage :

> "The law of the Lord is perfect,
> Converting the soul;
> The testimony of the Lord is sure,
> Making wise the simple, etc.,"

you will find substance to prove your excellence as a conductor.

Well, dear friend, you know what it is brilliantly to arouse a flaming spirit out of dead notes.

Accept the assurance of my sincere esteem and affection.

F. LISZT.

ROME, *June 9th*, 1868.

67. TO DR. FRANZ BRENDEL.[1]

DEAR FRIEND,

As might have been foreseen, I must unfortunately give up all thought of paying you and my friends of the *Tonkünstler-Versammlung* a visit this year. Were it possible for me to get away from here, I should to-day start for Munich, in honour of the *Meistersinger* which is to be performed next Sunday — and thence I should go to Weimar and Altenburg. In place of this I have to remain here till the end of the month.   After that I mean to go to the neighbourhood of Ancona for some sea baths.   Please send me at once, in a wrapper, the notices of the Altenburg

---

[1] This is the last of the many letters Liszt addressed to Brendel, who died a few months afterwards.

Musical Festival that have appeared in the *Neue Zeitschrift.*

Sgambati asks me to send you his kindest excuses. He would have much liked to wander to Germany, but he too is nailed here for this summer. His concerts in Florence with Wilhemj a few weeks ago were very successful. Sgambati is quite a phenomenal pianist for Italy, and is certain to do himself credit elsewhere on account of his sterling qualities, and his rare excellence as a virtuoso is combined with a personality of the greatest amiability and *reliable artistic feeling.* There is some talk of his getting an appointment in St. Petersburg.

A fortnight ago I heard from Paris that Berlioz was failing in health and suffering greatly. When I saw him last (in the spring of '66) he was then already physically and mentally broken down. Our personal relations always remained friendly, it is true, but on his side there was somewhat of a gloomy, cramped tone mixed with them. . . .

Neither Schumann nor Berlioz could rest satisfied at seeing the steady advance of Wagner's works. Both of them suffered from a suppressed enthusiasm for the *music of the future.*

I shall not be able to decide about my proposed stay in Weimar till the end of the year. Till then I shall keep quiet here or in the neighbourhood, the extreme boundary to which is indicated by the sea baths of Ancona. Several other invitations have had to be courteously declined. But next year a considerable change may take place in my outward circumstances, and may again draw me closer to

Germany. How this last chapter of my life will shape itself I cannot yet foresee.

The Vienna *Männergesang-Verein* have kindly asked me to provide a composition for their Jubilee Festival. This is the reason why I asked Kahnt for the score of the 18th Psalm ("The Heavens declare the glory of God"), which has at last come, and was despatched to Vienna the day before yesterday.[1] Kahnt has no doubt also received the *corrected* pianoforte score of the *Elizabeth*. And there happily remains only the full score to do, the proofs of which I am expecting now.

During the winter my innumerable social duties rendered it absolutely impossible for me to write any longer compositions. This enforced idleness vexes me extremely—and I intend to assume an air of rudeness to rid myself of a great many people. It is more especially intrusive correspondents who are a vexatious waste of time to me. Since the Coronation Mass, I have in fact only written one solitary work : a *Requiem* for male voices with simple organ accompaniment.[2]

How much I should like to hear Berlioz's colossal Requiem in *Altenburg* !—Think, when there, in all friendliness of

Your sincerely attached

F. LISZT.

ROME, *June 17th*, 1868.

Again I beg you to send me regularly the programmes and the notices of the Altenburg *T. K. V.* in the *Neue Zeitung*.

[1] Published by Schuberth, Leipzig.
[2] Published by Kahnt, Leipzig.

68. To E. Repos.

Dear Sir,

As you are kind enough still to remember about the " *Ave Maris Stella* " it would be inexcusable of me to forget it. My first manuscript having gone astray I spent the whole of yesterday in rewriting this very simple song, of which you will receive two versions at once by the next possible occasion ; one for *mezzo-soprano* voice with Piano or Harmonium accompaniment, the other for 4 *male voices* with a little Organ accompaniment. In this latter please excuse my very bad writing, over and above whatever there may be defective in the composition. I cannot, here, have several copyists at my disposal as in Germany. The only one whom I can employ is ill—and I have not time to wait till he gets well, for from to-morrow I undertake my pilgrimage to Assisi and Loretto—after which I shall make a *villeggiatura* of at least six weeks at Grotta-mare (near Ancona, on the shores of the Adriatic).

I depend on your kindness to send me the final proofs of the *Ave Maris Stella* to the address which I will give you shortly.

How shall I manage to get you my biographical notice published in 1843 in the voluminous collection of the *Biographie Pascallet*? I really do not know. This notice is both the most exact, the best edited, and the kindest of all that have appeared about me in *French*. Mr. Fétis quotes it in my article of the *Biographie univ. des Musiciens*, and I have asked Mr. le Chanoine Barbier de Montault to look for it at Angot the editor's.—The entire collection of the *Biographie Pascallet* must be, amongst others, in the library of Mr. Emile de Girardin, but the illustrious publicist has so many great matters to attend to that I should scruple to trouble him about such a trifle.

In any case it will be easy to unearth our unhappy little Opus in question in the Bibliothèque impériale, where, if necessary, it can be copied for the use of Mr. le Ch. de Montault.

Please, dear sir, count on my very sincerely affectionate and devoted sentiments.

ROME, *July 1st*, 1868.   F. LISZT.

A thousand thanks for your kind sending of the *Répertoire* of St. Sulpice, which is this moment come.

69. TO PROF. CARL RIEDEL IN LEIPZIG.[1]

DEAR FRIEND,

My sincere congratulation upon your glorious accomplishment—the performance of Berlioz's Requiem in Altenburg, and also my kindest thanks for all the trouble and care you have bestowed upon the *Elizabeth* and the 13th Psalm. I hope to hear Berlioz's Requiem next winter in Leipzig, and also some of Bach's contrapuntal *feste Burgen*. My ears thirst for them!

Meanwhile let me ask Frau Professor Riedel kindly to accept me herewith in *effigy* as an inmate.

With sincere esteem, I remain, dear friend,

Your gratefully attached

GROTTA MARE, *August 12th* [1868].   F. LISZT.

[1] 1827-88, founder and director of the celebrated *Riedel Verein* in Leipzig, and after Brendel's death President of the *Allgemeine Deutsche Musikverein*.

70. To E. Repos.

DEAR SIR,

By the same post I return you the proofs of the *Ave Maris Stella*, which reached me yesterday. Will you be kind enough to have the various errors of these first proofs corrected on the plates. Exactitude in editions is a duty of the profession, too often neglected.

I will send you, by the first opportunity, a short *Offertoire* (of some 40 bars) for men's voices. The text forms part of the *service of St. Francis—"Mihi autem adhærere Deo bonum est,"* and I composed it lately at Assisi.—In about a week's time I shall be back in Rome, where I left my manuscripts; amongst others a *Requiem* for men's voices with Organ accompaniment. The style of it is very simple, and whatever goodwill one brings to it the execution will also be very simple. If it would suit you to publish this *Requiem* (of about some thirty small pages of print) I will send it you with the *Offertoire* of St. Francis.

Accept, dear sir, the expression of my distinguished and devoted sentiments.

GROTTA MARE, *August 26th*, 1868.   F. LISZT.

Address *Rome.*—I have not received any letter from you for several months.

71. To Prof. Dr. Siegmund Lebert in Stuttgart.

DEAR FRIEND,

To satisfy rational and righteous people is the better part of my life. I am very glad that you approve

[1] The addressee was a distinguished pianoforte teacher (1822—1884), co-founder of the Stuttgart Conservatoire, co-editor of the *Grosse*

of the letter to the French edition of your *Method*, and that you find it appropriate. I have simply said what I think. I pledge myself always to be *true* in speech and action, however many annoyances and misinterpretations may be hurled at me in return. In confidence I will tell you what is the rule of my whole existence; it consists of the daily prayer: "O veritas Deus, fac me unum tecum in perpetua caritate!"—

Excuse the delay in the return of the 3rd part of the *Method*. I thought of making use of some favourable opportunity of sending it to Stuttgart to save you the expense of postage; but no such opportunity has presented itself, and so this concluding volume of the *Method* was despatched to you through the agency of Herr Kolb (Würtemberg consul in Rome). The added notes are very unimportant, because, in fact, I had no other weightier remarks to make. While playing through the Etudes I found myself put into a thorough good humour, and this must be my excuse for the few bad jokes which my mischievous pencil scribbled down. Please do not let them go further; such jests must be kept quietly *to ourselves*.

In Grotta mare I wrote about 20 pages of the technical exercises. Unfortunately a host of correspondence prevents my making progress with the work I have already begun and which is finished in my head. The Italians say: Give time, time ("dar tempo al tempo"), which often provokes me utterly!—

Clavierschule (Lebert and Stark), and of the instructive edition of Classical pianoforte-works published by Cotta, in which Liszt, Bülow and Faisst took part. It is to these last-mentioned works that the letters here given refer.

First of all I shall set to work at the Weber and
Schubert edition, which I hope to send you by the
beginning of November.

Please present my best thanks to Baron Reischach
for his kind letter.   The business point of it (the Weber
and Schubert edition) I herewith answer ; that I shall
redeem my promise by the beginning of November;
and that with an easy conscience I shall then give
proof of my gratitude by writing to Baron R. myself.

In sincere and friendly collaboratorship, I am

Yours most sincerely,

F. LISZT.

ROME, *September* 10*th*, 1868.

72. TO E. REPOS.

DEAR CHEVALIER AND FRIEND,

Your last letter interests me much, and I thank
you very sincerely for the confidence you show me.
Certainly I should ask nothing better than to reply
to it as you wish ; but there is the difficulty.   Shall
you reproach me with " claudicare in duas partes " ?
No, I do not think you will, for I do not intend to
have any hitch ; it is simply that the small influence
which, in certain given circumstances, I could exercise,
is paralysed by other circumstances that now pre-
dominate.   I should be obliged to explain various things
to make you understand my *extrinsic* inaptitude, and
consequently my obligatory abstention on some points
which touch me closely.   I prefer not to enter into
these details in writing ; perhaps we shall have an
opportunity of speaking about them : as to the present

time the following is my reply, reduced to the most
concise terms :

I entirely approve of your two projects of the
competition of sacred Music, and of the definitive,
normal and really Catholic edition of the Plain-Song
of the Church. These two enterprises are opportune and desirable, and may be carried out to your
honour and advantage. All the same I am not in a
position to serve you efficaciously *utraque*. Therefore
I ought not to be mixed up with it, . . . unless
any contingency as unforeseen as decisive should
supervene.

You will have read in the *Correspondance de Rome*
that the work of M. Sre. Alfieri has remained in
suspense. It is not a posthumous obstacle with which
your edition would have to contend, but another, which
might also be called *Legion*.

The *Requiem* and the *Offertoire* of St. Francis shall
be sent to you in a fortnight. Before sending them
to you I want carefully to look through the copy,
so as to save the engraver as many corrections as
possible.

I shall not leave Rome till Christmas ; from January
till the end of March I shall be at Weimar.—

Pray accept, dear Chevalier and friend, the assurance
of my affectionate devotion.

F. LISZT.

September 19th, 1868.

When will the 1st volume of your publication of the
History of the Popes and Cardinals come out ? I shall
be much obliged if you will send it me.

73. To C. F. Kahnt, the Musical Publisher.*

Dear Sir and Friend,

The delay in the receipt of your letter did not in any way lessen the very welcome news it contained, for which I thank you cordially. Herewith also my warm congratulations in regard to the little red-coloured Altenburg volume.

Of the gracious acceptance accorded to the dedication copy of the *Elizabeth* I have already received a full report, which is altogether satisfactory. The second copy *de luxe* please to keep for the present. I should like to present it to our Grand Duke *ad honorem* of the *Wartburg Library.*

Your intention of sending the third copy next Easter to the Exhibition of the German Products of the Printing Press, I, as the author, consider both very appropriate and a pleasant piece of news.

As I am expecting corrected proofs of the *Elizabeth* score, I beg you to enclose Wieseneder's "*Kindergarten Lieder-Büchlein.*" † Probably this will be your last sending to Rome for the year '68, as I shall be in Weimar again by the beginning of January. I shall, therefore, leave all further discussions *in extenso* till then. Meanwhile there is scarcely anything positive or *to the point* to write about.

My friendly greetings to Brendel; he knows how much it is my wish to obtain reliable *support* and some

* Facsimiles of this and No. 99 appeared in the *Neue Zeitschrift für Musik,* June 18th, 1890.

† Book of Kindergarten Songs.

profitable advantage for the endeavours of the *A. D. Musik-Verein.* Rest assured of this, dear friend, and count upon my sincere and unalterable attachment.

F. LISZT.

ROME, *September 20th* [1868].

Be quick with and out with the 69th Almanack !—

74. To E. REPOS.

DEAR MONSIEUR REPOS,

Here is the Requiem. If you think it would be well to publish the five parts separately (*Requiem, Dies iræ, Offertoire,* etc.) in the 5 numbers of the *Revue de Musique sacrée,* I have not the slightest objection to it, and will only ask you to announce the complete edition, to be had by itself, at the same time as the detached pages appear.

The copy is very distinct and correct ; please beg the engraver not to add any wrong notes of his own composition, and send me the proofs to Rome.

I should be glad if the *Offertoire* of St. Francis (added to the book of the Requiem) could come out *at once.* The manuscript is only two pages,—and I do not think I shall be infringing too much St. Francis's rule of poverty by reserving to myself, for this *Offertoire* as well as for *all my compositions* that you publish, author's rights for Germany and Italy, in order to keep my promise to several publishers.

Accept, dear Monsieur Repos, the expression of my very distinguished and devoted sentiments.

F. LISZT.

ROME, *September 22nd,* 1868.

75. To Prof. Dr. S. Lebert.

DEAR FRIEND,

To-day I deserve a little praise. The Weber task is finished, and hence I have kept my promise a few weeks in advance.

How I have understood my task you will see from the short Preface on the first page of the various readings to the *Conzertstück*. The printer will have to *act in strict conformity* with what is there stated, and to give the necessary letters and signs. Unfortunately I cannot help giving this unusual trouble, for *two kinds of letters and signs* are positively *indispensable*.

My responsibility with regard to Cotta's edition of Weber and Schubert I hold to be : fully and carefully to retain the original text together with provisory suggestions of *my* way of rendering it, by means of *distinguishing* letters, notes and signs,—and these I beg you will again have fully explained to the printer.

In the *various readings* you will probably find some things *not* inappropriate ;—I flatter myself that I have thus given performers greater licence, and have increased the effect without damaging or overloading Weber's style. Get Pruckner, who is acquainted with my bad musical handwriting, to play the various readings to you.

N.B.—They must be printed in small notes throughout the whole edition.

The parcel containing the Conzertstück, Momento capriccioso, 4 Sonatas of W[eber] (and the 2 Beethoven ones of the Bülow edition) will be despatched to you to-morrow by Kolb. Send me, at your early convenience,

Weber's 2 Polonaises (Härtel's last edition), which must not be omitted in Cotta's edition ; also let me have *all* Schubert's Dances (Valses, Ländler, Eccossaises, in Holle's edition revised by Markull). And as I have now got into the way of revising, I should like at once to prepare the Schubert volume and submit to you, before the end of November, the result of many years of most delightful communion with Weber's and Schubert's pianoforte compositions, with fingering, marks for pedal and expression, and various readings.

The Schubert volume I shall limit to 3 or 4 Sonatas, the great Fantasia, some 8 Impromptus, the Moments Musicals, and all his Dances. A few other pieces as duets may follow later, more especially his Marches and the Hungarian Divertissement.

Let me hope that my work may prove intelligible, *temperate* and satisfactory, and also of some service to ordinary pianists.

Any remarks and objections you may have to make in connection with these, I shall be quite willing to consider.

With friendly greetings and thanks,

Yours most sincerely,

Rome, *October 19th*, 1868.   F. Liszt.

P.S.—Let me hear from you at once, as soon as you receive the parcel.

76. To Richard Pohl at Baden-Baden.

Rome, *November 7th*, 1868.

. — . My very kind biographer La Mara writes me a few charming lines telling me that she is shortly sending me her volume "Studienköpfe." *   " *Das junge Volk hat Muth*," † as you say, and I quite approve of their not letting themselves be intimidated. Courage is the vital nerve of our best qualities; they fade away when it is wanting, and unless one is courageous one is not even sufficiently prudent. To examine, reflect calculate and weigh are assuredly necessary operations But after that one must determine and act without troubling too much about which way the wind blows and what clouds are passing.   . — .

77. To Johann von Herbeck.

Much esteemed Friend,

I have just answered the invitation of the " *Musikfreunde*," and trust you will agree with what I have written. I am quite aware that the performance of the *Elizabeth* in Vienna—which is considered a mark of honourable distinction to me—I owe to *you*. My not having complied with your offer before was mainly due to my desire to spare you any em-barrassments in connection with the performance, embarrassments which I, owing to my peculiar position and my distance from active circles of the Press, can readily ignore without the slightest "bitterness of feeling."

Well, let us hope that your favourable augury will prove true. Your earlier letter I have not received. But I was heartily delighted with your last. Shortly before receiving it I had been hearing a number of

---

* Studies of heads.
† Young folk have pluck.

excellent things about the composer, conductor and friend Herbeck, all of which tallied perfectly with what I remembered and of what I myself feel convinced. You will guess who communicated all this to me.

To return to the *Elizabeth* performance in Vienna; I should like to be present. The Committee of the *Musikfreunde* name two days in March; the last mentioned would be the most convenient one for me. I must tell you beforehand, in confidence, that on this occasion I should not be able to remain in Vienna beyond a couple of days, and that I wish especially to keep *quiet* while there, and to meet as few people as possible. It is no longer in any way appropriate that I should *appear* anywhere in person ;[1] it suits me much better, when necessary, to be *trodden down in effigy* by all the different chatter. And as you, much esteemed friend, are the one and only person who *shall* conduct the *Elizabeth* in Vienna, I wish to leave the distribution of the vocal parts entirely to your care. I would merely remind you that my two compatriots Bignio and Fräulein Rabatinsky (now in Vienna) sang splendidly in the parts of the Landgrave Ludwig and the spiteful Landgravine Sophie, at the first performances of the Oratorio in Pest. Hence, if no categorical objections are raised against them by the worthy theatrical potentates, it would seem advisable and well to secure these singers for parts for which they have already proved themselves competent.

As an unnecessary remark let me add that the small

---

[1] Liszt had been requested to conduct his *Elizabeth*, a request he declined (probably in consideration of his having taken holy orders).

Magyar Cantilena of the Magnate (in the first number) requires a powerful voice.

In sincere esteem, I remain yours in all friendliness,

F. LISZT.

VILLA D'ESTE, *December 1st,* 1868.

P.S.—I am expecting the promised manuscript of the "Tanzmomente."[1] By the beginning of January I hope to be in Weimar.

78. To Prof. Dr. S. Lebert.

DEAR FRIEND,

The annotations to Schubert's Sonatas demanded more time than I had anticipated. For some weeks past I have been working industriously at them—now they are finished *ad unguem.*

Our pianists scarcely realise what a glorious treasure they have in Schubert's pianoforte compositions. Most pianists play them over *en passant,* notice here and there repetitions, lengthinesses, apparent careless-nesses . . . and then lay them aside. It is true that Schubert himself is somewhat to blame for the very unsatisfactory manner in which his admirable pianoforte pieces are treated. He was too immoderately productive, wrote incessantly, mixing insignificant with important things, grand things with mediocre work, paid no heed to criticism, and always soared on his wings. Like a bird in the air, he lived in music and sang in angelic fashion.

O never-resting, ever-welling genius, full of tender-

---

[1] Composed by Herbeck for orchestra; transcribed by Liszt for the pianoforte.

ness ! O my cherished Hero of the Heaven of Youth !
Harmony, freshness, power, grace, dreamings, passion,
soothings, tears and flames pour forth from the depths
and heights of thy soul, and thou makest us almost
forget the greatness of thine excellence in the fascination
of thy spirit !— —

Let us limit our edition of Schubert's pianoforte
compositions to 2 Sonatas, the G major Fantasia (a
Virgilian poem !), the splendid *Wanderer*-dithyramb
(C major Fantasia), 2 books of Impromptus, Moments
Musicals and all his Valses (among which there are
gems of the first water). All this will be sent to you
forthwith ; and in addition Weber's Polonaises.

In the Sonatas you will find some various readings,
which appear to me tolerably *appropriate*. Several
passages, and the whole of the conclusion of the C
major Fantasia, I have re-written in modern pianoforte
form, and I flatter myself that Schubert would not be
displeased with it.

The pianoforte Duets of Schubert (Holle's edition)
please address to Weimar, as I have no time left for
revisings in Rome. Send me also a copy of the
" Aufforderung zum Tanz [Invitation to the Dance] "
that is so drummed at everywhere. You forgot to let
me have this piece of salon-fireworks with the other
music, and I too did not remember it at the time ; years
ago I had to play this " Invitation " over and over
again, times innumerable—without the smallest " invitation " on my part—and it became a detestable
nuisance to me. However, such a show-piece must not
be omitted in Cotta's edition of Weber.

Your visit to Weimar, dear friend, will be very

welcome and agreeable to me.   When there we shall
be able to discuss, weigh and settle a number of things
very conveniently.

With sincere thanks, I remain

Yours in all friendship,

F. Liszt.

VILLA D'ESTE, *December 2nd*, 1868.

P.S.—I have not received the French translation of
your Method.

79. To Eduard von Liszt.

DEAREST EDUARD,

Your promotion [1] is a real and great joy to me.
It does my heart good to see your continual services
receive recognition, and to know you about to
enter a more promising sphere.   Your new position
does not, indeed, free you from all effort and exertion,
but you have long since become accustomed to bear
the yoke on work-days like a man, and although the
yoke may not appear altogether enviable, still it is
always the most honourable and most secure.

I wish only that you may ever remain true to yourself, and by perfectly satisfying your own conscience you may deeply feel God's unfailing promise :
" Dominus non privabit bonis eos qui ambulant in
innocentia."—

. — . From the President and the Vice-President
of the Society of *Musikfreunde*, Drs. Egger and
Dumba, I received a very friendly letter inviting me

---

[1] Eduard von Liszt had been appointed *Oberstaatsanwalt* (Chief
State attorney) in Vienna.

to fix upon one of the three days—21st February, 7th
or 23rd March—for the *performance of the Elizabeth*
in Vienna, and to undertake to conduct the work.
To do the latter is absolutely *impossible* to me, for
reasons that you know; hence I shall decline to fix
upon a date.   My answer conveys to the above-named
gentlemen my thanks for this distinguishing mark of
their good-will, and, at the same time, I express my
wish to attend the performance, and mention that the
end of March would be the most convenient time for
me.

I also wrote to Herbeck pretty fully, saying that he,
and he alone, should conduct this performance; it is
to be hoped that under his direction the whole thing
will run a successful course.

Hearty greetings to all yours, and I look forward to
seeing you again soon.

F. L.

December 6th, 1868.   [VILLA D'ESTE.]

80. To Johann von Herbeck.

VERY DEAR FRIEND,

Although I feel absolutely sure that you will
conduct the *Elizabeth*-performance in a perfect and
brilliant style, I gladly comply with your wish that I
should be in Vienna a few days beforehand.   As I
have already said, it would be more convenient to me
to leave here towards the *end of March*.   Meanwhile
present my most gracious thanks to the Committee of
the "*Musikfreunde*," with the request that they will in
future regard me as quite *inadmissible* as a conductor.

Your question whether I attach "any special importance" as to how the different parts should be filled, I answer simply thus: arrange things wholly and entirely as you think best. The few indefinite suggestions in my last letter are of importance only in so far as they agree with your competent arrangement, otherwise in no way. One point only I should like adhered to in the Vienna performance, namely *that no foreign singers be engaged for it*. To have one's own house in good order is always the wisest and safest plan.

I have heard much in praise of Fräulein Ehnn;[1] and should feel specially indebted to her if she would undertake the Elizabeth: the part does not go against the grain, and should Fräulein Ehnn wish any alterations I should be quite willing to consider them.

With warm thanks, yours most sincerely,

Rome, *December 29th*, 1868.   F. Liszt.

The "Tanzmomente" are still dancing on their way here, for they have not yet come.

81. To Edvard Grieg.[*]

Sir,

I am very glad to tell you what pleasure it has given me to read your Sonata (Op. 8). It bears testimony to a talent of vigorous, reflective and inventive composition of excellent quality,—which has only to follow its natural bent in order to rise to a high

---

[1] A singer at the Royal Opera House in Vienna.

[*] Published in Grönvold "Norwegische Musiker" (Norwegian Musicians, Warmuth, Christiania).—The addressee was the clever leader of the Young School of Northern Composers. He was born at Bergen in 1843, and educated at Leipzig.

rank. I am pleased to think that in your own country you are meeting with the success and encouragement that you deserve : these will not be wanting elsewhere either ; and if you come to Germany this winter I cordially invite you to stay a little at Weimar, in order that we may thoroughly get to know each other.

Pray receive, sir, the assurance of my sentiments of esteem and very distinguished regard.

F. Liszt.

Rome, *December 29th*, 1868.

WEIMAR.—PEST.—ROME.

82. To Commerzienrath Carl Bechstein in Berlin.[1]

Very dear Sir,

Accept a seven-octaved chromatic scale of thanks for your kindness in sending your magnificent piano for the Grand-Ducal Hofgärtnerei in Weimar. I hope you will on some occasion allow me to have the pleasure of convincing you, *de visu et auditu*, how glorious the instrument looks and sounds here.

According to report we are shortly to see Tausig again in Weimar. Tell him he may be sure of a hearty welcome from me.

With sincere esteem and grateful thanks I remain

Yours most sincerely

Weimar, *January 19th*, 1869.   F. Liszt.

P.S.—Enclosed are a few lines for Tausig, which kindly forward to him.

83. To Johann von Herbeck.

Very dear Friend,

Fräulein Ehnn's amiable readiness to undertake the part has greatly pleased me, and I beg you to convey my sincerest thanks to *our Elizabeth*. The part will not cost her any immoderate effort; all

[1] Head of the famous pianoforte-manufactory; our "*Beflügler*," as Bülow and Tausig called him. (A play on the word *Flügel*, which means both a *grand piano* and *wings*.)

173

possible alterations, pauses, dotted notes, ornamentations, shall be left *ad libitum* and entirely to the pleasure of the gracious singer. Do not write to me further on this subject, and endeavour merely to get Fräulein Ehnn to feel herself comfortably and pleasantly at home with my poor tone-melodies.

Friend Reményi, whom I do not need now to introduce to you, will be the bearer of these lines to you. He has delighted and captivated every one here, the Court as well as the public, and this is verily no small matter, for in Weimar we are accustomed to the most distinguished violin-virtuosos. I requested him to tell you how grateful I feel to you for your idea of a concert of Liszt's compositions.

But, in order to avoid every appearance of indiscretion or forwardness, I consider it well and advisable to keep *exclusively* to the *Elizabeth* on this occasion.

Hold fast, therefore, to two points : *a.* all parts of the *Elizabeth* to be filled by *native talent.* *b.* Critics to be worried *only* with this one work.[1] I have also requested Reményi to ask you about the apartments I shall require. My stay in Vienna will be limited to eight or ten days, which I should like to spend in as quiet and peaceable a way as possible, and not within the circle of disturbing visitors.

With sincere esteem and friendly attachment yours,

WEIMAR, *January 27th,* 1869. F. LISZT.

---

[1] At the performance of the *Elizabeth* in the " *ausserordentlichen Gesellschafts-Concert* " [Company's special concert] on April 4th, 1869, Liszt met with a genuine triumph. Herbeck writes : "After every number, and at the end of every part, there was no end to the calls for Liszt." The performance was repeated on April 11th, and received with even greater enthusiasm.

84. To E. Repos.

Dear Sir and Friend,

A thousand sincere thanks for the kind zeal and love that you bestow upon the publication of my poor works. In order that the edition of the *Requiem* may be entirely correct, I will beg you to send me again proofs of the *Offertoire, Sanctus* and *Agnus Dei, either to Weimar before the 18th March, or to Vienna from the 25th March to the 12th April.* My address in Vienna is c/o *Mr. Herbeck,* Court conductor, etc., etc. *Graben, Trattnerhof. Vienna. Austria.*

I shall spend two or three days at Ratisbon towards the middle of April, in order to hear the Cathedral choir there, which has a great reputation in Germany. There also I shall find a manuscript of the highest interest, and one which up to now has been almost unknown : it is the *opus musicum magnum* of Orlandus Lassus. It is composed of more than *five hundred* pieces of music.

Are you in touch with Mr. Pustet, the most considerable publisher of religious music at Ratisbon ?—

Your visit to Rome will be extremely agreeable to me. I expect to be back at the end of April and to pass the summer at Santa Francesca Romana.

Your very affectionately devoted

F. Liszt.

Weimar, *March 3rd,* 1869.

Probably I shall profit by your kind proposition, and shall send you shortly a Mass (for 4 voices, with a simple Organ accompaniment).

85. To Laura Kahrer, in Vienna.[1]

DEAR AND ASTOUNDING ARTISTE,

Accept this small remembrance of the hour when your extraordinary talent so joyfully surprised me, and be assured of the sincere and friendly devotion of yours,

F. LISZT.

VIENNA, *April* 15*th*, 1869.

86. To Franz Servais.[2]

DEAR MONSIEUR FRANZ,

The sincere pleasure caused me by your letter, which reached me at Pest at the end of April, is completed by the one you have addressed to me here. I am delighted to hear that my prophecy has been realised and that you enjoyed yourself at Munich. At this time you would not find anywhere else an *ensemble* of ideas, works, acts and instruction so suited to your artist-nature, and, consequently, so favourable to the full development of your fine powers.

Thanks to M. de Bülow and his prodigious activity, on a par with his intelligence, Munich is becoming the

---

[1] Now married to *Concertmeister* Rappoldi in Dresden, and one of the lady-professors at the Conservatoire there. The above note, which was accompanied by a silver pen for composing, Liszt sent her after having been present at her first public appearance at a charity-concert in the Royal Opera House in Vienna. In 1870 she became a pupil of his in Weimar, and was soon considered one of the most distinguished lady-pianists; since 1879 she has enjoyed the title of *Kammervirtuosin* (Court pianist) of Saxony.

[2] Composer; conducted the Wagner performances in the Théâtre de la Monnaie, Brussels, in 1890-91.

new musical capital of Germany. You will therefore do well to stay some time there, in order vigorously to prepare yourself for the task which has devolved on you elsewhere.

Perhaps I may see you again this summer, for if, as announced, *Rheingold* is performed there on the 25th August I shall come to it.

Meanwhile I thank you for having so well listened to the *Elizabeth*; that is a presage to me that we shall meet more than once on the same path, in which I wish you the most complete success. . — .

Believe, dear Monsieur Franz, in my very devoted affection.

ROME, *May 21st*, 1869.   F. LISZT.

87. TO WILLIAM MASON.

ROME, *May 26th*, 1869.

DEAR MR. MASON,

Mr. Seward has given me your kind letter and several of your compositions. These give me a double pleasure in that they prove that you have not lost your time at Weimar, and that you continue to make good use of it elsewhere.

The Etude de Concert (Op. 9) and the Valse Caprice (Op. 17) are of a distinguished style and make a good effect. I shall also sincerely praise the 3 Préludes (Op. 8) and the two Ballades, but with some reservation. The first Ballade appears to me somewhat cut short ; it wants I know not what at the beginning and towards the middle (page 7) of something needed to make the melody stand out ; and the pastorale of the 2nd Ballade (page 7) figures like a too-cheap piece of "padding." . . .

And, since I am in the vein for criticising, let me ask why you call your "Ah! vous dirai-je, Maman"—"Caprice *grotesque*?" Apart from the fact that the grotesque style should not intrude into music, that title is unjust to the clever imitations and harmonies of the piece, very charming by the way, and which it would be more suitable to entitle "Divertissement" or "Variazione scherzose."—

As to the Méthode, you won't expect me to make a deep study of that. I am much too old for such a thing, and it is only in self-defence that I still work sometimes at the piano in view of the incessant botherations and indiscretions of a heap of people who imagine that nothing would be more flattering to me than to amuse them !—

Nevertheless, in looking through your Méthode I find some exercises much to be recommended, namely, the *interlocking passages* page 136 to 142 ;—and all the *accentual treatment* of *Exercises.**

May your pupils and the editor obtain from them all the profit that I wish them !

A thousand thanks, dear Mr. Mason, and count on my very affectionate and devoted sentiments of old.

F. LISZT.

88. TO THE COMPOSER HEINRICH SCHULZ-BEUTHEN.†

VERY DEAR SIR,

That you have dedicated your 42nd and 43rd Psalms to me I feel to be an honour in the artistic

* The italics in this sentence are written *in English and in italics* by Liszt.

† Printed in Gottschalg's "*Chorgesang*," 1890.—Schulz-Beuthen was born in 1838.

sense, for which I am sincerely grateful. It is long since any new composition has given me the impression of intellectual strength and musical completeness such as I find in yours. And this work stands even above eminent compositions of the kind. It appears to me even more fully rounded, pregnant and powerful than your 29th Psalm, which I justly recognised as a distinguished work upon first reading it through. The grand impression produced by your 29th Psalm on the occasion of the *Tonkünstler-Versammlung* in Dessau confirmed my predictions, and I am convinced that wherever the 42nd and 43rd Psalms are heard every person with any depth of soul will feel their sublime beauty, and offer you something more valuable than mere ordinary applause. Do not look for word-making from me ; I never knew much about it, and I can still less try my hand at it now in my old age. But allow me, very dear sir, to tell you quite frankly and briefly this :—

You must not hold yourself aloof and at a distance ; your splendid works must be performed, printed and circulated. And although—owing to the idle and impudent chatter of many leaders of the press—my influence in musical matters has been reduced to a minimum, still I hope shortly to arrange a performance of your Psalms in one or two places.

With sincere esteem I remain yours very truly,

WEIMAR, *June* 18*th*, 1869.   F. LISZT.

89. TO FRANZ SERVAIS.

DEAR MONSIEUR FRANZ,

        . —. Although older than you, yet my enthusiasm for "Tristan" is not second to yours.—I am delighted that the performance has come off so well, but I should not wish this marvellous *chef-d'œuvre* to become for you a sort of upas tree under the shadow of which you would go to sleep.—Great manifestations of genius ought to do the part of the sun,—to illuminate and fertilise.

Believe in my sentiments of devoted affection.

F. Liszt.

Rome, *July 4th*, 1869.

90. To Madame Jessie Laussot.

Dear Maëstra,

I do not know why the name of Boccherini always recalls to me the valley of *Tempe*. There could be nothing more flattering and more salutary for me than to be admitted into so fortunate an abode, and you have certainly made the stroke of a *Maëstra* in introducing me there (a little bit in a contraband way !). —I hope Mr. Delâtre will be kind enough to send me under cover the first number of the paper containing La Mara's article ;[1] directly afterwards I will subscribe to the Boccherini, so that I may get the whole of the biography regularly.

A thousand thanks for your intelligent solicitude ; I entirely approve of the word *tedesco* being left out on the title-page ; "tradotto dall' Autore" is evidently the better indication, and I guarantee you that the authoress will be perfectly satisfied and will add her thanks to mine, without thinking of making the slightest observation or difficulty about anything whatever.

[1] The Liszt-sketch from the first vol. of the "*Musikalischen Studienköpfe*," which the authoress had translated into Italian.

When you are passing through Leipzig I will make you acquainted with my very amiable panegyrist.

I am certainly intending to be present at the first performance of *Rheingold*, announced for the 25th August ; but I doubt whether they will be in a position to give this work so soon. Mr. de Bülow absolutely must take some rest after the Conservatoire examinations ; the Servais are pressing him much to settle down with them for the months of August and September at Hal (in Belgium) ; I want him to accept their invitation, and he will, I hope, decide to do so. Now without him *Rheingold* at Munich seems to me at least problematical. I will let you have positive tidings, which I myself shall receive shortly. Please tell me where to address you.

I have set to work again, and with the exception of the fortnight at Munich, in honour of *Rheingold*, I shall remain here, or else in the neighbourhood, until next spring.

Sgambati kisses your hands. Pinelli is at the baths of Lucca, where Buonamici[1] will probably join him.

Very cordially yours,
F. L.

I will write two words of thanks to Delâtre and beg you to give me his address.

In your walks at St. Gall make my salutations to the concert room in which were heard, some 10 or 12 years ago, the *Symphonie Héroïque* conducted by Wagner, and two *Symphonic Poems*, conducted by

[1] Giuseppe Buonamici, pupil of Liszt and Bülow, now one of the most celebrated pianists of Italy. Lives at Florence.

your very humble servant. Szadrowski was at that time conductor at St. Gall; since then he is settled in the Grisons (at Graubünden); if you should go that way do not fail to see him; I recommend him to you as one of our friends.

ROME, *July* 16*th*, 1869.

91. To Camille Saint-Saëns in Paris.[1]

VERY HONOURED FRIEND,

Your kind letter promised me several of your compositions; I have been expecting them, and, while waiting, I want to thank you again for your second Concerto, which I greatly applaud. The form of it is new and very happy; the interest of the three portions goes on increasing, and you take into just account the effect of the pianist without sacrificing anything of the ideas of the composer, which is an essential rule in this class of work.

At the very outset the *prelude* on the pedal *G* is striking and imposing: after a very happy inspiration you do wisely to reproduce it at the end of the first movement and to accompany it this time with some chords. Among the things which particularly please me I note: the chromatic progression (*last* line of the *prelude*) and that which alternates between the piano and orchestra (from the last bar of page 5—repeated then by the piano alone, page 15); the arrangement of thirds and sixths in demisemiquavers, charmingly

---

[1] The celebrated French composer, pianist and organist (born in Paris 1835) was, as is well known, in sympathy with the New German School, and fosters, amongst others, the *genre* of "Symphonic Poems" made known by Liszt.

sonorous, pages 8 and 9, which opens superbly on the
entry of the subject fortissimo ; the piquant rhythm
 of the second subject of the Allegro
scherzando, page 25.   Possibly this would have gained
somewhat by more combination and development,
either of the principal subject or of some secondary
subject ; for instance, a little anodyne counterpoint, it
seems to me, would not be out of place on pages 26, 27.

Violoncello pizzicato
and Bassoon.

etc.

etc., etc., and so on.   *Item* for pages 50 to 54, in which
the simple breadth of the period with the holding on
of the accompaniment chords leaves rather a void ;
I should like there to be some incidence and *polyphonic*
entanglement, as the Germanic *Polyphemuses* say.
Pardon me this detailed remark, dear Monsieur Saint-
Saëns, which I only venture to make while assuring
you in all sincerity that the *totàl* of your work pleases
me singularly.   I played it again the day before yesterday to Sgambati, of whom Planté [1] will speak to you,

[1] Francis Planté (born 1839), the exquisitely refined Pianist.

as of an artist above the common run and even more than ordinarily *distingué*. He will let the public hear your Concerto next winter, which ought to meet with success in every country.

When is the performance of the *Timbre*[1] to be? I wish it to give you abundantly all the satisfaction that you deserve, and shall only regret that I cannot be present at the performance of it. At my age the *rôle* of *young composer* is no longer suitable—and there would not be any other for me at Paris, as I cannot continue indefinitely that of an old disabled pianist. Thus I have judiciously made up my mind not to trouble myself about my compositions any further than the writing of them, without in the least thinking of spreading them. Supposing that they have any value it will always be found out soon enough either during my life or afterwards. The sympathy of my friends (a very well chosen sympathy, I flatter myself) amply suffices me; the rest of the world may talk in its own way. As to the *Elizabeth* I do not think it is adapted to the Parisian taste. I am moreover very tired of that score through the performances at the Wartburg, Pest and Vienna; and the difficult task of a suitable French translation, plus the rehearsals with a set of artists little disposed to take trouble, frightens me. I much prefer to employ my time in a manner less ungrateful and more agreeable; consequently I shall not put out anybody in Paris, which I shall not visit; and invite you to come and see me in Rome. Here, dear Monsieur St. Saëns, we can talk and *musiquer* [make music] at our ease. Try and procure me this

---

[1] Le timbre d'argent (the silver bell), an Opera.

great pleasure soon, and believe fully in my sentiments of high esteem and devoted affection.

F. LISZT.

ROME, *July* 19*th*, 1869.

92. TO CAMILLE SAINT-SAËNS.

VERY HONOURED FRIEND,

At last your compositions have come, and I spent all yesterday in their amiable society.

Let us speak first of the Mass : this is a capital, grand, beautiful, admirable work—so good that, among contemporary works of the same kind, I know perhaps of none so striking by the elevation of the sentiment, the religious character, the sustained, adequate, vigorous style and consummate mastery. It is like a magnificent Gothic Cathedral in which Bach would conduct his orchestra !

After having read your score three times I am so thoroughly imbued with it that I venture to risk a few remarks.

In the *Gloria* one should, I think, preserve the literal text *entire* : " Gratias agimus tibi *propter magnam gloriam tuam*."—Consequently add four or five bars.

At the beginning of the Sanctus it would be better to continue the voices, and to complete by them the sense of the orchestra ; similarly it would be advantageous to interlace, by means of an alto solo, the text of the Benedictus (which you have omitted) to the Organ melody, pages 77 and 78 after the Hosanna, as well as to add the chorus to the final phrase of the " Dona nobis pacem," pages 88 and 89.

You will find all these small matters carefully noted

down on your score, which I will venture to return to
you, begging you to let me have it back again soon,
for I must possess this extraordinary work, which has
its place between Bach and Beethoven.

Bear with one more liturgical question, and, in addition, a proposition boldly practical in the *Kyrie*, the
spire of your Cathedral.   The inspiration and structure
of it are certainly admirable . . . "omnia excelsa tua
et fluctus tui super me transierunt."   Nevertheless,
during these 300 bars, about, of a slow and almost
continuous movement, do you not lose sight of the
celebrant, who is obliged to remain standing motionless
at the altar ?   Do you not expose him to commit the
sin of impatience directly after he has said the con-
fiteor ? . . . Will not the composer be reproached with
having given way to his genius rather than to the
requirements of the worship ?

In order to obviate these unpleasant conjunctures
it would be necessary for you to resign yourself to an
enormous sacrifice as an artist, namely, to cut out
18 pages ! (*for church performance only*, for these
18 pages should be preserved in the edition to your
greater honour as a musician, and it would suffice to
indicate the " cut" *ad libitum*, as I have done in several
places in the score of the Gran Mass).

Sacrifice, then, 18 pages as I said, and put the
Christe eleison on page 6, instead of the *Kyrie eleison*,

concluding *pp* on page 10.

From the musical point of view exclusively, I should blush to make such a proposition ; but it is necessary to keep peace, especially in the Church, where one must learn to subordinate one's self in mind and deed. Art, there, should be only a correlative matter, and should tend to the most perfect *concomitance* possible with the rite.

Be assured, dear Monsieur Saint-Saëns, of the sentiments of high esteem and great sympathy which I entertain towards you.

Your very devoted

Rome, *August 4th*, 1869.   F. Liszt.

93. To Madame Jessie Laussot.

I have had to write a great many notes this last week. Pardon me for being so late in thanking you for your friendly lines, and kindly tell Mademoiselle Alexandrine Ritter how sincerely I feel for her in her affliction. Her mother expressed in a rare degree and in her whole personality the high and sweet dignity of the human soul. Respect attached itself to her naturally,—and she inspired the noble serenity of it.

In a few days a little surprise will reach you in the form of an *Ave Maria* written for the Cherubini Society, and dedicated to the society's dear Maëstra. However simple these few bars may be (in which there is not a single repetition of a word, nor ornamenting of any kind) I hope they will not be unpleasing to you, and I beg you to play them in the form of a prayer for

Your very affectionate

Rome, *October 7th*, 1869.   F. Liszt.

In acknowledging the receipt of the *Ave Maria* tell me when you expect Bülow, of whom I have had no tidings since Munich.

Sgambati returned here last week.

94. To Dr. Ludwig Nohl.[1]

DEAR FRIEND,

Let my best thanks for your letter be, to take it to heart—and to comply with it. Meanwhile this much is certain—that we shall see each other in Weimar next May, and that at the *Tonkünstler-Versammlung* there you will officiate as the worthy biographer of Beethoven.

In spite of too modest a remark in your letter I am convinced that you are peculiarly well qualified for thoroughly grasping, and making others comprehend, the question of the "more modern style of Art." Proofs of this have been gathered recently from all the admirable things you have said in your *brochure* on Wagner; for instance, in regard to the "refined, firm and proud position held by Music," its "most expressive physiognomy," and "that spirit of *love* which Music has created for itself"—and also, if you will allow me such presumption in contrast to your modesty, on p. 63, where you say, "The logos alone regulates the thought and gives life to the risings and fallings of the poetic idea"—

Sic vos non vobis—

Innumerable interruptions prevent my beginning the Beethoven Cantata to-day. But I have at last secured

[1] The well-known writer on musical subjects (1831—1885).

quiet : I shall remain all the winter at the Villa d'Este (3 or 4 hours out of Rome), and take care that I do not lose an immoderate amount of time.

With sincerest thanks and in all friendliness yours,

VILLA D'ESTE, *November 17th,* 1869. F. LISZT.

95. TO THE PRINCESS CAROLINE SAYN-WITTGENSTEIN.[1]

November 27th, 1869.

. —. The death of Overbeck reminds me of my own. I wish, and urgently entreat and command, that my burial may take place without show, and be as simple and economical as possible. I protest against a burial such as Rossini's was, and even against any sort of invitation for friends and acquaintances to assemble as was done at Overbeck's interment. Let there be no pomp, no music, no procession in my honour, no superfluous illuminations, or any kind of oration. Let my body be buried, not in a church, but in some cemetery, and let it not be removed from that grave to any other. I will not have any other place for my body than the cemetery in use in the place where I die, nor any other religious ceremony than a quiet Mass in the Parish Church (not any kind of Requiem to be sung). The inscription on my tomb might be : " Et habitabunt recti cum vultu suo." . — .

96. TO FRANZ SERVAIS.

Your kind letter has given me very sincere pleasure, dear Monsieur Franz. I hope your health

---

[1] According to the *Weimarer Zeitung* it was printed as above, fragmentarily, in the *Leipziger Tageblatt* of December 6th, 1888.

is quite re-established, and that you are plunging into
Bach to your heart's content,—that admirable chaly-
beate spring ! I will bear you company, and have
given myself, for a Christmas present, the little 8vo
edition of Peters of the two *Passions*, Masses and
Cantatas of Bach, whom one might designate as the
St. Thomas Aquinas of music. Kahnt, who sends me
these scores, tells me of his earnest desire to get
Cornelius settled at Leipzig, in the position of editor-
in-chief of the *Neue Zeitschrift*, founded, as you
know, by Schumann, and bravely carried on by
Brendel. It is the sole paper which has, for thirty
years past, sustained with steadfastness, knowledge
and consistency the works and the men of musical
progress. If, as I wish, Cornelius undertakes Brendel's
task, I think you would do well to follow out your
project of staying again in Leipzig.—In any case I hope
to see you again this spring at Weimar ; I shall arrive
there towards the middle of April, and shall stay till
the end of June. During the winter I shall abstain
from all travelling, and shall not leave my retreat at
the Villa d'Este except to stay a few days in Rome.
Many people have very kindly invited me to go to
Paris ; I have excused myself from doing so for
reasons of expediency which you know. Henceforth
it is not *myself* that I have to bring forward, but simply
to continue to write in perfect tranquillity and with a
free mind. To do this obliges me to seclude myself,
to avoid the *salons*, the half-opened pianos and the
society drudgery imposed by the large towns, where I
very easily feel myself out of place.

Thank you cordially for your propaganda of the

Missa Choralis ; I shall be much obliged if you will write me a couple of words after the performance. Will you also please tell M. Brassin that I thank him much for not having been afraid of compromising his success as a virtuoso by choosing my Concerto ? Up to the present time all the best-known French pianists— with the exception of Saint-Saëns—have not ventured to play anything of mine except *transcriptions*, my own compositions being necessarily considered absurd and insupportable. People know pretty well what to think by what they hear said, without any need of hearing the works.

How did the orchestra go with the piano in the Concerto ? Had they taken care to have enough rehearsals ? There are several passages that require minute care ; the modulations are abrupt, and the variety of the movements is somewhat disconcerting for the conductor. And, in addition to this, the traitor *triangle* (proh pudor !*), however excited he may be to strike strong with his cunning little rhythm, marked *pianis-simo*, provokes the most scandalous catastrophe. . . .

Notwithstanding all the regrettable parleying, for in such a matter all sensible people ought to be of the same opinion, I presume that Mr. Godebski's bust of Chopin will shortly be placed in the lobby of the theatre at Warsaw. Certainly Chopin well merits this mark of honour, which moreover need in no wise prevent people from busying themselves about a larger monument to Lemberg, and from collecting a sufficient sum for that purpose.

At Weimar we will talk of Hal and the pleasure it

* Oh shame !

will be to me to pay you a visit there.   Pray present my respectful thanks to your mother, and my affectionate remembrances to Madame Godebski,—and believe me, dear Monsieur Franz, your sincere friend,

F. Liszt.

Villa d'Este, *December 20th,* 1869.

(Address always Rome.)

97. To Dr. Franz Witt in Ratisbon.[1]

[Rome, *towards the end of* 1869.]

Very dear Sir and Friend,

Before I had the honour of knowing you personally the manuscript of your " Litaniæ lauretanæ " aroused in me sincere interest and religious sympathy towards you.   This first impression is now increased by my deeper knowledge of the substantial value of your compositions and my fuller appreciation of the great services you have rendered to Church Music. That you act as admirably in practice as in precept is evident in other of your works, but especially in the Mass and the Te Deum which were performed here on the Emperor of Austria's name-day in the Church of the Anima under the leadership of our dear friend Haberl.[2] Both of these works are of rare value—and, what is still more rare, both are equally devoted to Art and the Church.

---

[1] Like all the subsequent letters to Dr. Witt, this letter is without date or ending, as printed in Walter's biography of Witt (Ratisbon, Pustet, 1889).—Dr. Witt (1834–80) was a distinguished musical scholar, also a composer, the founder and first general president of the *Cäcilien-Verein* [St. Cecilia Society], and died as a clergyman in Landshut.

[2] On the 4th October, 1869.

The " Litaniæ lauretanæ " breathes also a spirit of nobility of soul, and diffuses its pleasant aroma notwithstanding the necessary musical limitation.   The collective character of the invocations shows uniformity ; and yet the lines of melody are very finely drawn ; especially touching to me is

Sa - lus infirmo — — rum Refugium peccatorum,
Conso-la-trix afflicto — — rum.

My hearty thanks for the dedication, my very dear friend ; it brings me justifiable and joyful pride, which your own exaggerated modesty should dispel.—Next summer I will again come to you for a few days on my way to Szegzard (Hungary), where my Mass for male voices (2nd *very much corrected* edition,—now published by Repos, Paris) is to be performed.   A few months after my visit you will I hope receive most satisfactory news (through Haberl) about the *Cäcilien-Verein*,[1] to which, in fullest conviction, I remain firmly attached—as well as to its much esteemed President.

98. To Prof. Dr. Siegmund Lebert.

Dear Friend,

The proofs of Weber's and Schubert's Sonatas were despatched to Stuttgart in two parcels *by rail* the day before yesterday.   This is the cheapest and quickest way of sending things, and I beg of you in

---

[1] Haberl had endeavoured, through the intervention of the Bishops assembled in Council in Rome, to obtain the Pope's approbation of the *Cäcilien-Verein*, and his efforts met with success.

future to send parcels in this way, as packages sent by *spediteur* come slowly and cost a great deal. N.B.— The parcels must not be too thick, and must have the address written on the *wrapper*. As soon as you send me the D minor Sonata, that is still wanting, and Weber's Conzertstück, I will revise them at once; ere long you will receive Schubert's Impromptus, Valses, etc.

My endeavour with this work is to avoid all quibbling and pretentiousness, and to make the edition a practical one for teachers and players. And for this reason at the very last I added a goodly amount of fingering and pedal marks; kindly get the printers to excuse this, and I trust that the trouble it causes will not prove superfluous.—With regard to the deceptive *Tempo rubato*, I have settled the matter provisionally in a brief note (in the finale of Weber's A♭ major Sonata); other occurrences of the *rubato* may be left to the taste and momentary feeling of gifted players. A metronomical performance is certainly tiresome and nonsensical; time and rhythm must be adapted to and identified with the melody, the harmony, the accent and the poetry. . . . But how indicate all this? I shudder at the thought of it.

Also kindly excuse me from writing a preface, and *write it yourself*, dear friend. For you know exactly what I should wish to say, and you would say it much more clearly than I could, for my very small amount of pedagogism is, for the most part, confined to the words of St. Paul: *Littera occidit, spiritus vivificat!*

Your success delights without surprising me. It is only what ought to be, that Lebert and Stark's

Pianoforte Method should meet with general acceptance, and that the Stuttgart Conservatoire should
continue to prosper. Both of these points of merit
I took the opportunity of mentioning with due honour
to H.M. the Queen of Würtemberg—on the occasion
of her visit to the Villa d'Este here.

Best thanks for sending the Bach Fugue, the 2
Etudes (separate edition) and the last volume of the
Method, which I found to contain many, to me, new
and praiseworthy items, among others the Etudes of
Hiller and Brahms.

Ever, in all friendship, yours

F. Liszt.

Villa d'Este, *January* 10*th*, 1870.

I shall remain here till the end of April, and then
go direct to Weimar.

99. To C. F. Kahnt, the Music Publisher.

Dear Friend,

The life's object of the *Neue Zeitschrift* remains :
firmly to stand by the colours of *Rheingold* and
the *Nibelungen*, and unfailingly to represent the interests
of the *Deutsche Musikverein*. This embraces all essential consequences for us.

At the end of next week I will send you the pianoforte score of the Beethoven Cantata, and write full
particulars to Riedel.

By the middle of April I hope to reach Weimar.

Best thanks for sending the *Ave maris stella*—and
in all friendliness I remain yours,

F. Liszt.

Rome, *February* 11*th*, 1870.

100. To Herr Gille, Councillor of Justice.

Dear Friend,

The best thing I have to tell you to-day is that we shall soon see each other again. At the beginning of April I shall visit Bülow in Florence, and then go direct to Weimar.

Last week I had a correspondence with Riedel about matters of the *Tonkünstler-Versammlung*. The most important points are as follows :—The utmost economy that is possible to making a perfectly suitable orchestra and chorus. The spaces at our disposal in Weimar (churches, theatre and refreshment room) will not allow of any great expenditure as regards the *personnel*. It is to be hoped that Müller-Hartung can obtain a respectable contingent for the Beethoven Mass, which will lessen the number of outside co-operators ; and I in like manner reckon chiefly on the Weimar Vocal Union for the more important numbers of the concert programme—Psalm by Schulz-Beuthen, Prometheus by Saint-Saëns, my Beethoven Cantata, etc. The arrangement of the orchestra is to be as it was at the Carl August Festival and at the *Tonkünstler-Versammlung* of '61—10 first violins, 6 to 7 double basses, etc. Riedel conducts Beethoven's Mass ; Lassen the concerts in the theatre ; and Müller-Hartung my Cantata. *Conzertmeister* David and Director Hellmesberger will *preside* over the 1st violins. Both gentlemen will also determine about the performance of the Beethoven Quartet. Any other *special* violin *virtuoso* would be superfluous *this time*.

Riedel must arrange the distribution of the solo parts of the Beethoven Mass according as he thinks best. Milde only requires, in my Cantata,

> " Dieser Brave sei verpflichtet
> Das zu thun, was wir gedichtet." *
>
> (Schober, 49. Goethe-Feier.)

I flatter myself, by-the-bye, that Milde will also find a pleasure in the *Sternen-Cantabile—*

Viel   tau - send hal - ten näch - tig   (Vide the accompanying page.) [1]

Riedel asks me who shall play the pianoforte?

If our meeting were at Jena I should decidedly invite Bülow to do it; he is the veritable Beethoven player and interpreter, the one who knows and who can do [*Kenner und Könner*]; but unfortunately the shades of Dingelstedt and Gutzkow warn him from Weimar's doors. . . .

Meanwhile there is no hurry about the choice of a pianist (*he* or *she*). Only arrange the principal things in a suitable manner, the chorus, orchestra, solo singers and the Beethoven Quartet; all the rest will soon be arranged after my arrival at Weimar in the middle of April.   Yours most faithfully,

F. Liszt.

Villa d'Este, *February 26th,* 1870.

* " May this brave one be constrained
  That to do which we ordained."

[1] It contained the Cantabile in question for Milde from Liszt's Beethoven Cantata.

The piano arrangement of my Cantata must be written out again, and cannot therefore be sent off for 8 or 10 days. The entire work lasts about three-quarters of an hour. I am so far ready with it, that there are only two or three more passages to be instrumented.

101. To the Baroness E. M. Schwartz in Crete.*

My winter *villeggiatura* at the Villa d'Este is drawing to its close; the day after to-morrow I return to Rome, and when you receive these lines I shall be at Weimar. Address to me there till the middle of June.

When will your Cretan volume, crowned † with erudition and philhellenism, be finished? Shall you return this summer for its publication? I hope you will, and I will confess to you without any compliments that you are among the very small number of my friends whose absence I feel to be a privation. Now, to accustom one's self to this kind of privation does not become easier with age.

You doubtless know the novel of your great historical friend, published now by the "Gaulois" (if I am not mistaken) under the title "La Domination du Moine" (or "Clélia.") I question whether another of your friends—less historical although very distinguished—M. St. Réné Taillandier, recently appointed Secretary General to the Minister of Public Instruction, would

* Autograph in the Liszt Museum at Weimar.—The addressee was widely known as the writer Elpis Melena.

† Untranslatable pun on the words "crétois" and "crété."

subscribe to many copies of G.'s novel for the Imperial libraries ; but he will have a fine opportunity of ministerial revenge when the biographer of the hero of *l'unità italiana* (not the "cattolica," relegated to Turin) brings out "*la Crète*," in which the Cretans will at last be relieved from the anathema of their Epimenides narrated in St. Paul's Epistle to Titus,—"Cretenses semper mendaces, malæ bestiæ, ventres pigri."—In the matter of "*mendaces*" and "*ventres pigri*" there would be a tremendous competition with the rest of Europe.

My plans for the spring and summer remain always the same. *Weimar*—from the 10th April till the 20th June—with the *Tonkünstler-Versammlung* (which has the honour of counting you amongst its illustrious members) ; then in the last week of May I should be very much tempted to be present at the famous "Passion Play" at *Ober-Ammergau* ; at the end of August I shall go to my old friend Augusz at Szegzard (Hungary), who is anxious that a new Mass of mine should be performed on the day of the dedication of a church (29th September) ; and in October I shall return to Rome.

I suppose you receive the *Allgemeine Zeitung*. It gives but too much news, and little edifying, about serious things here by its "Roman Letters," no less widespread than badly put together. If you want to obtain complete information on these difficult questions you must read *l'Univers* and the letters of Veuillot, or at least *l'Unità cattolica* ; but it would be exacting too much from your impartiality. Moreover you have better things to do than to read ; your chief duty is to make yourself read, consequently to write and to write again ;—in a secondary manner occupy yourself a little with your beautiful vines, and, above all, don't forget to bring soon some samples of their excellent product, which will enliven our material and intellectual "*substantials*," at which, hoping to participate again in the year of grace 1870, I am,

Your very affectionate and very devoted servant,

F. LISZT.

VILLA D'ESTE, *March 15th*, 1870.

As handy gossip I send you the following : they say that Odo Russel [*sic*] will shortly go to England for his wife's confinement, and will not return to his post in Rome.   It is also said that Schlözer will pay a visit here in the spring ;—and that the daughter of Countess Garcia is to marry a nephew of Cardinal Antonelli, and will bring a fortune of ten thousand pounds sterling.

Tarnowski will return to his Penates in Gallicia at Easter, and will write to you.   Wider continues to be president of the German circle.   Next door to one another, there are many concerts given at the *Sala Dante*, and our friend Sgambati is acquiring more and more the reputation of a great artist, which he merits. Reményi spent the winter in Hungary.   I should very much like to invite him to come to the *Tonkünstler-Versammlung* at Weimar ; but our programme is already over-full.   In any case I shall meet Rem. again at Szegzard.

102. TO CAMILLE SAINT-SAËNS.

DEAR FRIEND,

The rehearsals of your " Noces de Prométhée " (Marriage of Prometheus) are proceeding well at

Weimar and Jena; we shall pay particular attention
to the 4 harps, the saxophones, etc. But what is of
the greatest consequence is yourself. I have announced
your coming at the Court and in the town. *A revoir*
then! Try to be here on the *24th*,[1]—and believe me
yours ever in sincere friendship,

F. LISZT.

WEIMAR, *May* 12*th*, 1870.

103. TO JOHANN VON HERBECK.

VERY DEAR FRIEND,

Being perfectly convinced of your genuine
friendship I am quite willing to follow the instructions
you will briefly give me concerning the *Beethoven*
Festival [2] in Vienna. Whether, and in what way, I
may be able to take part in it will be decided when we
have discussed the subject. Meanwhile I most modestly
determine to consider myself unusable.*

About the beginning of August I shall pay you a
visit in Vienna, whence my road leads onwards to
Szegzard. My earlier halting points will be: 3rd July,
Leipzig—performance of my Missa choralis; 13th and

---

[1] Saint-Saëns came to Weimar for the *Tonkünstler-Versammlung*
of the "*Allgemeine Deutsche Musik-Verein*," with which the Beethoven
Centenary was simultaneously celebrated; and for the first time, on
the 27th May, 1870, Saint-Saëns' name appeared on the programme
of these concerts. He also appeared as a pianist, and Liszt played
with him at a Matinée on two grand pianos.

[2] For the benefit of the Beethoven Memorial. It took place in
Vienna on the 18th March, 1877. Liszt played the E♭ major Concerto
and the pianoforte Fantasia (with chorus), and accompanied the
Scotch songs sung by Caroline Bettelheim.

* There is here a play on the word *bescheiden*, the German being *ich
bescheide mich bescheidenst*, which is untranslatable.

17th July, *Rheingold* and the *Walküre* in Munich ; and
after that the Passion Play at Oberammergau.

The favourable reception accorded to the Coronation
Mass [1] is essentially due to your having conducted it.
My best thanks for this. The score is to be printed
shortly, and I must ask you to hand over to the
publisher Schuberth the manuscript which I gave you
in Munich last summer. Schuberth is going to Vienna
in a few weeks.

With sincerest esteem, I remain your ever gratefully
devoted   F. LISZT.

WEIMAR, *June 20th*, 1870.

104. TO SOPHIE MENTER.[2]

DEAR AND VERY HONOURED ONE,

A telegram from Abrányi informs me that an
invitation, addressed to *Capellmeister* O. B. in Salzburg,
has already been sent to you to ask you to take part in
the *Sängerfest* in Pest. Hence, after having triumphantly played in the Mozarteum on the 18th, your
triumphs are to be continued forthwith in Pest on the
20th. Baron Augusz and your humble servant expect
you there from the 19th. Kindly let me know (per
telegram) by which train you will arrive, and—a few
days afterwards—my rigidly adhered-to plan of carrying you off to Szegzard shall be brilliantly fulfilled.

---

[1] By Liszt.

[2] The favourite and most distinguished of Liszt's lady-pupils, of
whom he wrote to Navrátil on 29th September, 1881, that he had " for
many years past regarded her as the most brilliant and accomplished
of the lady-pianists of the day." Since 1874 she has held the
appointment of Court pianist at the Imperial Court of Austria.

Here in this house you will find rest, comfort, friendly sympathy and harmless affability, and, in addition, music too, and that not of the worst kind, for we shall arrange it ourselves.

Your sincerely attached and devoted

F. LISZT.

SZEGZARD, *August 11th*, 1870.

105. To SOPHIE MENTER.

Your hearty and humorous little note closes delightfully with the promise that you are soon coming to Szegzard. You will not find here any vestige of all the artistic enjoyments and glories of the *Mozarteum*; the whole symphonic contingent of Szegzard is limited to half a dozen gypsies with instruments out of tune and *harmonising* in pell mell fashion one with the other; the choruses are free and performed in the open air, namely: soprano and alto—flocks of geese; tenor and bass—cattle;—so that a conductor like O. B. would have nothing further to do than to pose as a mythological figure. . . .

Nevertheless I promise you, dear kind patroness, many pleasant and befitting things in this restful, genial and refined home of our mutual friend Baron Augusz.

You will be most heartily welcome to us all—especially to your most sincerely attached

F. LISZT.

SZEGZARD, *August 29th*, 1870.

Between the middle and the end of September Reményi, Mosonyi and Mihalovich will be staying here.

106. To Kornel von Abrányi in Budapest.*

DEAR FRIEND,

The death of Mosonyi puts our hearts in mourning.[1] It makes us sorrow also for Music in Hungary, of which Mosonyi was one of the noblest, most valiant and praiseworthy representatives. One might be proud of walking side by side with him in the right road.

In truth his name had not its *due éclat* and renown abroad ; but he did not trouble himself the least about that, and possibly he did not even take enough trouble about it,—as much by wisdom as by contempt of equivocal and vulgar means, which were repugnant to the elevated rectitude of his soul. He felt what esteem was due to him, and thought of nothing but real glory ; that which is attained by conscientious perseverance in the Good and the Beautiful.

Let us honour his memory by setting ourselves to make his examples and teaching bear further fruit !—

Many of the published compositions of Mosonyi deserve to be more and better known ; others, still in manuscript,—his last great dramatic work *Almos* in particular—will soon be spread abroad, I hope.

We will talk about this shortly at Pest. For to-day I wish merely to share with some friend, such as yourself, dear Abrányi, the grief at the loss which we have sustained.   Yours from my heart,

SZEGZARD, *November 2nd*, 1870.   F. LISZT.

* Autograph in the possession of Herr E. von Mihalovich in Budapest.—The addressee was a musician, writer and critic there.

[1] Michael Mosonyi, the friend of Liszt, and to whose sudden death the latter here refers, was famous in Hungary as a composer, teacher and author.

107. To Sophie Menter.

Dear Patroness,

Your dear little notes joyfully alarm the whole household. All beg you urgently to come as soon as possible, and I all the more urgently as I have to go to Vienna at the end of April.

Your bewitching description of the *Ambrosia*-Concerto makes me most inquisitive: be sure not to forget to bring the tremendous manuscript with you; we will arrange an historically memorable performance of it in the salon of the Town-Vicarage.

Hearty greetings, and in all friendliness yours,

F. Liszt.

Pest, *March 22nd*, 1871.

In musical matters as follows : this evening and Friday concerts by Reményi ; next Sunday and on the Wednesday before Easter Philharmonic concerts ;—in between a grand concert at the *Musik Academie* of Ofen, and on Good Friday a performance of the Stabat Mater, etc., etc.

Our programme shall be arranged here, forthwith, by word of mouth, at any quarter of an hour that my dear patroness Sophie may feel disposed to appoint.

108. To Edmund von Mihalovich in Budapest.[1]

. — . Augusz, in his last letter, speaks of fresh proposals on the subject of my settling in Hungary. I answer him, as before, that I am quite disposed to

[1] Composer of several operas and large orchestral works (born 1842), now director of the Music Academy in Budapest.

show myself accommodating, devoted, useful, obedient and grateful. The only condition that I make relative to my return to Pest next winter is—*a place to live in*;—for, on the one hand, the modesty of my income forbids me to increase my expenses, and, on the other hand, politeness demands, as it seems to me, that if they seriously want me they will also show me that they do, by sparing me the onerous trouble of having to find a home. On the four occasions on which I have stayed at Pest since 1865 Schwendtner has shown me the utmost and most cordial hospitality. I feel a most *true* gratitude to him, but should be afraid of showing it ill by taking too great advantage of his kindness to me.

. — . Mme. de Moukhanoff [1] writes, "Has Mihalovich received my letter of tender invectives and entreaties to make him come to Weimar ?"

It will be difficult to persuade her that walks on the shore at Ostend ought to be preferable to the charm of the talks on the "Goethe Platz," and even at the "Erb-Prinz," which she will again favour with her presence towards the middle of June, I hope. Tausig also promises me to spend a fortnight here.

Mlle. Brandt sang several songs admirably yesterday morning at the "Hofgärtnerei." I shall accompany her in yours to-morrow.

Yours in cordial friendship,

WEIMAR, *May 29th*, 1871.   F. LISZT.

Till the end of June address—Weimar.

---

[1] The cultivated musical friend of Liszt and Wagner, to whom the latter dedicated his "*Judenthum in der Musik*," whilst Liszt dedicated an Elegie to her memory.

109. To Marie Lipsius.

DEAR AND KINDEST BIOGRAPHER,

Again an excellent suggestion; follow it without hesitation and present us ere long with a pleasantly powerful and characteristic portrait of Tausig.[1] In what year of the fifties his father brought him to Weimar, I do not now recollect; but I do remember how greatly astonished I was at his extraordinary talent when I first heard him play. The intellectual claws and pinions were already giving signs of mighty power in the youth who was scarcely 14 years of age, and somewhat delicate in appearance. I felt some compunction in undertaking to give him further instruction, determined not to undertake the task, and therefore informed the father that in the case of such a stupendous organisation the wisest plan was to leave it free, independent development without a teacher. However Tausig insisted upon remaining with me. He studied immoderately; as a rule kept very much to himself while in Weimar, and got into various little scrapes in consequence of his quick, ironical humour. I was accused of being over-indulgent with him, and of thus *spoiling* him; but I really could not have acted otherwise, and I loved him with all my heart. On various occasions when I had to undertake short journeys in connection with the performances of my works he accompanied me; among other places to Dresden, Prague and Vienna. Subsequently he lived in Vienna for some length of time, and got up some

---

[1] Liszt's great pupil (born in 1841) had died in Leipzig on the 17th July, 1871.

concerts there with the view of having some Symphonic Poems performed which he himself conducted —but he was unable to get a proper start. He had to struggle on and to endure many privations before attaining the success he deserved. His brilliant vocation did not become firmly established till a few years ago, in Berlin, Leipzig, etc.

In the spring of '69 I met Tausig in Paris (after the *Tannhäuser* scandal), and returned with him to Weimar for the *Tonkünstler-Versammlung*. Bülow conducted the Faust Symphony *by heart* (at the rehearsals most accurately mentioning the *letters*!), and Tausig played the A major Concerto marvellously. Since then I have seen him only twice : last May at the *Tonkünstler-Versammlung* in Weimar (where he played Beethoven's E♭ major Concerto) and now. . . .

Countess Krokow could give you the most reliable information about him, and our friend R. Pohl may also be of use to you in your work. As far as I know, no one has understood Tausig's genius, his demoniacally ideal nature, with so quick a perception, so refined and—I might say—with such womanly intuition, as Frau von Moukhanoff (*née* Countess Nesselrode). Unfortunately the two letters in which she wrote me full particulars about Tausig are in Rome. Tausig dedicated his two lately published Etudes, Op. 1, to her, and she was ever a highly appreciative and kindly patroness of his. Remember to mention her specially in your delineation of his character.

Of Tausig's publications those chiefly deserving the highest praise are his masterly transcriptions of the

Beethoven Quartets, the Toccata and Fugue of Bach (D minor), Schubert's March ; the three pieces from "Tristan and Isolde," the pianoforte score of the "Meistersinger," of the Kaisermarsch, the "Nouvelles Soirées de Vienne" and his two last original Etudes. Recommend also, for the good of pianists, and as a very saleable work, an early publication of his very admirable and well-sustained arrangement of Chopin's first Concerto (E minor).

Accept the expression of my sincere esteem and gratitude.

F. LISZT.

SCHLOSS WILHELMSTHAL, *Sunday, July 23rd,* 1871.

In the middle of this week I return to Weimar and remain there till the 5th—10th of August.

110. TO FRANZ SERVAIS.

DEAR FRANZ,

In spite of the proverb " Every road leads to Rome " I shall not be able to return there by way of Hal this time. Will you give my very affectionate respects to your mother and tell her how much I regret to be unable to be present, except in thought, at the beautiful family *fête* at the time of the inauguration of the monument to your father, on the 10th September.—Shall you not invite the Prince de Chimay (the present governor of Mons, I believe) ? He would have a right there owing to his sincere interest for Art and his very distinguished musical talent.

I am persuaded that Lassen will express in noble music the inspiration of this *fête* intended to perpetuate the memory of an illustrious and sympathetic artist. But however successful may be his composition, it does not absolve you from yours, which filial affection demands of you and will dictate to you. Write it without delay, and afterwards take advantage of your leisure at Hal to fulfil the praiseworthy programme indicated in your letter :

a. To work hard at the Piano.

b. To help towards your independence by making yourself capable of cutting a good figure as conductor.

c. To venture on the performance of your *Macbeth* sorceries and other of your compositions, with the reservation of not hearing yourself immediately proclaimed *king* by the sorcerers of criticism.

Shall you make your appearance at the composition competition next year ? I invite you to do so.

You know that H. Richter has been appointed conductor to the National Theatre of Pest, and will conduct *Lohengrin* there at the end of September. He will find, I trust, honour and satisfaction in more firmly implanting in his country the sublime works of Wagner, and in making the orchestra, the stage and the public profit by the exemplary rules and practices of M. de Bülow at Munich. Needless to say that I shall endeavour to make Richter's task as easy as possible to him.

Count Tyszkiewicz, in passing lately through Weimar, was kind enough to explain to me his new system of musical mathematics, and to show me his tables of figures honoured with commendatory letters from Mr. Gevaert and several notabilities. If, by means of his figures and measures, Tysz. succeeds, as you claim for him, in demonstrating that X . . . is a "pyramid," this will be a more pyramidal glory even than the system.

Next Thursday I go to Eichstätt (Bavaria), where the (German) St. Cecilia Society meets. Its founder and president F. Witt—a much respected ecclesiastic, conductor of the Cathedral, composer and editor of two newspapers of sacred music published by Pustet at Ratisbon—gives evidence of a great capacity and a persevering zeal in endeavouring seriously to improve the uses and customs of Church music, and, by continuous publications, to propagate the old works of repute as well as the new ones of this class that are deserving of recommendation.—A pamphlet by Witt, which appeared in the spring, "über das Dirigiren der Kirchenmusik" ["about the conducting of Church music"], corrects some grievous errors and furnishes much profitable instruction.

I shall be much obliged if you will send me a printed account of your *fête* of the 10th September ; on that day I shall be in Rome, and shall not return thence till toward the end of October, to settle at Pest for the winter.

Remember me most kindly to your brother Joseph,[1] to Godebski and his wife, and believe, dear Franz, in my *steadfast* feelings of devoted affection.

WILHELMSTHAL, *August 25th*, 1871.   F. LISZT.

Address Rome, Santa Francesca Romana, Campo Vaccino.

What are Joseph's and your plans for the winter ?

---

[1] The excellent Violoncellist Joseph Servais, who died in 1885 at the age of 35.

III. To Walter Bache.

Dear Mr. Bache,

Your kind remembrance of the 22nd October has given me sincere pleasure, for which I thank you cordially. Please excuse me for not telling you oftener by letter my constant feelings of affection for you ; the hindrance of occupations and cares drives me, alas ! into an extreme parsimony as regards letter writing with my best friends, but I think that is my only omission towards them. To see M. de Bülow again was a real joy to me. His health is improving, and his prodigious *maëstria* is at its height. He is going to make a concert tour this winter in Vienna, Pest, Prague, Berlin, etc., and will come to London in May. I hope that the people there will be able to appreciate his superiority in its entirety. Bülow, more than any contemporary artist, takes the lead in celebrity. He is not only a very great virtuoso and musician, but also a veritable sovereign of music. Mme. Laussot, who has the genius of nobility of the heart, also came to *fête* me on Sunday. I shall see her again at Florence in a fortnight, on my way to Pest, where, as you know, I am henceforth fixed, by royal and national favour. Whether there or at Weimar, I hope we shall meet again next summer, dear Bache, in perfect harmony.

Your very cordially affectionate and devoted

F. Liszt.

Rome, *October 25th*, 1871.

Bravo and thanks for your concert programmes, which I beg you to continue sending me.

112. To Marie Lipsius.

Dear Patroness,

To your . —. sketch of Tausig only a single objection could be raised ; namely, that you bestow too high praise upon me. Pardon me if I cannot argue about it, and accept my cordial thanks for this new tribute of your generous kindness.

Last Sunday (22nd October) I had the great pleasure of a visit from Bülow. He is going to remain in Florence till the New Year, and he then begins a categorical concert tour in Vienna, Pest, Prague, Berlin, Leipzig, and at the end of April goes to London. His perfect mastery as a virtuoso—in the finest sense of the word—is in its zenith. To him one might apply Dante's words : "A master to those who know."

Again my hearty thanks, and wishing you an increase of La Mara's . —. writings, I remain with much esteem,

Yours very sincerely,

F. Liszt.

Rome, *October 25th*, 1871.

In a fortnight's time I travel to Pest.

113. To Breitkopf and Härtel.

Dear Sirs,

In order justly to decide the question of plagiarism between Messrs. Altschul and Joseffy,[1] one would need first of all to compare the manuscripts of

---

[1] Both were pupils of Liszt ; the former is now in Buda-Pest, the latter in New York.

the two disputants. Altschul was kind enough last winter to play me his *version* in thirds and sixths of Chopin's Valse (in D♭ major); the other, *questionable*, version by Joseffy I do not know. If you think it advisable to send me both versions I am quite ready to let you have my opinion on the subject. Meanwhile I will only remark that the multifarious forms of passages in thirds and sixths—upwards, downwards, to the right, to the left, or crossing, split up, etc., etc.—admit of a variety of forms of transcription in thirds and sixths of the Chopin Valse, and hence Herr Joseffy might quite innocently, in his love of sport as a virtuoso, have shot down *his own* bird even within Herr Altschul's range.

But whether *two birds* existed must be proved by the "corpus delicti."

With highest esteem I remain, dear sirs,

Most truly yours,

F. Liszt

Buda-Pest, *November 22nd*, 1871.   (Palatingasse 20.)

P.S.—Herewith is my yearly contribution to the " Bach-Gesellschaft."—

Allow me to reply, later on, to your kind inquiry in regard to a pianoforte piece.

114. To Madame A. Rubinstein in St. Petersburg.

Madame,

Your talent of observation is as incontestable as your very charming amiability. With a sagacious eye you observed my predilection for the silent "compatriot," apparently rather sombre, but of excellent composition at bottom.[1] Doubtless the advantages which appertain to it in its own right were peculiarly enhanced by the charm of your *salon*, where I hope to see it again and often. Meanwhile, since you are good enough to favour me with its *uninterrupted* company, I beg to assure you that I shall appreciate it even beyond its specific merits, which are moreover very real. Will you be so good as to renew to Rubinstein the expression of my old and admiring friendship, and accept, Madame, the most affectionate thanks and respects of your very devoted servant,

F. LISZT.

PEST, *Tuesday, January 9th*, 1872.

115. TO EDMUND VON MIHALOVICH.

VERY DEAR FRIEND,

Your new Song "Du bist wie eine Blume" ["Thou'rt like a tender flower"] is most welcome, and you have succeeded perfectly with it. It only remains to add a *ninth* to this No. 8, so that the volume may contain the number of the Muses. I hope that you will shortly bring me this No. 9 yourself, for we want you at the *Tonkünstler-Versammlung* (also the ninth), which will be held at Cassel from the 26th to the 30th June. Your *Geisterschiff* figures on the programme of the first concert, and Riedel (our President) will write to you officially to invite you to fill the post of pilot and captain of your "*phantom ship*," in other words, to conduct the orchestra. At the same concert Volkmann's Overture "*Richard III.*," Raff's

---

[1] A box of caviare, which Madame Rubinstein had sent to Liszt.

" *Waldsymphonie*," Rubinstein's Overture to "*Faust*" and a new Violin Concerto of Raff will be performed. Wilhelmj will play the violin part, and I hope that other soloists of renown will also lend us their assistance. The programme of this year's *Tonkünstler-Versammlung* contains, besides these, a new old piece of goods—the *Elizabeth*; and an antiquated new one—*The Seven Words of O[ur]. S[aviour]*., composed by Schütz at the end of the sixteenth century, and the manuscript of which was recently discovered at Cassel itself.

The *Elizabeth* will be given at Erfurt on the 2nd May, and on the 8th Riedel gives Berlioz's Requiem at Leipzig, for the benefit of our "Beethoven Scholarship." It goes without saying that I shall be present at these two performances.

. —. Schuberth has been very ill at New York, and is not yet sufficiently well to set out on his journey. I am expecting him here towards the middle of June: he will come to Cassel, where we will settle the little matter of your manuscripts in five minutes.

Yours in all friendship,

F. Liszt.

Weimar, *April 18th*, 1872.

My most affectionate thanks to Count Albert Apponyi for his kind remembrance, with the assurance of my cordial reciprocity.

P.S.—Augusz would give me great pleasure if he would send me a small provision of *Hungarian* tobacco (to smoke), for my old Weimar friend Grosse, the celebrated Trombonist.

Shall you not go to Bayreuth for the 22nd May? I shall invite you to do so.

116. To Johanna Wenzel.[1]

My dear Young Lady,

In reply to your friendly lines I beg of you earnestly no longer to think of having the barbarous operation performed upon your fingers ; rather all your life long play every octave and chord wrong than commit such a mad attack upon your hands.

With best thanks, I subscribe myself yours respect-fully,

F. Liszt.

Weimar, *June* 10*th*, 1872.

117. To Wilhelm von Lenz.

Very honoured Friend,

I owe you thanks in the 24 major and minor keys for the remembrance you keep of me, and the ardent style in which you publish it to the world. Your pamphlet[2] draws down upon itself a capital reproach ; it is that you make me out too grand and too fine. I am far from deserving it, and I confess it without any false modesty ; but since you have been pleased thus to overwhelm me I can but bow in silence, —and press your hand.

No one possesses less than myself the talent of talking with the pen, and the necessity of receiving more than a hundred letters a month (not counting

[1] The lady here addressed was a pupil of Liszt's at the time, and subsequently married Jules Zarembski, and is at present one of the teachers of the pianoforte at the Brussels Conservatoire.

[2] "Die grossen Pianoforte-Virtuosen unsrer Zeit" [The Great Pianoforte Players of our Day].

bills, and the numerous sendings of manuscript or
printed works which I have to read) makes correspondence again more than difficult for me.   It is all
I can do to get through the necessary epistolary work
imposed upon me. . . . Moreover the greater part of
the things which are easily said is indifferent to me,
and those that I wish to say resist ordinary language.
On this subject some one well said to me : " Words
seem to me to intercept feeling rather than to express
it ; and actions, alas ! seem to me sometimes like a
thick veil thrown over our soul : looks even seem to
be trammelled by phantom barriers, and souls which
seek one another across the sufferings of life only find
one another—such is my belief—in prayer and in
music."—

What wit, what sallies and what brilliant sparks in
your *Quartet* of Pianist Virtuosi !—Don't let us forget
the etymology of the word " Virtuoso," how it comes
from the " Cicerone " in Rome—and let us reascend to
Chopin, the enchanting aristocrat, the most refined in
his magic.   Pascal's epigraph, " One must not get one's
nourishment from it, but use it as one would an
essence," is only appropriate to a certain extent.   Let
us inhale the essence, and leave it to the druggists to
make use of it.   You also, I think, exaggerate the
influence which the Parisian *salons* exercised on
Chopin.   His soul was not in the least affected by
them, and his work as an artist remains transparent,
marvellous, ethereal, and of an incomparable genius—
quite outside the errors of a school and the silly trifling
of a *salon*.   He is akin to the angel and the fairy ;
more than this, he sets in motion the heroic string

which has nowhere else vibrated with so much grandeur, passion and fresh energy as in his *Polonaises,* which you brilliantly designate as "Pindaric Hymns of Victory."

No need to tell you that I fully share in your admiration and sympathy for Tausig and Henselt. Do you know Wagner's epigraph "*Für Carl Tausig's Grab*"? *

> "Reif sein zum Sterben,
> Des Lebens zögernd spriessende Frucht
> Früh reif sie erwerben,
> In Lenzes jäherblühender Flucht—
> War es dein Loos, war es dein Wagen:
> Wir müssen dein Loos wie dein Wagen beklagen."

Allow me to be particularly grateful to you for one very comprehensive expression in your pamphlet (page 4)—"es war *thematisch*" [it was *thematic*]—and accept, dear Lenz, the expression of my old and very cordial devotion.

F. LISZT.

WEIMAR, *September 20th,* 1872.

In three weeks I return to Hungary, and shall stay there for the winter. The remainder of my existence will be divided henceforth between Pest and Weimar. When you return to Berlin (in the summer) I invite you to come this way.

* For Carl Tausig's Grave:—

> "Ripe for Death's harvest,
> The fruits of life long tarrying,
> Full early to pluck them
> In the fleeting bloom of spring—
> Was it thy lot, was it thy bourn?
> Thy lot and thy destiny both must we mourn."

Are you in touch with the musical *young Russia* and its very notable leaders—Messrs. Balakireff, Cui, and Rimski-Korsakoff? I have lately read several of their works; they deserve attention, praise and propagation.

118. To Otto Lessmann in Charlottenburg.[1]

VERY DEAR SIR AND FRIEND,

My best thanks for presenting me with your admirable edition of Bach's Preludes. Such works are among the pleasant signs of the musical Present; inasmuch as they will drive away the old jog-trot style of pianoforte playing. Bülow's edition of Beethoven outweighs in the matter of instruction a dozen Conservatoires. And the editions by Kroll and Lebert also deserve praise and ought to be widely circulated; and to your Bach Preludes I wish plentiful successors in the *Suites, Inventions* and *Variations* (especially the 30 in G major) of grand old Herr Johann Sebastian— of Eisenach.

Allow me also to add that reading over your Songs enables me more and more thoroughly to enjoy them when I hear them—intelligent singers shall be found for them—and accept, dear friend, the expression of my sincere esteem and affection.

F. LISZT.

EISENACH, *September 26th*, 1872.

---

[1] Lessmann, a pupil of Bülow's and F. Kiel's, was at one time a teacher in Tausig's School for the Higher Instruction in Pianoforte Playing, and is now well known as editor of the *Allgemeine (deutsche) Musikzeitung*, representing the party of musical progress with energy and success.

119. To Eduard von Liszt.

Horpács, *November 6th*, 1872.

Dearest Eduard,

My stay here has been somewhat prolonged, and I shall not reach Pest till next Sunday.

Szechenyi's[1] residence here is most decidedly pleasant and convenient, without noise. In the chapel attached to the house, the house-chaplain (a cultured and estimable priest) daily reads Mass. At table an old house-physician, Dr. M., contributes a good deal to the entertainment. Among other amusing things he said one day: "As to the cholera, no one knows anything definite about it yet except myself, for I have fathomed its *nature*. And its nature consists solely and wholly . . . of nothing but *cholera*!"

The day before yesterday we drove with Szechenyi and Mihalovich to Raiding,[2] in less than two hours. A Herr Wittgenstein (probably an Israelite), who lives in Vienna, now rents this Esterhazy estate, and sublets it again. I found no perceptible changes in the house where I was born since my last visit there 24 years ago. The peasants recognised me at once, came to pay me their respects at the inn, and rang the church bell as we drove away.

. — . I wrote to Kahnt from here that he was to send you immediately the 9 *Kirchen-Chorgesänge* and my Mass for men's voices (" Editio nova ").

The three *Patronatsscheine* [tickets of membership] for the Nibelung performance in Bayreuth (*Bayern.*

[1] Count Szechenyi was Austrian ambassador in Berlin up to 1892.
[2] Liszt's birthplace.

N.B.—The King has commanded that henceforth *Baiern*
[Bavaria] shall be spelt with a *y*), and your letter to
Herr Feustel, please attend to without delay.

All cordial greetings to you and yours—from your
faithfully attached   F. Liszt.

Augusz I shall meet in Pest-Ofen.

Give Bösendorfer my friendly greetings, and at the
same time tell him how I praise the excellent piano
upon which I have been practising a little here.

If Zumbusch goes to Vienna, commission him—as
we arranged—to make a bust of me in marble and a
pedestal for Bösendorfer.

120. To Princess Caroline Sayn-Wittgenstein.[1]

Pest, *January* 10*th*, 1873.

Napoleon III. is dead! A great soul, an all-
embracing intelligence, experienced in the wisdom of
life, a gentle and noble character—with a disastrous
fate! He was a bound and gagged Cæsar, but still
closely related to the Divine Cæsar who was the ideal
embodiment of earthly power. In the year 1861, when
I had a pretty long interview with Napoleon, he said,
" Sometimes it seems to me as if I were over a hundred
years old." I replied, " You are the century yourself,
Sire !"—And, in fact, I honestly believed at the time,
and do so still, that Napoleon's reign was the one most
in keeping with the requirements and advances of our

---

[1] Printed by " order " in the *Signale*, 1873 (after the death of
Napoleon), in which form the letter is reproduced here, as the original
could not be procured. This letter does not indeed show us Liszt
as a far-sighted politician, but simply as a man of noble impulses.

era. He has set noble examples, and accomplished or undertaken great deeds: amnesties which were more complete under him than under other governments; the protection of the Church in Rome and in other countries; the rejuvenescence of Paris and other great cities in France; the Crimean war and the Italian war; the great Paris Exhibition, and the rise of local exhibitions; the earnest attention paid to the lot and to the interests of the country people, and of the working classes; the generosity and encouragement to scholars and artists,—all these things are historical facts, and are things in which the Emperor took the initiative, and which he carried out in spite of all the difficulties that stood in his way.

These things will not be eclipsed by the misfortunes that befell him, however terrible these may have been, and, on the day of judgment, France will fetch the coffin of Napoleon III. and place it in all honour beside that of Napoleon I. It can be affirmed without adulation that throughout life the Emperor unswervingly practised those great virtues which are in reality one and the same thing and are known by the names of benevolence, goodness, generosity, nobility of mind, love of splendour and munificence. One of the fine traits of his character that he is acknowledged to have possessed, was his never-failing kindheartedness and his deep gratitude towards those persons who had ever done him a service. In all humility and lowliness of spirit I will imitate him in this, and begin with himself by blessing his memory and addressing my prayers for him to the God of Mercy who has so ordered things that nations may recover from their wounds. .—.

121. To Eduard von Liszt.

Dearest Eduard,

Long since you ought to have heard from me. . . .
However, I have not been altogether idle, and during
the last weeks have been busy *blackening* some sheets
of music paper which you shall see in print and hear
me play. Bösendorfer heard some of it last night, and
will bring you word about it to Pest. Be good enough
to pay *Zumbusch* a visit, and beg him to have my
bust done in *good marble*, and to have it finished and
ready by the 2nd April (*Franciscus di Paula*). I intend to spend this name-day of mine with *you*
quietly,[1] and to take the bust to Bösendorfer "*in
persona.*"

I am told that the Gran Mass is to be performed
on Easter Sunday in Pressburg. If so, we will go
there together to hear it, with your wife, Marie[2] and
Franz.

As to the Bayreuth affair, I have already told you
what my wish and will is. It must remain thus. . — .

Probably Cosima will be going to Vienna in
February.

God's blessing abide with you and yours. Thine,
with all my heart,

F. Liszt.

Pest, *January 13th*, 1873.

---

[1] This was an established custom of Liszt's for many years, and
one to which—even after his cousin's death—he adhered, and spent
the day with the family up to the time of his death.

[2] Eduard von Liszt's daughter, now Baroness Saar in Vienna.

122. To Dr. Emil Thewrewk von Ponor, Professor at the University of Budapest.[1]

Much-esteemed and dear Herr Professor,

I regret that my reply to your request about the *Elizabeth-motive* can only be somewhat unsatisfactory. It was sent to me together with some others—referring to Saint Elizabeth—about 13 years ago, by Mosonyi and Baron Augusz, and the Hungarian text is published in the concluding notice to the score of my Oratorio. A copy of the "Lyra Cœlestis" I did not need; probably this (to me unknown) printed work will be readily found here, and is sure to be in the Library of the *Martinsberg* monastery.

If not inconvenient to you I should be glad to receive the honour of a visit from you; it would interest me greatly to hear of and to become acquainted with your researches concerning Hungarian rhythmic forms.

Meanwhile I thank you warmly for your friendly lines, and for communicating the *Volkslied* in the $\frac{5}{4}$ time :—

Yours with much esteem and sincerely,

Pest, *January* 14th, 1873.   F. Liszt.

---

[1] A classical philologist who published a little Hungarian work entitled "Die ungarische Rhythmik," the German edition of which was to be dedicated to Liszt. The two men differed in their opinion respecting the origin of Hungarian music; however, in consequence of Von Ponor's contribution to the subject, Liszt did in the end agree with the proof Von Ponor brought forward—with this reservation, that "the gypsies did bring harmony into Hungarian music," a point which—Ponor thinks—"may readily be conceded."

123. To Dr. Franz Witt.

January 20th, 1873.

MUCH-ESTEEMED FRIEND,

At New Year I sent you a copy of the Stabat Mater by Palestrina "for the lecture arranged by R. Wagner." The inaccuracies and errors of this copy I have carefully corrected, for in such a masterly and exemplary arrangement every iota is of importance. Wagner gave me his manuscript 18 years ago in Zürich, and forgot afterwards where it was. As regards its publication, which is much to be desired, it is not for me to interfere in the matter in any way, and I beg you to come to some understanding with Wagner about it. If he should wish to correct his old manuscript (the paper of which has become rather yellowish) I will gladly place it at his service.

124. To Eduard von Liszt.

DEAREST EDUARD,

Having considered the matter about the *certificate of death* which Rothschild wished to have, I shall not make use of Belloni in connection with it. If Emile Ollivier were still in Paris it would be *his* place to procure the certificate. My dear good mother died in his house (Rue St. Guillaume, Faubourg St. Germain) at the beginning of January 1866. He looked after her and took tender care of her for several years; and finally had her body taken to the Church of *St. Thomas d'Aquin* for the funeral service, and followed it thence to its last resting-place in the cemetery of *Montparnasse*.

This noble conduct and his speech at the grave I cherish in my innermost heart.

Since the winter of 1866 I have never been back in Paris, and my relations with *trustworthy* persons there are as good as entirely broken off. Hence I yesterday went and got good advice from friend Augusz, and have accepted his proposal, namely, to address a request to Count Alexander Apponyi—son of and Secretary to the Austrian ambassador in Paris—to procure the certificate of death of my mother and to send it to you. Let Rothschild know of this matter, which, let us hope, will soon be satisfactorily settled.

Many thanks for the trouble you are taking about the bust by Zumbusch, and which I very much wish personally to present to Bösendorfer in Vienna as an *Easter egg*. I know I can rely wholly upon your ever faithful and incomparable readiness to do me a favour.

Allow me one other request, which will cost you only half an hour's time and a visit. The visit is to an extremely interesting, learned and distinguished man —Dr. Ambros, formerly Imperial Solicitor-General in Prague, now professor and referendary to the *Officielle Zeitung* in Vienna, always an eminent writer on æsthetics, history, the history of music, a polygraphist, composer— in fact, a good friend of mine. Be kind enough to tell him that I am awaiting his answer in the *affirmative*, respecting a lecture by him on Robert Franz at the *extra Soirée* arranged in honour of and for the benefit of Robert Franz; Dr. Ambros was at my request respectfully invited by Herr Dunkl ("Firma Roszavölgyi") to give us his assistance. I take part too as pianist, collector and arranger of the Soirée, and

hope that Dr. Ambros—who is so specially competent
for the task, owing to his eloquent and valuable treatise
on Robert Franz—will give us brilliant assistance, and
give us a *speech* there without *talking himself out.* The
warmest welcome and appreciation will await him on
all sides. But obtain his kind consent *as soon as possible,*
together with a *written yea* to Dunkl (Musikverlag
Roszavölgyi, Christoph-Platz, Pest).

Heartiest greetings to your wife and children, and
au revoir on the 2nd April.

Thine,

F. LISZT.

PEST, *January 28th,* 1873.

125. TO EDUARD VON LISZT.

MY DEAREST FRIEND,

Zumbusch's letter seems to me pretty comforting,
and if you would have the kindness to write to him
again I hope the bust will reach Vienna by April 1st.
Have you asked what it costs? If not do so in your
next letter. Of course I do not mean to *bargain* with
Zumbusch (that is a thing I do only in case of dire
necessity—and even then am a bad hand at it). We
must simply pay what he asks, and leave ourselves to
his friendly feelings of *moderation,* which will not
fail. . . .

In spite of all your endeavours and persuasive
powers Dr. Ambros is not coming to the Robert Franz
Soirée in Pest. He wrote to Dunkl that he is unusually
busy in Vienna with urgent affairs connected with the
Zeitung—and hence cannot find any time to prepare an

address—and besides this is afraid of taking cold on the journey. . . . To all this we can raise no remonstrance, so I must just accept this refusal of Ambros, much as I should have liked a different answer. Some day I will tell you the preliminaries of this business.

Last week I received from Freiherr Suttner, President of the Vienna *Singakademie* and Imperial Chamberlain, an invitation to play a few pianoforte pieces in the concert arranged for Robert Franz's benefit. I replied that an interval of 25 years separated me from my last public appearance as a pianist, and that I considered it advisable for me to remain within the interval. As I told you last October, it is not my intention to officiate *in any way* this winter in Vienna.

Herewith I send you an extract from the sitting of the Chamber of the day before yesterday, the result of which is almost as unexpected as it is important. The deputies of the conservative party and of the opposition voted almost unanimously in favour of raising the funds for establishing a new *Musik-Akademie*. And an unusual honour was conferred upon me on the occasion,—for, although I have never come forward in the matter, it was nevertheless brought forward in my name, and this certainly puts rather a heavy burden upon me. I will endeavour conscientiously to do justice to the honour as well as the burden.

For the last couple of days a stupid feverish cold in the head has kept me in bed. To-morrow, however, I shall be up and about again.

Faithfully thine,
F. Liszt.

Pest, *February* 10th, [1873.]

126. To Eduard von Liszt.

My dear Friend,

Bösendorfer brings you tidings of the *Robert Franz* Soirée of yesterday.[1] In a fortnight's time I shall have a similar work before me as pianoforte player, at a charity concert which Countess Anna Zichy is patronising. Then follows, further, a matinée of the Liszt-Verein at the *Stadtpfarrei*,[2] and the performance of *Witt's* Mass, of which I undertake the conducting on the 25th March (in the church). At the beginning of April I shall be with you.

Heartfelt greetings to you and yours from your faithful   F. Liszt.

[Pest,] *March 3rd*, 1873.

127. To Madame Jessie Laussot.

Dear, excellent Friend,

Your *ideas* are always very wise, practical and noble; I participate in them beforehand, and esteem myself happy to have them communicated to me direct. With regard to Robert Franz's little capital, I presume that his zealous friends have already taken decisive measures; on my return to Weimar (before the end of April) I will learn whether it is possible to carry out your idea. . . . You know that a thousand thalers have been sent from here, the result of a soirée arranged in Franz's honour. Perhaps I shall find an opportunity to send him more soon. —

[1] At this soirée Liszt played Beethoven's A♭ major Sonata, Op. 26, No. 4; his own "Soirées de Vienne" (after F. Schubert); Schumann's "Wie aus der Ferne"; and R. Franz's "Lied."

[2] The town parsonage.

Walter Bache writes me word of his "*Ninth* Annual Concert" in London, with my 13th Psalm.   Bache behaves "eroicamente" with regard to me, and takes rank in the very small group of my friends who are the most determined to show the public—in spite of the contrary opinion, much believed by influential papers —that my music is not absolutely void of sense.   I should like to make the task of these friends a little easier, and I try not to increase the merit of their devotion by my faults.

Enclosed is the programme of the concert of our friend Mihalovich yesterday evening.   "Romeo and Juliet" was encored, and the "Geisterschiff" did not founder.   The audience, very aristocratic, was more select than numerous, which is a good sign for our friend. Item the *squashing* of some *learned* articles in the papers.

Will you kindly give my grateful acknowledgments to Mr. Hillebrand for his friendly remembrance, and for sending me his new volume on the French?   I had read bits of it in the *Augsburg Gazette*, and shall take a double pleasure in reading the entire work.   Hillebrand, like Alexander von Humboldt, has a passionate attachment to France ;—I am proud to feel that I am in accord with him *also* on this point.

The day after to-morrow I shall be in Vienna, and shall spend a fortnight with my near relative and friend Eduard Liszt.   After that I return to Weimar, and hope to see you there in the summer.   I will write to you in good time about the performance of the Oratorio *Christus*. . . .

Respectful homage and cordial friendship,

PEST, *March 30th*, 1873.   F. LISZT.

128. To Cäsar Cui.[1]

Sir,

Pray excuse my delay in thanking you for your very kind letter that Mr. Bessel brought me with the piano score of your Opera *William Ratcliff*. It is the work of a master who deserves consideration, renown and success, as much for the wealth and originality of the ideas as for the skilful handling of the form. As I am persuaded that all intelligent and honest musicians will be of this opinion, I should like to add to it some assurance on the next performance of your *Ratcliff* in Germany. It should be done at once at Weimar were I in active function at the theatre as in the preceding years (from 1848 to '59); but since my retirement I am not any longer in a position to take definite steps, and must confine myself to recommendations—more often counteracted than followed.

Accept, sir, my sincere thanks, and with every expression of high esteem I am, yours truly,

F. Liszt.

Weimar, *May*, 1873.

129. To Franz Servais.

Dear Monsieur Franz,

My best wishes accompany you "into your cage." * You do well to put yourself there, and, if the flight of your genius should find itself somewhat

---

[1] Russian composer and musical critic.

* This usually means "in durance vile," but the word "cage" is preserved here on account of the context.—Trans.

trammelled, for the time being, before the tribunal of
counterpoint and fugue, it will soar all the more
proudly afterwards.   I hope you will come out of your
cage glorious and crowned; in case of bad luck do
not be too much disappointed; more skilful and more
valuable men than you and I, dear Franz, have had
to have patience, and to have patience yet again.   M.
de Buffon, when he said "genius is patience," did
but make the mistake of an incomplete definition; he
took a part for the whole; but that part is absolutely
necessary in the practice of Art, as in that of earthly
life.

Please remember me very affectionately to your
mother; give a shake of the hand to your brother
from me,—and depend ever on my devoted and
affectionate feelings.

F. Liszt.

Weimar, *June 5th*, 1873.

130. To the Canoness Adelheid von Schorn.

Dear excellent One,

My little travelling plans have been upset by
a letter from Cosima.   I did not stop either at Salzungen (where I had arranged to meet Schuberth) or
at Meiningen, and came straight here on Saturday,
in accordance with an invitation from Cosima to a
little *fête* of the workpeople of the theatre of the
Nibelungen.

Many idle and gossiping people everywhere are
troubling their heads about this theatre, and are asking
when and how it will be finished building.   Instead of
descanting foolishly or maliciously about it (the two

things sometimes go together), it would be better to get a *"Patronats-Schein"* [a receipt of membership], and thus to join in the grandest and most sublime work of art of the century. The glory of having created, written and published it is Wagner's intact; his detractors have only to share the disgrace of having thwarted it and delayed the bringing of it to the full light of day, by performance. —

Next week I go to Schillingsfürst, and towards the middle of August I shall be back at Weimar.

A thousand very cordially affectionate and devoted regards.

F. LISZT.

BAYREUTH, *July* 30*th*, 1873.

131. TO EDUARD VON LISZT.

DEAREST EDUARD,

After an absence of 3 weeks I returned here yesterday. I remained first 10 days in Bayreuth, from August 26th to September 5th,[1] and then the same length of time in Schillingsfürst (with Cardinal Hohenlohe) and at Langenburg (with Prince Hermann Hohenlohe), whither I had the honour of accompanying the Cardinal.

Cosima, Wagner and the five children are in the best of health. The building of the *Nibelungen-Theatre* is progressing famously; if the necessary sum of 300,000 thalers [some £45,000], of which as yet only about 130,000 have been forthcoming, is got together

---

[1] The dates here ought certainly to be from July 26th to August 5th —as Liszt's letter is dated the 19th of August.

in time, the performance of the "Festival Drama"—
The Ring of the Nibelung—is to take place in the
summer of '75.

. —. Simultaneously with his theatre, Wagner is
building a beautiful and exquisitely situated house
close to the Hofgarten. The King of Bavaria has
given him 20,000 thalers [some £3,000] for this.
Next spring Wagner will take up his abode there.

My intercourse with Cardinal Hohenlohe is always
pleasant. He leads a very retired life in Schillingsfürst,
receives but few visits and pays only a few, and
occupies himself principally in building and arranging
a large schoolhouse and an institution for girls under
the superintendence of a Benedictine Sisterhood.

Great festivities are being arranged here in honour
of the marriage of the Hereditary Grand Duke. On
September 6th the entry of the bridal pair, on the 7th
a Court concert, on the 8th a Festival-play by Devrient
in the theatre and a performance of Beethoven's 9th
Symphony, etc., etc. I have undertaken to conduct
the Symphony and also to play a couple of pianoforte
pieces at the Court concert. A second Festival-play,
entitled "The Bride's Welcome to the Wartburg,"
written by Scheffel and set to music by me, is to be
given on September 21st in the Minnesänger Hall
in the Wartburg, where you heard the *Elizabeth*
Oratorio.

A few days after this I shall travel to Rome, and
remain there 3 or 4 weeks. Before the end of October
I shall come to you again for a couple of days before
returning to Pest on November 1st.

The dedication-copies of the "Szószat" and the

"Hymnus" for Count Andrassy are not yet ready, it seems. Roszavölgyi (Dunkl) has sent me only a few ordinary copies of the pianoforte version, and not one of the score. I shall therefore have to wait till November before sending or presenting it to Count Andrassy.

From the Grand Duchess I received 1,000 thalers—but these together with your 500 have all been spent. Be so good as to send me another 300 thalers *next week!* For my journey to Rome I shall probably, towards the middle of September, again have to ask you for a note of 500 francs. Although I do not go in for any luxuries, money vanishes quickly and readily in my hands.

Heartiest greetings to your wife and children, and *au revoir* in Vienna at the end of October.

Faithfully thine,

F. LISZT.

WEIMAR, *August* 19*th*, 1873.

132. TO FRANZ SERVAIS.

DEAR VICTORIOUS ONE,

Your letter had been travelling several days in Bavaria before it reached me here yesterday morning. I thank you for letting me take an affectionate part in the success you have obtained, and I wish to keep that part throughout your future successes—and even failures. The latter will not do you any great harm, provided that you know how to keep that attachment to work, and that perseverance in noble ideas, which are the chief heirloom of the artist.

Lassen tells me that we are shortly to hear your *Tasso* here: my attentive sympathy is wide awake; so fulfil your promise, dear Franz, by coming *before* the end of this month, and we will talk at our ease at the *Hofgärtnerei* of our aims and plans.

Please give my respects to your mother, and my cordial remembrances to Joseph and Godebski.

Your affectionate and devoted

F. LISZT.

WEIMAR, *August* 19*th*, 1873.

133. TO WALTER BACHE.

DEAR FRIEND,

Often I am behindhand and stop short of thanks with you, but it is certainly not for want of sincere affection and esteem.

Your "9th Annual Concert" has again shown the worth of your talents and the firm constancy of your character. Now in our artistic world character is still more rare than talent.

You nobly unite the two; it is a pleasure to me to acknowledge it, and to count you amongst the most devoted champions of progress and of musical good sense.

At their head, by right of age and capability, walks imperturbably and gloriously Hans de Bülow.

Will you give him the enclosed letter? and believe me ever, dear Bache,

Your very cordially affectionate

F. LISZT.

WEIMAR, *August* 20*th*, 1873.

134. To Max Erdmannsdörfer, Hofcapellmeister
     in Sondershausen.[1]

VERY DEAR HERR CAPELLMEISTER,

Your friendly invitation for me to attend the
performance of your "Schneewittchen" I am unfortunately unable to accept. Owing to the festivities at
the Wartburg it is impossible for me to get away next
week. Will you kindly convey to the Princess Elizabeth my regrets as well as my most gracious thanks?

On Sunday, September 28th, I shall have the pleasure
of thanking you personally in Sondershausen for
arranging and carrying out the extraordinary concert
programme. It is my special wish that the two *Faust
Episodes* should not be separated—even at the risk
of wearying the public for a few minutes with the
Nächtlicher Zug.[2] But this piece does not appear
to me altogether so bad. . . .

I beg you again to repeat my sincere praise to the
Sondershausen artists who played so admirably here
last Monday in the 9th Symphony, and remain, very
dear Sir, with marked feelings of esteem,

Yours in all friendship,

WEIMAR, *September 16th*, 1873.   F. LISZT.

Kahnt, Gille, J. Schuberth, Lassen and several other
friends of mine are going to attend the Sondershausen
concerts on the 28th and 29th September.

The Weimar presentation I will bring you.

---

[1] At present *Capellmeister* in Bremen; he has rendered good
service to the cause of the New-German musical tendency both in
Germany and Russia.

[2] Two Episodes from Lenau's *Faust* (Leipzig, Schuberth).

135. To Otto Lessmann.

Dear Friend,

Best thanks for sending Kiel's *Christus*—a work full of spiritual substance, of noble and fine sentiments, and masterly in execution. Riedel proposes to give a performance of it next winter in Leipzig.

With such a clause as Joachim introduces for the "*Novitäten-Concerten*"—"that only such composers shall be taken into consideration in the programmes whose renown as artistic representatives of the German nation is established"—Händel, Bach, Mozart, nay even Beethoven, would have come off badly in their life-time!

Whether it is appropriate for the Berlin Hochschule to act in so specially a high and mighty manner remains to be seen. Still it is to be expected that such procedure is likely itself to meet with some other restricting "clauses."

Of the arrangement for 8 hands of the Pastorale and March[1] which I *wish* to have from you, you will have already heard from Schuberth. Likewise from Kahnt of the couple of pieces from the *Elizabeth*.

Au revoir on Sunday, the 28th September, in Sondershausen, where we shall have a curious (*sonderliches*) Programme. Receive herewith, dear friend, a special invitation, together with the assurance of my friendly attachment.

F. Liszt.

Weimar, *September 24th*, 1873.

---

[1] From Liszt's Oratorio *Christus*.

I shall bring you back your copy of Kiel's *Christus* to Sondershausen.

136. To Kornel von Abrányi.

Dear valiant Friend,

Your letter, and the printed paper of great fame which accompanies it, recalls to me the saying, "*La joie fait peur.*"[1] Nevertheless I could not suit myself to the *rôle* of a coward; I will therefore endeavour to surmount my fear and to make myself worthy to share with my brave compatriots in the joy they have prepared for me.

I beg you, in your capacity of secretary of the Festival Committee, to present my most grateful thanks, in good Hungarian, to the most illustrious and most reverend President, Monseigneur Haynald,[2] and to the members of the Committee.

Baron Augusz had written me word that he would come here in the middle of September, to be present at the "*Festspiel*" [Festival Play] at the Wartburg. He shall soon receive news from me from Rome, where I shall arrive on Sunday.

---

[1] Abrányi, who was the Secretary of the Festival Committee which had been formed for the celebration of Liszt's Artist-Jubilee in November 1873 at Budapest, had in their name invited Liszt to take part in this.

[2] The Archbishop of Kalocsa, afterwards Cardinal, Liszt's friend of many years. (Being interested in the present collection, he promised to contribute to it the letters addressed to him "by the great artist and noble man." His death unfortunately prevented the fulfilment of his promise, and the Archiepiscopal Chapter of Kalocsa did not accede to the request of the editor to be allowed to have these letters.)

Schuberth is sending you the score and the piano score of the "*Christ*," together with the biographical notices for which you asked me. My cousin Eduard will send you the "postscript" immediately.

Cordial friendship and fruitful collaboration.

WEIMAR, *October 1st,* 1873.   F. LISZT.

Herewith the programmes of the 2 concerts at Sondershausen at which I was present. This afternoon I start for Rome,—and on the 1st November shall be at Pest.

137. TO MARTHA REMMERT.[1]

PEST, *December 27th,* 1873.

DEAR FRÄULEIN,

The best "solution" in reply to the ministerial order lies in your *hands*. Merely play the first page of Henselt's Concerto and no one will doubt that I am very kindly disposed towards you. And I shall be glad to render you further service in your zeal for study and your ambition as a virtuosa. No matter whether I be in Pest or in Weimar.

In all friendliness yours,

F. LISZT.

138. TO ?*

VERY DEAR FRÄULEIN,

Please reply at once *per telegram* :—

"*Please* do not come.—Liszt does not need or wish

---

[1] A pupil of Liszt's; became later *Kammervirtuosin* (court-pianist) in Weimar, and lives now in Berlin.

* Autograph without address or date in the possession of Count Albert Amadei in Vienna.—According to him the letter belongs to the year 1873.

to be heard, as he has no one for whom he must strike up."

To-morrow evening more by word of mouth.

Sincerely yours,

F. LISZT.

Monday.

139. TO COUNTESS MARIE DÖNHOFF IN VIENNA.*

[*Beginning of January,* 1874.]

DEAR COUNTESS,

You speak to me so eloquently of the merit, talent and superiority of Madame L. B. that I am quite ashamed of not fulfilling her wish *subito.* But in reality that would be more difficult than she imagines ; a "petit morceau de piano" would only be a small part of the matter ; the public is a very exacting master, even in its days of favour ; the more it gives the more it expects. . . .

Half a dozen such requests as that of Madame L. B. have been addressed to me at Vienna this week. How can one suffice for such a business, which, be it said in passing, is at once outside and far beyond my duties ?—At my age one must try to behave reasonably, and to avoid excess ; I shall therefore limit myself in Vienna to the *one concert* of the "Kaiser Franz Joseph Stiftung," † which reasons of great propriety, easy to understand, have led me to accept with alacrity. I am told that it will take place on Sunday, 11th January ; so be it : I shall willingly conform to the arrangements

* Sketch of a letter in the possession of Herr O. A. Schulz, bookseller in Leipzig.—The addressee, the wife of the German ambassador Von Bülow, lives now in Bucharest.

† Emperor Francis Joseph Scholarship.

of the Committee and have no other wish in this matter than . . . not to inconvenience anybody.[1]

Permit me to hope, dear Countess, that you will not, under the pretext of "*discretion*," inflict upon me the immense punishment of seeing you less often this time than formerly, and that you will not retract any of your kindness, on which I place the greatest store.

A thousand and a thousand sincere and most respectfully devoted expressions of homage.

F. LISZT.

140. TO B. BESSEL, MUSIC PUBLISHER IN ST. PETERSBURG.

HORPÁCS (CHEZ LE COMTE SZECHÉNYI), *February 2nd*, 1874.

DEAR SIR,

Pray excuse me for being so late in thanking you,—you and all those who signed the telegram sent to Pest on the occasion of my Jubilee fête. I am deeply touched with the noble sentiments it expresses with a chivalrous eloquence, and beg you to convey the tribute of my most sincere gratitude to Messrs. Balakireff, Borodine, Cui, Moussorsky, Rimski-Korsakoff, Scherbatcheff, and Stassoff.

You were kind enough, Sir, to let me see several of their works at Weimar; I appreciate and esteem them highly, and as far as depends on myself I will do all I can to make them known, and shall feel

---

[1] The concert for the "Emperor Francis Joseph Scholarship" did not take place till April; and Liszt did actually play, in the Easter week, for the Countess's *protegée*, though not in the Concert Room, but in the Palais Auersperg.

honoured thus to respond to the sympathetic kindness
which brave colleagues such as these accord to
Their very devoted
F. LISZT.

141. To Professor Skiwa in Vienna.*

VERY DEAR SIR,
Kindly excuse the delay in my sending you my
sincere thanks, which I shall very shortly take the
liberty of expressing to you personally in Vienna. I
shall then also ask you to do me the favour of making
me more intimately acquainted with your excellent
transcriptions. In reading them through one at once
observes the author's masterly style and his care and
artistic handling of the characteristic peculiarities of
the harmonium, especially in the management of the
basses and the mid-voice parts. But still the mere
reading your transcriptions does not satisfy me, and
I should like to hear them, so as to be able fully to
enjoy them.

Herr Bösendorfer will bring you the manuscript of
the Consolation, the dedication of which is very acceptable to me. The transcription of this small piece into
A major appears to me very appropriate, and the
arrangement excellent.

With marked esteem and friendly thanks,
F. LISZT.

PEST, *March 21st,* 1874.

* Printed in the *Signale*, 1874, No. 20.— Skiwa had dedicated his
"Beiträge zur Literatur des Harmoniums" [Contribution to Harmonium Literature] to Liszt.

142. To C. F. Kahnt, the Music Publisher.*

Dear Friend,

The day after to-morrow I again go to Vienna, and remain there about a week. In case the *Prometheus* proofs are ready send them to me to my usual address (" Schottenhof bei Hofrath E. v. Liszt ") by the middle of *Easter week*; after that my address will be rather uncertain, as I intend spending a few days in Pressburg and Kalocsa (with Archbishop Haynald), and do not return here till after April 20th. Hence, if the *Prometheus* proofs are not ready within the next few days, do not send them till after my return to Pest (April 21).

Please send the proofs of Mihalovich's songs as soon as possible to the composer, addressed to

" Servitenplatz, im Teleky'schen Haus."

The Vienna concert in the " Palais Auersperg" is announced for Easter Monday, April 6th. The following Sunday, or at latest on Sunday the 19th April, the concert of the " *Kirchenmusik-Verein* " is to be given in Pressburg, at which I take a part in piano-playing—it is to be hoped for the last time this year!—

I think of remaining here from April 21st to the beginning of May, and then of wandering straightway to Rome, and to the *Villa d'Este.*

I wish you in all friendliness a happy Easter, with satisfactory business at the Easter's fair, and remain your sincerely attached

F. Liszt.

Pest, *March 29th,* 1874.

* Published in the *Neue Zeitung für Musik,* 14th September, 1892.

Have you sent Countess Oriolla the omitted copy of the " Wartburg Songs " ?

143. To Dr. Franz Witt.   [1874?]

I look forward with eager interest to the realisation of your scheme to found a Catholic School of Music. The numerous and important services you have rendered as composer, conductor, teacher, promoter and president of the *Cäcilien-Verein* proclaim and mark you as pre-eminently fitted to organize and direct this highly important kind of School. I should wish that Hungary, my fatherland, might set a good example, and might offer you, my very dear friend, an honourable and influential post in the *Musik-Akademie* that was voted for last year in the Chamber. This wish of mine was seconded with cordiality by His Eminence the Cardinal Primate, His Excellency the Archbishop of Kalocsa, Haynald, and H. E. Trefort, the Minister of Public Instruction. Various political circumstances interfered with the plan of starting a *Musik-Akademie* in Pest ; but the idea has by no means been given up, and I have still the hope that you may yet at some future day be called upon to give your powerful assistance in connection with the teaching and practice of Church music in Hungary.

144. To Professor Carl Riedel.

Dear Friend,

As at all preceding *Tonkünstler-Versammlungen*, you have again this year in Brunswick done the best that was possible.[1] *Five* concerts sound almost alarm-

[1] The Meeting took place in Halle, instead of in Brunswick.

ing, but the programmes are drawn up and arranged with so much forethought and care that your master-hand and that indescribable "with *avec*" (as dear Frau Dr. Pohl called it) are at once to be recognised. It certainly was advisable to check the "democratic movements" of the orchestra without interfering with the well-meant "command." That the Sondershausen set continue to prove themselves reliable and friendly I am delighted to hear. I wish all possible success to Erdmannsdörfer's "Schneewittchen." The youthful and captivating Frau Kapellmeisterin Erdmannsdörfer is especially capable of doing justice to Raff's Trio (or Concerto) and other pianoforte pieces.[1]

Will Bülow be able to be present? We have not written to each other for some time past. Do you know where to address him just now?

In case my Faust Symphony is given at the 5th concert (as your programme announces), I beg you to ask Bülow to be conductor. This work has become his property since he conducted it so magnificently at the Weimar *Tonkünstler-Versammlung* ('61), when the whole orchestra was amazed and astounded at his fabulous memory. You will remember that not only did he not use a score, but at the rehearsal referred to the numberless *letters* and *double letters* with unerring accuracy.

With regard to two other matters I wish: A, that Steinway may have the kindness to lend one of his excellent harmoniums for the *Hunnenschlacht*, and that the instrument may be so placed as to be invisible to

---

[1] Pauline Fichtner, who married Erdmannsdörfer, was a pupil of Liszt's, and became court-pianist at Weimar and Hesse.

the public and yet distinctly heard. B, that the performance of the Sanctus from the Mass for men's voices be taken from the *editio nova* (published a few years ago by Härtel), *and not from the earlier edition.* Here, too, Steinway's harmonium would render excellent service, *visible* and placed close to the chorus. Perhaps our friend Stade would have the kindness to play the harmonium part of the Hunnenschlacht and of the Sanctus. —

I truly regret that I shall not be able to hear that sublime, grand and overpowering Requiem by Berlioz, nor to attend the Musical Festival in Brunswick. I am physically and mentally very exhausted, and need several months' rest ; besides my remaining away from Weimar forbids me from meanwhile visiting any other German towns.—Before the middle of May I shall go direct to Rome, and remain there till the end of the year in my former residence at the Villa d'Este ($3\frac{1}{2}$ hours from Rome).

With friendly greetings to your wife, I remain,

Yours ever in esteem and sincere attachment,

F. Liszt.

Pest, *April 17th,* 1874.

Accept my best thanks for cancelling my promise to Metzdorff (in regard to the performance of his Symphony).

I agree perfectly, of course, with your *desideria* for the *Musik-Verein*, and hope next year to be able to contribute something towards their realisation.

" In patientia vestra possidebitis animas vestras."

To Kahnt I wrote at once on my return from Pressburg on Monday.

145. To Dom-Capellmeister * Dr. Franz Haberl in Ratisbon.†   [1874 ?]

Pardon me if I again come with claims upon your kindness. You may know that I am working at an Oratorio on St. Stanislaus, and perhaps might be able to give me some assistance with it by communicating to me the liturgic hymns referring to the feast of St. Stanislaus. The Enchyrydion and Directorium Chori designate the Mass, Protexisti, etc., on May 7th. To receive fuller information from you on this point would greatly oblige me.[1]

Pray accept, reverend Sir and friend, the expression of my marked esteem, and believe me yours gratefully and sincerely,

F. Liszt.

146. To Professor Carl Riedel.

Dear Friend,

Herzogenberg's [2] *Deutsches Liederspiel* pleases me very much. The very first chorus with its mixed species of tempi $\frac{6}{4}$—$\frac{3}{2}$ and $\frac{6}{4}$—$\frac{3}{2}$ is fresh and pithy, and the whole work seems to me excellent, pleasant and

* Cathedral Conductor.

† This letter, like the subsequent one to Haberl, is a copy of the draft of a letter of Liszt's by Dr. Mirus in Weimar.—Haberl is a distinguished musical scholar (born in 1840).

[1] Haberl also gave Liszt aural communications regarding the Stanislaus legend. "On one occasion," says Haberl, "Liszt was specially and greatly delighted to hear of the man whom Stanislaus summoned out of the grave as a witness that the field had been paid for, and gave me a sketch of his proposed motives and tone pictures."

[2] Formerly Director of the Leipzig *Bach-Verein*, then Kiel's successor at the Berlin *Hochschule*, which post he lately resigned.

effective.   Hence I should much like to recommend its being performed.

Where does Herzogenberg live ?   Has he any appointment anywhere ?   Let me know, when you can, something of his former and present work.

(N.B.—It would be worth while, later, carefully to arrange the *Deutsches Liederspiel* for orchestra.)

I observe with special pleasure that Grützmacher has chosen a Suite of St. Saëns'.   St. Saëns will not, however, *be able* to come,—the less so as a few years ago his appearance in quite a harmless concert in Baden-Baden brought down upon him hideous rebukes and reproaches from the Parisian Press.   And the tone in France is not yet more temperate ; still it is right that German artists should prove themselves fair and just towards foreigners, and, as long as Auber's and Gounod's Operas are given in all German theatres, I see no good reason against considering and performing other works by French composers.   Among modern composers I regard St. Saëns as the ablest and most gifted.

I am much satisfied with the choice you have made of my things, dear friend, and thank you cordially for it—at the same time I must express my sincere regret that I am unable to attend the *Tonkünstler-Versammlung*, and remain, with much esteem, yours most sincerely,

PEST, *May 5th*, 1874.   F. LISZT.

147. TO PRINCESS JULIE WALDBURG AT CASTLE WURZACH.

MADAME LA PRINCESSE,

I feel that I am quite inexcusable.   You have been so kind as to send me some charming *Lieder*, and

to accompany them with the most gracious lines in
the world. How could I fail to thank you for them
immediately? What rusticity!—Deign to think of
this no longer, Princess; and permit me not to "judge"
your songs,—magisterial competency would fail me
utterly,—but to tell you that I have read them with
much pleasure. The one of which the style and
impassioned accent please me particularly is dedicated
to Mme. Ehnn—"Liebeshoffnung"; but I do not
mean to depreciate the others.

The *oriental* interval of the augmented fourth, which
I scent in the "*Mondlied*," would be written, I think,
more simply thus:—

(*C* instead of *B♯*). And to prove to you, Princess, my
attention in reading your works, I will venture to
observe to you that in the French Romance "Comme
à vingt ans" the prosody is neglected in the third
couplet. Instead of the printed version (with two
syllables omitted) it should run something like this:—

Je vis le len - de - main, non plus au bord de
l'onde mais as - si - se au che-min la jeune fi - le blonde

If I still had, as in Vienna, the honour of finding
myself in your neighbourhood, I hope you would

grant me a word of indulgence; and meanwhile, Madame la Princesse, I venture to beg you to accept the most respectful homage of

Your very humble and inexcusable servant,

F. LISZT.

PEST, *May 10th*, 1874.

148. TO PETER CORNELIUS.

DEAREST FRIEND OF MY HEART,

Again a request. You alone can help me, and give me *in German* a faithful poetical rendering of Lamartine's " Hymne de l'enfant à son réveil."

Years ago I used to sing this hymn, from my inmost heart, to my three children; you remember them. . . .

And now the *composition* (what an unknown word for it!) is to appear in print, and the publisher *Taborszky* in Pest will send you my manuscript together with a copy of the poem. In case any prosodical alterations should seem appropriate, be kind enough to write them down distinctly in *notes* on a separate sheet of paper.

To-morrow I travel direct to Rome, and shall spend the summer and autumn in the Villa d'Este (Tivoli). There, at length, our *Stanislaus* shall be pushed forward.[1]

With friendliest greetings to all your circle, I am, dearest Cornelius, ever your heartily devoted

F. LISZT.

PEST, *May 16th*, 1874.

---

[1] Cornelius translated the text to the Oratorio *Stanislaus*.

149. To A. F. Eggers in Liverpool.*

[Villa d'Este, *June 21st*, 1874.]

Dear Sir,

Your friendly communication rests upon a harmless mistake. You do not seem to know that for 26 years past I have altogether ceased to be regarded as a pianist; hence I have for a long time not given any concerts, and only very occasionally played the piano in public, for some very special reason, to aid some charity or to further some artistic object, and then only in Rome, Hungary (my native country), and in Vienna—nowhere else. And on these rare and very exceptional occasions no one has ever thought of offering me any remuneration in money. Excuse me therefore, dear Sir, that I cannot accept your invitation to the Liverpool Musical Festival, inasmuch as I cannot in any way think of wearying the public with my *whilom* piano-playing.

Respectfully yours,

F. Liszt.

150. To Walter Bache.

Dear and honoured Friend,

I am often with you in kindest remembrance and cordial sympathy with your admirable *efforts*, but unfortunately I rarely get any letters written to the friends I value most, for my time is wasted with a number of wearisome and useless notes. I have just despatched one of this sort to a Mr. E. in L. The good man invites me to the Festival to be held there,

---

* From a copy of the draft of a letter by Dr. Mirus, Weimar.

asks me to consider the matter, and even offers me a remuneration in money for *playing*—without imagining that I have anything else or better to do than to accept such invitations. To me concert tours would be absolutely senseless; to fulfil my duties in Pest and Weimar gives me trouble and interruptions enough. All the other things need not be enumerated.

The summer and autumn (till my return to Pest in January '75) I mean to spend here quietly and at work. Last Monday and Tuesday I had the special pleasure of a visit from Bülow. And we thought of you in all friendship.—Bülow is now going to Salzungen (near Meiningen) for a couple of months, to recover from the terrible fatigues of his concert tour, and next October goes again to London.

Remember me most kindly to Mr. Dannreuther with assurances of faithful attachment, and do me the favour to give the enclosed notes of thanks to Messrs. Hueffer and Gounod.

Our very able and dear patroness, Madame Laussot, told me that you, dear Bache, will probably soon be wandering towards Italy.

A hearty welcome, therefore, to the old place where again is resting your old and sincere friend,

June 21st, 1874.   F. LISZT.

(Villa d'Este,—Tivoli, per Roma—Italia.)

151. TO DR. FRANZ WITT.

[VILLA D'ESTE, *Early Summer,* 1874.]

MUCH-ESTEEMED SIR AND FRIEND,

The lively recollection I entertain of the truly edifying Church-music performances in Eichstätt under your direction [1] increases my regret that I am unable to accept your friendly invitation to the 5th General Assembly of the *Cäcilien-Verein* in Ratisbon (between the 1st and 7th August).[2] A wearisome piece of work will keep me here till my return to Pest in January '75. Next summer, however, I hope again to pay you a visit, and to gather excellent precepts and examples from you. Meanwhile I am reading your Essays with peculiar satisfaction, and more especially your compositions in the "Musica sacra" and the "Fliegende Blätter." "Fliegend" [flying] must here be taken in the higher, angelic sense ; in the latter sense O salutaris hostia sounds altogether comforting Musica angelorum, such as pleasantly animates all your Church toneworks.

152. To Dr. Franz Haberl.*

[VILLA D'ESTE, *Early Summer*, 1874.]

MUCH-ESTEEMED SIR AND FRIEND,

To my sincere regret I find myself prevented from attending the *Cäcilien-Verein* in Ratisbon.

The efforts and performances of the *Verein* I follow with the deepest interest, and anticipate that its promoters—who are so capable, careful and learned— will accomplish all that is truly of advantage in Church music.

---

[1] On the occasion of the 3rd General Assembly of the *Cäcilien-Verein* in Eichstätt, August 1871.

[2] The Assembly was held on the above-mentioned days.

* A portion of this letter is printed in Dr. Mirus' *brochure*, "Das Liszt-Museum in Weimar" (1892), which contains many interesting relics of Liszt.

And in this Ratisbon has for many years past deserved to rank first, and you, my much-esteemed friend, deserve the fullest recognition that can be offered for the abundant services you have rendered in the cause. Accept my grateful thanks for kindly sending Vittoria's Missa pro defunctis,[1] which was brought to me by the Chaplain of the Anima Church. Will you be so kind as to get Herr Pustet to send me also, through Leukoch,[2] "Mannuale breve canticum," etc. ?[3]

In spite of the grievous news of your continued sufferings I do not give up the hope of seeing you here again soon, and of taking all friendly care of you ; and you shall not in the least degree be troubled or wearied ; merely recruit from your over-exertions by living simply and comfortably amid quiet and congenial surroundings.

Hence I take the liberty again of inviting your Reverence to spend the next months with me here in the Villa d'Este, where you will find rest, quiet and cosiness, mild air, glorious scenery, pleasant walks, good eating, good wine, books, music, pianos to make use of ad libitum, and a temperature mentally agreeable.

Cardinal Hohenlohe requests me to say that you will be heartily welcome, and this message is communicated with unmixed pleasure by your very respectful and sincerely grateful

F. Liszt.

[1] A six-voiced Requiem given by Dr. Haberl at the 5th General Assembly of the *Cäcilien-Verein* in Ratisbon in 1874, and published in the "Musica divina," Annus II., Tom. 1, by Pustet.

[2] Perhaps ought to read Leuckart ?

[3] A little book of Chorales by Joh. Georg Mettenleiter.

153. To Edmund von Mihalovich.

Very dear Friend,

Your Prologue to the *Nibelungen* in course of performance at the Walhalla-Roszàvölgyi has royally amused me.[1] I wish that Wagner may find in Messrs. Betz, Scaria, Niemann, etc., interpreters as well suited to their *rôles* as Richter-Wotan, Dunkl-Loge, Abrányi-Thor and Gobbi-Mime.

At Bayreuth "fervet opus." The preparatory piano rehearsals are going on ; celebrated artists are growing thick on the ground, like the suitors at Penelope's court. Joseph Rubinstein suspends his commercial occupations, and returns from Cracow to drive the four-in-hand accompaniment of *Rheingold.* The architects, painters, decorators, machinists, costumiers and their people are continuing their work; therefore, in spite of difficulties and obstacles, the great work of Art of this century—Wagner's Tetralogy of the *Nibelungen*—will come to pass, and I hope to be present at the first performance with my very dear friends Mi and Do.[2]—Meanwhile let us go on patiently at our own modest work, and endeavour to make it as suitable as possible. Next winter we will make an exchange of our latest sheets of music. I will bring a pretty thick packet to Sir Hagbar.[3]

Schuberth promises me the "Geisterschiff" in the autumn ; we will then launch it at once with Sgambati,

[1] A joke of Mihalovich, who had nicknamed several mutually known people with the names and characters out of the *Nibelungen.*

[2] Mihalovich was called *Mi* by Liszt, and Count Apponyi *Do.*

[3] An Opera by Mihalovich (*Hagbar and Sigurd*).

who has just composed several *Lieder*, exquisite in sentiment.   I have recently written, as an Impromptu, without any forethought, an *Elégie* in memory of Mme. de Moukhanoff, entitled "Schlummerlied im Grabe" [Slumber Song in the Grave].

Your kind wishes for my repose are being realised here.   I pass my days very peaceably, and my evenings alone, in reading, writing or playing.   Since the departure of Bülow, who gave me his most eminent company for two days (in the middle of June), I have, so to say, seen nobody.   He is now making his *villeggiatura* at Salzungen near Meiningen, returns to England in the month of November, and will not go to America till the autumn of '75.

Pay me a visit sometimes in thought, dear Mi, and believe me ever your very cordially devoted friend,

F. LISZT.

VILLA D'ESTE (TIVOLI), *July 30th*, 1874.

Let me hear something about Do and Horpács.[1]   I will write to them later.

154. TO PETER CORNELIUS.*

DEAR AND VALUED FRIEND,

You have again presented me with a marvellous gift.   Your German translation of Lamartine's "Hymne de l'enfant à son réveil" is exquisitely successful, and

---

[1] An estate of Count Emmerich Szechényi, the former Austro-Hungarian ambassador in Berlin, whom Liszt frequently visited.

* The letter is addressed to Neuenahr, where Cornelius had gone for a water-cure, shortly before his death.   The translation of the *Cäcilia-legend* he did not accomplish.

retains all the fragrance and aroma of the original poem.

> "Kein Würmlein vergissest Du. . . .
> Das Zicklein an Staude und Beere. . . .
> Am Milchkrug Mücklein saugt den Saft. . . .
> Und die Lerche das Körnlein picket." . . . *

All and everything fits in so exactly with the music, syllable by syllable, that it seems as if the poem and music had sprung up together. Verily, dear friend, you are an extremely kind and most perfect magician. Now do not be vexed with me if my grateful appreciation of your skill should prove somewhat covetous, and I again ask you to do me a favour. A little French poem of 48 short lines, "Sainte Cécile, Légende," by Madame Emile Girardin (Delphine Gay) is awaiting your poetic courtesy. Allow me to send you my finished composition of this *Cäcilia*, the musical foundation of which is furnished by the Gregorian antiphone : "Cantantibus organis, Caecilia Domino decantabat." It is to be hoped that I have not spoilt it, and I trust to your friendly kindliness to send me a German translation of it before the next *Cäcilia Festival* (22nd November), soon after which it shall be printed, and a performance of it given in Pest.

The delay with the edition of your two Operas I sincerely regret. They deserve much greater appreciation and a much wider circulation than hundreds of others that are printed, and the publication of the pianoforte scores is sure to effect this for them. Meanwhile

---

> * "No worm dost Thou e'er forget. . . .
> The kid amid the shrubs and berries. . . .
> The fly that sips the sweetest juice. . . .
> And the lark that pecks the blade of corn." . . .

I am glad that you have made use of my suggestion to base the Overture of the *Barber* on the pleasantly characteristic motive—

Next summer we shall meet in Munich.—With hearty thanks,   Your sincerely attached   F. Liszt.

Villa d'Este (Tivoli), *August 23rd,* 1874.

If you should see Frau Schott in Mainz, give her my kindest remembrances. For some time past various manuscripts have been lying ready which I should have liked to hand over to Schott's house of business ; but fear that they might arrive at an inopportune moment. The very title, " Drei symphonische Trauer-Oden " [Three Symphonic Funeral Odes] might prove alarming ; and besides, the scores—all about 20 pages in length—would have to be published simultaneously with the pianoforte transcriptions (for one or two performers).

Well, " we can wait." . . .

I am working pretty industriously at the *Sanct Stanislaus.* Of this you will to-morrow receive a full report—and an urgent request for speedy, *energetically* accentuated pains over the essential but not lengthy alterations of the text.

155. To Ludwig Bösendorfer in Vienna.[1]

Dear Friend,

With my sincere thanks for your interesting reports of the Vienna musical world I would gladly have

[1] Head of the celebrated pianoforte manufactory, now *Commerzien-rath* (Councillor of Commerce).

given you something of the same kind in return. But there is here nothing whatever in the way of novelties or specialities in the way of concerts ; be content, therefore, if my letter to-day mentions only one, but to me a very important artistic item—namely, the frequent use of your piano, which, among other virtues, possesses a wondrous power of *not getting out of tune* [Unverstimmtheit]. Since its despatch from Vienna not a tuner has touched it, and yet it keeps in beautiful tune, and steadily resists all variations and effects of temperature.

Till the end of January I shall remain quietly at work here ; then go direct to Pest—and by the middle of April on to Weimar. My thoughts and efforts require now only peace and seclusion. These are things that suit me best in my old age, and uphold me in spiritual intercourse with my dear and true friends. As such I greet you and your wife heartily and sincerely.

F. LISZT.

VILLA D'ESTE, *August 28th*, 1874.

156. TO ADELHEID VON SCHORN IN WEIMAR.

DEAR AND MOST EXCELLENT ONE,

For our grand *coup* you come in completely in your *rôle* of *providence*, which you fill with such complete good grace, and with an admirable mastery ! I cannot tell you what immense comfort your letter brings me, with its assurance of your speedy arrival in Rome. Try not to delay it beyond the 25th—30th November, and if possible come sooner. Princess Wittgenstein is still very suffering, and has kept her bed entirely for six weeks ; your company and the inspirations of your solicitude will do her more good than all the Allo- and Homœopaths put together.

I beg that you will write to her speedily to announce your coming, for she is ignorant and *must* be kept in complete ignorance of the plot we have hatched with Princess Marie,[1] the happy success of which you will crown. Questions of detail will be easily settled to your satisfaction, in such a manner that the stay in Rome will be thoroughly pleasant to you.

It is understood that you will not mention the question of where you will live to Princess W., who has already only too much worry about her own rooms. In my opinion it would be best for you to go to the Hôtel d'Amérique, Via Babuino (close by the house of the Princess and of the one where I live), and to spend some days there, until you see where you can settle yourself comfortably, whether at the Pension (also very near the Babuino) where your cousin Octavie stayed, or elsewhere.

When you reach Bologna, please let me know by telegram on what day you will arrive ; I will meet you at the station, and it will be a real joy to me to escort you to your first abode in Rome.

Thank you with all my heart, and yours ever,

F. LISZT.

ROME, *October 12th*, 1874.   (VICOLO DE' GRECI, 43.)

The Princess is living at Via Babuino 89.

Your letter was only returned to me from Tivoli yesterday evening.

I shall remain here, or at the Villa d'Este, till the end of January.—

[1] The daughter of Princess Wittgenstein.

157. To Breitkopf and Härtel.

VERY DEAR SIRS,

The kind reception you gave the last sending of my somewhat cumbersome manuscripts and revisions pleased me greatly.   I will always gladly do what I can not to increase the *publishers' worries,* and henceforth print only what has been carefully worked out and will prove tolerably acceptable.

With regard to the form in which the Songs and Wagner-transcriptions are to be published, you may act altogether as you think best.   I did certainly think that the convenient and neat edition in *small octavo* would be preferable (like the last edition of Chopin and my *Etudes transcendantes*) : hence in from 5 to 6 little volumes :—

1. Beethoven (The Adelaide and other Songs) ;
2. Mendelssohn (6 Songs) ;
3. Robert and Clara Schumann ;
4. Robert Franz ;
5 to 6 (?). Wagner-transcriptions.

This would in no way prevent the songs and pieces of several pages (such as the Adelaide, Mendelssohn's Songs, the Tannhäuser-March, the Rienzi-Fantasia, etc.) being sold *singly*—in the same small 8vo form which, candidly speaking, I always like best.   As long ago as the year '39 I induced Haslinger to publish Schubert's songs in an edition of this kind—and at that time it seemed rather a doubtful innovation.   Also about placing the words *below the music.*   I wish this, for the sake of the poetical delivery in all of the songs, *except the Adelaide,* because the poem roams about rather too freely in rococo style. Let us leave " *the flow'ret at the grave* " to bloom on quietly without *retouching* it again.

I must unfortunately again trouble you to send me *all* the proofs. It is a matter of great moment to me to have the things arranged as accurately and as appropriately for the piano as possible. And for this I require the last proofs, in order finally to revise them in reading and playing them over. (For the printer's consolation be it remarked that no new alterations shall now crop up again; my zeal in correcting shall be confined to making some pedal marks and fingerings.) First of all I should like to try over Sgambati's duet arrangement of the "Ideale" with *him*; and you will doubtless do me the favour of sending me the proof sheets *stitched together* before I leave here (at the end of January). —

I leave the matter concerning the small honorarium confidently to your well-known kindly disposition, and remain, very dear Sirs,

Yours respectfully and most obediently,

F. LISZT.

VILLA D'ESTE, *November 24th,* 1874.

158. TO COUNT ALBERT APPONYI IN BUDAPEST.[*]

[VILLA D'ESTE, *December 6th,* 1874.]

DEAR AND VERY HONOURED FRIEND,

Your excellent letter of the 27th November reached me here yesterday evening. I hasten to give

* From an undated rough draft of a letter in the possession of Herr O. A. Schulz, bookseller in Leipzig. (The date has been ascertained from a letter to Mihalovich.)—The addressee was the well-known Hungarian statesman.

you my very sincere thanks, and to add a frank reply on the question of the Academy of Music.

First of all I think the "moyen violent" [violent means] of Huszar, which will deliver us from barren tittle-tattle, is right; let us throw the *Seeschlange* [sea serpent] into the Danube, and if he wants an epitaph here is one : "It is better to do nothing than to do stupidities."

Now, are we the stupid ones ?—The Government is much interested in this affair; the Sovereign's decision has been obtained ; I know not what official publication has followed. You yourself, dear Count, have brilliantly persuaded the Chamber of Deputies that the said Academy would be of use in raising Art in Hungary; my necessary humble reserve has been taken by the public as consent.—Is it possible now to take no account of such precedents, and to draw back when it is a question of advancing ? I do not think so, and I am quite of your opinion, as wise as it is opportune.

In spite of the difficulties of a position embroiled with divers worries, and in spite of the scantiness of the financial means, we ought to stick to our affirmative position and not in the least to give way.

As to my "personal convenience," which you are good enough to take into such kind consideration, permit me to assure you anew that I aspire to one only blessing—quiet time for work in my own room. Orare et laborare. The *point of honour*, which no one understands better than yourself, attaches me to Hungary, our country. May I fulfil there all my duty of gratitude !—

I shall be back at Pest (Fischplatz) on the 10th February, and shall rejoice to hear the Ballade of our valiant friend Mihalovich, to whom I shall write to-morrow.

Yours from my heart,

F. LISZT.

159. TO EDMUND VON MIHALOVICH.

DEAR EXCELLENT FRIEND,

I wrote the day before yesterday to Do, and was about to continue with a letter to *you* when a telegram called me *subitissimo* back to Rome. The thread of my ideas has not been broken on the journey, and I resume our conversation, *à trois*, on the long gestation — omen of abortion — of the Hungarian Academy of Music.

I trust that my very dear and honoured friends will be convinced of my perfect disinterestedness in the question; the idea of an Academy is in no way mine: if I become sponsor to it, it will be in self-defence and without any connivance at paternity whatever; I even refuse to help in the procreation of the *marmot* [brat]; and, far from making myself, before my time, in any way its champion or propagandist, I hesitate over the difficulties which are opposed to its birth. I have explained these many a time to my Budapest friends, and the difficulties have increased rather than diminished during these last three years. . . .

1stly. The financial situation of the country appears to be such that one must scruple to burden the budget with an expenditure beyond urgent needs. My patriotism is sufficiently sincere and lively to counsel me to abstention, including every renunciation that is compatible with my strict duty.

2ndly. It would be a poor luxury to add a third music school to the two schools already existing (meagrely) at Pest. If one cannot emulate with honour the similar establishments of Vienna, Leipzig, etc.—what is the good of troubling any further about it? Now, to give a vigorous impulse to Art among us, we must first unite and fuse into one spirit a set of professors of well-known capability,—a very arduous and ungrateful task, the accomplishment of which demands much intelligence, and a sufficient amount of cleverness and of money.

Other minor, local considerations complicate the matter still further ; I pass them over in silence to-day, and will not repeat myself any more except on one point,—my religious devotion to our country and our art. To serve them somewhat, according to the moderate degree of my talent, whether it be in working *by myself* at my manuscripts (which is what I much prefer), or in co-operating with my friends in public things, this is my simple and exclusive desire, totally removed from the personal pretensions or anxieties of vanity which are wrongly imputed to me.

" Tiszta lélek, tiszta szándék, akár siker, akár nem." [" Pure soul, pure intention, whether the results be favourable or not."—Maxim of Stephan Szechényi.]

My friends are those who haunt the *Ideal* ; there, dear friend, we " *recognise* " each other, and shall always do so,—but not " in the mud," illustrated by a fascinating poet, too much celebrated and tainted by the triviality of vulgar applause—Heine. Amongst other things he had predicted that the Cathedral of Cologne would never be finished. "In vain will Franz Liszt give his concerts," etc.—

You know that Wagner is coming to Pest in Lent. It is only right that several of your compositions— especially the last, "Sello"—should be performed in public at that time. Talk the matter over with Richter. I on my side will ring the "*Bells*." Please beg Abrányi to hurry with the Hungarian translation of Longfellow's poem (the Prologue to the "Golden Legend"), and to follow, not the German translation of the "Pianoforte score," which I have sent to Engesser, but the original English text.[1]

Yours in cordial friendship,
F. LISZT.

VILLA D'ESTE, *December 8th*, 1874.

I will write to-morrow to the very gracious châtelaine of Horpács.

160. TO CARL HOFFBAUER IN MUNICH.*

[End of 1874.]

My hearty thanks for the kindly zeal with which you have taken up the *Christus* Oratorio. But a performance of it in Munich appears to me so doubtful, and connected with so much trouble, expense,

---

[1] Liszt had set to music the Prologue to the "Golden Legend," under the title "Die Glocken des Strassburger Münsters" [The Bells of Strassburg Cathedral].

* From a copy belonging to Dir. Aug. Göllerich.—Hoffbauer, born in 1850, became in 1872 Director of the *Gesang-Verein* in Munich, went to Frankfort in 1880, and put an end to his own life. He composed, among other things, the Operas *Comata* and *Demetrius*.

and difficulty, that I must for the present dissuade you from the undertaking. Besides, it would not be possible for me to accept your invitation for the end of February, as several engagements will keep me in Pest till Easter. And, if ever you give a performance of the *Christus* in Munich, I should much like to be present. As yet the whole work has been only twice heard, in Weimar and Pest (in May and last November, '73).

In reply to your inquiry, I must mention Herr and Frau von Milde and Frau Dr. Merian as specially well acquainted with and capable of taking the solo parts.

Accept the assurance of my utmost gratitude for your eagerness to give a performance of the *Christus* in Munich.

Most respectfully and sincerely yours,

F. LISZT.

161. To EDMUND VON MIHALOVICH.

VERY DEAR FRIEND,

In spite of the legion of Dessoff, calm plains or storms, go on roaring bravely in the waters of the "Phantom Ship." Even should we not succeed in arriving safely in port, and should we meet no other *Senta* than Her Highness Madam Criticism, it matters not; those who follow us in the *same waters* of the Ideal will be more fortunate. . . .

" Et quasi cursores vitai lampada tradunt ! " —-

We will talk about all this fully in February, in the *Fischplatz.*

Will you be so kind as to send the enclosed letter to

my gracious and admired translator of the " *Chopin* "—
Mme. la Comtesse Ottilia Wast ?[1]

Further, I beg that you will recommend Taborszky
to publish before Easter my *St. François de Paule*,
which our very dear friend Albert Apponyi has been
good enough to adorn with his poetry,—and also
"L'hymne de l'enfant à son réveil," which Taborszky
must have received in November (with the German
words by Cornelius and the addition of a harp part).

Schuberth has been seriously ill. I shall be after
him to bring out your *Geisterschiff* [Phantom Ship]
without any more delay.

A revoir in six weeks, and always

Very cordially yours,

VILLA D'ESTE, *December 29th,* 1874.   F. LISZT.

On the occasion of the Wagner concert in Pest I
should like my "Bells" to ring, and beg Abrányi to
attune the Hungarian *Klingklang* [ding-dong] of them
speedily and beautifully.[2]

162. TO CARL HOFFBAUER IN MUNICH.*

[Probably PEST, at the beginning of 1875.]

VERY DEAR SIR,

Your last letter exhibits so convincing a
character of truth and noble-mindedness that I sincerely
rejoice at the prospect of becoming personally and

---

[1] A translation into Hungarian from the old edition of the book.

[2] Liszt's "Glockengeläute " [Bell-ringing] consisted in this—that
he played the Beethoven E♭ Concerto at the Wagner concert in Pest.
He allowed himself to be persuaded to do this, as people were afraid
that, on account of the high prices, the concert would not be full.—
The "Bells of Strassburg Cathedral " were not performed.

* From the copy of a draft of a letter by Dr. Mirus.

in spirit better acquainted with you.   And first of all
be assured of my special interest in your Opera
Comata.   Whatever I may be able to do as regards a
representation of it in a theatre I shall not fail to do.
In Munich we will read the score over together, and
discuss further details.

Of your persistence in wishing to have the *Christus*
performed I wrote to Schuberth yesterday, and shall
in full confidence leave the whole matter to your considerate zeal.   You will best know whether and how
a successful performance can be made possible, and
please therefore arrange matters altogether according
as you think fit.   I beg you merely to let me know the
day you fix upon some 10 or 12 days previously, and
address me to Pest (at Easter), if earlier to Weimar,
and I will then come for the full rehearsal.[1]

Respectful greetings to the poetess of the *Comata*,
and believe me, with marked esteem, yours gratefully
and sincerely,

F. Liszt.

163. To Professor Julius Stern in Berlin.

Dear Friend,

For years past and again lately I have been
very much indebted to you.   Our eminently learned
and dear friend Weitzmann[2] told me of the careful
rehearsals, and of the admirable manner in which you
conducted the Faust Symphony.

[1] The performance took place on the 12th April, 1875.   As a
result of this King Ludwig II. ordered a separate performance in the
Court theatre, and this again was followed by a public one.

[2] Theorist and contrapuntist in Berlin (1808—1880).

Owing to *critical* circumstances and negativings I
have, as a rule, to dissuade people everywhere from
giving performances of **my** scores. All the more
pleasantly am I affected by the goodwill of the few
friends who carefully and courageously march on in
front.

Therefore, while offering you my sincerest thanks, I
beg you to excuse my not being just now able to accept
the tempting invitation to Berlin.

Yours most respectfully and sincerely,

F. LISZT.

ROME, *February 4th,* 1875.

(Next week I return to Pest, and at the beginning of
April go to Weimar, where I should be delighted to
welcome you again.)

164. TO COUNT ALBERT APPONYI.*

February 18*th,* [1875 ?]

This morning the *Politische Volksblatt* † brings
me your portrait, my honoured and dear friend. The
notice accompanying it pleases me only in so far as it
predicts a great future for you, based on your very
evident merits and great talents. People are agreed
upon your great height (*" Haupteslänge "*)—all the better,
for it corresponds to the height of your character, and
I bet a hundred to one that you will never combat " the
spirit of the times " (*" Herr von Zeitgeist und Frau von
öffentliche Meinung,"* ‡ as the honourable Count Gozzi

---

* From a rough copy of a letter in the possession of Herr O. A.
Schulz, bookseller in Leipzig.

† The Political People's-Paper.

‡ Mr. Spirit of the Times and Mrs. Public Opinion.

ceremoniously said), except when you meet with stupidities and adventures on which this spirit of the times is astride.

A friendly invitation for to-morrow evening at the house of

Your very devoted and grateful

F. LISZT.

165. To JOHANN VON HERBECK.

VERY DEAR FRIEND,

My sincere thanks for your letter ; gladly would I follow your very kind and *"unselfish"* request. To say "nay" to my friends always comes hard to me. But how can I act otherwise in face of the negativings of critics ? And why should I not prefer abiding my time *in peace* alone ?

Now-a-days an artist is reckoning without his host if he places honest faith in the public. For people now-a-days hear and judge only by reading the newspapers.

I mean to take advantage of this in so far that the leading and favourite papers of Vienna, Pest, Leipzig, Berlin, Paris, London, etc.—which abhor my humble compositions and have declared them worthless and objectionable—shall be relieved of all further outward trouble concerning them. What is the good of *performances* to people who only care to read newspapers ?

Hence, dear good friend, let the "Gran Mass"[1] and the "Glocken"[2] remain unperformed in Vienna, where

---

[1] Herbeck, however, did have them performed.

[2] "Die Glocken des Strassburger Münsters" [The Bells of Strassburg Cathedral].

(in Easter week) you shall receive a visit from yours most warmly and gratefully,

F. LISZT.

BUDAPEST, *March 3rd*, 1875.

166. To EDUARD VON LISZT.

DEAREST EDUARD,

Give Lenbach my kindest thanks, and at the same time ask him to send his extremely poetical portrait of Frau von Moukhanoff here *soon* in honour of the noble lady and of the musical Commemoration Festival which we have announced for the middle of May.[1]

To-morrow morning early I go to Hanover; my address there till May 29th[2] will be: "at Freiherr von Bronsart's, Intendant of the Hoftheater." On Saturday is the performance of the *Elizabeth*, and on the 29th the concert for the benefit of the *Bach* monument.

My gracious Grand Duke is very urgent about my speedy return; I shall, therefore, probably spend only 8 or 10 days at Schloss Loo (from the 2nd to the 12th May), and then return here forthwith.

The *Tonkünstler-Versammlung* is to be held in Dresden at the end of June. I long for some rest and quiet work.

Thine with all my heart,

F. LISZT.

WEIMAR, *April 22nd*, 1875.

[1] Liszt dedicated an *Élégie* to the memory of this gifted lady.
[2] This must mean the 29th April.

167. To Adelheid von Schorn in Rome.

Dear excellent One,

I come to keep you company a little in your convalescence,—far advanced, I hope, so as to be something like a complete cure. For a *tisane** I offer you some news of your cara patria. There are few variations at Weimar : the Grand Duke and Grand Duchess remain there till the end of June; the Emperor of Russia is announced for the 25th June ; the *Hereditary* Highnesses are going to the waters (Marienbad and Pyrmont) in a few days, and will return before the Grand Duke's *fête* (24th June) ; Gutschen Watzdorf is going on his own account independently to Carlsbad, Mme. de Loën to Reme (in Westphalia).

At the theatre a tempered, but lively activity ; during these latter weeks a new Drama by Otto Roquette has been given—*Der Feind im Hause.*† The subject is taken from the quarrel of the Colonna in Rome ; the success of the piece will not occasion any fresh quarrels ; nor will that of two new Operas that I have seen—*Der Widerspänstigen Bezähmung*‡ by Götz and *Golo* of Scholz, which have come inopportunely into competition with Schumann's *Genoveva*—a work which has been taken up again with marked success this year (after it had been prudently ignored for twenty years—except at Leipzig and Weimar) at Leipzig and Wiesbaden. Other theatres will mix themselves up with it, in spite of the non-success of *Genoveva* at

---

* A soothing drink.
† The enemy in the house.
‡ The subduing of the refractory ones.

Vienna, where it was put on the stage in the winter of '74 with a most praiseworthy luxury of decoration and costumes.

At the time of the performance which I conducted, and that is some twenty years ago, I said : Genoveva is musically the sister of Fidelio ; only *Leonora's* pistol is wanting.

Tristan and Isolde, announced here for the 15th and 19th May, . . . have remained at Munich with M. and Mme. Vogel, who have lost a child. Loën[1] and all the public are very much put out at this untimely mourning; possibly the Vogels will be able to come towards the end of June ; I don't reckon on it much, but have written to them on the subject at Loën's request. If they accept, the Commemoration Matinée of Mme. Moukhanoff will take place between the two performances of *Tristan*, and the " *Tempelherrenhaus* " in our park has been chosen by us as the spot for this musical commemoration. I will send you the programme.

Meanwhile here is that of Saturday last at the "Orchestral School"—a very useful establishment, well adapted to our modestly proud situation of Weimar, and which Müller-Hartung conducts according to my wishes.[2] Bruch's *Odysseus*—a musical illustration of Preller's admirable pictures in the Weimar museum —was performed last Thursday, conducted also by Müller-Hartung.

Lassen is in the middle of composing some fine

---

[1] The Weimar Intendant.

[2] The concert "in honour of Liszt's first visit to the School " consisted entirely of works by him.

choruses for the two *Fausts*, which Devrient is intending to get up here in two evenings, in conformity with
his new scenic arrangement.

Very cordially yours,
F. Liszt.

WEIMAR, *May* 17*th*, 1875.

168. To Eduard von Liszt.

DEAREST EDUARD,

. — . The day after to-morrow I join the Duke
of Weimar's party at Schloss Wilhelmsthal, and shall
remain there several days.   After that I should have
liked to wait upon Cardinal Hohenlohe in Schillingsfürst; but His Eminence is at present at Bad Ragaz
(Switzerland) undergoing some after-cure for a foot-
trouble, the result of some accident he met with last
winter.   When I receive his answer I shall so arrange
things that my visit to Schillingsfürst is paid as is
agreeable *in tempore opportuno.*

From the 3rd to the 15th August I shall be in
Bayreuth; after that I shall this year end with Weimar
(without playing *Tannhäuser* there, as a guest !) at the
Carl-August Festival on September 3rd, for which I
have written a short and simple chorus in popular
style, the text of which is furnished by King David:
"The Lord preserveth the souls of His saints, and
light is sown for the righteous."

In contemplating this light in all humility,

I am, in true affection,
Thine,
F. Liszt.

WEIMAR, *July* 17*th*, 1875.

Enclosed are a few words for our Marie. If I had to choose a cousin I should choose her. Hence I confess my innermost *elective*-affinity with papa and daughter.

Lenbach's wondrously inspired portrait of Madame Moukhanoff will to-morrow be sent back to Vienna to the Countess Coudenhoven.

169. To Louis Köhler.

VERY DEAR FRIEND,

Merit and success, in your case, would seem always to stand in perfectly delightful harmony. Best thanks for your kindly letter and for sending your Opus 147: "Technische Künstler-Studien." * And although I am more disposed to turn away from than towards Methods and Pedagogics, still I have read this work of yours with interest. The entrance of the pedal after the striking of the chords as indicated by you at the beginning of page 3, and as consistently carried through by you almost to the utmost extreme, seems to me an ingenious idea, the application of which is greatly to be recommended to pianoforte players, teachers and composers—especially in slow *tempi.*

I regret that we are *geographically* so far apart; but sympathetically I remain in sincere esteem and in all friendliness yours,

F. LISZT.

SCHLOSS WILHELMSTHAL, *July 27th,* 1875.

My friendly greetings to your very talented pupil

* Technical Artist-Studies.

Alfred Reisenauer. Perhaps you may be coming to Weimar again shortly ; I should be pleased to hear this.

One line in your friendly letter I answer herewith : proud of my Königsberg title of doctor, and anxious to do it credit, I willingly refrain from giving performances of my humble compositions anywhere.

170. To Carl Hillebrand in Florence.[1]

Dear and very honoured Friend,

Your friendly letter leaves me a good hope . . . for next year. I have just transmitted your thanks and the data relative to our *concerted idea* to the Grand Duke, who arrived at Ostend on Thursday last, with his daughters, his son and his daughter-in-law. Their Royal Highnesses return to Weimar the 1st September for the *fête* of Carl August, which the Emperor and Empress of Germany will solemnise with their presence. Monseigneur tells me to invite you to it. I observe to him that you will probably be detained elsewhere ; nevertheless, if you should come to Germany at that moment, be assured that you will be warmly welcomed and received at the Court of Weimar.

The monument of Carl August will be inaugurated on the 3rd September. The ceremony of the *Toison d'Or* [Golden Fleece], at which the Emperor will be the sponsor of his brother-in-law, our Grand Duke,

---

[1] The celebrated author of "Zeiten, Völker und Menschen" [Times, People and Mankind] and other works ; born 1820 ; lived, from 1870 until his death, in Florence, where a memorial tablet, in gratitude to his memory, was erected over his house in the Lung' Arno.

will take place on the 4th.   Then T.R.H. will leave
Weimar, and my poor self return to the Villa d'Este
(towards the middle of September) for as long a
time as my very dear compatriots will allow of it.
They press me strongly to return to Pest on the 1st
November; before obeying them I shall come and see
you at Florence.

Please count always on the feelings of sincere and
high esteem of your very cordially devoted

F. LISZT.

BAYREUTH, *August 2nd*, 1875.

The papers keep you *au courant* of the marvels
of Wagner's theatre here.   The performances (announced for the month of August '76) of the
Tetralogy, *Der Ring des Nibelungen*, will be the
chief event of dramatic Art, thus royally made manifest for the first time in this century in its *ensemble* and
unification of Poetry, Music, Acting, and their decorations of Painting and *mise-en-scène*.

There is not merely the chance, but the guarantee
of a grand and striking success, in view of the sublimity
of the work itself, and also of the enthusiasm which
it already excites amongst the numerous staff of
artists chosen to interpret it.   In spite of the difficulties
of this new transcendental style of Wagner, the
preparatory study and rehearsals are an enchantment
for the singers and the musicians of the orchestra.

By the 18th August I shall be back at Weimar, and
shall stay there till the 6th September.

To Madame Laussot my tender and grateful regards.

171. To Adelheid von Schorn.

DEAR EXCELLENT ONE,

It is not without regret that I have given up the very sincere pleasure of meeting you now at Nuremberg. If you remained there till towards the middle of September I should come and ask you what commissions you have for Rome, where I expect to arrive before the 20th September.

Here we are sailing in the full tide of the marvels of art. Every day, morning and evening, one act of the *Ring des Nibelungen* is rehearsed in Wagner's new theatre. The enthusiasm of the whole staff of singers and orchestral players, to the number of about 150, is as sincere as it is abundant, and everything augurs for next year some prodigious performances of the immense and sublime work which royally dominates all contemporary Art, including the former works of Wagner.

Cosima sends you a thousand affectionate messages, and is expecting to see you at the time of the definite succession of the *Nibelungen-Ring* in the month of August 1876. You were present at the laying of the first stone of the monument, and must not be absent at the crowning moment. . — .

Mme. de Schleinitz is staying here a fortnight longer, and is living at the castle. She keeps herself continually at the highest diapason of grace and charm, without ever missing the opportunity of effectually obliging her friends.

A revoir soon, dear and very excellent one ; and ever from my heart your devoted

BAYREUTH, *August 7th*, 1875.   F. LISZT.

I shall be back at Weimar by the 18th August.

172. To Dr. Franz Witt.

[*Probably August or September*, 1875.]

Much-esteemed Friend,

While greatly regretting to hear of your indisposition and thanking you sincerely for your last letter, I now ask you: How are you going to answer the ministerial communication of Trefort?—Are you willing to render important help as regards Church music in Hungary? Superfluous words are unbecoming to me; let us onward and act; and may your noble and stimulating influence be granted to Hungary. Assuredly you will find there admiration, affection, and the necessary assistance in the great services you will render.

In a word: Come to us, and let us work together in Budapest!

173. To Lina Ramann.[1]

Dear Friend,

Thanks to your care I had excellent and very inspired company during my two days' journey from Nuremberg to Rome. Your parallel "Bach and Händel" delighted me more than the famous landscapes of the Brenner. Allow me specially to praise your fine insight into and correct interpretation of the various musical forms of culture from the Motet to the Mass and the Oratorio.

Some portions also of the "Allgemeine musikalische

---

[1] Authoress of "F. Liszt als Künstler und Mensch" [F. Liszt as Artist and Man], 2 vols. (Leipzig, Breitkopf and Härtel, 1880 and 1887).

Erzieh- und Unterrichtslehre" [Universal Musical Instruction] pleased me—(in spite of my inaptitude in things pedagogical), especially the main idea of the work :—that musical instruction should not be separated from, but form a part in, the course of education ; a relevant thought, the practical application of which will essentially benefit, and prove useful to, art as well as education.

Again my cordial thanks for the hours at Nuremberg, and best greetings to the amiable comrades in art Fräulein Ida and Auguste.

Yours respectfully and sincerely,

F. LISZT.

ROME, *September* 28*th*, 1875.

174. TO EDUARD VON LISZT.

ROME, *September* 29*th*, 1875.

DEAREST EDUARD,

Wherever we may be we ever remain one in heart. Probably I shall be in Budapest as early as the middle of November, on account of the *Musik-Akademie*, which it is my duty to shape in accordance with the standard of somewhat difficult local circumstances. Appointments have already been made by the Minister Trefort : Franz Erkel as Director, Volkmann as Professor of Composition, and Abrányi as Secretary. Witt and Bülow had the first offers from Trefort : unfortunately Witt is still too ill, and Bülow could not come till later, after his return from America. Of course Bülow would have received the largest possible sphere of action—somewhat the same as he occupied in Munich, where, for a couple of years, he acted as Director of the Conservatoire in the most successful manner. . . .

All hearty greetings to your circle, and believe me ever your gratefully and sincerely attached

F. LISZT.

Address : 43, Vicolo dei Greci, Roma (Italia). Till the beginning of November I stay here or at the *Villa d'Este*, and then travel direct to Pest.

Pray send me news of our dear and amiable Marie.

175. TO KORNEL VON ABRÁNYI.

DEAR FRIEND,

A thousand thanks for your letter with its weighty contents.[1] All things considered, it does not appear to me advisable to hurry my return. As I did this year, I mean next year also to reach Pest towards the *middle of February*—in time for Lent and the concert season. By that time the work at the *Musik-Akademie* ought to have fairly established itself.

I gladly undertake to conduct a pianoforte-class for virtuosi and teachers,—first of all from the 1st March to Easter 1876. And should the undertaking give indications of proving a success, I would be willing to devote several months a year to this species of instruction in the *Musik-Akademie* of Budapest.

I look forward to being on the best and most cordial

---

[1] Abrányi had informed Liszt that the Hungarian *Landes-Musik-Akademie*—which had been called into existence by Trefort, the Minister of Education—had already been organised and was shortly to be opened, and that Liszt was invited to the inauguration ceremony.

terms with Erkel.[1]   Also with Volkmann and the other professors.

As regards the very worthy Secretary, I rejoice to *labour* with him as next-door neighbour (on the *Fischplatz*, where assuredly we shall not dry up " like fish out of water "), and remain always

His grateful and truly attached friend,

F. LISZT.

VILLA D'ESTE, *October 14th,* 1875.

My friendly greetings, please, to Engessers,[2] Zimay,[3] Siposz,[4] and to our dear composer of the " Liszt-Cantata," Gobbi.

176. TO WALTER BACHE.

HIGHLY ESTEEMED AND DEAR FRIEND,

Hearty thanks for your kindly remembrance of the 22nd October.

With regard to the *Elizabeth* performance (at your " Twelfth Annual Concert" on the 24th February) I am somewhat anxious on account of the great exertions and expense which the performance will entail upon you. Still I will not make any further objection to your characteristically firm *incorrigibleness* in your steadfast wish and endeavour to do the *utmost possible* for the good of your old friend, now 64 years of age.

To Frau Blume (whom I often called upon in Rome) please give my friendliest remembrances. If the part

[1] Franz Erkel (born 1810), a celebrated Hungarian composer, at that time Director of the *Musik-Akademie* and *Capellmeister* at the National Theatre in Pest. Died 15th June, 1893.

[2] [3] [4] All Hungarian musicians.

of Elizabeth does not displease her she is certain to give an excellent interpretation of it.

I am most glad to grant friend Banz the permission he desires, and am grateful to him for his kindly sentiments.

Till the middle of February I shall stay here—and then go direct to Budapest—and remain your faithfully attached

                                                    F. LISZT.

VILLA D'ESTE, *October 26th*, 1875.

In case you receive direct news of Von Bülow, please let me know.

177. TO EDUARD VON LISZT.

MOST DEAR FRIEND,

Your letters are as full of heart as they are of mind. They both comfort and exalt me. My prayers always include you. May the "Supreme Spirit" strengthen us!

For me to appear at the opening of the *Musik-Akademie* in Pest on November 7th, is, I think, neither necessary nor desirable. It will be better that the undertaking (the official part of which I did not call into existence!) should be more fully started before I take any part in it. Hence till the middle of February I remain at the Villa d'Este (quietly finishing a few compositions) and then return direct to Pest.

Herbeck is said to have promised to conduct a concert there. I trust we may meet in friendship on the "Fischplatz" during Lent. How could he manage to have the Gran Mass performed in the Burgkapelle? The dimensions of the work require rather a goodly amount of space for chorus and orchestra. . . . Next summer it is proposed to give a grand concert-performance of the Gran Mass in Düsseldorf (where they have a splendid hall, admirably adapted for musical festivals). I shall look for your report of the *Vienna* performance.

As regards the *Prometheus*, I beg you to *fix* with Her-beck that in Vienna the new improved edition, published by Kahnt (Leipzig), shall be used, and get him to procure it from Kahnt: pianoforte score, full score, and voice parts. If Herbeck should entertain any doubt about the new edition on account of the expense, I shall be quite ready to settle the small "*difference*" with a few gulden, which you will advance me[1] for the purpose.

I am very anxious that this *Prometheus*—who is ready to "unchain" himself next summer in Düsseldorf and at the Musical Festival at Altenburg—should not again be a failure in Vienna, after his late want of success there.—

Give Kulke my best thanks for his excellent essay with its kindly sentiments (in the *Vaterland* of September 17th); I am specially pleased with the close: "In the same way as Sebastian Bach could not conceive a musical thought in any other way than from a contrapuntal point of view, Liszt cannot conceive a theme in any other way than from a thematic point of view," etc.

Heartiest greetings to all your circle: Marie will always prove herself noble and firm.

Your faithfully attached

(VILLA D'ESTE,) *October* 31st, 1875.　　　　　　F. L.

---

[1] Eduard von Liszt managed Liszt's money affairs for him.

178. To Madame Jessie Laussot.

Very dear and kind Friend,

Although I scarcely know how sufficiently to express my gratitude to you for all the proofs of friendship you have constantly shown me during twenty years, I am quite convinced that no misunderstanding would ever be possible between us. You know my good intentions from the outset, and in case of necessity you divine them with the heart's most penetrating and delicate intelligence.

I add to my thanks for your last letter a request which you will certainly grant, by assuring our very honoured friend Hillebrand of my sincere devotedness. In addition, assure him also that my zeal in serving my gracious master, the Grand Duke of Saxony, will never be used to the detriment of any one, and that I especially take into consideration the proprieties appropriate to the merits and position of *individualities* that I esteem and love.

So then we will discuss "academicamente," at your house in Florence (after my return from Hungary, towards the middle of February), the subject of Hillebrand's spending some months each year at Weimar.

This could be brought about under reciprocally pleasant conditions; I confess that I take a rather egotistical interest in it . . . but without failing in the duties of friendship.

In a week's time, Mdlle. Adelheid de Schorn accompanies her aunt—"the Lady Abbess von Stein"—

back to Germany.   She will bring you two or three
books of music from me.

Sgambati has finished a second, very remarkable
Quintet (for Piano and Strings), which will soon be
heard in Rome.

Zarembski (whom I introduced to you) works
valiantly, and deserves to be reckoned as an unusually
excellent pianist of the first rank.

A revoir in February, and yours very devotedly,

VILLA D'ESTE, *November 17th*, 1875.   F. LISZT.

If you should see the Jaells before their concerts in
Rome, give them my most affectionate remembrances.

179. TO EDUARD VON LISZT.

MY HONOURED FRIEND,

What you felt at the performance of the Gran
Mass has extremely rejoiced me.   "He who loves
understands."

Give Herbeck my warmest thanks for the carefulness
of the rehearsals and performance of this work, about
which I allowed myself to make the remark (in Paris
1866), to a personage of the very highest rank, that
" it had been more criticised than heard."

On no account would I press Herbeck to give a
performance of the "Prometheus-choruses"; according
to my thinking, it would be better to wait and see how
these choruses are done next spring in Düsseldorf and
at the *Tonkünstler-Versammlung* in Altenburg before
bringing them back to Vienna.   I should also like to
be present at the Vienna performance, which will not
be possible *this* winter.   I shall probably only be able
to stay one day with you (at the beginning of April).

I almost doubt whether the "*Hunnenschlacht*" could be performed amongst the "*Philharmoniker*" [lovers of harmony] without defeat to me. Nevertheless, "vincit qui patitur."

Heartiest greetings to our *Franz*, who will prove himself worthy of you.

Most faithfully thy

(VILLA D'ESTE, TIVOLI,) *November 26th*, 1875.   F. LISZT.

. — . As I already told you, I shall remain here till the middle of February, and then return direct to Budapest. From next April I am threatened with much travelling about. My *threefold* domicile, Pest, Weimar and Villa d'Este, and all that is connected with it, makes my life very onerous. Even the well-known consolation, "Tu l'as voulu, Georges Dandin" [it is your own doing], fails me. . . . Still there is hope in the proclamation "Et in terra pax, hominibus bonæ voluntatis."

Once more thanks for your kind intercession in my friend Vincenz Kirchmayer's [1] affairs. When the decision has been given let me know it.

180. TO HANS SCHMITT, PROFESSOR AT THE CONSERVATORIUM OF MUSIC IN VIENNA. [2]

MY DEAR SIR,   [*End of* 1875.]

It is well known how much mischief is done to the piano both with hands and feet. May your instructive pamphlet on the right use of the pedal duly

---

[1] Liszt's former travelling companion in Spain and Portugal during the forties, and especially recommended by Liszt to his cousin Eduard.

[2] Well known as an excellent teacher of the pianoforte, also as a writer on music.

benefit pianoforte players.[1] With best thanks for sending me the pamphlet, I remain

Yours respectfully,

F. LISZT.

181. TO KORNEL VON ABRÁNYI.

DEAR HONOURED FRIEND,

In the affairs of the Academy of Music I had till now simply to wait.[2] Now comes the time when a different, an active line of conduct presents itself to me. I shall always endeavour to come up to the expectations of my friends. First of all in the middle of February we begin our peaceful *academical* conferences, and, as I have already written to you, I willingly undertake, from the 1*st March*, to conduct a pianoforte class (for virtuosi and teachers)—provided that Erkel and you, dear friend, agree to this harmless proposal. My further activity in the Royal Hungarian Academy of Music had better be favoured, measured and decided by the *circumstances*. I can only lay claim to be the well-intentioned zealous servant of Art and of Hungary.

Please to give Erkel my heartiest thanks for the *Liszt-paragraph* in the " Inaugural Address." The kindly confidence which Erkel has reposed in me for more than 30 years shall never be abused.

The notice "Count Geza Zichy, President, and Bartay, Director of the Pest Conservatorium," affects me very pleasantly. Engesser's constancy in conducting the *Liszt-Verein*[3] particularly rejoices me. Is Gobbi's

---

[1] "The Pedal of the Piano." Vienna, Döblinger (3rd ed. 1892).

[2] The opening of the Academy of Music had taken place meanwhile in the middle of November, 1875.

[3] Engesser founded the *Liszt-Verein* in Pest (for mixed voices).

Cantata come out ?   Friendly greetings to the composer
and recently " well-known composer of *album-leaf*
waltzes," from your old, truly attached

F. LISZT.

VILLA D'ESTE, *January 20th*, 1876.

(Before my arrival—16th February—I will telegraph
to you from Venice, where I shall visit Count Imre
Széchenyi.)   In case there were anything to write
to me, address, till February 5th, *Rome*, Vicolo dei
Greci, 43.

182. TO EDUARD VON LISZT.

(VILLA D'ESTE,) January 23rd, 1876.

MY DEAR, BELOVED FRIEND,

Your letter has deeply affected me.   I preserve
it in the secret cell of the heart, where the last words
of my dear mother remain—and give me consolation.
I cannot thank you in words.   My thanks rise in
prayer to God.   May His blessing ever be with your
generosity and constancy in all that is good.

At the " Decisions of the Court of Cassation " (the
2nd October and 16th November) you spoke so forcibly
and beautifully clearly about blasphemy, and of the
symbol of redemption, the crucifix—and thus truly
fulfilled the teaching of our Saviour : " Thesaurizate
autem vobis thesauros in Cœlo."   Let us continue to
the end, dearest Eduard, in the love of Christ !

I absolutely wrote the " *Hunnenschlacht* " for the
sake of the hymn " Crux fidelis."   Kulke in a very
generous manner determined on the production of this
work in Vienna.   For very many years Kulke has
always been well-affected towards me.   I enclose a few

lines of thanks which I beg you to hand to him.   His "Moses before Pharaoh" I have, alas, not the *power* to compose.   To compose philosophy and politics in music appears to me an all-too-difficult task.   I almost doubt whether it could be accomplished.

Heartiest greetings to your family, and most truly yours,   F. LISZT.

I shall arrive in Pest again in the middle of February.

183. To Dr. EDUARD KULKE IN VIENNA.

MY DEAR SIR,

During long years you have constantly shown me so much kindness that I cannot sufficiently thank you for it.   I am also ashamed not to compose better works, so as to make the kindly interpretation of them more easy and pleasanter to you.   Nevertheless all the more valuable is your insight and indulgence.

The "feathered thief"[1] reconciles me with the "newspaper geese."   It will, without plagiarism, win its laurels on the stage.   The dialogue and action are full of humour and wit . . . and the final catastrophe of the thrashing must make an impression on the public.—

Excuse me, my dear Sir, if I do not feel myself equal to the task of an *Old-Testament* Oratorio.[2] Michael Angelo represented his *Moses* mighty and *horned* (perhaps as a most excellent ideal forerunner of Pope Julius II. ?); Rossini sang exquisitely the

---

[1] A comedy by the addressee, a well-known and meritorious author, and sent by him shortly before to Liszt.

[2] Kulke had sent a poem, "Moses before Pharaoh," to Liszt in Rome, with the question whether he would be inclined to make it the subject of an Oratorio.

"*preghiera di Mosè*," with which Europe is still enraptured; and Marx's Oratorio *Moses*, less well-known, contains many excellent parts.

"Non omnia possumus omnes." My humble self can do but little, and remains most humbly grateful to the "*Caritas Christi.*"

With especial regards and thanks, yours most truly,

VILLA D'ESTE, *January 23rd*, 1876.   F. LISZT.

184. TO MARIE LIPSIUS.

MY HONOURED PATRONESS,

Your kind promise to translate the "Chopin" into beautiful German rejoices me extremely. Hearty thanks for it. I will soon send the revised (French) copy, and I hope the work will be easy and pleasant to you. In the 3rd edition of "*Musikalische Studienköpfe*" I lately read "Berlioz"—an excellent characterisation and recognition of this extraordinarily great master, who perhaps hovers more in the untrodden regions of *genius* than anywhere else.

The addition of the "*index*" is a valuable completion of this third edition. Its success augurs well for *what will follow.*

With much respect and gratitude,

(VILLA D'ESTE,) *February 3rd*, 1876.   F. LISZT.

185. TO AUGUST VON TREFORT, THE HUNGARIAN MINISTER OF EDUCATION IN BUDAPEST.*

HERR MINISTER,

Although I scruple to weary the extraordinary good-will which the public of Budapest has evinced

---

* Printed in the *Pester Lloyd* of that date.—Addressee died 1888.

towards me, I nevertheless make so bold as to offer
the assistance of my two hands for the concert
shortly to be given in aid of the sufferers by the floods,
if Your Excellency is of opinion that this could still be
at all useful.   In the year 1838, when I returned for
the first time to Vienna, I gave my *first* concert there
in aid of the sufferers by the inundation at Pest.   It
will be a comfort to me if I can now *close* my
protracted career as virtuoso by the fulfilment of a
similar duty.[1]   I remain, until death, Hungary's true
and grateful son.

Your Excellency's most obedient

BUDAPEST, *March 1st,* 1876.   F. LISZT.

186. TO WALTER BACHE.

HONOURED AND DEAR FRIEND,

You, in your London "Annual Concerts," have
for 12 years worked more wonders than I was able
to compose in the *"Rosenwunder"* [Rose miracle] of
Elizabeth.   Hearty thanks for your account of the
12th concert, and all the exertions connected with it!

I beg you to present my most respectful compliments to Mrs. Osgood ("Elizabeth"), and, before
all, to Constance Bache, the kind translator of the
Legend.

Entirely approving of the use of the *mute* in the
passage

---

[1] The concert in aid of the sufferers by the floods in Budapest
took place with Liszt's co-operation on the 13th March, 1876.

and during the chorus of angels, remains, in sincere esteem for the steadfast conductor and friend Walter Bache, his faithful and grateful

F. Liszt.

Budapest, *March 8th,* 1876.

187. To Madame Jessie Laussot.

Dear excellent Friend,

The Commander Casamorata has written to me again about the *fête* of Bartolomeo Cristofori. I have replied to him that my answer had been already received by you in the month of January '75, and that I can only repeat the same · excuses. I copy the last lines of my letter to Casamorata that you may have the exact particulars :—

" Without reckoning that for more than thirty years I have not belonged to the active lists of pianists and only desire the honourable repose of an invalid, I permit myself to remark that the duty of celebrating the inventor of the pianoforte in Italy belongs by preference to Italian pianists of note, such as M. Buonamici (in Florence) and M. Sgambati (in Rome), etc."—

In conclusion, I scarcely could leave Germany all this summer (except for the visit to the Château de Loo), and I shall probably be obliged to return to Hungary after Bayreuth, where I hope still to find you.

Yours very devotedly,

F. Liszt.

Budapest, *March 9th,* 1876.

188. To Dr. Leopold Damrosch in New York.*

My dear honoured Friend,   *April 15th*, 1876.

    You have recommended our young friend Max
Pinner to me. He shows himself to be an excellent
artist, and I have become much attached to him.[1] I
beg you to accept through him the renewed expression
of my former faithful friendship.

    Your beautifully conceived and nobly executed work
Ruth I have read with sympathetic interest and pleasure.
I will not fail to suggest its performance in Germany.

    How shall I thank you for the edifying goodwill
which you manifest towards my compositions ? Your
intelligent enthusiastic conducting of my scores prevents
any one noticing the defects of the composition.

    A hearty greeting to your wife, and with warmest
esteem ever yours,   F. Liszt.

189. To Friedrich von Bodenstedt.†

My very honoured Friend,   *June 8th*, 1876.

    Your very agreeable and genial friend, Frau
Major von L., sends the September leaflet about the
concert in Hanover. A thousand thanks for it. . — .

    On the occasion of my happy 50 years' jubilee you
rejoiced me with a poem, of which I am proud. You
have admirably succeeded in coaxing such poetical

---

  * Draft of a letter from a copy by Dr. Mirus in Weimar.—Addressee
(1832—1885) came to Weimar in 1855 as a violinist under Liszt,
went to Breslau in 1858, and in 1871 to New York, where he had
great success and influence as a conductor.

  [1] Died young.

  † From a copy by Director Aug. Göllerich in Nürnberg.—Addressee,
who died in April 1892, the poet of Mirza Schaffy.

euphony from an old worn-out instrument like my humble self.

Au revoir in Hanover, and friendly greetings to your family.

With thanks, yours sincerely,   F. LISZT.

190. TO THE MUSIC PUBLISHER BESSEL.

SIR,

Although the music which you have been so obliging as to send me through Mr. Kahnt has not yet reached me, I hasten to assure you again of the strong interest which I take in the works of the new Russian composers—Rimski-Korsakoff, Cui, Tschaikowski, Balakireff, Borodine—which you edit. You know that lately, at the *Tonkünstler-Versammlung* at Altenburg, the Ballade "Sadko" was well performed and received. Next year I shall propose that other works of the above-named Russian composers be produced. They are worth serious attention in musical Europe.

When you return to Weimar in July I shall better express to you my thanks and regards.

WEIMAR, *June 20th*, 1876.   F. LISZT.

Kindly give the accompanying note to Mr. Cui.

191. TO PRINCE CARL LICHNOWSKY.*

YOUR MOST SERENE HIGHNESS AND FRIEND,

In old attachment I thank you heartily for your kind lines.

* Communicated to the *Musical Chronicle*, 20th February, 1888, by A. Göllerich.—Addressee is the brother of Liszt's intimate friend, Prince Felix Lichnowsky, who, as a member of the Parliament of Frankfort, fell on the Heath at Bornheim [Bornheimer Haide], a sacrifice to the Revolution of 1848.

The most grateful recollections ever bind me to the House of *Lichnowsky*. Your highly endowed father and your admirable brother *Feliz* showed not less kindness to me, than Prince Carl Lichnowsky showed before that to the young Beethoven, who dedicated his Opus I. (3 Trios) to the Prince *Lichnowsky*, and felt himself quite at home in the so-called *Krzizanowitz* "Palace," and in the Castle of *Grätz*.[1] May it be permitted, dear Prince, to find you again there (perhaps next year) to

Your faithful and most devoted

F. LISZT.

June 21st, 1876.

192. To HOFCAPELLMEISTER MAX ERDMANNSDÖRFER.

VERY HONOURED FRIEND,

Thanking you very much for your kind invitation, I shall willingly come next Sunday, and rejoice that I shall again hear a special *Sondershausen* concert. Berlioz's Harold-Symphony is to me an old, ever-fresh recollection : the Sondershausen orchestra played it capitally at the first Festival of the *Music of the Future* in Ballenstedt, which I conducted.

Send me *soon* the whole printed programme. Can you already conduct Wagner's new *Fest Marsch* ?

I beg for Bülow's " Nirwana," if possible, and in case there should be room for anything, not long, of mine, I would most modestly suggest the Symphonic Poem " *Hamlet*," which I never heard.

---

[1] Krzizanowitz is Lichnowsky's inherited estate in Prussian Silesia, the Castle of Grätz his dominion in Austrian Silesia. Franz Liszt like Beethoven, was a guest in both these places.

Most friendly greetings to your wife, and believe
me always

Yours most sincerely,

F. Liszt.

Weimar, *June 27th,* 1876.

I suppose the concert takes place on Sunday *afternoon,* so that the visitors from Weimar can get back
here again ?

Which train, in the lately altered railway guide—
as I was told yesterday—will bring me *in tempo* (non
rubato) [in time—not broken] to Sondershausen and
back ?—

193. To Kornel von Abrányi.

Dear honoured Friend,

Best thanks for your letter. Please to make my
apologies to the mayor Herr Károly and to the Festival
Committee in Szégédin.[1] With reference to the first
invitation to Szégédin (last March) I made the observation immediately that " During the whole month of
August I belong to Bayreuth." Consequently it is no
fault to remain there,—if the principle is correct.

Now, dear faithful friend, I invite you once again to
come hither. The *" Festival-Play "* is of the very
most serious historical significance. . . . So do come at
the latest from the 27th till the 30th August for the
third series of these stupendous performances of the
Nibelung's Ring.

[1] The town of Szégédin and the Hungarian Vocal Society had
begged Liszt's active sympathy for the Musical and Singers' Festival
about to be held in that place. Karl Wagner was president of the
Festival Committee.

The *Montecuculi*-an matters will be gladly arranged for you here [1] by

Your old, most sincerely faithful

F. LISZT.

BAYREUTH, *August 6th*, 1876.

194. TO RICHARD WAGNER.*

INCREDIBLE ONE,

Hast thou a moment's time for the Leipzig "*affaire*"? then please come down here (where Herr Neumann *now* is) to thine own

F. L.[2]

[BAYREUTH, *August*, 1876.]

195. TO THE KAMMERSÄNGERIN [PRIVATE CONCERT SINGER TO THE COURT] MARIE BREIDENSTEIN IN ERFURT.[3]

DEAR HONOURED ONE,

Perhaps the Schubert songs with my most modest instrumentation would suit somewhere in your programme. Here are the printed scores with the orchestral parts.

---

[1] *I.e.* the expenses.

* Autograph of this curiosity in possession of Herrn Commerzienrath Bösendorfer in Vienna.

[2] This referred to the performance of the *Nibelungen* in Leipzig, striven for by Angelo Neumann and interceded for by Liszt, for which purpose the former came to Bayreuth.—Wagner wrote in pencil on Liszt's letter as follows:—

"STILL MORE INCREDIBLE ONE!

"I am in my shirt-sleeves, and under *no* circumstances inclined to give my work to Leipzig or anywhere else!

"Love me!   Thy   R. W."

[3] Died 1892. She dedicated herself with satisfaction to the rendering of Liszt's compositions, and was also his pupil for piano.

"Gretchen" and "Erlkönig" have been much used and are played out. This is not so much the case with the "Young Nun"; and Mignon's wonderful song, "*So lasst mich scheinen bis ich werde*" [So let me seem till I become], is scarcely heard—or appreciated !

But if you will once more spare me an hour in Weimar, I will accompany these 4 *instrumented* Schubert-Songs for you.

Next Saturday departs from here

Your sincerely devoted
F. LISZT.

WEIMAR, *Monday, September* 18*th*, 1876.

N.B.—The instrumentation compelled me to a few little different readings in Schubert's four songs : on this account the singer must go by my score-edition as regards the rests and the very slight alterations.

196. To CAMILLE SAINT-SAËNS.

VERY DEAR FRIEND,

In sending you to-day the transcription of your "Danse macabre," I beg you to excuse my unskilfulness in reducing the marvellous colouring of the score to the possibilities of the piano. No one is bound by the impossible. To play an orchestra on the piano is not yet given to any one. Nevertheless we must always stretch towards the *Ideal* across all the more or less dogged and insufficient forms. It seems to me that Life and Art are only good for that.

In sincere admiration and friendship,

Your very devoted
F. LISZT.

HANOVER, *October* 2*nd*, 1876.

197. TO PROFESSOR L. A. ZELLNER, GENERAL SECRETARY OF THE CONSERVATOIRE OF MUSIC IN VIENNA.*

October 31st, 1876.

HONOURED FRIEND,

Be so very kind as to convey my sincere thanks to Directors Mosenthal and Herbeck for the friendly communication about the Beethoven-Monument Concerts in Vienna next March.   A few weeks earlier I beg you to send me the programmes, to which Beethoven's Concerto in E♭ major, and also as a Finale, in case the " Hammerclavier " appears admissible, the Choral Fantasia, will willingly be added with his old hands by

Your faithful and most obedient

F. LISZT.

198. TO HANS RICHTER, CONDUCTOR OF THE ROYAL OPERA IN VIENNA.†

November 10th, 1876.

I thank you most sincerely for your friendly intention of giving my Beethoven-Cantata in the performance at the Royal Opera House for the benefit of the monument to Beethoven.   By to-day's post you will receive the whole printed score, together with a separate edition of the orchestrated Andante (from the B♭ major Trio), which shines, like a guiding star, above my insignificant work.

* From a copy of a draft by Dr. Mirus in Weimar.

† From a copy by Dr. Mirus in Weimar.—Addressee (born 1843 in Hungary) the renowned conductor, since 1876, of the Bayreuth *Festspiel*, and, in addition to his opera work in Vienna, conductor of the Philharmonic Concerts there and of the Richter-Concerts in London.

The Cantata was published by Kahnt, Leipzig, in the year 1870, and was also first brought out in Weimar, then in Pest, on the occasion of the Beethoven Jubilee Celebration. If, my dear Sir, the orchestration to some extent pleases you, I should advise you to take up this *alone* in your programme on the 15th December. The remaining movements might meet with many hindrances in Vienna . . . and, frankly, I have become altogether somewhat shy as regards the performance of my compositions. Although I quietly endure their foregone want of success with prevailing criticism, it is my duty not to let my friends be injured by it.

Once again hearty thanks for your goodwill and meritorious conducting of Wagner.

F. Liszt.

199. To Breitkopf and Härtel.

Dear Sirs,

Your communication to me of the 25th October has been very much delayed, owing to my change of residence several times during the past weeks. There is surely no need to assure you that I never thought of causing any unpleasantness at all to any one—more especially judicially.[1] In particular my connection with your very honourable house for more than 30 years has ever been most simple and honest. This is also shown by my two quoted letters of the 17th February and 3rd April, 1853, with reference to the publication by your firm of the "Tannhäuser and Lohengrin pieces,"

---

[1] The publisher of *Tannhäuser* had tried to make out that Liszt's arrangement of the March was a "piracy."

whose publication at that time I was quite "*in agree-ment*" with Richard Wagner in suggesting.

Certainly I could not, without injuring the Tann-häuser March, go all through the original, *loading it with shakes*, and here and there adding *arpeggios*.   However, if "connoisseurs" will look through my transcription in detail, they will easily discover that neither the varia-tion on the principal theme, nor the modulating of the second, nor in any manner the whole setting of the pianoforte arrangement, could be found fault with as a "*piracy*."

With much esteem,

Very sincerely yours,

F. LISZT.

November 12th, 1876.
BUDAPEST (where I stay the whole winter).

200. TO CONSTANTIN SANDER, MUSIC PUBLISHER IN LEIPZIG.[*]

VERY HONOURED SIR,

Best thanks for kindly sending me the "collected writings of Hector Berlioz" and some novelties of your firm.   The compositions of Tschaikowsky interest me.   A few of my pupils here play his Concerto and several of his pieces really capitally.   I have also recommended Riedel to include Tschaikowsky's Symphony in the programme of the next *Tonkünstler-Versammlung.*

Otto Reubke's arrangement of the Schubert Quartet [1] for one performer on the pianoforte seems to me well

---

[*] Autograph in possession of M. Alfred Bovet in Valentigney.
[1] In A minor, published by Sander (F. E. C. Leuckart).

done, though the 3rd bar of the first Allegro should
stand thus,—

because in the latter case the important E of the melody
cannot be held on, etc.—

I know the manuscript of an *excellent* arrangement
of Schubert's D minor Quartet for 2 hands, the author
of which, a man of very high standing, I do not to-day
mention by name. But should you be inclined to
publish this Quartet (arranged for 2 hands on the P.F.)
I will gladly give you further particulars.—

By to-day's post you receive my last revision of
Berlioz's *Symphonie fantastique.* I have added two
remarks to the title which I beg you to notice and
adhere to. Thus " *Piano Score"*—not *Arrangement. . . .*
Then it is absolutely necessary to insert the whole
programme of Berlioz, French and German, in your
2nd edition (on the 1st page after the title-page). If
necessary my friend Richard Pohl will give you the
original French text and the translation.

With sincere regard, yours in all friendship,

BUDAPEST, *November 15th,* 1876.   F. LISZT.

P.S.—I keep the copy of the *Witzendorf* edition for
a while, and send you to-day only the Paris edition,
together with the last proof copy of the Symphonie
fantastique.

201. TO BREITKOPF AND HÄRTEL.

November 23rd, 1876.

DEAR SIR AND FRIEND,

Before Herr W. Juranyi handed me your letter I had replied to the earlier communication from your esteemed house with reference to the same matter.

Accept once again the assurance that I lay great stress upon the continuation of our friendly relations, which have now existed for 36 years. As far as this depends on me it shall never cease.

Your letter contains two proposals :—

1. To recommend Wagner to sign a legal document.

This is entirely opposed to my peaceable practices.

2. To prepare an *enlarged* version of the transcription of the " Tannhäuser-March."

Acquiescing in this, I will send you the day after to-morrow a couple of pages of notes [musical] for the purpose of an enlarged edition. I cannot decide whether these acquire a *legal* value, but in any case they prove to you, dear Sir, my sincere readiness.

My *Wagner-Transcriptions,* by-the-by, were not in any way a matter of speculation to me. Appearing at the beginning of the fifties, when only the Weimar theatre had the honour of performing *Tannhäuser, Lohengrin* and the *Flying Dutchman,* such transcriptions only served as modest propaganda on the inadequate Piano for the sublime genius of Wagner, whose radiating glory now and henceforth belongs to the Pride of Germany.

With high esteem most sincerely yours,

BUDAPEST, *November 23rd,* 1876.   F. LISZT.

202. To the Music Publisher Constantin Sander.

Very honoured Sir,

You have rightly guessed that Herr von Keudell's "*excellent*" transcription of Schubert's D minor Quartet is finished. It now only remains for you to write to His Excellency, that you may put this work in your window.

Reubke has succeeded very well with the B minor Rondo of Schubert, only, to my thinking, he should add the now indispensable pedal marks to it. By the same post I send you his manuscript together with a few remarks, and beg you to thank Reubke for his friendly dedication, and also to compliment him especially on the refined and beautifully effective carrying out of the subject—

Yours most truly,
F. Liszt.

Budapest, *November 29th*, 1876.

203. To Vera Timanoff.[1]

Dear Virtuosa,

I telegraphed immediately to you at Laibach, to tell you to come without ceremony. Your talent is such that it would convert even the Turks, and I assure

[1] First Tausig's pupil (also Rubinstein's for a little while), from 1875 she studied every summer with Liszt as long as he remained in Weimar. In 1880 she became pianist to the Court at Weimar.

you that the audience at the Pest concerts will be
delighted to applaud you. As to the title which you
propose to take, I think it is too modest for you, but
there would be an excess of modesty on my part in
saying anything against it . . . so let us be reciprocally
proud of it and don't let us advertise it !

A revoir soon,—and always

Your affectionately devoted

F. Liszt.

Budapest, *November 29th*, 1876.

Be so kind as to give my most cordial regards to
Monsieur and Madame Bösendorfer.

204. To Otto Reubke at Halle-on-the-Saale.[1]

Dear Herr Reubke,

Your Arrangement[2] pleases me uncommonly. I
beg you to notice the alterations I have made on the
accompanying sheet of music-paper. This version is
not quite so much like the original as yours, but, as
the great thing is to bring out a *fortissimo*, we may well
allow inaccuracies of this kind in favour of the performer
and of effect.—

You are requested to add to your *excellent* Arrangement of the Schubert Rondo much *pedal* and some
fingering,

By your warmly attached

F. Liszt.

Budapest, *November*, 1876.

[1] Now Music Director at the University there.
[2] Of Schubert's B minor duet for pianoforte alone.

205. To Marianne Brandt, Kammersängerin in Berlin.

December 3rd, 1876.

Dear honoured Friend,

What is always very pleasant and dear to me is your goodwill. With my hearty thanks for it I send to-day the little notice. "*Jeanne d'Arc au bûcher*" * came out a few months ago at Schott's (Mainz). This short dramatic Scena can be sung with either pianoforte or orchestral accompaniment. The chorus is conspicuous by its absence. Johanna [*Jeanne*] alone has to perform. N.B.—Only the second edition (published 1876) is to be used ; not the first, which also came out at Schott's 30 years ago. Schott sent me no copy of it ; it was too much trouble for Berlin to correspond with Mainz viâ Budapest. Herr Capellmeister Mannstädt [1] will therefore be so kind as to order the " Johanna " (full score and piano score) at Schott's, if you really have the goodness to sing it. [2] There might possibly be special feelings now in Berlin against it, in spite of Schiller's Tragedy, "*Die Jungfrau von Orleans.*" Therefore think the matter over.

For years past I have been mostly obliged to dissuade people from the performance of my large works. The general public usually goes by what is said by the critics, whose most prominent organs among the newspapers are hostile to me. Why should I go into useless quarrels and thereby compromise my friends ? Peace

---

* Joan of Arc at the Stake.

[1] Now Capellmeister at the Court theatre in Wiesbaden.

[2] It was done in honour of Liszt's presence in Berlin, which was celebrated by the performance of some of his works.

and order are the first duties of citizens, which I have doubly to fulfil both as honourable citizen and artist.

As for the rest, dear friend, if it suits you to sing any one of my musical compositions, be assured of the sincerest thanks of

Yours most truly,

F. LISZT.

206. TO THE COMMITTEE OF THE BEETHOVEN MONUMENT IN VIENNA.*

December 10th, 1876.

HONOURED GENTLEMEN,

Rejoiced to be able to help you, I will work with you with a full heart and both hands in the concert for the Beethoven Monument.

Allow me to answer your friendly remark about the performance of Beethoven's Choral Fantasia thus,— that I should not think of performing any other work at this concert than one absolutely written by Beethoven, and consequently my share in the concert programme will consist of the E♭ major Concerto.[1]

I beg you will kindly communicate to the honoured Secretary of the Committee, Herr Zellner, my hints with regard to the Beethoven Scholarship in Leipzig.

Accept, Gentlemen, the expression of my high esteem.

F. LISZT.

* From a copy by Dr. Mirus in Weimar.

[1] It did not consist of that. Liszt did after all play the Pianoforte Part of the Choral Fantasia, Op. 80.

207. To Eduard von Liszt.

BUDAPEST, *January 2nd,* 1877.

DEAREST, MOST HONOURED COUSIN,

I always remain faithful to thee in heartiest agreement with thy thoughts and feelings. Every year brings us nearer to the fulfilment of our hope in Jesus Christ the Saviour !

" He that endureth to the end shall be saved ! "—

I am now quite recovered from my little attack. If there were nothing worse in this world than sprained legs and physical suffering, one could be quite satisfied. Moreover I belong to the very favoured and happy ones, even as regards physical suffering.

There is nothing particular going on here which I need mention. Four times weekly I have a class for pianists and pianistes, native and foreign. Half a dozen of these distinguish themselves and will be able to grow into capable public artists. Unfortunately there are far too many concerts and concert-players. As Dingelstedt quite truly said, " The theatre is a necessary evil, the concert a superfluous one." I am trying to impress this sentence on my disciples of the Hungarian Academy of Music.

As you know, Budapest possesses three musical Institutions : the Conservatorium (which has existed 36 years and counts several hundred scholars), the Hungarian Theatrical School, and the new and still small Academy of Music. An excellent younger friend of mine, Count Geza Zichy, is president of the Conservatorium ; an older one, Count Leo Festetics, president of the Theatrical School ; and my humble self acts in

the same position at the Academy of Music, whose
Director Franz Erkel and General Secretary Abrányi
proceed most zealously and judiciously. I have only
pleasant relations with them both, and the Minister
Trefort is already well-disposed towards me, because
he knows that I save him unnecessary annoyance and
expense. Most likely the Academy of Music will in
two years' time be so flourishing that there will be more
to say about it; in the meantime let us study—and be
silent. . — .

Heartiest greetings to thy family, and *au revoir* in
Schottenhof[1] in the middle of March, on the occasion
of the " Beethoven-Monument Concerts."

Thy
F. Liszt.

The Christmas week has beggared me. Be so good
as to send me very quickly 500 gulden, for I have
hardly 60 left.

208. To Walter Bache.

Truly, dear Bache, you are a *wonder-working*
friend. Your persevering trouble, exertions, expenditure of time and money for the production of my bitterly-
criticised compositions in London during the past
fifteen years, are among the most uncommon occurrences
in the annals of Art. Once again heartiest thanks;
please also to thank Mr. Manns properly for his excellent
conducting of " Mazeppa." Things of that kind are
awkward both for conductors and performers. But
how can one go on making music with what is idly

---

[1] Eduard Liszt's home in Vienna.

convenient, even when this is raised into importance under the guise of being classical ?

Hueffer's translation of Wagner's letter pleases me. Friendly greeting to Hueffer [1] and Dannreuther [2] from
Your grateful and very devoted
F. Liszt.

Budapest, *March 9th*, 1877.

At the beginning of April I shall be back in Weimar. I am pleased that you included the old "Loreley," with fresh orchestral accompaniments, in your concert programme. Give my respectful compliments to the friendly singer Mrs. Osgood.

209. To Eduard von Liszt.

Weimar, *July 3rd*, 1877.

Dearest Eduard,

For some weeks I have been much on the go and disturbed in many ways. Several musical performances occasioned me to go about in the neighbourhood. On the 17th June some portions of the *Christus* Oratorio were splendidly sung in the Thomaskirche (Leipzig) by the *Riedel Verein*. Last Friday *Elizabeth* came brilliantly to the fore again in Eisenach, and yesterday Gille, my untiring friend of many years' standing, arranged a large concert of sacred music (with several items of mine), at which I was present.

I do indeed regret that I am not able to accept *in person* the kind invitation of my beloved nephew Franz for his wedding-day. It would be much better for me

---

[1] Musical author in London, lately deceased.
[2] Musician in London

to be more with you all ! . . . Enclosed are a few words to Franz. Arrange for my proxy as a *witness* at the marriage ceremony. Whoever is chosen by you will be worthy and right to me : as for me I should choose my friend Bösendorfer.

I go the day after to-morrow to Berlin for two days ; then I am bidden farther and nearer till the end of July. I shall respectfully announce to the *Frau Fürstin* [Princess] my arrival in Rome—beginning of August. Please send me here on the 20th July the money for the journey, and something over—about 1200 marks [about £60]. I must not have any other debts except *moral ones.* Our name Liszt in the Hungarian language means *Flour* : we will provide good wheaten meal " ex adipe frumenti " with thee, Franz, and thy children.

Truly devoted,

F. L.

. — . I shall visit you in the middle of November on the return journey from Rome to Pest,—where I think of spending the winter, as formerly.

Heartiest greetings to your wife and Marie.

210. TO LUDWIG BÖSENDORFER.

HONOURED FRIEND,

You have been just as much a pianoforte maker as I have been, and still remain, alas ! an almost *posthumous* pianoforte player.

My friend Berlioz asked : " Do you believe that I can listen to music for my pleasure ? " Nevertheless we intend to continue our Music and Piano "for our good pleasure."

Thanks for letter and telegram.

Heartily devoted,

F. LISZT.

WEIMAR, *July 12th,* 1877.

211. TO EDMUND VON MIHALOVICH.

. ‒‒. In order to obtain this performance [1] I think it necessary and indispensable (as I have already told you) that you should lay a regular siege *in person* to the Intendant, the Capellmeister, and the singers, male and female, of the theatre which you choose.

The new *serious* Operas are now regarded with suspicion and are in disgrace everywhere. Several trials have been made of them here and there of late years. In the happiest of them the public applauded warmly during the first performances, and abstained from attending the following ones. Consequently the coffers remained empty : ergo, it is the receipts which prove real success. If Wagner's marvellous *chefs d'œuvre* hold their own in the *repertoire*, it is because they make money and continue to draw even a large contingent of detractors. . ‒‒.

WEIMAR, *July 20th,* 1877.

Towards the middle of August I shall be in Rome, and shall stay at the Villa d'Este until my return to Pest in November.

[1] Of Mihalovich's Opera *Hagbar.*

212. To Kornel von Abrányi.

WEIMAR, *July 28th*, 1877.

HONOURED FRIEND,

Dear Secretary-General of the "Zene Akadémia,"[1] Sincere thanks for your significant communication, which I answer immediately, point by point.[2]

1. The conclusion of the year '77 with the examination concerts (25 to 28 June—and the "Magyar Hangverseny"[3] on the 30th June) has been very gratifying. Let us rejoice in the praiseworthy performances of Messrs. Juhász, Agghází, Swoboda, and of the ladies Frau Knapp, Fräulein Lépessy,[4] etc., in Counterpoint, Harmony, Composition, Æsthetics, Hungarian music and the indispensable Piano-playing.

The work best praises the Master: in like manner do the pupils, when preparing themselves for preeminence, praise their teacher. The "Zene Akadémia" has not to work for the universally usual kind of musical study, but has indeed a weightier, higher task to fulfil.

2. The publication of your "Academic lectures" I had especially recommended to His Excellency Minister Trefort. "Suitable teaching and departmental books" *printed* in the Hungarian language are inaccessible. You, my honoured Secretary-General,

---

[1] *I.e.* Academy of Music of the Country.

[2] Abrányi had informed Liszt, as President of the Academy, of the course of instruction (1877) and concerts, and had also asked him for his opinion on several Art questions.

[3] An Hungarian Concert.

[4] The above-mentioned were favourite pupils of the Master at the Academy.

have to look after that,—and the Minister will certainly support your scientific-patriotic work for the use and benefit of learners and teachers at the " Zene Akadémia " —and further, in all Hungary.

3. As to the " Plan of classes in the department for Church music, Singing and Organ," I can now only repeat my previously expressed wish that the right and able person of good working capability may be found for conducting these classes. Neither invalids nor dabblers may officiate at No. 4, Fischplatz![1]— If unfortunately the right reverend Herr F. Witt should continue unable to fill the post offered to him in Budapest, I shall propose that the new director should come for a year *on trial*. And a complaisant sort of Protection is thereby to be avoided, for the matter in question is nothing less than the worthy thriving and culture of Church music in Hungary.

4. I consider as necessary the appointment of an experienced Pianoforte Professor, one who is pushing forwards, and who will be able to relieve our highly honoured Director Herr F. Erkel of a part of his very meritorious but excessive exertions. Meanwhile I protest *strongly* against desiring to have a professorship without salary. Fees with *honour*; judicious restrictions without beggarly management; otherwise we shall come to grief.

5. I beg that my " jubilee-stipend," entrusted to me in the most honourable manner by the municipality of Budapest, may next year ('78) be apportioned to *the same* artists as this year. I will gladly sign all the papers having reference to this.

[1] Liszt's house, and, for the time, the *locale* of the Academy.

Looking forward to the speedy appearance of your *Study of Harmony*, and of the collected writings of our never-to-be-forgotten friend Mosonyi, together with his biography and Abrányi's new compositions, and greeting your laudable and persistent endeavours in the cause of Art with sympathetic recognition,

I remain, with best regards, yours truly,

F. LISZT.

Next week I journey farther—shall be in Rome by the middle of August—and in November in Pest, where I intend to spend the winter again. Write to me in September: my address will be Villa d'Este, Tivoli, (presso) *Roma, Italia.*

I beg you to give the enclosed lines to Frau Knapp.

213. TO THE MUSIC PUBLISHER CONSTANTIN SANDER.

VERY DEAR SIR,

I shall have much pleasure in preparing the re-discovered manuscript of the Harold Symphony (Score for Piano and Alto) *for the press* and in entrusting it to you. Send me the manuscript soon, together with the *original score* of Berlioz, which is necessary for the accurate revision of the arrangement. My fee shall be a moderate one, as I am pleased that your firm is going to publish this arrangement, which was finished in Switzerland forty years ago. I would have made it public long since, if the manuscript had not been lost.

Sincerely yours,

F. LISZT.

VILLA D'ESTE, TIVOLI (near *Rome*), *September 5th*, 1877.

Please send with it a copy of the excellent Trio of Eduard Nápravnik. My friend Sgambati will produce it publicly in Rome, and make it a success.

214. To Adelheid von Schorn at Weimar.

Dear and honoured One,

When one is at a loss what to say or write, well—one tries to help oneself with music.

Enclosed I forward you the song of your noble-hearted mother : " Ach, was ist Leben doch so schwer ! " [Ah, why is life so burdensome !] My *setting* is so managed that you will easily master it, as well in the singing as in the accompaniment.[1]

Faithfully yours,

F. Liszt.

Rome, *September 15th,* 1877.

215. To Breitkopf and Härtel.

Honoured Sirs,

. — . May my slight share in your edition of Chopin's works, which nearly all belong to your firm, be of use to you. I remarked before how little really remains to be done to Chopin's compositions, as he himself, with praiseworthy and exceptional accuracy, added every possible instruction to the performer—even to the pedal indications, which in no other author appear so frequently.—Your collaborators will certainly find accuracy and authenticity of the original text in Karl Klindworth's Moscow edition of Chopin.

[1] Published in the 8th book of Songs under the title " Sei still " [Be still].

I chose the *Etudes*, because the first volume was dedicated to me, and the second too for the matter of that (at that time). I gladly dispense with a revision of both, and beg you particularly, dear Sirs, not to expose me to an unseemly rivalry. I will always maintain a most peaceful attitude towards my honoured colleagues, and, wherever they please, allow their influence and opinion to have free play.

According to your letter, you repudiate the idea of " an instructive edition with other additions " of Chopin's works. Are then the directions for fingering also to be omitted ? . . . All the more undisturbed will the leisure of the collaborators be.—

Last week I sent you the corrections of the "Triomphe funèbre du Tasse," as well as the " Impromptu." To-morrow "Héroïde funèbre" (for four hands) will follow, and very soon I am expecting the " Hunnenschlacht," which completes all the arrangements for four hands of the 12 *Symphonic Poems*. A complete edition of them in 3 or 4 volumes (as you may judge best) will be a pleasure to me.

In spite of the much criticising, ignoring, and de-nunciation, which these things have had to suffer for 20 years, they are perhaps not yet quite done to death.

I beg you to add the *Prefaces* and *Poems* (French and German) to the edition for four hands, as well as to the scores, and also to the further editions for 2 pianos. The same with regard to the transcription for piano of the " Triomphe funèbre " (Italian and German), because, as a matter of fact, a well-disposed *programme composer* uses such hints more than is generally supposed.

Of course the dedication of the "Impromptu"—"à Madame la Baronne Olga de Meyendorff, née Princesse Gortschakoff"—must not be left out.

With distinguished respect,

Your obedient

F. LISZT.

VILLA D'ESTE, *September 26th,* 1877.

Till the end of October my address will be: 43, Via dei Greci, Roma (Italia). From the middle of November: Budapest (Hungary).

216. TO FRAU INGEBORG VON BRONSART IN HANOVER.

DEAR KIND FRIEND,

I am much touched by your charming letter, and grieved at not being able to accept your friendly invitation. That would certainly be more agreeable than to attend to all sorts of duties; but, since three parts of these are self-imposed, I am all the more bent upon fulfilling them; and, in order to keep faith with *myself,* I am returning to Budapest before the middle of November, and shall remain there till April. Perhaps I am less useless there than elsewhere; it is an idea or an illusion of mine.

What excellent and beautiful things the *two Hans* are going to do at Hanover![1] It is a matter of lively joy to me, and next summer I hope that my ears will benefit by the new musical régime all in honour of Art, and the example of which will be of service and bear fruit far and wide.

Last week I forwarded from the author to your

---

[1] Hans von Bülow had been appointed Hofcapellmeister in Hanover, where Hans von Bronsart was Intendant of the theatre.

address a copy of Sgambati's Quintet, dedicated to Bülow ; and also a Fugue (preceded by a grand Prelude and ending in a Chorale—the same which Guido d'Arezzo made use of to name the six notes of the gamut : " *Ut* queant laxis *re*sonare fibris, etc. ! " . . . One of the two Hans will tell you the rest of the hymn, which is always chanted on the 24th June, the feast of St. John the Baptist).

Once on a time you used to cultivate fugues with *maèstria* : will that of Sgambati seem to you classical enough ? I almost doubt it, since in these matters your strictness is extreme. In consequence of H.M. the Queen of the Netherlands being in mourning, the "auditions" at the château of Loo do not take place this year. I shall therefore go straight from here to Pest.

Please give my love to your children, and believe me to be for all time the heartily devoted friend of their papa and mamma.

F. LISZT.

(VILLA D'ESTE,) *October 21st,* 1877.

217. TO EDUARD VON LISZT.

DEAREST EDUARD,

. — . I am told that one or two newspapers announce that I am going to Paris. I have no thought of doing so, and am moreover very weary of travelling. What I should prefer would be to remain firmly fixed in one place, it matters not what, village or city, till my end, and to go on as quietly as possible with my work. As this is not permitted to me, I try at least to avoid unnecessary perambulations, do not go (in spite of various invitations) to Paris or London, and keep within that already far too extensive and troublesome triangle, Pest, Weimar, Rome !—So I shall again spend the next four months here, and then, at the beginning of April, pay you a week's visit.

Write and tell me where my dear cousin Marie is.[1] Is her husband established in Wiener-Neustadt, and in what capacity ?

How are *our* Franz in Graz and his wife ?

Heartiest greetings to the Frau *Generalissimus-Procuratorin* [2] from your heartily and faithfully affectionate

F. Liszt.

Budapest (Fischplatz, 4), *November 23rd, 1877.*

All friendly greetings to Bösendorfer.

218. To Jules de Zarembski.[3]

Dear Friend,

Thinking that you would spend some weeks at Berlin, I sent the day before yesterday a letter for you to our friend Bösendorfer, begging him to have it punctually delivered to you. This letter enclosed another, which you will remit to Paris to Madame la Comtesse Taida Rczewazska. She promised me lately at Rome to take an interest in your success at Paris, and I assured her that your talent and intellectual gifts would not make her patronage irksome. Therefore be careful not to give me the lie, and to show

---

[1] She had shortly before married Baron von Saar, an officer.

[2] Eduard v. L. had in December 1875 become General Procurator. Liszt called his wife in joke "Generalissima" or "Generalin."

[3] A highly gifted pupil of Liszt, born in 1854 in Russian Poland, died in 1885 at Brussels, where he was Professor in the Conservatoire.

yourself of an amiable disposition at Countess Rcze-wazska's.

I forgot to ask her where she lives in Paris ; but you will find out without difficulty from some compatriot, or from other people of the world, which is society.

Enclosed are a few lines of introduction to the illustrious, indefatigable and unageing publicist, Emile de Girardin. They say of him in joke that he has an idea every day. If he were to reach the age of Methuselah ideas would certainly never fail him.

At one time there used to be music in his *salon;* he understands it quite as well as the late M. Thiers or the Maréchal MacMahon. However, if M. de Girardin invites you, play there, as I did when I was last in Paris (in the year '66).—

An excellent recipe against unjust criticisms (of the kind like that of M. X. which you quote to me) is to criticise oneself thoroughly before and after—and finally to remain perfectly calm and follow one's own road !

Cordially yours,

BUDAPEST, *December* 13*th*, 1877. F. LISZT.

An enthusiastic account of your success at Vienna was given me by Mme. Tony Raal, who yesterday evening played Tausig's " Zigeunerweisen " admirably at a concert of M. de Swert.[1]

219. To MADAME JESSIE LAUSSOT.

DEAR AND MOST EXCELLENT FRIEND,

Your " intrigues " are noble, salutary, beneficent, and would win every advantage in the broad light of

---

[1] A Belgian violoncellist, recently deceased.

day.[1]   To take my part in them, at your command, is one of my most agreeable duties.

I sent my letter direct to Rome to Baron de Keudell yesterday. . — . Bazzini deserves the post of director of the Conservatoire at Milan, which ought to be offered to him at the first onset.

Your most heartily devoted

F. LISZT.

BUDAPEST, *January 29th*, 1878.

Our friend Mihalovich will give you news of Budapest. As elsewhere, I am absorbed here in the most difficult of tasks—to put up with myself. Happily I receive plenty of help; noble friendships and dear and beautiful memories light up the path which I still have to follow before I reach the grave.

220. To MADAME JESSIE LAUSSOT.

DEAR AND EXCELLENT FRIEND,

Under present circumstances (indicated in your note of this evening) I doubt whether your just and noble efforts will attain their end.[2]

Without pretending to Catonism, it is a good thing to attach oneself to good causes, whether favoured by the gods or not.

"Victrix causa diis placuit." . . . So, if you are

---

[1] Mme. Laussot was trying to obtain the nomination of Antonio Bazzini, the excellent violinist and composer (born 1818), as director of the Conservatoire at Milan, and begged Liszt to support this choice through the German ambassador Baron Keudell in Rome, which he did. Bazzini however did not at that time receive the office, which he at present holds.

[2] Refers to the as yet unsuccessful candidature of Bazzini for the directorship of the Milan Conservatoire. See the preceding letter.

vanquished on the battle-field between the Cathedral
and the Conservatoire of Milan, I shall remain on *your*
side, in spite of my reasonable leaning towards *Cæsar*,
and the lawful inheritors of his *idea*, . . . not towards
the others, please, because that would drag me too low
and roll me in the mire.

From my heart your old servant and friend,

F. Liszt.

Budapest, *February 3rd,* 1878.

221. To the Music Publisher B. Bessel.

Dear Sir,

You have been unusually parsimonious in only
sending me a single copy of the Ballade of Count
Tolstoy.[1] Allow me then to make use of this copy to
indicate the *version* which I think should be put into
the arrangement for piano (alone without declamation).
I add the necessary notes and alterations, for you to
publish or not, as you think best, the *version* subjoined.
I have no claim to the sale of my wares, and am only
manufacturing them . . . for the honour of Castile!—
Count Tolstoy understood this sentiment; he only has
to make a bargain: that is why I have sung with
Tolstoy his Ballade of the " Blind Bard," hoping too
for " peace " at last " for all noble boyars."* You sent
me some other publications of your house: " six
morceaux pour piano " by Liadoff; they are pleasantly
refined; and the " Russian national songs edited by N.
Rimsky-Korsakoff," for whom I feel high esteem and

---

[1] "The Blind Bard." Liszt wrote the melodramatic piano accompaniment to it (1874).

* Slavonic noblemen.

sympathy. To speak frankly, Russian national music could not be more felt or better understood than by Rimsky-Korsakoff. His *notation* of the "*popular songs*" is most intelligent and most musical; and the accompaniment and harmonies seem to me admirably *adequate*. If you publish the version for piano of Tolstoy's Ballades I beg you to send me the proofs beforehand.

A thousand affectionate compliments.

F. LISZT.

BUDAPEST, *March 11th,* 1878.

Please send me in any case half a dozen copies of the "Ballade," already printed, to Weimar, where I remain from mid-April till the end of July.

222. TO WALTER BACHE.

VERY HONOURED AND DEAR FRIEND,

I have always to be thanking you; it is from my heart, and will ever be so.

The programme of your fourteenth "Annual Concert" is again an act of courage; particularly in London, where my compositions meet with all manner of obstructions—almost more than elsewhere, from the Leipzig *Gewandhaus* down to many greater and smaller *Gewandhäusler.*

It stands clearly written, a hundred times over, that I cannot compose; without indulging in unseemly protests against this, I quietly go on writing, and set all the greater store by the constancy of some of my friends, particularly Walter Bache, for the stoutheartedness which till fourteen times fourteen he has for so many years displayed.

In the introduction to your fourteenth Programme F. Niecks,[1] *à propos* of F. Liszt, said very truly :—

1. " Form is an abstract idea."

2. " A harmonic combination or progression may be against the rules of a system," etc.

3. " Programm-music is a *legitimate genre of the art*." *

Give Niecks my sincere thanks ; also to Mr. Manns and *courtoisement* Miss Williams.[2] The " Funeral Pyre of Joan of Arc " will, I trust, have done away with her coolness.

With regard to the *Tempi* I am very yielding in my small pieces, and gladly allow well-disposed artists to decide this.

Sophie Menter-Popper was recently here and will probably (middle of May) play in Sir Benedict's model monster-concert, which for forty years has wielded the sceptre of London successes. Call on my honoured friend Sophie Menter—a rarely natural and excellently schooled musical individuality. You will feel yourself quite at home with her, and I told her this beforehand.

Yours affectionately,

BUDAPEST, *March* 19*th*, 1878.   F. LISZT.

From the middle of April till the end of July I remain in Weimar ; later, at the end of August, I go again to the Villa d'Este.

---

[1] Friedrich Niecks, Professor of Music at the University of Edinburgh ; the writer of the excellent work " F. Chopin as Man and Musician."

* Written in English by Liszt.

[2] The well-known vocalist Miss Anna Williams.

223. To Professor Dr. Ludwig Nohl.

HONOURED AND DEAR FRIEND,

Of the many pictures of the remarkable group of cypresses in the Villa d'Este your brother's [1] beautiful poetical drawing is my favourite. For the present of this and the *inscription* on it I thank you most heartily. I attempted (last October) to put down on music paper the conversation which I frequently hold with these same cypresses.[2] Ah ! how dry and unsatisfactory on the piano, and even in the orchestra,—Beethoven and Wagner excepted—sounds the woe and the sighing * of almighty nature !—

Nevertheless I will most modestly show you this Cypress-*Memento* at the piano when we next see each other—I hope in Vienna, where I am staying during the *first week* of April with my dear cousin as usual. Afterwards I go to Bayreuth and Weimar.

Sincerely yours,
F. LISZT.

BUDAPEST, *March 20th*, 1878.

224. To Professor Dr. Siegmund Lebert.

HONOURED FRIEND,

Quite excellent so. Let us divide the revision of the *Cotta edition* of the 4-handed Schubert, and for your part look after all the Sonatas, " Lebensstürme," Scherzi, etc.—If you wish it, a few pedal marks and fingerings shall willingly be added to the Variations

---

[1] Max Nohl, painter.

[2] " Au Cyprès de la Villa d'Este" [To the Cypress of the Villa d'Este). 2 numbers. Schott, Mainz.

* Das Weh und Wehen.

Op. 10 and 82.   Send me both works to Weimar, with the rest of Schubert's Waltzes for four hands, which show more creative power than many big compositions —old or new.

With the few Schubert pieces send me also the scores of the Beethoven Concertos and their accompaniments, arranged for a second piano by Moscheles.   My arrangement I will forward you at the beginning of August.   Meanwhile I beg you to give the Freiherr von Cotta my most grateful thanks.

Very respectfully yours,

F. LISZT.

BUDAPEST, *March 27th*, 1878.

From the middle of April till the end of July I remain in Weimar.

225. TO EDMUND VON MIHALOVICH.

VERY DEAR FRIEND,

I most sincerely feel with you in your grief. " Non ignara mali " . . . for I too have wept at the grave of my mother.

A sad but well-written book, " *Stello* " (" Consultations of the black doctor "), depicts the sufferings and death of three young poets,—Millevoye, André Chénier, Chatterton,—gathered home before they had acquired glory here below.

In these moving pages of Alfred de Vigny he asks, " What is one to think of a world which one enters with the hope of seeing one's father and mother die ? " . . . Prayer alone can answer this question.   Let us then pray our heavenly Father that His Will may be done on earth as it is in heaven, and that the work of our life may be ever conformed to the Divine Will.

Ever yours,

F. LISZT.

BAYREUTH, *April* 13*th*, 1878.

226. TO KORNEL VON ABRÁNYI.

. — . What could I write to you about Wagner's *Parsifal* ? The composition of the first act is finished : in it are revealed the most wondrous depths and the most celestial heights of Art.

Ever very sincerely yours,

F. LISZT.

BAYREUTH, *April* 14*th*, 1878.

227. TO FRAU INGEBORG VON BRONSART.

DEAR KIND FRIEND,

If you have not already done so, you will end by having a bad opinion of your old and very affectionate servant. My share of free locomotion is very limited. Having arrived at Weimar last Wednesday I could not pack off again immediately without inconvenience. I must therefore await a favourable week for my Hanover wish. In May *Rheingold* is to be given here, and St. Saëns's *Dalila* again, which I wish to hear and see. Monseigneur the Grand Duke assured me yesterday that this work made a success at its first performances ; and several people, who often hold a contrary opinion, agree in their praises of *Dalila*.

From the 13th to the 15th June (Whit week) a *Tonkünstler-Versammlung* is announced at Erfurt. It will seem pale as compared with that of Hanover of last year; but I want to be present at it, considering my unvarying interest in the work undertaken by the late Brendel and bravely continued by Riedel and Gille.   After having said A, and even B and C, I ought to go through the whole alphabet.

Formerly, in the first period of your success, I had the pleasure of applauding and admiring you at the old theatre of Erfurt.   Now there is a new and very handsome one, I am told, with more than 1100 seats; besides that a new concert room which I do not know, any more than I do the theatre.   I dare not invite you to favour them with your presence, but if you should come with Hans it would be charming.

The next time I see X. I shall come upon him to show himself an editor rather than a shopkeeper ("*Krämer*") in the little negotiation of which you speak.

A thousand sincere wishes for the finishing of *Hiarne*,[1] and my constant and very devoted homage to the persevering composer.

F. LISZT.

WEIMAR, *Saturday, April 20th,* 1878.

228. TO EDUARD VON LISZT.

DEAREST AND MOST HONOURED COUSIN,

The accompanying copy of the Budapest telegram will tell you that I must go to Paris probably at the end of May.   I had indeed refused several private invitations to visit the Paris Exhibition; for years past both long and short journeys—unless there

---

[1] The Opera composed by Frau von Bronsart, which was given for the first time in 1892 in Berlin with great success.

is some special reason for them—have been inconvenient, difficult and repugnant to me. It was on that
account that I told you and others of my having given
up the collective-wonder of Paris.

Now the telegram from Trefort and Szapary (President of the Hungarian Exhibition in Paris) alters my
negative decision.[1] Without ever talking *twaddle about
patriotism*, yet in all modesty I will not be wanting
where there is something to be done for Hungary.

As soon as my duty in Paris as an Hungarian Member
in the *International Jury* is fulfilled I shall return here.
I have promised to be present at the *Tonkünstler-Versammlung* in Erfurt in the last week of June, and on
the 8th July Weimar celebrates the Jubilee of the
25th year of the accession of the Grand Duke.

.—. I shall be much pleased to make the acquaintance of Herr Adalbert Goldschmidt. I have several
times hankered after the score or pianoforte score of
his grand work "*Die Todsünden*" [The Mortal Sins],
which, so I am told, has not yet appeared in print.
Is the composer staying long in Hanover? Probably
I shall go to see Bülow and Bronsart there immediately
after the Erfurt *Tonkünstler-Versammlung*, at the end
of June.

You remember that I categorically dissuaded Fräulein

---

[1] The telegram, dated 21st April, is as follows: "Abbé Franz Liszt,
Weimar. Universal wish that you should represent Hungary in
International Jury of Paris Universal Exhibition. Jury begins on
1st June, lasts about 2 to 3 weeks. Please accept confidential mission,
and wire reply immediately to Presidential Bureau, *Handelsminis-
terium*, Budapest. Minister Trefort. Count Julius Szapary." To
this Liszt replied: "Most ready for service, Liszt begs for full particulars of his duties."

Remmert from giving an *orchestral* concert in Vienna. In spite of that she had it announced and advertised, . . . and in the end there only came of it a vexatious *mancando, perdendosi !*

Ah ! the artist-world is full of troubles !

Thy faithful and heartfelt-devoted

F. LISZT.

WEIMAR, *April 26th*, 1878.

229. TO HOFCONCERTMEISTER EDMUND SINGER.

DEAR HONOURED FRIEND,

Your charming, gifted illustration of my little *Quelle* [spring] [1] delights me anew. The three violins flow, splash, bubble and sing—and sound like rainbow colours.

With friendly thanks for this Artist-gift, I remain your ever respectfully obliged

F. LISZT.

WEIMAR, *May 10th*, 1878.

230. TO ADOLF VON HENSELT IN ST. PETERSBURG. [2]

MY HONOURED FRIEND,

The original works of Adolf Henselt's are the noblest jewels of Art. One longs for more of them. . . .

By-the-by, when Henselt gives a hope of arranging, " interpreting," " making an effect with" other compositions, he succeeds so admirably that the public,

[1] Liszt's "Au bord d'une source " (Années de pèlerinage), for three violins concertante (Schott, Mainz).

[2] The " German Chopin," as Henselt has been called (1814—1889), lived in St. Petersburg from the year 1838, where, after Liszt's first visit there in 1842, they became warm friends. Henselt sent his " interpretation " of Liszt's Lucia-Fantasia to the latter " for correction." The above letter is in answer to that.

the pianists, and the compositions in question are thereby enriched and favoured. Even my little *Lucia-transcription* has gained much by thine "interpretation," dear friend. Hearty thanks for this *reminiscence* of our Petersburg intimacy.

The proof-copy I simply sent back to you, unaltered and nothing crossed out, as all the *various readings* are admirably suitable, and henceforth I leave it to your good pleasure to decide about the publishing. (In Russia Hofmeister's German copyright holds good, does it not ? . . .)

To-morrow I go to Paris, and will observe there your recommendation of the Russian instrument.

Many of your admirers frequently tell me about you ; above all Zschocher and Töpfer. You come backwards and forwards to Dresden and Leipzig ; why not also to Weimar ? . . . Answer this modest question *in person* here to thine old and most faithful

F. Liszt.

Weimar, *June 5th*, 1878.

231. To Eduard von Liszt.

[Weimar, *June 6th*, 1878.]

Dearest Eduard,

Adalbert Goldschmidt has brought you Weimar news. I consider his "*Todsünden*" a remarkable Art-work. If the composer maintains himself on these heights in his next Opera his name will become famous in spite of all the critics. . . .

Nowadays, more than ever, the public thirst for Opera alone. Everything else in music is nonsense to them.

There is a French saying—" There is some one who is wittier than Mr. de Voltaire ; that is *everybody*"—and when all the world gets a fancy into its head one must certainly consider it either reasonable, or stupid,—but necessary.—

With regard to the delay of the Jury (Class 13, " *Instruments de Musique*") I go to Paris next Sunday, 8th June, remain there till the 19th, and return here on the 20th June on account of the Erfurt Musical Festival. . . .

Thy faithful, loving

F. LISZT.

To simplify our correspondence call me also "Dearest Franz."

My Grand Duke much wishes to have the photograph of your son-in-law's cousin, the poet Saar. Send me this speedily.

232. To PROFESSOR CARL RIEDEL.

DEAR FRIEND,

The further carrying out and arranging of the Erfurt programme I leave to your long-tried and complete mastery.

I once more recommend Borodin's Symphony ; the quartet parts that are wanting can certainly be speedily written out next week (at my expense).

The study of the numerous works will offer no difficulties in Sondershausen ; there they are accustomed to step boldly forward.

Friend Riedel conducts my 13th Psalm ; Bülow undertakes the two Faust-episodes (in case these are not struck out, as I did advise you to do); and I retain the "*Hungaria*" and Bronsart's Concerto; but for several reasons I beg that my name may *not* be put on the programme as conductor.

I told Concertmeister Kömpel [1] and L. Grützmacher [2] (the Weimarer) yesterday that Bülow wishes to play the Bronsart Trio with them. Both gentlemen are quite agreed about this.

If Frau Erdmannsdörfer would play some other brilliant piano piece (*not of my* composition), rather than the often-heard Hungarian Fantasie, I should prefer it, just because the programme already contains too many Liszt things, and I could not myself bear the false appearance of making use of the *Tonkünstler-Versammlungen* for bringing forward my compositions. . . .

My real feeling on this matter has been known to you for years past.—

Early on Saturday, at half-past nine, I go direct from here to Paris—and on the 21st June arrives in Erfurt

Yours ever with sincere esteem,

F. Liszt.

Weimar, *Thursday, June 7th,* 1878.

My Paris address (from the 10th to the 18th June) will be : Maison Erard, Rue du Mail, 13.

Do publish the programme in the next number of the *Zeitschrift*; two or three slight alterations will not matter in the least.

---

[1] A pupil of Spohr's ; died not long ago at Weimar.
[2] Solo violoncellist.

233. To Vera Timanoff.

DEAR ILLUSTRIOUS ONE,

I don't know how you will manage to adapt the "Sonnambula" to your little hands; they will have to trot about on the roofs in the style of somnambulists.

A revoir, wide awake, the day after to-morrow,— and a thousand affectionate and devoted regards.

F. LISZT.

Thursday [*Summer*, 1878].

234. To Eduard von Liszt.

DEAREST EDUARD,

I have very little in the way of musical matter to tell you about my stay in Paris from the 9th to the 18th June. I scarcely found time to hear the two last acts of Gounod's *Faust* at the Grand Opera. I was prevented from attending concerts by invitations and visits elsewhere. But I was able to follow attentively the *plain-song* during High Mass at Notre Dame on Trinity Sunday, together with a very intelligent friend, R. P. Joseph Mohr (Societate Jesu), a competent judge and promoter of Church music.

Hanslick—who showed himself friendly to me in Paris—will report in the *Neue Freie Presse* concerning the 13th class (musical instruments, etc.), of which he is vice-president.

Madame Erard placed at my disposal a princely suite in her house, Rue du Mail, 13 (with which Spiridion[1] was quite satisfied); a carriage also in addition. Thanks to this hospitality my expenses

---

[1] Liszt's valet.

were very much diminished, and I only required 1500 francs. . — .

My old friend Belloni has also proved himself most faithful this time in Paris, and saved me many expenses. It is wonderful how honest and disinterested he remains, with all his constant contact with the artist-world !—

Immediately on my return I went to Erfurt for the *Tonkünstler-Versammlung* (from the 22nd to the 25th July). The whole affair went off well. I send you in addition the whole programme. Bülow played in a marvellous and *masterly* manner.

Everything in Weimar is now in a state of commotion over the Ducal-Jubilee-Festivities, which begin the day after to-morrow. The King of the Netherlands, the King of Saxony, Prince Friedrich Carl of Prussia, several reigning German Dukes and foreign Princes are expected. Our Emperor and King is sending Prince Windischgrätz with congratulations to the Grand Duke. Victor Scheffel (the author of " Ekkehard," the " Trompeter von Säckingen," the " Bergpsalmen," etc.) has written the Festival Play, which is to be performed in the theatre here on the 9th July. My *Carl-Alexander* March, which was published 20 years ago (by Bote and Bock) in Berlin, is to serve as Prelude.

For 30 years past I have been *incrustated* into the Royal house of Weimar, and shall remain faithful to it.—

My dearest cousin Marie wrote me a loving, witty note with respect to the photograph of her cousin, Ferd. von Saar, which I wanted for my Grand Duke. I will write my thanks to Marie shortly.

Send the accompanying lines to Franz in Gratz; I am congratulating him, in them, that you are now grandpapa.

Heartfelt greetings to the Generalissima.

Thy

F. L.

235. TO ROBERT FRANZ.*

MY MUCH-HONOURED FRIEND,

How beautiful, how deep, how fervently and truly finished are, once more, your *Six Songs* (Opus 48)!

Heartfelt thanks for so kindly sending them. You well know that for thirty years past your genius—a fixed star in German lyrics—has been sincerely admired by your ever most faithful

WEIMAR, *July 12th*, 1878. F. LISZT.

236. TO KORNEL VON ABRÁNYI.

DEAR AND HONOURED FRIEND,

On arriving here yesterday evening I found your letter, together with the enclosure to Minister Trefort, which I return immediately to you, signed. Agghazy deserves to be helped, because his hands and his head are very musically endowed.[1] Juhász and he

---

* A facsimile appeared in the "Musikalisches Wochenblatt." Liszt worked untiringly, like no other of his contemporaries in art, to make the great German Master of Song, Robert Franz (1815—1892), understood and appreciated (See "Robert Franz." *Gesammelte Schriften*, IV.); and, when increasing deafness prevented this artist from practical musical work, Liszt founded the fund in his honour which is mentioned on page 227.

[1] Agghazy (now teacher of pianoforte playing at Stern's Conservatorium in Berlin) received a stipendium from the Hungarian Government, through Liszt's intercession, in order to make a livelihood in Paris·

will certainly do honour everywhere to the Budapest Academy of Music. Aggházy must have some letters of introduction for Paris. Advise him to ask for them from Minister Trefort, Ministerial-Counsel Hegedüs, Friedrich Harkany and Count Geza Zichy. Before his departure I will send him a few lines to Madame Erard, and to my loyal old friend Belloni, who is ever ready to do me a service.

I need scarcely ask, dear Abrányi, how you have passed your summer. The chief thing is to hold out steadfastly, and you show this in the noblest manner by your unwearied, meritorious endeavours after the high goal of Art. "*Persévérons !*"

I think of staying here till the beginning of January, and of returning then direct to Budapest. First of all I must finish a little extra work : as soon as the new setting of the text for the dramatic Oratorio "*Der heilige Stanislaus,*" which Baron Dingelstedt has kindly promised me, comes to hand the composition shall proceed. I am often quite anxious about further writing of music, but I do not give it up, although I do not imagine at all that I can express that which floats before my mind. But my self-dissatisfaction finds ample consolation in the ever-fresh joy at the master-works of the Past and Present :—most of all in Wagner's majestic *word-tone-creations*. King Ludwig II. of Bavaria rightly addressed " to the Tone-poet Master Richard Wagner."—

Hearty greetings to your family, and ever yours
Sincerely and gratefully,
F. LISZT.

September 13*th*, 1878.   (VILLA D'ESTE, TIVOLI.)

The loss of Augusz touches me most painfully. Since the first performance of the Gran Mass, more than twenty years ago, we have been *one in* heart. He it was also who especially decided me to carry out my wish to settle myself in Budapest.

After the opening of the new Academical Course write to me about it.

237.   To Eduard von Liszt.

Dearest Eduard,

I give my heartiest thanks to the highly-honoured friendly Frau General for writing at your dictation.

We take the heartiest interest here in your recovery. It is to be hoped you are already on the best road to vigour.

My dearest cousin Marie has now happily made me a great-uncle.   Enclosed are two words of thanks to Marie.

I am now waiting for the new setting of the poem of "Stanislaus" from Dingelstedt in order to take up my interrupted composition again—I want at least a year and something over to finish it.

Meanwhile I have not quite lost my time.   In the last two months I have completed a *Via crucis* (the 14 Stations) and pretty full responses to the 7 Sacraments (for Chorus and Organ).   I rejoice [to think] that I shall play them to you on the 2nd April, '79, at the Schottenhof.

Thy faithful

F. Liszt.

Rome *November 4th,* 1878.

238. To Freiherr Hans von Wolzogen in Bayreuth.[1]

Highly-honoured Baron,

The October number of your *Bayreuther Blätter* brought me the highest intellectual gift.[2] No temporal ruler can bestow one like it. The estimation of it lays me all the more under an obligation to that true humility with which I have long and most devoutly paid homage to our incomparable master, Richard Wagner.

Accept my sincere thanks for the friendly words in remembrance of the performance of the Dante Symphony in your house, and kindly recall to the good graces of the Frau Baronin von Wolzogen

Yours most respectfully and devotedly,

F. Liszt.

November 15th, 1878.   (Villa d'Este, Tivoli.)

239. To Eduard von Liszt.

. — . I take a hearty interest in the improvement of your health. You are the younger, the more sensible and useful of us two; therefore you should outlive me many years in good health.

I have been dreadfully industrious with my music-writing since the middle of September. I sit and walk in it like one possessed!

The *Via crucis* (now finished) has brought me back to a long-cherished idea—namely, the composition of

---

[1] The well-known writer on Wagner and publisher of the *Bayreuther Blätter*.

[2] Wagner's Essay "The Public in Time and Space."

choruses to be made use of at Church festivals during the giving of the 7 holy sacraments; thus 7 pieces of music of about a hundred bars each. These have now been 8 days at the copyist's, and, according to my thinking, are not quite a failure. If you also think this it will heartily rejoice

Your most faithfully devoted

F. LISZT.

November 21st, 1878.   [TIVOLI.]

This evening I shall be in Rome, and will have this letter and the signed enclosure attended to at the post.

Hearty greetings and thanks to the dear Frau *Generalissima.*

240. TO EDUARD VON LISZT.

BUDAPEST, January 22nd, 1879

DEAREST EDUARD,

. —. On Sunday, the 12th January, His Holiness was so gracious as to give me, for the second time, a private audience. I will tell you shortly, by word of mouth, the friendly sentiments of the Pope towards me.

I spent last Wednesday evening in Görz with Frau Baronin Augusz, and arrived again at Fischplatz, No. 4, early on Friday. The roof is already on the new Music Academy building, Radialstrasse, and is said to look very well. In November of this year I shall inhabit it.

My friends in Budapest, Abrányi, Mihalovich, Count Albert Apponyi, Count Geza Zichy and several others, are strongly and heartily attached to me. Archbishop Haynald only comes to Pest in the beginning of January.

I was not caught in the other base spider's web. "Honesty is the best policy!"

Bösendorfer called on me yesterday and told me of the intention of the Vienna *Friends of Music* to perform the Gran Mass at the end of March. If Bösendorfer's intimations are correct I am not disinclined to conduct this performance, although for many years I have refused all such invitations—and only a little while ago to London, Aix-la-Chapelle, Berlin, etc. I should be rejoiced if at last the Gran Mass had a fair hearing *in Vienna*.

A hearty greeting to Frau Generalissima from thy faithfully devoted

F. LISZT.

Looking forward to our speedy meeting at the end of March.[1]

241. TO LUDWIG BÖSENDORFER.

DEAR AND HONOURED FRIEND,

I take your friendly hint by enclosing these lines to Hellmesberger; please to give them to him. During many years, in Vienna, Weimar and Budapest, Hellmesberger has always shown himself kindly disposed towards me. In ingratitude there is, alas, only too much rivalry; the matter grows contemptible, and contemptible people like to find amusement in it. My nature absolutely forbids me such despicable behaviour.

---

[1] It did not come to pass. Councillor E. von Liszt died on the 8th February, 1879. "It is for me a constant sorrow at the heart that Eduard is no longer with us," wrote Liszt to the widow a year after Eduard's death.

Count Geza Zichy tells me, dear friend, that he expects you shortly.   Perhaps you will come with Hellmesberger to our *Künstlerabend* [Artists' Evening] here on the 7th March, when we shall be honoured by the fine composer and splendid virtuoso, my excellent friend, Saint-Saëns.

Count Zichy writes you the rest about the Klausenburg journey.

A hearty greeting to your wife.

Truly devoted,

F. LISZT.

BUDAPEST, *February* 19*th*, 1879.

I have just received Zellner's letter.   Give him my hearty thanks for it.

Sophie Menter went to Warsaw the day before yesterday, and gives a concert there to-morrow with her husband Popper,—and afterwards in St. Petersburg.

242. To ADOLF VON HENSELT.

VERY DEAR FRIEND,

Hast thou still pleasure in beautiful, distinguished virtuoso piano-playing ?   If so then go and hear the eminent pianiste Frau Menter.   She brings thee the hearty greeting of thy old friend

F. LISZT.

BUDAPEST, *February*, 1879.

243. To MARIE LIPSIUS.

MY DEAR FRIEND,

Hearty thanks for your dear lines of sympathy. The loss of my cousin and most intimate friend Eduard von Liszt is a deep grief to me.

You wish for the dates of the Budapest and Vienna concerts; for this I was obliged to ask the help of my excellent friend Kornel Abrányi. He knows these and other things far better than I. For ten years he edited the Hungarian musical paper, and now officiates as General Secretary and Professor at the Royal Academy of Music in Budapest, the Director being Franz Erkel, and my humble self the President.

Here is the result of Abrányi's researches, by which it is evident that I have neither been idle nor used anything for my own benefit.

At the same time let it be mentioned to the praiseworthy and amiable authoress of " *Musikalische Studienköpfe*," La Mara, that since the end of '47 I have not earned a farthing by pianoforte playing, teaching or conducting. All this rather cost me time and money.

Since the year '47 I only played *in public* twice in Rome—'63 and '64—at the gracious command of Pope Pius IX.; often in Budapest later on, twice in Vienna, once in Pressburg and Oedenburg (my native town) as a child of the country. Nowhere else. May my poor pianoforte performing at last come to an end! It has long been a torment to me. Therefore—Amen!—

On the occasion of the celebration of their Majesties' silver wedding I shall have the honour, in accordance with the invitation of the *Gesellschaft der Musikfreunde* [Society of friends of music], of conducting the "Gran Mass" in Vienna on the 8th April (the Tuesday before Good Friday). Performances of this Mass (after the first at Gran in '56) took place in Pest, Prague, Vienna, later in Leipzig and Amsterdam, in '66 in Paris, and again in Amsterdam, as also in '77 in Weimar and

Düsseldorf, the latter under the conductorship of Ratzenberger. This Mass has also been heard in America.

In conclusion also the following memoranda for La Mara : Without a written engagement, yet indeed morally bound, since '71 I spend several months of every winter in Budapest, from April to July in Weimar, then the autumn months, and more, chiefly in the Villa d'Este near Rome, where His Eminence Cardinal Hohenlohe affords me the kindest reception. There I wrote the "Christmas-tree," the "Via Crucis," the "Responses to the Seven Sacraments," etc. These three works are quite ready, and indeed beautifully copied, as well as the "Cantico del Sole" of the marvellous St. Francis of Assisi. Their publication troubles me little, for they are not suitable to the usual musical customs and trade. . . .

So why bargain with them ?

I have only fragmentarily sketched the Oratorio "Stanislaus," but wish to finish it, which will take at least a year.

My "Technical Piano-Exercises"—improperly advertised in the papers as "Pianoforte-School"—still require a few months for revision and arrangement with fingering, etc., but could come out next year if I have no hindrances.

Accept, my dear friend, my sincere and grateful attachment.

F. Liszt.

Budapest, *March 2nd*, 1879.

The middle of April I shall be in Weimar again

244. To Otto Lessmann.

My dear Friend,

The enclosed programme proves to you that in spite of all fatigue my *invalided* piano-playing still contributes in a small degree to the relief of the sufferers of Szégedin.[1]

To assist in other concerts than in this country would not become me, and I have already declined many invitations of that sort with excuses and thanks.

For the celebrations preceding the silver wedding of their Majesties I shall have the honour of conducting the *Gran Mass* in Vienna on the 8th April (" Society of the friends of music ").

To our speedy meeting in Weimar, and ever yours in all friendship,

F. Liszt.

BUDAPEST, *March 23rd*, 1879.

245. To Von Trefort, the Hungarian Minister of Instruction.*

Monsieur le Ministre,

I learn through M. Abrányi that Your Excellency continues to show your solicitude for the Royal Academy of Music at Budapest. The work of this institution is to serve Art in Hungary, and thus to help, in this connection, in making your patriotic, grand intentions fruitful.

---

[1] According to the programme, Liszt played Schubert's Funeral March ; "To the memory of Petőfi," and " *Cantique d'Amour* " of his own composition, as well as, with Mihalovich, Schubert's Fantaisie (C major) for two pianofortes.

* From a copy in the possession of K. v. Abrányi.

My colleagues at the Academy of Music are of one mind and devoted in their activity.

I permit myself to recommend once more particularly to your kindness M. Abrányi. He perseveres in his meritorious career as writer, theorist, composer, translator, professor, and Magyar character of the noblest stamp. The evidence of his merits will assuredly be recognised in many languages by a heap of laudatory phrases . . . after his death. A brilliant obituary is assured to Abrányi, but I hope that Your Excellency will accord him the modest satisfaction that he claims while he is alive.

I have the honour to be, Monsieur le Ministre, your very humble and very devoted servant,

F. LISZT.

WEIMAR, *May 12th*, 1879.

246. TO WALTER BACHE.

VERY HONOURED, DEAR FRIEND,

Hearty thanks for your letter and for letting me see Manns's Commentary on the " *Hunnenschlacht.*" Please give to Manns the accompanying short explanation of the idea of my "Symphonic Poem." In spite of my spending several hours in letter-writing almost every day, it is impossible for me to be regarded as a punctual correspondent. Intelligent and kindly-disposed persons will excuse me, and the many others I can scarcely entertain any longer, because I don't require any such entertainment ! *

Next Whit-week " *Tonkünstler-Versammlung* " in

* Play upon the words "wirthschaften" (to manage) and " Wirthschaft " (housekeeping, or a public house).

Wiesbaden.   On the 5th June Bülow conducts the first
concert there, at which Bronsart's beautiful and valuable
" Frühlings-Fantasie," Bülow's music to Shakespeare's
" Julius Cæsar," and my " Faust Symphony " will be
performed.   Bülow kindly plays the piano the same
evening, and has chosen Tschaikowsky's Concerto.
Besides this his favourite pupil Schwarz produces
several " Etudes transcendantes." [1]   Till the middle
of July I stay here.   Then Bayreuth, and at the end
of August Villa d'Este.   To Frau Jessie Hillebrand
and her husband [2] give heartfelt and faithful devotion,
with respectful thanks, from

Theirs in old friendship,

F. LISZT.

WEIMAR, *May 25th*, 1879.

[The explanation, accompanying this letter, of the
idea of the " *Hunnenschlacht*" is as follows :]

Kaulbach's world-renowned picture presents two
battles—the one on earth, the other in the air, according
to the legend that warriors, after their death, continue
fighting incessantly as spirits.   In the middle of the
picture appears the *Cross* and its mystic light ; on this
my " Symphonic Poem " is founded.   The chorale
" Crux fidelis," which is gradually developed, illustrates
the idea of the final victory of Christianity in its
effectual love to God and man.

247. To LUDMILLA SCHESTAKOFF.

MADAME,

Your illustrious brother Glinka is one of the
well-chosen admirations of my youth.   His genius has

---

[1] By Liszt.   [2] Who were just then in London.

been known to me ever since the year 1842 ; and at my last concert in St. Petersburg (in '43) I played the "Marche tscherkesse" from "*Russlan and Ludmilla*," and a brilliant transcription by Vollweiler of several themes from the same Opera.

Glinka remains the Patriarch-prophet of music in Russia.

With my sincere thanks to you for sending me the beautiful score of "*Russlan*," carefully edited and well arranged by Messrs. Rimsky-Korsakoff, Balakireff and Liadoff,[1] I beg you to accept, Madame, the expression of very respectful homage of your very humble servant,

WEIMAR, *June 14th*, 1879.   F. LISZT.

248. TO ALEXANDER BORODIN, CÆSAR CUI, ANATOLE LIADOFF AND NICOLAS RIMSKY-KORSAKOFF IN ST. PETERSBURG.

VERY HONOURED GENTLEMEN,

You have done a work of serious value under the form of a jest. Your "*Paraphrases*" charm me : nothing can be more ingenious than these 24 Variations and the 16 little pieces upon the favourite and *obligato* subject

In short, here we have an admirable compendium of the science of harmony, of counterpoint, of rhythms, of figuration, and of what in German is called "The Theory of Form" (Formenlehre) ! I shall gladly suggest to the teachers of composition at all the

---

[1] The score was published in 1879.

Conservatoires in Europe and America to adopt your *Paraphrases* as a practical guide in their teaching. From the very first page, the Variations II. and III. are true gems; and not less the other numbers continuously, up to the grotesque Fugue and the *Cortège* which crown the whole work gloriously. Thanks for this dainty feast, gentlemen, and I beg that when any one of you brings out a new composition he will let me know it. My most lively, my highest and most sympathising esteem has for many years been assured to you; pray accept also the expression of my sincere devotion.

F. LISZT.

WEIMAR, *June 15th*, 1879.

249. TO CAPELLMEISTER PROFESSOR JOS. BÖHM IN VIENNA.

HONOURED HERR VEREINSLEITER,*

I follow your edifying endeavours in the *Cäcilien-Verein* with sincere interest. It seems singular that they should stumble on obstacles. What is in question? Innovations? . . . By no means. The noblest Conservatism remains the essence and aim of the *Cäcilien-Verein*; it merely demands a serious study and proper performances of the most dignified classical authors in Church music, Palestrina and Lassus at the head. Nothing can reasonably be objected to this, and you may confidently maintain, dear sir, that "recognition must take place and the good cause prove victorious."

I beg you will put down my name as a subscriber to

---

* Conductor of a *Verein* (Society).

your "Vienna journal for Catholic Church music,"[1] and have the numbers which have already appeared addressed to me in Weimar.

Be so good as to employ the enclosed hundred florins for the gravestone of my highly esteemed friend the late A. W. Ambros.

Yours with all esteem,

F. LISZT.

WEIMAR, *June 22nd*, 1879.

250. TO VERA TIMANOFF.

A hearty welcome to you, Illustrissima, and pray tell M. Sauret that I shall be delighted to make closer acquaintance with him. I greatly admired his superb talent in Vienna.—You know my rule never to bother any one, and least of all artistes ; but if M. Sauret should feel inclined to play something at the *Hofgärtnerei* this morning, it would give me great pleasure.

In any case I invite him to come (at eleven) with you, and I shall request you to fulfil your promise of captivating us by your performance (not by dancing, but by your superior fingering) of Rubinstein's Ballet, " Feramors."

Yours affectionately,

F. LISZT.

Sunday Morning [*Summer*, 1879].

251. TO ADOLF VON HENSELT.

VERY DEAR FRIEND,

Our meeting once more is a cordial pleasure to me. According to your last letter, you purposed

---

[1] Professor Böhm was at that time the editor of it, and had invited subscriptions for a monument to the musical historian Ambros.

arriving on the 19th inst.   Why delay ?   Still, arrange
it entirely according to your own convenience.   Only
allow me to make one observation : on Wednesday
evening, 23rd July, I am invited by somebody where a
refusal would be wrong and stupid.   But if you were
favourably inclined, our extra three-handed whist
might be quite well arranged at the house of this
somebody.[1]

Your version with the grace note [passing note ?] B♭

pleases me best.[2]

In expectation of seeing you, and in faithful and
admiring friendship,

WEIMAR, *July 12th*, 1879.   F. LISZT.

252. TO DR. SIEGMUND LEBERT.

DEAR FRIEND,

I keep a long-standing promise to-day, by sending you the 3 last Concerti by Beethoven arranged

[1] Henselt was in Weimar the 19th and 20th July.   "We played
together, not on the piano, but certainly half a dozen games of
whist, of which I fortunately lost five at least," wrote Liszt to
Fräulein von Schorn.

[2] The two bars of music refer to C. M. v. Weber's "Episodic
Thought," which Henselt had transcribed for piano and amplified ;
he published it in March, 1879, dedicating it to "his friend Franz
Liszt."   Henselt at first meditated calling it "Hymn of Love."   But
Liszt found "the term rather too highflown for this favourite melody."
"Episodic thought is more suitable," he wrote, and so that title
remained.

for 2 pianos. This arrangement is distinctly different from all other existing arrangements of the same Concerti for 2 pianos. Till now it has been the habit of arrangers to content themselves with setting the Tutti (or better, the orchestral parts) for the 2nd piano only, leaving the 1st to rest entirely or to support the 2nd according to inclination. By this a grievous disproportion in the effect of the orchestral parts is induced, let alone the fact that some of the arrangements are exceedingly scanty.

In my opinion this sort of proceeding belongs to the past and is *hackneyed*. What good is there in the first player sitting there at all, if he does not know how to take part in the whole? Ergo, I had to occupy him almost constantly.

As a matter of course I have not altered a single note of Beethoven's original version (of the so-called *Soli* parts), and have only added a tolerable amount of indications for pedal and fingering, for the convenience of pupils and teachers.

2 identical copies (printed on 4 lines—excepting the Cadenzas) are necessary for the performance of this arrangement.

It may prove useful and effective, as well in studying at the " homely fireside " and in musical schools, as also in performances in small concerts (where there is no orchestra), in Conservatoires, at examinations and drawing-room performances.

The chief title stands on the first page; on the 2 following ones are remarks for the printer, which I leave to your masterly hand as a *pedagogue*, dear friend, to render more distinct and to complete.

With special regard I remain always yours sincerely,

F. LISZT.

ROME, *September 25th*, 1879.

I have great pleasure in the perusal of the 2nd edition of Weitzmann's "History of Pianoforte Playing."

253. TO PROFESSOR BASSANI IN VENICE.[1]

MUCH-ESTEEMED COLLEAGUE,

You are so forcibly exceptional a person, and prove this by truly uncommon musical and poetical works.

Mademoiselle Giuli has already written to tell you the lively pleasure I have had in hearing her play one of your compositions remarkably well ; several others, for piano or for the voice, deserve a similar success, and will obtain it as soon as they are known.

Pray accept, dear Monsieur Bassani, the very sincere esteem and sympathy which is offered to you, together with best wishes for the extension and widespread fame of your " Armonie dell' Anima," by

F. LISZT.

(VILLA D'ESTE,) *October 28th*, 1879.

254. TO THE COMPOSER ANATOLE LIADOFF IN ST. PETERSBURG.

DEAR SIR,

All your compositions bear the stamp of distinction and of good taste. This one is charmed to find again in the "*Arabesques*" you are kind enough to

[1] A well-known teacher of the pianoforte in Venice, and friend of Liszt's.

send me.   Pray accept my thanks and the expression
of my very sincere and devoted esteem.

F. Liszt.

(Villa d'Este,) *December 25th,* 1879.

255. To Frau Reisenauer-Pauly [1] in Rome.

Dear Madame,

My best thanks for your kind notice of the
Roman concert of January 23rd.   It seems to me that
"*populations nécessiteuses*" [distressed population] would
have been better on the programme than "*populations
affamées*" [starving population] *of Silesia.*

Mendelssohn's excellent Concerti always hold their
ground without risk, especially since Berlioz's witty
article (published nearly 30 years ago), according to
which they are occasionally performed by the pianos
alone, without further trouble on the part of the pianist.

While taking affectionate part in the success achieved
by your son Alfred, whose talents are duly valued by
me, I remain, dear Madame,

Yours truly,

Budapest, *January 30th,* 1880.   F. Liszt.

My cordial greetings to Madame Helbig.

256. To Professor Klindworth in Moscow.

Much-esteemed dear Friend,

My sincere thanks for your masterly arrangement of Chopin's Concerto.[2]   You showed me the first
movement of it some years ago in Munich.   I consider

---

[1] The mother of Liszt's pupil, Alfred Reisenauer.

[2] The Concerto in F minor ; score, orchestral parts and arrangement
for 2 pianos published by Jürgenson (Moscow) and Bock (Berlin).

the modifications in the instrumentation and in the piano part successful. As much *transparency* as possible should be preserved in the melodious parts.

I conclude that you will impress on M. Jürgenson the necessity of not giving way to the ancient careless abuses of publishers in the 2-piano edition. Thus *four lines* and two *identical copies* are requisite for performance.

As leader and head of the now numerous Chopin-Editors, your excellent *Jürgenson-Edition* authorises you to advance a proudly modest "*Sic vos non vobis*."

Au revoir this summer in Hall, dear Klindworth. Give my kind regards to your wife.

Yours faithfully,

F. Liszt.

The last corrected proofsheets of Tschaikowsky's Polonaise dedicated to you leave by to-day's post addressed to Jürgenson.

257. To the Kammervirtuoso Professor Hermann Scholtz in Dresden.[1]

Much-esteemed Sir and Friend,

I have sincere pleasure in praising and recommending your *Chopin*-Edition. To Klindworth belongs the merit of having preceded you by his intelligent and practical work. Your publisher, Peters, might be advised in the next thousand copies he issues of the Chopin-Edition signed Hermann Scholtz :—

A. Not to fill up the first volume with Waltzes. Why make this paltry concession to the trifling requirements of the drawing-room ? Chopin's Waltzes

---

[1] Pianist and composer (born 1845, pupil of Bülow and Rheinberger), is especially famous as an admirable player of Chopin.

are certainly charming, elegant and full of invention . . .
still his Polonaises and Mazurkas have a far higher
importance.

Chopin is the bewitching musical genius in which
the heroically chivalrous Polish nationality finds expression. This chief characteristic ought to be distinctly
emphasised in classifying his works. So, *first volume* :
Polonaises, Mazurkas and the Fantasia upon Polish
motives.

B. The clear notation of the melodies (indicated by
tails turned upwards !), as in the Klindworth-Edition,
should be maintained.

C. In works having an orchestral accompaniment
an arrangement of that accompaniment for a second
piano ought to be printed under the Solo part of the
first piano.

(The brains of most pianists become addled by the
usual editions, where the essentially melodious and
rhythmical character, nay often even the correct bass,
is wanting.)

D. This is again addressed to Mr. Peters. He
ought not to withhold from the audience your *admirable*
version of the Recitative in the Adagio of the F minor
Concerto for Piano Solo, and should add these few
pages to your Chopin-Edition.

Yours faithfully,

F. Liszt.

Weimar, *April 29th*, 1880.

258. To Sophie Menter.

Dear Friend,

The signature of the telegram *from Rome*
announced to me your return to " Hungaria." I met

friend Bösendorfer the day before yesterday in Frankfort : we began at once of course to talk about Sophie Menter and her new thickly-leaved Petersburg laurels. Similar plants will bloom for you everywhere according to the capacity of the soil, and will always shade your artistic peregrinations through Europe and America.

Give my kindest regards to Neuschul, from yours cordially,

F. LISZT.

WEIMAR, *May 26th*, 1880.

259. TO JULES DE ZAREMBSKI.

DEAR FRIEND,

You have made an excellent choice ; and M. Gevaërt also. The Brussels Conservatoire keeps in the first ranks : its very active and intelligent Director will take good care not to allow it to degenerate or to sink into idleness ; on the contrary, he gives and will give it an entirely progressive impulse. You will have to see that your piano class does honour to the Conservatoire, to its head and to your own name. This will take some years to do ; therefore, persevere.

Your three studies are most uncommon, remarkable and successful. The second, in F minor, might be signed *Chopin*. This exceedingly high praise does not imply that you have in any way been guilty of plagiarism, for in your works original power is manifest.

Perhaps there may be a slight falling-off towards the middle of the third Study ; still this does not disturb the total good impression.

When we are chatting together again about music I will explain to you *vivâ voce* my antiquated ideas concerning the whys and wherefores of matters belonging to our profession.

I am sending Simon at Berlin at once the good copy of your three Studies. He has sent me the rather bad one of your Mazurkas for two performers. These I played over with the Baroness von Meyendorff yesterday evening. She begs me to tell you our very favourable opinion of these charming productions of your Polish muse.

I am telling Simon that publishers cannot do better than bring out works of value such as Zarembski writes.

Pray, dear friend, present the sincere regards to Mme. Zarembska of your cordially attached

F. LISZT.

WEIMAR, *June 1st*, 1880.

I am just sending off the copies of the Studies and Mazurkas to Simon.

260. To Professor Bassani.

DEAR FRIEND,

Your " Studio sinfonico " is fine poetry in music. It reminds me of Venice when I was twenty. The solemn, sad motive $\left(\frac{5}{4}\right)$ corresponds to the lagoons and to the gloomy stroke of their waves round the Bridge of Sighs : the other subject soars on high accompanied by the gentle sound of the belfries, announcing, as it were, from a distance the joyfulness of divine hopes.

My cordial sympathy and friendship.

F. LISZT.

WEIMAR, *June 4th*, 1880.

261. To Marie Lipsius.

Dear Friend,

Hearty thanks for your persistent kindness ;
" Carmen " has just arrived, and I now beg you to
find out for and send to me another tale of Mérimée's,
called " *Les âmes du Purgatoire* " [Souls in Purgatory].
It narrates the adventures of Don Juan de Marana,
immortalised by Mozart and Lord Byron. Grabbe
has also turned his poetical attention towards this
mauvais sujet, and gives him as a companion to Faust,
which might perplex His Excellency von Goethe.

I hope soon to see you either in Leipzig or Weimar.

Ever yours gratefully,

F. Liszt.

Weimar, *June 10th,* 1880.

To-morrow I shall write to Härtel's that the edition
of my " *Gesammelte Schriften* " could not do better than
begin with your excellent version of the " Chopin."

262. To Kornel von Abranyi.

Highly esteemed dear Friend,

My hearty thanks for the dedication copy of
your charming " *Nocturnes.*" " Near the chapel " and
" Starry night " belong to my *most select intimate
Programme.*

Aladàr Juhász needs but health to stand forth and
hold his own as an excellent artist, virtuoso and
composer. The matter of his stipend is now arranged
—as we wished it. Juhász will certainly also greatly
distinguish himself at the Klausenburg Musical Festival.
My lines of introduction to Trefort, the Minister, must

no longer be presented to His Excellency as *mustard after dinner*. The less scribbling and gossiping the better. " Vitam impendere vero."—

I request that the two accompanying letters in Hungarian may be answered by the General Secretary of the Royal Hungarian National Academy of Music, Abrányi Kornel, in my name. Before I left Budapest we read together the polyphone *tattoo* by J. K., and I then requested you to make the composer understand that Meyerbeer's far-famed Rataplan, Rataplan, plan, plan (in the *Huguenots*) is quite enough henceforth for the audience.

Do not delay any longer returning his score to J.

Beg Herr P. A. to excuse me for not being a *millionaire*.

Till the end of July remains in Weimar

Yours most faithfully and gratefully,

F. Liszt.

Weimar, *June 20th*, 1880.

263. To Freiherr Hans von Wolzogen.

Highly esteemed Freiherr and Friend,

. — . Wagner has shown and taught us triumphantly " what style is." You explain the mighty matter admirably in your last writing, dear Sir. That a "School for the culture of style in Bayreuth" should be established, is wished by no one more seriously than by

Yours most sincerely,

F. Liszt.

Weimar, *July 28th* 1880.

264. To Friedrich Hofmeister, Music Publisher in Leipzig.

WEIMAR, *August 17th*, 1880.

DEAR SIR,

For the last twenty years or more Kirchner has known how sincerely I esteem his compositions. I rejoice to see that he continues adding to their number with freshness and vigour, and am much obliged to you for sending me his "Toys," "Caprices," "Leaves," etc., which you have brought out.

Yours truly,

F. LISZT.

265. To Baroness Helen Augusz, Sister of Mercy in Graz.[1]

MOST REVERED SISTER OF ST. VINCENT DE PAULE,

Pray always dispose of my feeble services. I am writing to the Baroness de Roner according to your instructions, and request that you will send her the enclosed lines.

M. Tirindelli's[2] abilities deserve attention, consideration and encouragement. This you have well understood, and it will be a pleasure to me to second you.

How can I be of use to him?

By recommending him to some publisher in Germany?

Does he intend to travel and give concerts? Your protégé, M. Tirindelli, may count upon my sincere readiness to oblige him: the only thing I ask is, that

---

[1] Daughter of Liszt's late friend, Baron Anton Augusz, of Szegzard in Hungary.

[2] Professor at the "Liceo Marcello" in Venice; violinist and composer.

he should write me *distinctly* in what way I can be of service to him.   Yesterday I took the liberty of noting several alterations in his melody "*All' Ideale,*" his Mazurka, and in the Adagio of the Trio which pleases you by its fine feeling.

By the way, this Adagio has been so badly copied that another less faulty one will have to be made before sending it to print.   By this same post you will receive the three works with my alterations.

Having arrived here last Saturday, I shall remain at the Villa d'Este till New Year.   In the middle of January will return to Budapest

Your very respectful and devoted servant,

ROME, *September 1st,* 1880.   F. LISZT.

The most convenient address for me during the next months is : Albergo e Via Alibert, Roma.

266. To MADAME A. RUBINSTEIN.

Allow me, dear Madame Rubinstein, to dedicate to you my transcription of your husband's charming and very famous *Lied.*   To the very conservative burden "*Ach! wenn es doch immer so bliebe*" [Ah! could it remain so for ever!] I add that what will certainly always remain as now is, your most respectfully and affectionately obedient servant,

F. LISZT.

(VILLA D'ESTE,) *October 24th,* 1880.

267. To FRAU AMALIE VON FABRY IN BUDAPEST.

DEAR MADAME,

I do not know whether I talk too much; but I certainly write too little to those who remain constantly in possession of my sincere gratitude. I crave your kindly indulgence therefore for my involuntary short-comings.

Through your nephew Imre [1] I hear that his mother, Baroness von Augusz, has been so good as to look at my new dwelling in the Academy of Music, and that the arrangement of it, as yet unknown to me, meets her approval. The solicitude you have shown, Madame, in this matter—as well as in other similar ones in the Palatingasse and Fischmarkt during the last 8 years—I beg to acknowledge with warmest thanks. It never enters my head to make exaggerated pretensions with regard to my residential requirements. Decency without display continues to be the right thing for me. I only have one wish at all times : never to be a trouble to my friends anywhere.

It will be agreeable to me if Fanny feels disposed to undertake my modest household service again this winter. She adapts herself well to it with her pretty smiling face.

Pray accept, dear Frau von Fabry, the renewed expression of my old devoted affection.

F. LISZT.

VILLA D'ESTE, TIVOLI, *November 1st,* 1880.

On the 15th January I shall again arrive at Budapest.

268. TO FRAU ANNA BENFEY-SCHUPPE.*

DEAR MADAM,

A thousand apologies. I ought long ere this to have written you and my esteemed friend, Dr. Benfey,

[1] Baron Augusz, son of Anton Augusz. He died at an early age.

* Autograph belonging to Herr Fritz Donebauer at Prague.—The addressee is an authoress residing at Weimar.

a letter of thanks, and to have sent your sheetful of
questions back answered.[1] Pray excuse this delay.—

I frankly confess that the title of the pamphlet,
"Beethoven and Liszt,"[2] at first frightened me. It
called to my mind a reminiscence of my childhood.
Nearly fifty years ago, at the *Jardin des Plantes* in Paris,
I used often to notice a harmless poodle keeping company in the same cage with a majestic lion, who seemed
to be kindly disposed towards the little chamberlain.
I have exactly the same feeling towards Beethoven as
the poodle towards that forest-king.

With sincere thanks and regards,

Yours, F. LISZT.

November 11th, 1880. (VILLA D'ESTE, TIVOLI.)

At the end of September, Breitkopf and Härtel sent
my own duet arrangements of my twelve *Poèmes Symphoniques* at my request to Gottschalg (Weimar). *This
copy is intended for Dr. Benfey.* Gottschalg will likewise willingly place the scores of the *Dante* and *Faust*
Symphonies, as well as the arrangement for two pianos
of both these works, at your disposal.

The names of the greatest performers figure in the
Court concerts, such as, Joachim, Ernst, Vieuxtemps,
Bülow, Rubinstein, Bronsart, Tausig, Madame Viardot-
Garcia, etc., etc. A few of these concerts were con-
ducted by Berlioz, and their programmes in every case
contained *nova et vetera* (as prescribed in the gospel).

During my direction of the Opera at Weimar, from
'49 to '58, the following works were performed there,

---

[1] The answers follow in the letter.

[2] Alludes to a pamphlet contemplated by the late husband of the
lady addressed.

together with the standing *répertoire* of Mozart's,
Weber's, Rossini's, Meyerbeer's Operas, etc.

February '49 *Tannhäuser*; August 28th, '50, *Lohengrin* (first performance); later on *The Flying Dutchman*,
and Wagner's splendid edition of Gluck's *Iphigenia
in Aulis.*—Berlioz's *Benvenuto Cellini*, Schumann's
Manfred (first performance), Raff's *King Alfred*, two of
Lassen's Operas, Spohr's *Faust* (with the recitatives),
Sobolewski's *Comala*, Dorn's *Nibelungen* (first performance), etc., etc.—Finally, Peter Cornelius' *Barber of
Bagdad*—the last operatic performance which I
directed there.

This short list will suffice for your purpose of the
pamphlet; to it we may add that several Oratorios
and Symphonic works were performed under my
direction, such as Marx' *Moses*, Rubinstein's *Paradise
Lost*, Schumann's *Paradise and the Peri* and his concluding scenes in *Faust*, etc.; as for Symphonies,
the Great Pyramid—Beethoven's Ninth (for Goethe's
Jubilee in '49), nearly all Berlioz's Symphonies and
Overtures, besides other Symphonies and Overtures by
Schumann, Raff, Hiller, Bronsart, Joachim, Bülow, etc.,
most of which were at that time scarcely known or
entirely new.

You might obtain better and more detailed information concerning musical life at Weimar (from '49 to
'58) from some who took part in it either as performers or friends, especially Gille, Lassen, Gottschalg,
Grosse (trombone-player and contrapuntist), Wahlbrüll,
Milde and his wife, and Frau Dr. Emilie Merian, than
from the theatre archives.

I have no doubt, moreover, that the present Intendant, Baron von Loën, will readily permit you to inspect the archives of the theatre and see any programmes of the Court concerts of that time which may still be forthcoming. You may likewise count upon the obliging readiness of Lassen and Müller-Hartung in making your pamphlet known.

During my summer stay in Weimar in latter years, some pianists have taken to coming there regularly who play my Symphonic Poems well and willingly. I am not able to name any of those who come during the winter. Ask Lassen and Müller-Hartung about this. Enclosed you will find an introduction from me to Madame Merian. She sings my songs with fervent intelligence, from heart to heart.

F. Liszt.

November 11th, 1880. (Villa d'Este.)

269. To the Committee of the Antwerp Musical Society.

Very honoured Gentlemen,

The expression of my sincere gratitude for your very kind letter has been delayed owing to a circumstance which was independent of my will.

I am acquainted with the high character which the Antwerp Musical Society bears; many of those who were present at your *Festivals* in 1876, '77, and '79 have spoken to me in the liveliest terms of praise of those great musical performances, of the far-famed merits of your director, Peter Benoit, of his *Rubens Cantata* and of his *Oratorio,*[1] recently sung at Brussels on the occasion of the national commemoration by 900 members of your Society.

[1] La Guerre, De Oorlog.

Greatly flattered by your invitation, I hope, Gentlemen, that my answer to it may not appear discourteous to you. Allow me to decline the honour of directing the *Festival* you have in view for 1881 and to be present at it as a simple listener.[1] Should any work of mine have been admitted to your programme, I would fain request M. Peter Benoit[2] to conduct it, since for the last fifteen years I have declared myself unfit for this work in all countries.

My engagements keep me at Budapest till Easter. After that time I shall be charmed to have the opportunity of assuring you again personally at Antwerp of the sentiments of high consideration and distinguished esteem with which I remain,

Yours faithfully,

November 16*th*, 1880. (VILLA D'ESTE,) TIVOLI.   F. LISZT.

[1] The *Liszt-Festival* given by the *Société de Musique d'Anvers* took place on the 26th May, 1881, under Benoit's direction, in Antwerp. The programme comprised the Gran Mass; the E flat Concerto, played by Frau Falk-Mehlig; the Dance of Death, played by Zarembski; Mignon and other songs, sung by the ladies Kufferath and Schauenburg; and the *Préludes*.

In a second Festival-Concert on 29th May, arranged by Liszt's former pupil F. von Servais and Jules de Zarembski, *Tasso* and the Faust Symphony, the Concerto Pathétique (played by M. and Mme. Zarembski), and *Loreley* with orchestra (Mdlle. Kufferath) were performed. Gevaert, the celebrated musical *savant*, apostrophised Liszt in the opening speech as "*the incomparable Virtuoso* whose prestige has never been surpassed, nor even equalled; *the prolific and inspired composer*, who in the numerous domains of Art which he has touched has opened new roads, explored new shores, and left everywhere the luminous imprint of his bold and innovating genius; *the eminent head of a School*, who may without exaggeration be described as the initiator, *par excellence*, of the musical movement of our epoch; one of those rare favourites of the gods for whom posterity begins even during their life-time," etc.

[2] One of the chief representatives of Belgian national music (born 1834), Director of the Antwerp Conservatoire.

270. To Sophie Menter.

DEAR, HIGHLY VALUED FRIEND,

If I rightly understand your letter and telegram you are soon going to Paris and London, and also soon coming to Rome. When ?—tell me this clearly.

A Roman Sophie Menter Concert is easily arranged and will be a great pleasure for me.

Although introductions from me are quite superfluous for *you*, I beg you to consider them always at your disposal. The best person to safeguard your interests with the German Ambassadors in France and England will be Frau Gräfin Schleinitz. Alter, shorten and improve anything you like in the Fantaisie on the Huguenots. Pieces of this sort ought only to be brought forward by super-eminent *virtuosi*—Sophie Menter, for instance. The transcriber then hardly serves as " *Klecks*." [1]

Yours cordially,

F. LISZT.

December 2nd, 1880.   (VILLA D'ESTE, ROME.)

Maybe you will tell me yourself soon in Rome where I am to send the letters ; if not, send me your address. I shall remain here till January 5th and be at Budapest on the 15th.

271. To Dr. Friedrich Stade in Leipzig. [2]

VERY DEAR SIR AND FRIEND,

Your transcription of "Gretchen" [3] for pianoforte and harmonium is *capital*, just as I wished. I only take the liberty of very slightly altering it, and have

---

[1] Klecks is the name of Mme. Menter's favourite cat.

[2] Musical writer (born 1844) in Leipzig.

[3] Out of Liszt's Faust Symphony.

added ten bars at the end, which are to be henceforth inserted in the score and in my own arrangements or the Faust Symphony.[1]

If you will kindly take the trouble to arrange the entire Faust Symphony for two performers on one piano, I shall be greatly indebted to you.[2] Deal as freely as possible with the figurations and also with the distribution among the seven octaves of the odious keyboard. It seems to me that what may be more *literally* accurate ought often to give way to what sounds better and even to what is more convenient for the players at the piano.

Thanking you once more, I remain,

Yours most cordially,

Rome, *December 11th*, 1880.   F. Liszt.

We will play your duet arrangement together before it is published, in Weimar—next spring.

[1] They follow herewith in the orchestral movement, according to Dr. Stade's copy.   [2] This was done.

272. To Professor S. Jadassohn in Leipzig.[1]

Dear Sir,

Your setting of the 100th Psalm is nobly religious in feeling and excellent in style. The working out of the choruses is masterly throughout, from beginning to end; a passage which comes out with especial brilliancy is that on pages 14, 15-19, 20, "with rejoicing," where the trombones, and then the trumpets and trombones, joyously repeat the subject of the fugue in augmentation.

The Arioso too which follows, "He made us," is most fervent in expression. There is a fine field here for beautiful contralto voices to rejoice in.

My sincere thanks, dear sir, for the dedication of

[1] Composer (born in 1831), teacher at the Leipzig Conservatoire since 1871.

this excellent work. I shall recommend it for performance to such of my friends as are conductors; above
all, to Hofcapellmeister Müller-Hartung, whom I shall
request to bring out your Psalm at Weimar.

Yours sincerely,

VILLA D'ESTE, *January* 10*th*, 1881.   F. LISZT.

273. To Frau Reisenauer-Pauly in Königsberg.

DEAR MADAM,

It is one of my duties to deal sparingly in letters
of introduction. Still I am quite willing to repeat my
opinion that your son Alfred is a highly gifted and
brilliantly aspiring pianoforte-player.

Should this conscientious opinion enable him to
obtain further recommendations, he is free to make
use of it.

Yours sincerely,   F. LISZT.

BUDAPEST, *January* 29*th*, 1881.

274. To Dionys von Pazmandy,
Editor of the *Gazette de Hongrie.*[1]

DEAR SIR AND FRIEND,

You want to know my impression of yesterday's Bülow Concert ? Yet it must have been yours,
that of all of us, that of the whole of the intelligent
audiences of Europe. To define it in two words :
admiration, enthusiasm. Bülow was my pupil in
music five-and-twenty years ago, as I myself, five-and-
twenty years before, had been the pupil of my much
respected and beloved master, Czerny. But to Bülow

---

[1] This letter is printed in French in the *Gazette de Hongrie*, but
is only known to the Editor in the German translation (*Neue Zeitschrift für Musik* ?).

it was given to do battle better and with greater perseverance than I did. His admirable Beethoven-
Edition is dedicated to me as the "fruit of my tuition."
Here however it was for the master to learn from the
pupil, and Bülow continues to teach by his astonishing performances as *virtuoso*, as well as by his extraordinary learning as a musician, and now too by his
matchless direction of the Meiningen Orchestra.—Here
you have the musical progress of our time !

Yours cordially,

BUDAPEST, *February* 15*th*, 1881.   F. LISZT.

275. TO FRAU CÖLESTINE BÖSENDORFER IN VIENNA.[1]

Not to see you in Vienna this time, Madame,
was a grief to me. It cast, as it were, a melancholy
shadow over my stay there, which otherwise was
brightened by so cordial a reception.—

I am accompanied by the roses without thorns of
my pleasant recollections of you, and my hearty and
respectful devotion remains unaltered.

F. LISZT.

WEIMAR, *Easter Sunday, April* 17*th*, 1881.

Have the kindness to repeat to Bösendorfer the
assurance of my very cordial friendship.

276. TO THE MOST HONOURABLE COMMITTEE OF THE WAGNER-VEREIN, BERLIN.

Addressed to Professor Otto Lessmann.

GENTLEMEN,

A distinction such as that which was conferred
upon me yesterday by the Berlin "Wagner-Verein"

---

[1] The wife of the celebrated pianoforte-maker, who died young.

and by the audience has seldom been received by the highest masters in the musical art, among whom I can only count as an apprentice.[1]

Accept my warmest thanks for the "*Liszt Festival Concert*" of Sunday, 24th April; it remains as a joyous incentive to lifelong continuous work with

Yours respectfully,

BERLIN, *Monday, April 25th*, 1881.   F. LISZT.

277. TO KORNEL VON ABRÁNYI.

WEIMAR, *May 13th*, 1881.

MY DEAR FRIEND,

Rather more than half of my concert-engagements for this year have now been fulfilled. The two performances of *Christus* in Berlin and Freiburg were admirable; the *Liszt-Concerts* in Freiburg and Baden-Baden likewise; in the first of these the three-part hymn "*L'enfant au réveil*" was also given, charmingly sung by deliciously clear voices. By way of a rehearsal of this piece the ladies gave a morning serenade in honour of me at the house of my friendly hosts the Rieslers, whose villa will remain most pleasantly in my remembrance. Felix Mottl conducted the Liszt concert in Baden-Baden with *Mazeppa*, the "Mephisto-Waltz," the "Hunnenschlacht," and three pieces from the Oratorio *Christus* in a most praiseworthy manner.

---

[1] "Les Préludes" and "Festklänge," the former under Lessmann's, the latter under Mannstädt's direction, had been performed in the winter garden of the Central Hotel before a numerous audience assembled by invitation. Between the two symphonies, Marianne Brandt sang "Jeanne d'Arc au bûcher," and Heinrich Ernst some of Liszt's songs. A banquet concluded the festival.

Bülow's *Liszt-evening* in Berlin glorious as at Pest and Vienna. . — .

I shall stay here till Sunday, 22nd May. On the 24th I shall be at Antwerp. On the 26th is the performance of the *Gran Mass* there.

I am very glad that the Committee of the Musical Festival has chosen just *this* particular work, which has hitherto been more talked about and abused by the critics than heard. Of course I had left the programme entirely to the discretion of the Committee, for I really have no wish to recommend any work of my own for performance anywhere. My mission is to work on unpretendingly and without troubling myself about advancement.

Yours faithfully,

F. Liszt.

My best regards to your wife and sons. I will send you programmes from Antwerp and Brussels. I shall be back here again on the 4th June. From the 9th to the 12th June *Tonkünstler-Versammlung* in Magdeburg.

278. To Kornel von Abrányi.

Much esteemed, dear Friend,

The second copy (with the additional few hundred bars) of the score of my *second* Mephisto-Waltz is admirably done. Thank Gyula Erkel very particularly in my name for it. I request his acceptance of the enclosed forty florins, as a slight remuneration for the time he has spent on it. I depend upon your firm friendship, which has stood the test of so many years, to find a delicate mode of presenting them to

him.   The score of the second Mephisto-Waltz will be
published next autumn by Fürstner (Berlin), and then
performances can take place at Budapest and elsewhere.

I am writing to our esteemed Director of the Royal
Hungarian Academy of National Music, Franz Erkel,
to have Chickering's grand pianoforte, as an excellent
and kind gift from America, placed in the music-hall
in the Radial-Strasse.   This piano, as well as the whole
of my possessions in Budapest, will belong to the Royal
Hungarian Academy of Music at my death, which is not
far off.   *Correctness* remains the motto of

Yours most faithfully,

WEIMAR, *May 22nd*, 1881.   F. LISZT.

To-morrow evening I shall be at Antwerp.   The
Committee there have decided for the *Gran Mass* to
be performed on the 26th May without any pressure
on my part.   Therefore Éljen Hungaria—in all countries.
You may address to Weimar in the beginning of June.

279. TO FRAU CHARLOTTE BLUME-ARENDS.[1]

DEAR MADAM,   WEIMAR, *August 29th*, 1881.

A good deal of irregularity has crept into my
housekeeping during my long indisposition.   Your kind
letter only reached me yesterday.   Thank you heartily
for it ; I accept the office of godfather.   So your son
is to be named Franz, and to walk the waters of life
firmly and serenely, trusting securely in God, like
my patron Saint François de Paule, whose motto is :
" Caritas."

---

[1] A pupil of Liszt's now in Berlin.

I have long been wishing to thank you by letter for the charming present which decorates my study in the new wing of the Musical Academy at Pest. That elegant work of art is greatly admired by my numerous visitors.

It would be charming, were the amiable donor to return and inspect it. The remembrance of you is still vivid in Pest.

Best compliments to your husband from

Yours gratefully and truly,

F. LISZT.

I hope to be quite recovered in ten days, and shall then go to Rome.

280. TO OTTO LESSMANN.

WEIMAR, *September 8th*, 1881.

DEAR FRIEND,

I have still to undergo a supplementary treatment of baths and sweatings.[1] This I shall do at Weimar.

From the 21st to the 30th September I shall be at Bayreuth, and from October till New Year in Rome.

I am sending off the duet version of my Symphonic Poem " From cradle to grave " to Bock to day. . — . I shall send him the score from Bayreuth, because just now I am not able to work more than a few hours a day continuously.

There is so much admirable music written that one is ashamed to write any more. With me it only happens in cases of urgency and from inner necessity.

Thanking you heartily,

Yours ever,

F. LISZT.

---

[1] In consequence of a fall, Liszt had been seriously ill all summer.

281. To François Auguste Gevaërt, Director of
    the Brussels Conservatoire.[1]

VERY HONOURED, DEAR FRIEND,

Among the recollections of my long artistic life
one of the dearest to me is that of your kind sympathy.
I cherish sincere gratitude for it, of which I should be
glad to give you a proof. Allow me, to begin with,
to dedicate to you the Symphonic Poem I have just
written, which was suggested by a drawing by Michel
Zichy entitled " From the cradle to the grave."—The
score is short enough, and, it seems to me, free from
superfluous repetition.

Lassen has spoken to you about the performance
of your *Quentin Durward* at Weimar. The Grand
Duke desires it to take place ; his Theatre-Intendant,
Baron von Loën, was preparing for it, and the singers
are certain to take great pains and show all alacrity in
performing their several parts well.

To my own regret, in which his Royal Highness
shares, as well as his theatre company and the
audience, the performance has to be adjourned ; for
the German translation is not forthcoming, and some
dawdling on the part of your publisher throws obstacles
in the way. Let him soon turn over a new leaf. As
for the German translation, I particularly recommend
to you my friend Richard Pohl (who is living at
Baden-Baden, where he is editor-in-chief of the local
newspaper of that charming place). Pohl is distinguished by great musical intelligence and cleverness

---

[1] Celebrated Belgian music teacher and composer, born 1828.

in translating, of both of which he has given proof in Berlioz's *Beatrice and Benedict* and Saint-Saëns' *Samson.*

Lassen and Baron Loën will continue to correspond with you concerning the *mise-en-scène* of *Quentin Durward* at Weimar. Small towns have but small successes to offer. You are entitled by right to both large and small ones. Accept them.—

I do not scruple to ask a favour of you, my dear friend. The decoration of the Order of Leopold arrived at a time when I was ill in bed. It was accompanied by a few complimentary lines from the Secretary of the Foreign Office, Baron de Lambermont, as well as by the official document which was to be signed by me. It would have been my most agreeably imperative duty to have thanked Baron de L., and to have expressed my lively feelings of gratitude for this royal favour. This I could not immediately do, owing to the state of my health, which did not allow of my writing, and still renders that occupation very difficult. Add to this that a good deal of disorder had got into my household ; several letters and manuscripts have been mislaid, and, notwithstanding all my endeavours, I have not been able to find Baron de L.'s lines again or the document they enclosed. I therefore beg you, dear and highly esteemed friend, to present my apologies to the Baron, and to ask him to send me a duplicate of the document I have to sign.

My address from 22nd September to 2nd October will be : Bayreuth (Bavaria) ; after that, Via and Hôtel Alibert, Rome.

Yours, in high esteem and cordial friendship,

Weimar, *September 19th,* 1881.　　　　　　F. Liszt.

282. To François Auguste Gevaërt.

Highly honoured Master and dear Friend,

Thanks to your kind help I have at last put my business with Baron Lambermont in order and have just written him a letter of very grateful acknowledgment.

Permit me to *revenir à nos moutons*. Panurge has nothing to do with them, nor has the honourable biscuit-seller of the Gymnase, still less his peaceable neighbour, your publisher Mr. Grus. What we want is the score of your *Quentin Durward* and composer's consent to the performance of it at Weimar. The Grand Duke's Theatre-Intendant undertakes the payment of the German translator, my old friend, Richard Pohl, who will certainly take great pleasure in performing his task in the most satisfactory way possible. Baron Loën and Lassen will correspond with you concerning the performance, which is intended to take place in December '82.

My cordial thanks for your favourable acceptance of my dedication. Some months are still necessary for the copying and publishing of the score together with the orchestral parts. Before this is finished I will send you the printed pianoforte arrangement for one and for two performers.

Be good enough, dear friend, to give my affectionate regards to Madame Gevaërt and to your sons, and ever count upon my very grateful devotion.

F. Liszt.

Bayreuth, *October 8th*, 1881.

I shall be in Rome in eight days.

283. To Edmund von Mihalovich.

DEAREST FRIEND,

I must be found guilty [of negligence ?]. I do not apologise. My aversion to letter-writing has grown excessive. But who could answer more than two thousand letters a year without becoming an idiot ?

I have been ailing a good deal for the last three months. As soon as there was an improvement, something else appeared. Do not let us mention this any more, for you know how little my health occupies my thoughts, and how disagreeable it is to me to hear it talked of. In short, I feel sufficiently recovered to set out for Rome the day after to-morrow. My very dear granddaughter Daniela goes with me, and will remain till the beginning of January. This is a providential pleasure on which I did not count at all, but for which I thank the good angels.

I will tell you by word of mouth the minor reasons which prevented me from sooner communicating your two splendid scores and the pianoforte duet arrangements of them to the publishers, Breitkopf and Härtel. Your fine manuscripts have at last reached Leipzig, and you will soon have a letter from the present proprietors of the ancient and illustrious house Breitkopf and Härtel, with their conditions for publication, which will be their *ultimatum*. They are aware of the sincere interest I take in your works, and will, I trust, share it, without leading you into any expense.

Stern[1] has given me fairly good news as to the

---

[1] Adolph Stern in Dresden, author of the libretto.

preparations for the performance of your *Hagbar* at Dresden. Young composers are always too impatient.—

Pray remember me cordially to our excellent friends the Véghs, Albert Apponyi, Madame d'Eötvös and her daughter, Mademoiselle Polyxena, and . . . I was just going to add the name of a charming woman with whom I am out of favour.

Yours ever,

F. LISZT.

BAYREUTH, *October 8th*, 1881.

My address from the middle of October to the 1st of January : Via and Hôtel Alibert, Rome.

You are held in affectionate remembrance at *Wahnfried.* Wagner is finishing the instrumentation of the 2nd act of *Parsifal*, and gives it his most passionate attention. We shall have something new, marvellous, unheard of, to hear.

M. Humperdink, the lucky *triple* laureate of the three scholarships, " Mozart," " Meyerbeer," " Mendelssohn," is at work here copying the score of *Parsifal* ;[1] Joseph Rubinstein[2] is continuing his arrangement of it for piano at Palermo just now, and will complete it later on at Bayreuth. Other artists on the high road to celebrity are also employed in copying this same *Opus magnum*, the performance of which we shall applaud

---

[1] E. Humperdink, born in 1854, made Wagner's acquaintance in 1880 at Naples, and at the first performance of *Parsifal* conducted the choruses from on high and the music on the stage. He has been teacher at the Barcelona Conservatoire since 1885.

[2] Born 1847 in Russia, he lived a great deal in Wagner's society after 1872, and took an active part in the rehearsals for the Bayreuth Festival Performances in 1875 and 1876. He died by his own hand the 15th of September, 1884, at Lucerne.

in July 1882. It will be a next to miraculous and highly fashionable pilgrimage.

P.S.—The busybody Spiridion has been so careless as to carry off a little gold watch of mine that I had merely given him leave to wear while he was in my service. Please ask Spiridion to give you this watch on New Year's Day. You will return it to me about the middle of January 1882, when I go back to Budapest.

284. To Jules de Zarembski.

Dearest Friend,

I have rarely done a minor work—big ones bother me—with as much pleasure as that of setting your two Galician Dances for Orchestra. It is quite finished, with a few additions of which I hope you will not disapprove; but my scrawl of a manuscript cannot possibly be sent you: therefore I have asked Friedheim[1] to undertake to copy it, and I will send you this copy before the New Year. If the publisher Simon is inclined to publish this orchestration I will let him have it for a thousand marks; if not, keep it yourself, and make any use you like of it; first of all at the concert in which you are going to bring forward your own compositions exclusively. I wish I could be present at it, and on this occasion I renew to you the sincere and sympathetic esteem in which I hold your noble and rare talents. They will fructify by means of perseverance.

Friedheim's copy will reach you in time to have

---

[1] One of the most pre-eminent among the younger pupils of the Master.

the parts copied and to add the necessary *nuances*. Please send me a programme of the concert of which Zarembski as composer is to fill the list. The other programme you are meditating, to be devoted to my works for the pianoforte, seems to me to be too long ; this is a defect for which I can only be very thankful to you, and yet I am going to ask you to reduce your recital to the average proportion. An hour and a half of pianoforte music of mine, however admirably played, is more than sufficient.

M. Becquet, President of the Brussels Musical Society, writes to me concerning the performance of my *Elizabeth*, and M. Radoux, Director of the Liège Conservatoire, likewise. I fear the translation of the libretto and its proper adaptation to the work will be impediments. Nevertheless, if your friend Franz Servais were good enough to undertake the work of revision and of intelligent adaptation to the vocal parts, I should be more easy in my mind, and should only wish to look through the whole before the publisher, Kahnt, prints the French version under the German original. I am now writing this to M. Becquet.

Pray give my cordial regards to Franz Servais and my grateful remembrances to Maître Gevaërt.

Enclosed are the photographs with signature for MM. Dumon and Dufour ; to which I add a third (recently taken in Rome) for yourself.

I am honoured, flattered, and also . . . overwhelmed by numbers of letters. I have received more than a hundred during the last six weeks ; I should have to give ten hours a day to letter-writing if I were to attempt to pay my debts of correspondence : this I cannot do. Even the state of my health, which is not bad but forbids any continuous occupation, is opposed to it. Besides, when my old mania for writing music lays hold of me—as is the case just now—I feel quite unable to use my pen in any other way. I therefore beg you to convey my apologies and very affectionate thanks to M. and Mme. Tardieu for the kindness they show me.

I hope to repeat all this to them personally, for it is not said that I shall not return to Brussels, although travelling is becoming arduous for me. M. Tardieu's present of spirituous *liquid* has restored me several evenings during my work, . . . which may be superfluous, but completes what has gone before.

Your very devoted friend,

F. LISZT.

ROME, *December 4th*, 1881.

I remain here till the first week in January at *Via* and *Hôtel Alibert.*

285. To CAMILLE SAINT-SAËNS.

MUCH-ESTEEMED DEAR FRIEND,

You are not one of those who are easily forgotten, and you have won your fame valiantly. My feelings of sincere admiration and gratitude have followed you for many years; they are confirmed and increased by the proofs you give of constant and active sympathy.

I wrote to you last summer from Magdeburg on the occasion of the festival. Your remarkable work "La Lyre et la Harpe" figured on the programme; a delay in the translation and in the study of the choruses

obliged me, to my great regret, to defer the performance of it till next summer, when the *Tonkünstler-
Versammlung*, which is honoured by your active
membership and has just named me its Honorary
President, will again meet.

Before Christmas Fürstner, the publisher, will send
you, from me, three copies (score and arrangements for
pianoforte solo and duet) of my second Mephistopheles
Waltz, dedicated to Camille Saint-Saëns.   I thank you
cordially for giving it so hearty a welcome.   No one
more than myself feels the disproportion in my compositions between the good-will and the effective result.
Yet I go on writing—not without fatigue—from inner
necessity and old habit.   We are not forbidden to
aspire towards higher things: it is the attainment of
our end which remains the note of interrogation, being
in this something like the end to the Mephistopheles
Waltz on *b, f*—

intervals which are indicated in the first bars of the
piece.

You intimate the friendly desire that I should revisit
Paris.   Travelling at my age becomes burdensome,
and I greatly fear that I should be found out of place
in capitals like Paris or London, where no immediate
obligation calls me.   This fear does not make me less
grateful towards the public, and especially towards my
Parisian friends, to whom I acknowledge myself to be
so greatly indebted.   Besides, I should not like completely to give up the thought of ever seeing them

again, although the deplorable performance of the Gran Mass in 1866 left a painful impression upon me. This is easily explained on both sides. Nevertheless, it would be too much for me in future to expose myself to such misapprehensions. Without false modesty or foolish vanity I cannot allow myself to be classed among the celebrated pianists who have gone astray in composing failures.

By the way, allow me to ask a question. If I were to return to Paris, would you feel disposed, dear friend, to repeat your former offence by conducting any of my works in I know not what orchestral concert? I dare not ask you to do it, but, supposing that a favourable opportunity should occur, I should be very proud to be present. Meanwhile be so good as to remember me very kindly to Viscount Delaborde, and to thank your colleague of the Institute, Massenet, sincerely for his telegram. He will excuse me for not answering him at once. To fulfil the duties of a correspondent is an insoluble problem for your very grateful and devoted friend,

F. LISZT.

ROME, *December 6th*, 1881.

286. TO LUDWIG BÖSENDORFER.

VERY DEAR FRIEND,

I was raised to a very exhilarated state of mind by the many tokens of sympathy and friendship on the 22nd October.[1] To give it expression, I wrote several pages of music, but no letters at all. Antipathy to letter-writing is becoming a malady with me. . . .

Have the kindness to beg my friends in Vienna to

[1] Liszt's 70th birthday.

excuse this.   Perhaps I may yet live long enough to prove my affection to them in a better way than by words.

My health does not preoccupy me at all ; it is fairly good and only requires care, a thing which is at times irksome to me.

As usual for the last 10 years, I shall return to Budapest in the middle of January '82.

My best regards to your wife.

Yours faithfully and gratefully,

F. Liszt.

Rome, *December 8th*, 1881.

I repeat especially my hearty thanks to Zellner.

287. To Pauline Viardot-Garcia.[1]

Most illustrious and gracious Friend,

A woman distinguished by her shrewdness and talents, the authoress of several volumes which have had the good fortune to pass through several editions, has asked me for a line of introduction to you.   I have told her what she and all the world besides already knows : that Pauline Viardot is the most exquisite dramatic singer of our time, and besides this a consummate musician and a composer of the most delicate and lively intelligence.   To which opinion, as merited as it is universal, Madame X. is prepared to give ample and elegant expression in a notice she meditates publishing upon you.

Pray give a kind reception to your new correspondent, and keep a friendly remembrance of your old and most devoted admirer,

F. Liszt.

Rome, *December 12th*, 1881.

[1] The great singer, who still teaches in Paris, was Liszt's pupil for piano.

288. To Madame Malwine Tardieu in Brussels.[1]

How good of you, Madame, to make such ready allowance for my delays and shortcomings in correspondence. It is a disagreeable infirmity of mine not to be able to write longer and better letters. Your last kind lines delighted me, and I thank you for them most affectionately. The brilliant success of Massenet's *Hérodiade* [2] gives me sincere pleasure ; *all Paris*, after having applauded the work on its first appearance at Brussels, will be all the more ready to applaud it again in Paris itself. For my own part let me confess to you quite in a whisper that I am inclined rather to hold back with respect to certain love-scenes, which, it seems, are necessary on the stage, when introduced into biblical subjects. They jar on my feelings— excepting in our admirable and valiant friend St. Saëns' Dalila, where he has made a glorious love duet which is quite in place ; for Dalila and Samson are bound to give themselves to the devil for love's sake, whilst in Massenet's Magdalen and *Hérodiade* the whole thing is merely conventional . . . theatrical.

Pray forgive me, Madame, for this opinion, which is slightly pedantic, but without any pretension.

When you see Madame Viardot again, tell her that I still cherish an enthusiastic recollection of her—a typical Orpheus, Fidès and Rosina,—and, besides, an enchanting composer and a pianist full of ingenious dexterity. Have you heard anything of her daughter,

[1] The wife of the chief editor of the *Indépendance Belge*.
[2] The first performance of the Opera took place at the Théâtre de la Monnaie in Brussels, 19th December, 1881.

Madame Héritte ?   Do you know her remarkable setting
of Victor Hugo's " Feu du Ciel " ?   Monsieur Becquet [1]
has sent me an excellent French translation of my
Elizabeth,[2] quite adapted to the sense and rhythm of
the music.   When this *Legend of St. Elizabeth* was first
performed at Budapest (end of August 1865) the *Indépendance Belge* published a most flattering article on
the work. . — .

Pray remember most kindly to M. Tardieu your
affectionate and devoted servant,

F. Liszt.

Rome, *January 20th*, 1882.

Zarembski has received my orchestration of his
charming " *Danses Polonaises*." [3]

289. To Colonel Alexander Wereschagin.[4]

Dear M. de Wereschagin,

I am very grateful to you for sending me the
photograph of one of your brother's admirable pictures.
His " Forgotten " is a dismal, ghastly symphony of
crows and vultures ; I understand it, and deeply enter
into his marvellous inspiration.

Be so good as to tell your brother how great is my
admiration for his genius, and accept, dear Sir, the
expression of my best and most devoted regards.

F. Liszt.

Budapest. *February 5th*, 1882.

[1] President of the Brussels Musical Society (since dissolved).
[2] By Gustave Lagye.
[3] " Danses Galiciennes."
[4] The brother of the celebrated painter ; formerly adjutant to the
Russian General Skobeleff, also an author.

290. To the Kammervirtuosin Martha Remmert.

Dear Martha,

Enclosed are the various readings [*Varianten*] to my "*Todtentanz.*" * I noted them down after hearing the piece last May for the first time with Orchestra at the Antwerp Musical Festival (played by Zarembski in a masterly way). The brief alterations are easy to insert into the instrumental parts, for they only apply to the *Horns,* and consist in the addition of 7 bars; the rest are pauses in the orchestra while the pianoforte *solo* continues.

All is accurately indicated in the enclosed copy, so that, should the publisher Siegel (Leipzig) feel disposed to add a complementary sheet to the score, it might be easily printed from this copy. I should not like to trouble Siegel about this; but I authorise you, dear Martha, to communicate the complementary pages A, B, C, to Siegel.[1]

I wish you all the success you deserve in your concert productions, and remain always,

Yours sincerely,

F. Liszt.

Budapest, *February 20th,* 1882.

291. To Madame Malwine Tardieu.

Dear Madame,

You were beforehand with me in knowing that the performance of my *St. Elizabeth* is to take place, for the first time in French, at Brussels on Sunday,

---

* Dance of Death.

[1] The alterations alluded to did not appear in print.

30th April. If the date is not changed, I shall arrive on the 27th for the last rehearsals.

I hardly venture to accept the hospitality you are so good as to offer me, from delicacy; if, however, you help me ever so little to overcome my scruples, they will vanish. A thousand thanks for the good news you give me of the success of *Samson* and of other works by St. Saëns in Germany. He has possessed my admiring friendship for many years.

My very affectionate and grateful regards.

F. LISZT.

BUDAPEST, *April 11th*, 1882.

I shall return to Weimar in about ten days, where I shall expect to receive the *printed* programme from M. Becquet, which is to fix my arrival in Brussels.

Pray thank M. Tardieu for his obliging intention of reproducing the article of the *Indépendance* upon the first performance of the *St. Elizabeth* at Budapest in August 1865. I will tell you by word of mouth who penned those lines.[1]

292. TO FRANZ SERVAIS.

VERY DEAR FRIEND,

It is a grief to me that you will be conspicuous by your absence on the approaching occasion of my return to Brussels. The Liszt-Concert set afloat and directed by you last spring remains one of my

[1] This article, which was signed Reményi, was written by Frau Cosima Wagner, Liszt's daughter, and (according to Madame Tardieu's opinion) had "a high interest on account of its poetical and brilliant conception."

pleasantest recollections during my too long artistic
career. Even at that time you suggested a performance of my *Elizabeth*, and I did not think that it would
take place during your absence. My approaching
second visit to Brussels is entirely one of gratitude for
the sympathetic reception granted to me there at the
concert which you directed—an excellent performance
of some works of mine. Perhaps the *Elizabeth* may
likewise be favoured by good luck. . . . M. Lagye has
made an excellent French translation of it.

The one thing important for you, my dear Franz, is
to complete your *Ion*.[1] This will be your advent as
composer, for a complete and resounding success in
which you have the best wishes of

Yours ever devotedly,

F. LISZT.

WEIMAR, *April 22nd*, 1882.

Write to me at Brussels, where I shall be from
May 1st to 4th, and address your letter to Zarembski.

293. TO MADAME MALWINE TARDIEU.

Unless I receive a countermand from you, I
shall be in Brussels on Sunday evening.[2] I shall take
the liberty of sending you a telegram on the road to
give you the hour of my arrival. It will interest me
greatly to hear the *Hérodiade*.[3]

[1] The original title of the Opera now called *L'Apollonide*, which
Servais still keeps in his portfolio, though it is finished.

[2] The first performance of *St. Elizabeth* in French took place on
the 3rd of May. Saint-Saëns, Massenet, Francis Planté, and others
besides were present.

[3] Liszt heard Massenet's opera on the 2nd of May.

Bülow's exceedingly witty article on Saint-Saëns' *Samson*, which Bülow declares to be the best and most successful of all the Operas that have been performed for the last fifteen years (excepting Wagner's),—this article, which creates a sensation and makes a noise at " Landerneau," will reach you at the same time as these lines from your affectionate servant,

F. LISZT.

WEIMAR, *April 23rd*, 1882.

294. To OTTO LESSMANN.

I owe you so many thanks, dear, esteemed friend, that I could never get to the end of them. If the canon form were less unfamiliar to me, I would dedicate a symphonic *Canone perpetuo* of thanksgiving to you.

Our friend Adelheid von Schorn tells me that you are likely to spend your holidays at Weimar. A hearty welcome to you.

This year the *Tonkünstler-Versammlung*, at which I am accustomed to appear as a superfluous necessity (" *le superflu, chose si nécessaire*," according to Voltaire), ever since the foundation of these gatherings twenty years ago with Brendel—takes place at Zürich from the 9th to the 12th July.

Let us go there together, dear friend, from Weimar. I read by preference your excellent newspaper, and am making a lively propaganda for it.

Yours gratefully and cordially,

F. LISZT.

WEIMAR, *April 23rd*, 1882.

295. To Frau Charlotte Blume-Arends.

WEIMAR, *April 23rd*, 1882.

DEAR MADAME,

Poetry is your domain. As a pretty French verse has it, *" Même quand l'oiseau marche, on sent qu'il a des ailes"* [Even when it walks, we feel that a bird has wings].—My most cordial thanks therefore for the gift which you call prosaic, and my best regards to your husband. It would be charming if you came to Weimar again. From the middle of June to the 12th of July remains here uninterruptedly

Yours very truly,

F. LISZT.

296. To Freiherr Hans von Wolzogen.

MUCH-ESTEEMED FREIHERR,

Your *" Leitfäden"* are a salutary enrichment to musical literature. They essentially promote the spiritual comprehension of the great, sublime, unique works of Wagner. The *" Leitfäden"* are already considered *classical*, and rightly so, because, as a masterly piece of work, they establish a school.

Pray accept my very best thanks for the numerous proofs of kindness you have given me, to correspond in some degree to which is the wish of

Yours sincerely,

F. LISZT.

WEIMAR, *April 25th*, 1882.

A cordial and friendly meeting at *Parsifal!*

297. To Frau Henriette von Liszt in Vienna.

Weimar, *May 11th*, 1882.

My dear Cousin,

Our dear Hedwig[1] has not been forgotten. Immediately on arriving here I ordered Overbeck's edifying drawings for her, "The Seven Sacraments," a serious study of which, as well as of the commentary, is to be highly recommended. The work is published at Ratisbon; my bookseller here is wont to do business in *Tempo moderato molto commodo.* He kept me waiting, and I had to go to Belgium (on the 30th of April). I only received the above-mentioned work here yesterday, and send it you to-day together with the "Ave Maria" for Harmonium and Meyer's excellent "Manual of Universal Knowledge." Eduard and Hedwig may extend their knowledge by means of it.

My Belgian week—from May 1st to 8th, Brussels and Antwerp—was of the pleasantest. Enclosed are the moderate articles (on the performance of *St. Elizabeth*) by the Brussels Schelle and Hanslick[2]—Eduard Fétis, the son of the renowned and meritorious author of the many-volumed "Biographie universelle des Musiciens" and of the "Universal History of Music." Thirty years ago I said to that same Fétis somewhat arrogantly, nay almost insolently: "My aspirations are directed not merely towards obtaining articles, but rather towards acquiring a durable position in the History of Art."

Till the beginning of July will remain in Weimar

Yours most cordially,

F. Liszt.

---

[1] The daughter of E. von Liszt, who studied a whole summer under Liszt in Weimar.   [2] In the *Indépendance Belge.*

P.S.—The arrival of the "*Kaiser Virginia*" has just been announced to me.   Please send me the little bill.

298. To Camille Saint-Saëns.

VERY DEAR FRIEND,

I am still quite struck with wonder at your "*Prédication aux oiseaux de St. François*."[1] You use your organ as an orchestra in an incredible way, as only a great composer and a great performer, like yourself, could do.   The most proficient organists in all countries have only to take off their hats to you.

I am sending you by this post a parcel of things of mine for organ.   If you should find an opportunity at Brussels of producing the Introduction to *St. Elizabeth*, it would, under your fingers, have the effect I intended.

Cordial thanks for your visit to Brussels, and ever yours in admiration and friendship.

F. LISZT.

WEIMAR, *May 14th*, 1882.

299. To Madame Malwine Tardieu.

DEAR KIND FRIEND,*

The telegram Tardieu-Lynen-Lessmann sent from Aix-la-Chapelle has given me extreme pleasure.[2]

My *padrone di casa* (Lessmann is this through his paper) are always most excellent.

Daniela de Bülow, my darling granddaughter, writes

---

[1] "St. Francis preaching to the birds." Composed by Liszt for pianoforte alone. (Roszavölgyi.)

* "Chère bienveillante."

[2] The Tardieus, the Lynens (Antwerp friends of Liszt), and Otto Lessmann were present at the Musical Festival at Aix-la-Chapelle.

how kind you are, and will come with us shortly to Villa " Fantaisie " (Bayreuth).[1]

At *Parsifal* we shall be 30,000 ; that will be the best chance of seeing one another again.

The Opera of *Hamlet*, by Stadtfeld,[2] written in transition years (50), and twice given here, not without success, is one of the best that I know of the Meyerbeer-Donizetti *genre*. The Wagner invasion is strangely modifying theatrical requirements at the present time. It is no longer possible to write a " Hamlet " according to the style of a Duprez, some absolute tenor with the famous " *ut de poitrine*," nor to make the ghost of Hamlet's father benevolently intervene in order to effect a Trio or Quartet, even of a pretty musical manufacture. The distinguished work of Stadtfeld belongs, then, to the theatrical Past, so rich in oblivion. . — .

As you are so kind as to undertake my books, I will ask you to send me soon the following works :—

    1st, Gevaërt—History of Music in ancient times : 2 volumes. (Publisher, Annoot Braekmann, at Ghent.)

    2nd, Charles Clément—Michael Angelo, Leonardo da Vinci, Raphael,—a magnificent volume illustrated by 167 drawings. Price, bound, 15 francs. (Publisher, Hetzel, Paris.)

    3rd, J. D. Lewis—" *Bons Mots* of the Greeks and Romans": 1 volume in 16—Charavay library.

[1] She had accompanied her father, Dr. Hans v. Bülow, who played (under Wüllner's conductorship) Brahms' first Pianoforte Concerto, and Beethoven's 15 Variations (on a theme out of the Eroica).

[2] The first performance of the Opera. The composer, a Wiesbaden man (born 1826), had studied at the Brussels Conservatoire, and died there in 1853.

A thousand pardons for thus using and abusing your amiable kindness.

I have read with pleasure the article in the " *Guide Musical*" on the Festival at Aix-la-Chapelle, and beg you to repeat to the author [1] my sincere friendship.

Till our happy meeting at Bayreuth, at the end of July, farewell.

In affectionate gratitude,

F. Liszt.

I add the article from the official paper of Weimar on Stadtfeld's *Hamlet*.

WEIMAR, *June 10th,* 1882.

300. To the Honourable Committee of the *Allgemeine Deutsche Musikverein.**

DEAR SIRS,

The *Allgemeine Deutsche Musikverein* confers a high distinction on me by electing me as its Honorary President.

Since the starting of this *Verein*, 20 years ago, I have the honour of feeling that I have been of service to it. Its aim is a worthy one,—the advancement of music and musicians in an unprejudiced manner, and in accordance with the spirit of the time. Its ways have always been known as pure and worthy of recognition, regardless of opposition and silence.

Let us therefore go boldly forwards on our noble road !

Accept, dear Sirs, my heartiest thanks, together with

---

[1] Presumably Monsieur Tardieu.

* Printed in the *Neue Zeitschrift für Musik,* 1882, No. 23.

the assurance that, ever conscious of my task, I remain, with high esteem,

Yours most faithfully,

F. LISZT.

ROME, [*June*, 1882.]

301. TO THE COMMENDATORE F. VON JAGEMANN AT FREIBURG IN BREISGAU.*

DEAR SIR AND COMMENDATORE,

You ask me if L. Ramann's biography is "classical"? To belong to the classical means, first of all, to be dead, then to be to the world immortal. Neither of these is claimed at present by yours,

F. LISZT.

FREIBURG, *July 6th*, 1882.

302. TO NICOLAUS OESTERLEIN IN VIENNA.[1]

MY DEAR SIR,

I have already heard the praise of your "Catalogue of a Richard Wagner Library." It will be a pleasure to me to make its acquaintance, and while awaiting your kind sending of the work accept thanks for your accompanying lines,

From yours very truly,

F. LISZT.

BAYREUTH, *July 16th*, 1882.

---

* From a copy of Liszt's in the possession of Otto Lessmann at Charlottenburg.

[1] The addressee was the able founder and possessor of the Richard Wagner Museum in Vienna, a unique collection, in its way, of musical and historical importance. The bibliography mentioned in the letter came out (at Breitkopf and Härtel's) shortly before the first performance of *Parsifal*.

303. TO KORNEL VON ABRÁNYI.

BAYREUTH, *July 23rd*, 1882.

DEAR HONOURED FRIEND,

By the same post you will receive the instrumentation of the "A magyarok istene" for the Musical Festival at Debreczin. . — . I beg the directors carefully to try over the small instrumentation *before* the full rehearsal, with the instruments (*plus* the brilliant cymbals), without the vocal parts.

The *solo trumpeter* must perform his part, as a Hungarian Magnate, in a noble manner, and not blow the trumpet as though it were a trade.

I also beg that the directors will be so good as to correct any chance mistakes there may be in my hastily written and unrevised manuscript score. Though I trouble myself but little about the spread of my compositions, yet I do not wish them to be offered to the public in a mutilated form. As I flatter myself that I possess a sufficient portion of self-criticism, other criticism remains only valuable and instructive to me.

Your son Kornel is heartily welcome to me at Bayreuth.

I will discuss here with Vegh [1] the ministerial affairs of your "academic, historical manual." The matter will assuredly be settled to your satisfaction.

Yours most faithfully,

F. LISZT.

Wagner's *Parsifal* far surpasses the master-works which the theatre boasts up to the present time. May the public be educated up to it.

[1] Formerly Vice-president of the Hungarian Academy of Music.

304. To Freiherr Hans von Wolzogen.

My dear Freiherr,

Both at and after yesterday's performance of Wagner's *Parsifal* it was the universal feeling that about this *wonder-work* it is impossible to speak.

It has indeed struck dumb those who were so deeply impressed by it; its sacred pendulum swings from the sublime to the sublimest.

Yours ever,

F. Liszt.

Bayreuth, *July 27th*, 1882.

305. To Madame Malwine Tardieu.

Weimar, *September 12th*, 1882.

Dear Madame and Friend,

How I reproach myself for the delay in my *written* thanks! Those *preceding my letter* have not been wanting, and your friendly kindness touches me deeply. Lassen assures me of your indulgence. He has lately heard at Brussels " l'hymne à la beauté," [1] and (between ourselves) did not think it particularly beautiful. In this kind of music even the greatest masters have seldom succeeded in freeing themselves from lukewarm conventionality. This [conventionality] affords matter for academical prizes such as have been carried off several times by Madame Louise Collet of inglorious memory.

Our friend Benoit shall follow his vocation of musical *Rubens*.

[1] By Benoit. Performed at the Brussels Musical Festival in August 1882.

And Gounod's " Redemption " !   Ought one to speak
of success or non-success in a work of that kind ?
Gounod has always kept the Catholic religious incentive
with a turn towards the sublime.   His *Polyeucte* is a
witness for him.

May that abominable quibbler and bloodthirsty
" doctrinaire," Henry VIII., be the means of a brilliant
and lasting success to St. Saëns, who richly deserves
it ; but in the matter of serious opera the public has
reached that *blasé* point which is explained in the
words of Ronge, a naïve German reformer :—

" What we have we don't want any more ; and
what we would have we don't quite know."   Wagner
has known how to want and to act—gloriously,
although and because.*   His work is already becoming
immortal.

Let us speak of some modest things, concerning
your humble servant.   The three Psalms have been
admirably translated into French by Mr. Lagye ; I
will write my thanks to him fully, as soon as I have
entirely finished the work of *adapting* the text to the
music.   For this it is necessary to modify and rewrite
about fifteen pages, a dozen of which are ready.   I
shall send the whole to Kahnt, the publisher, on Sunday
next, and shall inform Lagye, in whose debt I am, of
the remainder of the arrangements.

His translations appear to me really excellent, very
carefully made, and prosodically well suited to the
music.   I only regret to have to give him so much
trouble, but I hope that in the end he will be satisfied

---

* Wagner a su vouloir et perpétrer—glorieusement, quoique et
parce que.

with me. He shall have the second copy of my *Lieder*; if he succeeds as well in putting them into French as he has done with the three Psalms, they may with advantage make their way in Belgium and still farther.

All my articles of musical criticism, lately published by L. Ramann under the title of " Essays " (Breitkopf and Härtel, Leipzig), were written *in French*. Three or four appeared long ago in the *Débats* and the *Constitutionnel*. The most extensive of these, on Berlioz's Harold Symphony, was to have been put into a celebrated review in Paris, but in the fifties it was considered *too eulogistic*, and I refused any curtailments for Berlioz. . . . Consequently this article has only appeared in a German translation (*Neue Zeitschrift für Musik*, Leipzig). What has become of the original French manuscripts of my complete articles I don't in the least know. The introduction to Härtel's for which Mr. Kufferath[1] asks will not serve his end at all. The only person who could give him some particulars would be Mademoiselle L. Ramann, my biographer, who has been for many years past on the look-out for everything relative to my prose and music. She is the directress of a Pianoforte School in the *Dürerplatz* at *Nuremberg* (*Bavaria*).

Please thank Kufferath for his kind interest, and assure him that, if I abstain from writing to the firm of Härtel, it is from no want of willingness on my part.

---

[1] Moritz Kufferath, a writer on music, reviewer of the " *Guide musical*" (Schott), and translator of many of Wagner's writings, wanted to translate Liszt's Essays into French.

A thousand friendly regards to your husband, and ever cordial and devoted expressions to yourself.

F. Liszt.

I stay here till the beginning of October.

306. To Otto Lessmann.

My very dear Friend,

It is only through your kindness that I learn of Hellmesberger's intention to perform shortly in Vienna a new *Mass* of my composition. Hellmesberger has indeed always been very well disposed towards me, and has frequently conducted the Hungarian Coronation-Mass in the *Hofkapelle*, and several of my longer works at concerts ; but it would be rather difficult for him to conduct a *new* Mass, because I have not composed one. I should think it must be the *Missa choralis* (with Organ accompaniment only). . . .

Here is the list of my Masses, and the order in which they were composed :—

1. For men's voices (with Organ), Anno 48—*Editio nova* at Härtel's.
2. The Gran Mass.
3. Missa choralis (with Organ) at Kahnt's.
4. Hungarian Coronation-Mass (performed at the coronation in Buda).
5. Requiem for men's voices (with Organ). Rome, latter half of the sixties. Published by Kahnt.

Perhaps I shall yet write a Requiem at special command.[1]

---

[1] A requiem, composed on the death of the Emperor Maximilian of Mexico, still exists in manuscript.

I beg you to give my thanks to the friendly publisher of the Symphonic Poem " From the cradle to the grave," for sending me the pianoforte version of this composition. Before the end of October I will send Bock the completed score.

A short piece from *Parsifal*, " Solemn March to the Holy Grail," will reach Schott to-day at Mainz.

Three weeks longer remains here

Yours ever faithfully,

F. Liszt.

Weimar, *September* 16*th*, 1882.

Ever heartily welcome in Weimar ; that is to say, if the visit suits you as *Allegro commodo*. It would be dreadful to me to incommode my friends.

307. To Otto Lessmann.

Dear Friend,

If one wants to be just, he must see that he speaks only with high respect of Hans von Bülow. His knowledge, ability, experience are astounding, and border on the fabulous. Especially has he, by long years of study, so thoroughly steeped himself in the understanding of Beethoven, that it seems scarcely possible for any one else to approach near him in that respect. One must read his commentary on the pianoforte works of Beethoven (Cotta's edition), and hear his interpretations of them—(what other virtuoso could have ventured to play the 5 last Sonatas of Beethoven before the public in one evening ?), and follow Bülow's conducting in the orchestral works of Beethoven.

To set one's back up against such remarkable deeds as these, I call feeble or malicious nonsense.

Yours ever in friendship,

WEIMAR, *September 20th,* 1882.   F. LISZT.

308. TO FRAU CHARLOTTE BLUME-ARENDS.

MY DEAR FRIEND,   WEIMAR, *September 27th,* 1882.

I thank you again for a beautiful, kind gift—"The Oberammergau Passion Play," described by Franz Schöberl, a clergyman in Laibstadt. The little book has been composed with reverence, and gives an exact description of the Oberammergau production, which seems to me especially deserving of notice on account of the *agreement* between the Old Testament *representations*—beginning from Adam and Eve to the Brazen Serpent and further—and their fulfilment in the *facts* of the gospel. This agreement is no simple peasant's invention, but indeed a significant, most touching parallel, thought out by cultured priests, familiar with the Christian tradition. The grouping, and the mute performance of the life-like Old Testament *representations* and of the Crucifixion of Christ in Oberammergau, deserve full praise, in contrast to the music, which is beneath criticism, and very much spoiled the whole performance for me. And even such esteemed and highly honoured Catholic musicians and divines as F. Witt, Haberl, etc., protest against such inane musical stuff and rubbish.

Thank you once more, and with heartfelt greetings to you and yours,

Yours most truly,

F. LISZT.

309. To Otto Lessmann.

Dear Friend,

At the Musical Festival which I had the honour of conducting some twenty-five years ago at Aix-la-Chapelle, Hiller, the friend of my young days in Paris, took up quite a critical attitude against the conductor and his compositions.

I took no particular notice of his behaviour, but I heard that it displeased many people, who made no secret of it to him. I was also told that at one of the rehearsals Hiller did not exactly leave of his own accord. As I was engaged at the conductor's desk I did not observe the occasion of his leaving, and contented myself with reading, some days later, his witty report of the Aix-la-Chapelle Musical Festival in the Cologne paper. My excellent friend, Freiherr Hans von Bronsart, replied to Hiller's article with no less wit and with a different opinion. Unhappily the musical chronicle is overflowing with unresolved discords.

To you, dear friend, I am ever *harmoniously,*

F. Liszt.

Weimar, *October 14th,* 1882.

310. To Otto Lessmann.

[Weimar,] *November 4th,* 1882.

Dear Friend,

I shall be delighted if the *Tannhäuser*-Songs[1] give you satisfaction. Find a pianist of the fair sex, or the other sex, in Berlin, who will set about his task

---

[1] Composed by Lessmann, transcribed by Liszt for piano, and published by Barth, Berlin (now Junne, Leipzig).

well of playing these songs in public. As far as I can tell I should think they would bring the player applause.

I will answer your two questions at once.

Of my " continuously written autobiography " I have as yet heard nothing. Publishers have frequently asked me to write memoirs, but I put it off with the excuse that it was more than enough for me to live through my life, without transcribing it to paper. If I were married I could certainly dictate somewhat of it to my wife now and then. But I am glad to keep out of the bothers of penmanship, which I dislike.

The dramatic performance of the *Elizabeth* in Cologne is to take place after my return from Budapest, next April or May. (I have promised to be present at it.)

Yesterday evening I wrote a couple of lines of thanks and commendation to Herr Duysen, for Fräulein Spiring, whom you met here.[1] She is a pianist and teacher deserving of recommendation, and is trying to establish herself in Berlin, and I commend her to your good graces.

With thanks, yours ever,
F. Liszt.

Rubinstein is coming to see me next Tuesday after the Leipzig performance of the *Maccabees*.

311. To Madame Malwine Tardieu.

Weimar, November 6th, 1882.

Dear friendly One,*

I am still detained here, partly on account of a stupid indisposition,—nothing serious, but disagreeably

---

[1] Lives now in Jena.   * Chère bienveillante.

prolonged.   I make a rule of never bothering my head about my health, and I beg my friends never to trouble about it.

Thank you for sending the 3rd volume of the correspondence of George Sand.   The long letter of 20 pages to Mazzini, dated the 23rd May, '52, appears to me to be a *chef d'œuvre* of judgment and foresight. In 1852 few political men were placed in a sufficiently elevated position to rule the fluctuations of socialism and to understand its necessary value.   Mazzini himself was mistaken in this, as well as in regard to the importance of the acquisition of universal suffrage. Forgive me for wandering off thus into political matters, of which I don't understand anything, and of which it does not concern me to talk.   But I will just quote to you a *mot* which in 1842 was rather widely spread on the sly in Petersburg.   A fair lady of my acquaintance told me that the Emperor Nicholas had said to her of me, "As to his hair and his political opinions, they displease me."   I begged the same lady to transmit my reply, which was as follows : His Majesty has every right in the world to judge me as seemeth well to him, nevertheless I venture to beg him not to think that I am an idiot.   Now it would be idiocy on my part to proclaim political opinions.   The Emperor shall know them when he deigns to put 300,000 soldiers at my disposal.—

To return to the letters of George Sand.   Those addressed in '52 to Prince Jerome Bonaparte and to Louis Napoleon about the *pardoning* of several democrats are in exquisite taste ; the genius of a great heart appears in them.

Allow me to beg for the little account of the books that you have been so kind as to send me, dear Madame Tardieu, and please add to it the price of the subscription to the *Bien public*. I suppose you only took it for one quarter, and I will not go on with it, not having time to read half the papers which my profession and my tastes would lead me to peruse. Besides this my eyes, without having exactly anything the matter with them, do not any longer adapt themselves either to reading or writing without reprieve ; and by evening I often feel extremely tired. . . .

Has the *Indépendance Belge* spoken of a most interesting and superb volume,

"The Correspondence and Musical Works of Constantin Huygens" (17th century), published by Jonckbloet and Land, professors at the University of Leyden, magnificently edited by Brill at Leyden ?

The work is worthy of notice.

To the kind remarks which the *Indépendance* has inserted on the concert of the 23rd October with the Liszt programme,[1] I add the observation that the real title of my "Transcription" of the Rakoczy March should be—*Paraphrase symphonique*. It has more than double the number of pages of Berlioz's well-known one, and was written *before* his. From delicacy of feeling for my illustrious friend I delayed the publication of it until after his death ; for he had dedicated to me his orchestral version of the Rakoczy, for which, however, one of my previous transcriptions served him, chiefly for the harmonisation, which differs, as is well known,

---

[1] A Liszt-concert in the Weimar theatre in celebration of his birthday.

from the rudimentary chords usually employed in the performances of the Tsiganes and other little orchestras on the same lines.   Without any vanity I simply intimate the fact, which any musician can verify for himself.

At last I have just written to my most honoured and more than obliging collaborator, Mr. Lagye. His excellent French translation of my four Psalms is being engraved.   As soon as it is out you shall have it.

In about ten days I shall join the Wagners, and shall spend more than a month with them at the Palazzo Vendramin, Venice.

Cordial regards to your husband, from your

Very grateful and affectionate

F. Liszt.

The director of the subscription concerts at Weimar is going to give Benoit's " La Guerre," and at the next *Musical Festival* Benoit's *Sanctus* and *Benedictus* will be heard.[1]

312. To the Editor of the "Allgemeine Musikzeitung," Otto Lessmann, at Charlottenburg.

Dear Mr. Editor,

As I am very much hindered in my work by overmuch sending of scores, other compositions, and suchlike writings, I beg you to make it known that I wish in future not to have my attention claimed in

---

[1] Both these intentions of Liszt came to nothing, owing to external causes.

this manner. I have modestly refrained for many years past from contributing to collections of autographs.

Yours truly,

F. LISZT.

WEIMAR, *November*, 1882.

313. TO ADELHEID VON SCHORN.

Monday, November 20th, 1882.

Venezia la bella : PALAZZO VENDRAMIN.

DEAR FRIEND,

I don't intend you to hear first through others of my safe arrival here. Thank Heaven! the Wagners and all the family are in perfect health.

Your brother will write you word from Nuremberg that the method of whist, so to say invented and certainly perfected by you, is being spread on to the Dürerplatz also under your name at L. Ramann's. To get rid of all the aces first of all is really glorious.

With the exception of one incident, which stricter people than myself would call a regular fleecing on the part of the Custom House at Milan, whereby I parted with about 70 francs as a fine for having brought 50 cigars (!), all my journey passed off very well. At Zürich I met with the same kind reception on the part of several members of the Committee—with the President of the town, Mr. Roemer, at their head—as at the *Musical Festival* last July. The proprietor of the Bellevue Hotel, Mr. Pohl (no relation to his namesake at Baden), insisted on my accepting gratis a charming room, with dinners, suppers and excellent wines. Such munificence would have given a fit of fever to the late Hemleb of the *Erbprinz*, and his associates will scarcely imitate Mr. Pohl's amiable proceeding. So I will

beg you to recommend the very comfortable Hotel
Bellevue, in the front ranks, to any of your friends
and acquaintances who may pass through Zürich.
Without promising that they will be received *gratis*,
I can assure them that they will find the beautiful view
on to the lake, good rooms, an excellent *cuisine*, and
attentive service. The Duke of Altenburg and other
princes have stayed in it, and inscribed their names in
the hotel album.

Your friend Ada Pinelli is still here with the Princess
Hatzfeld, at Palazzo Malipieri. I shall go and see her
to-morrow. I shall, however, practise great sobriety
in the matter of visits. Wagner does not pay any,
and I shall imitate him on this point to the best of my
ability. My illustrious friend has lodged me splendidly
in a spacious apartment of the Palazzo Vendramin,
which formerly belonged to Madame la Duchesse de
Berry. Her son, the Duke della Grazia, is at present
the owner of it, and Wagner is the tenant for one year.
The beautiful furniture still bears the impress of the
old princely *régime*, and is perfectly preserved. The
main inhabited part of the Palazzo Vendramin is in the
best possible condition, so that Wagner did not have
to go to any special expense, not even for stoves and
other requisites, which are often neglected.

Ever since my first stay in 1837 I have been
enamoured of Venice : this feeling will not grow less
this time, but quite the contrary.

Cordial and very devoted friendship.

F. LISZT.

Try to learn something about Bülow, and send me

word. It was heart-breaking to me not to see him again at Meiningen.

314. To Freiherr Hans von Wolzogen.

MY DEAR FREIHERR,

. —. Wagner is perfectly within the truth when he says that without the extraordinary munificence of H.M. the King of Bavaria the performances of *Parsifal* at Bayreuth would have been endangered, and only the sympathy of the public, outside the Wagner Societies, made the continuance of them possible. But does it follow from this that the Wagner Societies are useless, and that this is the opportunity for disbanding them? To my thinking, No, for they keep up a wholesome agitation, and support the "*Bayreuther Blätter*," which essentially promote the good cause. There does not seem to me to be any advantage in changing the name *Society* [*Verein*] into *Fellowship* [*Genossenschaft*]. Wagner's great name and most important personality are what are most needed here. Moreover the *parliamentariness* of the Societies will not be averse to the absolute authority of the creator of so many immortal works. In merely minor matters variety of opinions may be made apparent; in all essentials we are really and truly one. On this account I desire the continuance, consistency, and increasing welfare of the Societies.—

It goes without saying that Wagner must reign and govern as legitimate monarch, until the complete outward realization of his Bayreuth conception—namely, the model performance of his entire works, under his own *ægis* and directions at Bayreuth.

It behoves all who sympathise in the historico-civilised culture of Art in the coming years of the closing 19th century to endeavour to promote this aim.

When we have attained the end in question let us sing with Schiller and Beethoven,

"Freude, schöner Götterfunken!" *

Accept, dear Freiherr, the assurance of my true and high esteem.

F. Liszt.

Pray remember me most kindly to your family.

315. To Franz Servais.

Dear Franz,

Your welcome lines reached me at Weimar and I thank you cordially for them. . . .

I tell you again, dear Franz, that you were "born with a silver spoon in your mouth"; after the hearing of your Opera with the piano the success of a performance will follow.—Don't get impatient at a little delay; the most illustrious composers, including Meyerbeer, could not say, like Louis XIV., "*J'ai failli attendre.*" †. . . But I hope that the saying "*Tout vient à point ā qui sait attendre*" ‡ will be realised in your case without much delay. Good courage then and Mistress Patience.

Will you remember me very affectionately to Godebski; his graceful bust, so perfect in its likeness

---

* "Joy, thou spark from heaven descending!"
† "I nearly had to wait."
‡ "All comes to him who can wait."

to the never-to-be-forgotten Madame Moukhanoff, is ever the precious ornament of my little *salon* at the "*Hofgärtnerei*" in Weimar.

The large bust of Rossini which Godebski presented to the Grand Duke ornaments the lobby of the theatre, where it blooms like a god from Olympus. Tell me what works Godebski has been doing lately.

When next you see Madame Judith Gautier, please express to her anew the admiring homage of your very faithful

F. Liszt.

Venezia, *November 26th*, 1882.

P.S.—Our friends * * * might, I think, do you good service with M. Vaucorbeil, and could tell him also, as a "by the way," that I take a lively interest in your work. Would you perhaps think it advisable to let some fragment of it be given at a public concert?

I am remaining here till New Year's Day with the Wagners, at the superb Palazzo Vendramin; then I shall return direct to Budapest.

316. To Adelheid von Schorn.

Venezia, *December 8th*, 1882.

Dear Friend,

Your sad news about Bülow's bad state of health are much the same as his wife gave to Daniela. Let us hope for more reassuring news!

Here, in Palazzo Vendramin, a peaceful and most united family life goes on without monotony. But I cannot speak of the things which touch me most, except clumsily. So it is better to keep from doing so.

The Princess writes to me from Rome that she

shall be delighted to obtain possession of the two water-colours of Gleichen for the splendid portfolios of drawings belonging to her daughter, of which the mother, since the years at Weimar, has regally provided the greater part.   These portfolios are among the finest collections in Europe.

Joukowski,[1] who has been delayed by a funeral and by the floods, will arrive here to-day.   Neither funerals nor floods have been able to prevent Lassen from scoring our Symphonic Intermezzo " *Über allen Zauber Liebe.*" *   I hope Lassen will conduct it at the Court concert on New Year's Day, and I beg you to go and hear it and let me know about it. . — .

I beg Gille to send me the volume " *Die deutsche Bühne von einem Weimaraner.*" †   Do you know who it is ?   According to the index he seems to ignore the doings of the Weimar theatre during the last thirty years, which is not very honourable to a Weimarer, and looks very like a cowardly action of a low standard.

Your cordially devoted

F. LISZT.

Saturday Morning, December 9th.

Joukowski arrived last night, and we began at once to sound your praises.

Daniela has written to you.   I will send you the programme of the performance of Goethe's *Geschwister*,‡ which will take place to-morrow at Princess Hatzfeld's.

[1] Widely known by his *Parsifal* sketches and the portraits of Liszt and of Wagner's family.

* "Above all magic Love."

† "The German stage, by a Weimarer."

‡ "Brothers and Sisters."

Those old books of operas, such as "*Les Indes galantes*," * and other antiquities, re-edited in Paris, may peaceably repose at the "*Hofgärtnerei*," unless you prefer to lend them to some one who likes works of that kind, which are sought by some.

317. To Professor Carl Riedel.

Dear Friend,

Dräseke's *Requiem* is such a first-rate work, and is so likely to obtain a good reception from the public, that I again recommend the performance of it at the next *Tonkünstler-Versammlung*. Dräseke will presumably also agree to it in the end.

Gustav Weber's Trio, Op. 5, published by Siegel, and dedicated to me, I consider an eminent work, worthy of recommendation and performance. I am sure you think the same.

I should like to add to the vocal programme of the *Tonkünstler-Versammlung* two songs by your namesake Riedel,[1] now *Hofkapellmeister* in Brunswick. If they should be ascribed to you they will please you all the better for that. And *à propos*, why do you let your valuable, excellent works be so seldom heard in public ? I shall reproach you further with this injustice to yourself when we come to talk over the programme, and I hope that you won't continue to overdo your reserve as a composer. Without pushing one's-self forward one must still maintain one's position, to which you, dear friend, are fully entitled.

---

* "The gallant Indies."

[1] Hermann Riedel, born 1847, made a special success with songs from Scheffel's "*Trompeter von Säkkingen*."

Will you be so kind as to tell Härtel to send me here quickly 25 sheets of 10 line, and 25 sheets of 12 line music paper (oblong shape, not square) for cash, together with a few of the small *books of samples,* containing all kinds of music paper, which I have recommended several musical friends of mine here and elsewhere to buy. One can rub out easily on this paper, which is one of the most important things—that is to say, unless one tears up the whole manuscript, which would often be advisable.

A happy Christmas, and a brave New Year '83.

Ever your faithfully attached

F. Liszt.

Venezia, Palazzo Vendramin, *December 9th,* 1882.

318. To Arthur Meyer in Paris, President of the Committee of the " Presse Parisienne." *

Monsieur le Directeur,

My telegram of this morning expressed to you my excuses and deep regret at being unable to be of use in the programme of your Festival.[1]

It would certainly be an honour to me to take part in it, and I am by no means oblivious of the gratitude I owe to Paris, where my youthful years were passed.

Moreover it would be, it seems to me, a becoming thing that, after the generous and striking sympathy shown by Paris—also by a festival at the Grand

---

* Copied in the *Gazette de Hongrie* at Budapest, February 1st, 1883.

[1] Liszt had been asked to take part in a Festival which was given at the Grand Opera for the benefit of the sufferers from the inundations in Alsace-Lorraine. " The name of Liszt in France," they wrote, " is synonymous with triumph, and we know that it is also synonymous with kindness."

Opera—to my compatriots on the occasion of the inundation of Szeged, an artist from Hungary, who has been favoured by so much French kindness, should make his public acknowledgments at your approaching grand performance.

Unfortunately my age of 72 years invalidates me as a pianist. I could no longer risk in public my ten fingers—which have been out of practice for years—without incurring just censure. There is no doubt on this point ; and I am perfectly resolved to abstain from any exhibition of my old age at the piano in any country.

Please accept, Monsieur le Directeur, my thanks and best compliments.

F. Liszt.

BUDAPEST, *January 28th*, 1883.

319. To the Composer Albert Fuchs.

Your Hungarian Suite[1] is an excellent and effective work. While springing from the musical ground of Hungary, it nevertheless remains your own property, as there are no imitations or used-up ornamentations in it, but rather much new employment of harmonies, and always a national colouring. For the dedication you are heartily thanked by

F. Liszt.

BUDAPEST, *February 4th*, 1883.

320. To Saissy, Editor of the " Gazette de Hongrie" in Budapest.*

I come to ask your advice, dear Monsieur Saissy ; please give it me quite frankly, without any

---

[1] For Orchestra, dedicated to Liszt.

* From a rough copy in the possession of Herr O. A. Schulz, bookseller in Leipzig.

reserve, and tell me whether you think it is an opportune moment for my letter (which I enclose), relative to my *pretended* animadversion against the Israelites, to be published or not. If you think it is, I beg you to insert it in the next number of the *Gazette de Hongrie*; otherwise it shall remain unprinted, as I shall not send it to any other paper.

As the proverb says, "Silence is gold"; but perhaps, under the given circumstances, in view of the serious question of the Israelites in Hungary, it would be better to speak in the current silver money in the papers.

Let us rectify errors, and remain modest but not timid. In faithful devotion,

F. LISZT.

BUDAPEST, *February 6th,* 1883.

321. TO THE EDITOR OF THE "GAZETTE DE HONGRIE." *

MR. EDITOR,

It is not without regret that I address these lines to you; but, as there has been some report spread here about my pretended hostility to the Israelites, I ought to rectify the mistake of this false report.

As is well known in the musical world, many illustrious Israelites, Meyerbeer first and foremost, have given me their esteem and friendship, and the same in the literary world with Heine and others.

It seems to me that it would be superfluous to

---

* Published in the *Gazette de Hongrie* of February 8th, 1883, Budapest. A translation of it also appeared in German papers; amongst others, in Lessmann's *Allgemeine Musikzeitung*, at the wish of the Master, who was annoyed with the aspersion against himself of having promoted the Antisemitic movement.

enumerate the many proofs I have given, during fifty years, of my active loyalty towards Israelites of talent and capacity, and I abstain in like manner from speaking of my voluntary contributions to the charitable institutions of Judaism in various countries.

The motto of my patron saint, St. François de Paule, is " Caritas ! " I will remain faithful to this throughout my life !

If, by some mutilated quotations from my book on the *Gipsies* in Hungary, it has been sought to pick a quarrel with me, and to make what is called in French *une querelle d'Allemand*, I can in all good conscience affirm that I feel myself to be guiltless of any other misdeed than that of having feebly reproduced the argument of the kingdom of Jerusalem, set forth by Disraeli (Lord Beaconsfield), George Eliot (Mrs. Lewes), and Crémieux, three Israelites of high degree.

Accept, Sir, etc.,

F. LISZT.

February 6th, 1883.

322. To Rich and Mason in Toronto.*

[1883.]

DEAR SIRS,

The Rich and Mason Grand Piano which you have so kindly sent me here is a pattern one. And as such will artists, judges, and the public recognise it.

Together with my hearty thanks I wanted at the same time to send you the Liszt portrait for which you wished. It was painted by Baron Joukowski, son of the highly honoured tutor and friend of Alexander II.,

---

* From a rough copy in the possession of Herr O. A. Schulz bookseller in Leipzig.

a man who will also be ever famous in Russian literature. Now, however, this Liszt portrait has been such a success that they wanted to have a second one like it for the Joukowski Museum. The painter kindly consented to the request, which has necessitated a delay of 2 to 3 months in my sending off the first portrait to Toronto.

Joukowski had also prepared the sketches for the *Parsifal* scenery in Bayreuth, which were followed by a successful performance.

Excuse, dear Sirs, the delay in my acknowledgments, and accept the assurance of my high esteem.

F. LISZT.

323. TO MADAME MARIE JAELL IN VIENNA.*

CHÈRE ADMIRABLE [DEAR ADMIRABLE ONE],

I give you at once a most cordial welcome to Budapest. Have you already made your arrangements for concerts here? Can my very excellent friend Bösendorfer be of use to you as an agent? To my regret I am not in a position to help you in that, on account of my being so very decidedly out of touch with the principal concert arrangers of the neighbourhood, who impertinently make a pitiable trade for the benefit of Art . . . the art of their own pocket and predominance.

To our right speedy meeting! Will you let me make acquaintance with your new compositions, and

* Autograph in possession of Herr Commerzienrath Bösendorfer in Vienna.—The addressee was the widow of Alfred Jaell, and was a pianiste and composer in Paris.

accept the homage of my admiring sympathy and affection?

F. LISZT.

BUDAPEST, *February 12th,* 1883.

Have you had anything to do with a serious and really distinguished composer,—Rendano? He is giving his concert in Vienna one of these next days.

324. TO ADELHEID VON SCHORN.

If you were here, dear friend, you would perhaps find means to put into some sort of order the hundreds of letters that rain upon me from everywhere. These bothers and burdens of the amiability with which I am credited are becoming insupportable, and I really long, some fine day, to cry from the housetops that I beg the public to consider me as one of the most disagreeable, whimsical and disobliging of men.

To our cordial meeting at Weimar in the early days of April.

Ever your very affectionate and grateful

F. LISZT.

BUDAPEST, *February 14th,* 1883.

325. TO OTTO LESSMANN.

Your sad news [1] pierces my heart. Worthily have you said of the great, undying hero of Art, " May the memory of him lead us on the right road to truth !"

I abstained from going at once to Venice and Bayreuth, but no sensible man will on that account doubt my feelings.

---

[1] After Wagner's death on the 13th February.

Until Passion Week I remain here ; then according to what my daughter arranges I shall either go to Bayreuth or elsewhere, wherever my dearly beloved daughter may be.

Hearty thanks, dear friend, for your satisfactory, truthful adjustment of my position, which is neither a doubtful nor a cowardly one, in the Jewish question.

The watchword and solution of that question is a matter for the perseverance of the Israelites and for the all-ruling Divine Providence.

Yours faithfully and gratefully,

F. Liszt.

BUDAPEST, *February 18th,* 1883.

I shall send that number of your weekly paper (16th February) to Cardinal Haynald, my gracious patron of many years' standing—who was also the President of the Liszt-Jubilee Festival in Budapest.

326. To Lina Ramann.

MY VERY DEAR FRIEND,

Ever since the days of my youth I have considered dying much simpler than living. Even if often there is fearful and protracted suffering before death, yet is death none the less the deliverance from our involuntary yoke of existence.

Religion assuages this yoke, yet our heart bleeds under it continually !—

" Sursum corda ! "

In my " Requiem " (for men's voices) I endeavoured to give expression to the mild, redeeming character of death. It is shown in the " Dies iræ," in which the

domination of fear could not be avoided ; in the three-
part strophe

> " Qui Mariam absolvisti,
> Et latronem exaudisti,
> Mihi autem spem dedisti "

lies the fervent, tender accent, which is not easily
attained by ordinary singers. . . . The execution is
also made more difficult by the 2 semitones, ascending
in the 1st Tenor, and descending in the 2nd Tenor
and 1st Bass. Progressions of this kind are indeed
not new, but singers so seldom possess the requisite
crystal-clear intonation without which the unhappy
composer comes to grief.

Our 3rd *Élégie*, " The funeral gondola " ("la gondola
funèbre"), written unawares last December in Venice,
is to be brought out this summer by Kahnt, who has
already published my 2 earlier Elegies.

Heartfelt greetings to your respected collaborators,
and ever yours gratefully,

F. LISZT.

BUDAPEST, *February 22nd*, 1883.

327. TO MADAME MALWINE TARDIEU.

DEAR BENEVOLENT ONE,

To great grief silence is best suited. I will
be silent on Wagner, the prototype of an initiatory
genius.

Thank you cordially for your telegram of yesterday.[1]
No one rejoices more than I in the success of Saint-
Saëns. There is no doubt that he deserves it ; but

---

[1] On the success of Saint-Saëns' Opera *Henry VIII.* at the opera
in Paris.

fortune, grand sovereign of doubtful manners, is often in no hurry to array herself on the side of merit.

One has to keep on tenaciously pulling her by the ear (as Saint-Saëns has done) to make her listen to reason.

Be so good as to send me the number of the *Indépendance* with the article on *Henry VIII.* I will ask M. Saissy, the director of the *Gazette* (French) *de Hongrie*, professor of French literature at the University of Budapest, to reproduce this article in his Gazette. Saissy is one of my friends; consequently he will publish what is favourable to *Henry VIII.*

Saint-Saëns has sent me the score of his *beautiful* work "La Lyre et la Harpe." Alas! everything that is not of the *theatre* and does not belong to the *répertoire* of the old classical masters Händel, Bach, Palestrina, etc., does not yet gain any attentive and paying consideration—the decisive criterion—of the public. Berlioz, during his lifetime, furnished the proof of this.

Please give my love to your husband, and accept my devoted and grateful affection.

F. LISZT.

BUDAPEST, *March 6th*, 1883.

With regard to Lagye, I am contrite. Various things which I had to send off with care have prevented me from going on with the revision of the French edition of my *Lieder*. It shall be done next month.

328. TO FERDINAND TABORSZKY, MUSIC PUBLISHER IN BUDAPEST.

DEAR TABORSZKY,

As it is uncertain whether I shall still be alive next year, I have just written an Hungarian *Königslied*

[Royal Song] according to an old mode, for the opening of the New Hungarian Theatre in Radialstrasse.

Herewith is the manuscript for pianoforte, two hands, and the score with text by Kornel Abrányi[1] will follow in Easter week.

The publishing of my *Königslied* ought not to take place till the first performance in the new theatre in '84. Until then we will keep quiet about it.—

Yours in all friendship,
F. Liszt.

Budapest, *March* 11*th*, 1883.

329. To Baroness M. E. Schwartz.*

Budapest, March 22nd, 1883.

Dear and most excellent One,†

It is really extraordinary that after so many years of constant practice in works of mercy you are not ruined. Your life seems to me one vast *symphony* of generosity, munificence, charities, gifts and attentions as delicate as they are costly. To begin with, there are Garibaldi and his people, and to continue indefinitely there are those poor German fellows, ill at Rome, and buried there at your expense ; and then the fighting Cretans, the infirm people in your hospital at Jena, the societies for the protection of animals, etc., etc.

I admire you and bow before your perpetual kindnesses and goodness,—all the more because you exercise them unobtrusively, as it were in the shade, without any flourish of trumpets and drums.

Do not scold me for having divided the gift you

---

[1] German translation by Ladislaus Neugebauer.

* Autograph in the Liszt Museum at Weimar.

† Chère excellentissime.

confided to me for the sufferers from the inundations at Raab. 300 florins were amply sufficient for them, and the other 300 florins of your 50 pounds sterling were well employed for the children's gardens (an admirable institution of Fröbel's), of which Madame Tisza, the wife of the President of Council of the Ministers of Hungary, is the president in this country.

I send you herewith Madame Tisza's thanks (in Hungarian, with a German translation), and the receipt of Count Thun,—supreme Count (an ancient title still preserved,—"Obergespan" in German) of the Committee of Raab.

I preferred to send your gift in the name of Madame E. de Schwartz, and not to mix up your *nom de plume* of Elpis Melena with it. Pardon me this innocent bit of arbitrariness.

Shall I see you again, my very dear friend, this summer at Weimar? I hope so, and I remain *semper ubique*
Your grateful and attached
F. LISZT.

From the middle of April until August I shall stay at Weimar, with the exception of some excursions of a few days' duration. Please let me know a couple of weeks beforehand when your friendly visit will take place.

330. To BARONESS WRANGEL IN ST. PETERSBURG.[1]
MADAME LA BARONNE,

For thirty years past I have entirely abstained from adding to collections of autographs and of writing my name in any albums whatever.

[1] This lady had begged Liszt for a contribution to an album which

Nevertheless I willingly make an exception to-day, while thanking you for your kind words, and begging you to transmit to my honoured friend A. Henselt the short copy enclosed herewith.

A renowned diplomatist once said to me, " To princes one should offer only flowers gathered from their own gardens."

Henselt belongs to the princes, and will accept the souvenir of one of the most beautiful flowers of his own noble gardening.

Very humble respects.

F. Liszt.

Weimar, *May 20th,* 1883.

"Albumblatt" for Henselt.

Motive of the wonderful *Larghetto* in A. Henselt's Concerto.

it was intended to present to Henselt on the occasion of a festival in honour of his having been 25 years General Music Inspector of the Imperial Schools in St. Petersburg, Moscow, etc. This is Liszt's answer.

etc. (ever more and more beautiful)

For 40 years the composer's admiring and truly attached

F. LISZT.

WEIMAR, *May,* 1883.

331. TO MASON AND HAMLIN IN BOSTON.*

MY DEAR SIRS,

For what a magnificent Organ I have to thank your kindness! It is worthy of all praise and admiration! Even average players could attain much success on it.—I should gladly have kept this splendid instrument in my own house, but, alas! there is not sufficient room for it. It is now looking grand in the large room of the Orchestral School here, an institution of importance, the excellent director of which is *Herr Professor* and *Hofcapellmeister* K. Müller-Hartung —he has published some beautiful Organ Sonatas and plays them no less beautifully.—On the evening of its opening two renowned organists played upon it, the Court organist A. W. Gottschalg (the publisher of the considerable Organ *répertoire,* etc., etc.), and the town organist B. Sulze, who has attained a great name through many valuable compositions and transcriptions.—I shall probably have a visit this summer from Prof. Dr. Naumann from Jena, Walter Bache

* Printed in Gottschalg's " Urania."

from London, and Saint-Saëns from Paris, who, according to my opinion, continues to be the most eminent and extraordinary king of organists. I shall not fail to beg the three above-mentioned virtuosi to make a closer acquaintance with your organ. For the rest it shall not be misused and shall remain closed to ordinary players.

Accept, etc.,

F. Liszt.

WEIMAR, *June 12th*, 1883.

332. To Madame Malwine Tardieu.

Chère Bienveillante,

Thank you for the very agreeable news of the resumption and continuation of the performances of *Henry VIII.* No one wishes Saint-Saëns, more than I do, all the success that he grandly deserves, both in the theatre and in concerts.

In the matter of concerts, those of the Meiningen orchestra, under Bülow's conductorship, are astonishing, and very instructive for the due comprehension of the works and the *rendering* of them. I send you a copy of some lines written to a friend ; these will give you my impression,—one which you would share if you heard these concerts of the highest artistic lineage. —The parallel between the Sigurd of Reyer [1] and the Siegfried of Wagner is ingeniously traced by your husband, and renders good preparatory service to the success of the performances of Sigurd. As to the Nibelungen tetralogy of Wagner—it shines with an immortal glory.

---

[1] Performed for the first time on 7th January, 1884, at the Théâtre de la Monnaie, Brussels.

In the course of the winter season the Weimar theatre will give Gevaërt's *Quentin Durward*. Lassen will take the utmost pains in directing the study and performance of it. To my regret I shall not be able to be present at the *première* here, as I am obliged to be at Budapest before the middle of January.

Please give Tardieu the cordial love of

Your much attached

F. LISZT.

WEIMAR, *December 14th*, 1883.

Yet another young pianist, but one of the best kind, —M. Siloti, a Russian by birth, and of good education. He was said to be the best pupil of Nicholas Rubinstein before he came to work with me. He obtained a marked success at Leipzig lately, which he will continue next week at Antwerp. In spite of my aversion to letters of introduction, I am giving him a couple of words for the Lynens, and I recommend him to your kind attention.

333. To CASAR CUI.

VERY HONOURED FRIEND,

It is well known in various countries in what high esteem I hold your works. As I am convinced that the "*Suite*" of which you speak will prove itself worthy of your preceding compositions, I feel that I am honoured by the dedication, and thank you for it with gratitude. Your musical style is raised far above ordinary phraseology; you do not cultivate the convenient and barren field of the commonplace. . . . Doubtless *form* in Art *is* necessary to the expression of ideas and sentiments; it must be adequate, supple, free, now energetic, now graceful, delicate ; sometimes even subtle and complex, but always to the exclusion of the ancient remains of decrepit *formalism.*

At Meiningen, where Bülow's admirable conducting is working wonders of rhythm and *nuances* with the orchestra, I lately had the honour of a conversation with the Grand Duke Constantine Constantinowitch, on the actual development of music in Russia and of the well-known capacity of its courageous promoters. His Imperial Highness justly appreciates their serious worth, their noble character and intense originality ; consequently, dear Monsieur Cui, the Grand Duke accords full praise to your talents and deserts.

I take pleasure in repeating this to you, at the same time renewing to you the assurance of my very sincere regard.

F. Liszt.

WEIMAR, *December 30th,* 1883.

A young Russian pianist, M. Siloti, who has been brought to a high state of virtuosity by the lessons and example of Nicholas Rubinstein, is now gaining a real success in Germany. When he comes to Petersburg I recommend him to your kindness.

334. To Otto Lessmann.

WEIMAR, *January 10th,* 1884.

Dear Friend,

The remarkable concerts of the Meiningen Court orchestra led me to the attempt to write a *Bülow March.* I send you herewith a Preface to this, and also an article (in French), in the form of a letter, on my impressions in Meiningen.

Will you insert both these in your paper? Also kindly translate the French letter.[1]

Faithfully yours,

F. LISZT.

I shall stay ten days to a fortnight longer in Weimar on account of the severe illness of Achilles.[2]

Preface to the Bülow March.

For thirty years Hans von Bülow has been expressing and actively furthering everything that is noble, right, high-minded and free-minded in the regions of creative Art. As virtuoso, teacher, conductor, commentator, propagandist—indeed even sometimes as a humorous journalist—Bülow remains the *Chief* of musical progress, with the initiative born in and belonging to him by the grace of God, with an impassioned perseverance, incessantly striving heroically after the Ideal, and attaining the utmost possible.

His conducting of the Meiningen Court orchestra is a fresh proof of this. To that same orchestra this *Bülow March* is dedicated in high esteem for their model symphonic performances, by

F. LISZT.

WEIMAR, *January*, 1884.

MEININGEN, *December*, 1883.

At seven o'clock people were at the rehearsal of the *Beethoven concert*. Under Bülow's conducting the Meiningen orchestra accomplishes wonders. Nowhere

---

[1] It follows here after the Preface in the original. A German translation of it appeared in Lessmann's *Allgemeine Musikzeitung* on the 18th January, 1884, under the title of "Letter to a friend."

[2] Liszt's servant.

is there to be found such intelligence in different works; precision in the performance with the most correct and subtle rhythmic and dynamic *nuances*. The fact of the opera having been abolished at Meiningen by the Duke some twenty years ago is most favourable to the concerts. In this way the orchestra has time to have a fair number of partial and full rehearsals without too much fatigue, as the opera work has been done away with. Bülow is almost as lavish of rehearsals as Berlioz would have been if he had had the means to be. . . . The result is admirable and in certain respects matchless, not excepting the Paris *Conservatoire* and other celebrated concert-institutions. The little Meiningen phalanx, thanks to its present General, is in advance of the largest battalions. It is said that Rubinstein and some others have expressed themselves disapprovingly about some of the unusual *tempi* and *nuances* of Bülow, but to my thinking their criticism is devoid of foundation. . . .

Besides the programme of the Beethoven concert, in the morning there was an *extra séance* of the orchestra for the performance of the Overtures to " King Lear " (Berlioz) and to the " *Meistersinger*," my march " *Vom Fels zum Meer*," the " *Ideales*," and Brahms' Variations on a theme of Haydn. Always the same and complete understanding in the *ensemble* and the details of the scores,—the same vigour, energy, refinement, accuracy, *relief*, vitality and superior *characteristics* in the interpretation.

An extraordinary thing! the most difficult Quartet of Beethoven, one which on account of its complications never figures on any programme, the grand fugue,

Op. 133, is played by the Meiningen orchestra with a perfect *ensemble*. On a previous occasion I also heard at Meiningen Bach's celebrated Chaconne played *in unison* with a real virtuosity by some ten violins.

F. LISZT.

335. TO FELIX MOTTL, HOFCAPELLMEISTER AT CARLSRUHE.[1]

MY VERY DEAR FRIEND,

You have done a noble artistic deed in reinstating Cornelius's charming Opera "The Barber of Bagdad." I hardly know of any other comic opera of so much refined humour and spirit. This champagne has the real *sparkle* and great worth.

The *one-act* arrangement seems to me the most propitious. As in Carlsruhe so elsewhere it will make its way. Write about this to Hans Richter. "The Barber of Bagdad" might perhaps, *in one act*, become a stock-opera in Vienna, and then return once more to Weimar, where, at the first performance long ago, they behaved so ill about it.

Friendly thanks, and yours ever,
F. LISZT.

BUDAPEST, *February 8th*, 1884.

336. TO FRAU HOFRÄTHIN HENRIETTE VON LISZT.

MY VERY DEAR COUSIN,

This time I was not able to have a thorough rest in Vienna. Such an extra [luxury] is hardly my

[1] The addressee, born in 1856, has been since 1880 at Carlsruhe, where he was recently appointed to the post of Court opera conductor, and since 1886 one of the conductors of the Bayreuth Festivals. He is one of the most important conductors of the present day, and has also come forward as a composer.

lot anywhere. My life is one continued fatigue.
Some one once asked the celebrated Catholic champion
Arnauld (the Jansenist) why he did not allow himself
some rest. "We have eternity for that," answered he.

I hear for the first time through you of a cousin or
niece, Mary Liszt, a concert giver. Concert givers
have frequently misused our name by playing under
it in provincial towns. A pianist in Constantinople,
Herr Listmann, apologised to me for having knocked
off the second syllable of his name. On this account
he received a valuable present from the then Sultan
Abdul Medgid. . — .

Farewell till our next meeting in Easter week, dear
cousin, from yours ever affectionately,

F. Liszt.

BUDAPEST, *February 8th*, 1884.

One, and even two, letters from the Princess in the
month of January have been lost.

337. To Camille Saint-Saëns.

VERY DEAR AND MOST EXCELLENT FRIEND,

Before I received your kind letter I had intimated
to Baron Podmaniczki, the Intendant of the theatre of
Budapest, that he ought to esteem it an honour to give
your *Henry VIII.*—a frightful personage in history,
but brilliantly illustrated by your beautiful music.[1]
The inauguration of the new theatre will take place at
the end of September with the *St. Etienne*, a new
Opera by Erkel, the popular dramatic composer *par
excellence* in Hungary. His *Hunyadi Laszlo* was per-

---

[1] Opera by Saint-Saëns.

formed 250 times, and his *Bankban* more than 100, without ever over-reaching the mark. Two other works are promised after the *St. Etienne*, so that your *Henry VIII.* cannot appear till '85, for it still has to be translated into Hungarian.

I spoke about it in Vienna to his Excellency Baron Hoffmann, the Intendant of the Imperial Theatres. He told me that your work is going to be given shortly at Prague, and that he will send his own conductor, M. Jahn, there, in order that it may be better looked after. I beg that you will send the piano score of *Henry VIII.* at once to M. *le directeur* Jahn (very influential), with a few polite lines; also to do the same to M. Erkel Sandor (son of the composer), conductor of the National Opera of Budapest. Address to him "Théâtre National," Budapest.

Very much vexed to be unable to make a place for one of your grand works—such as your superb Mass or some Poëme symphonique—in the programme of our next *Tonkünstler-Versammlung* at Weimar from the 23rd to the 28th May. Sauret is going to play your third Concerto, and I will send you this overloaded programme. If you came to hear it, it would be a very great pleasure to

Your admiringly and cordially attached
F. LISZT.

WEIMAR, *April 29th*, 1884.

338. TO OTTO LESSMAMN.

[WEIMAR,] *May 7th*, 1884.

DEAR FRIEND,

The motto of my Oratorio "Stanislaus" is "Religion and Fatherland."

In the fragment (Orchestral Interlude) which will be given here at the next *Tonkünstler-Versammlung* the whole meaning of the work is made plain.[1]

Farewell till our speedy meeting.

Ever faithfully yours,

F. LISZT.

339. TO CAMILLE SAINT-SAËNS.

VERY DEAR FRIEND AND CONFRÈRE,

I refused to suspect that there could be any ill-will against you at Budapest. Nevertheless I think it is strange and most unjust that your dramatic and symphonic works have not yet taken the place which is due to them in Hungary. I have explained myself clearly about them several times, but the theatre *ménage*, and even that of the Philharmonic Concerts, is formed outside of my influence. They are quite ready to accord me a general consideration, with the exception of arranging particular cases otherwise than I wished. For many people doubtful profits and manœuvres contrary to their dignity exercise an irresistible attraction. The idea of honour seems to them too troublesome.

I shall not desist in the least from my conscientious propaganda of your *Henry VIII.* and other of your works. The new theatre at Budapest will open (at the end of September) with the *Roi St. Etienne,** a grand Hungarian Opera by Erkel (senior). After that Baron Podmaniczky, the Intendant, has promised to

[1] This remained unfinished, as is well known.

* King Stephen.

give a new Opera by Goldmark, also Hungarian in subject, and another by Delibes. The *Henry VIII.* should appear somewhere between these three.   Its performance at Prague will determine that at Vienna, which will be soon, I hope. His Excellency Baron Hoffmann, the Intendant of the Imperial Theatres in Vienna, told me that he would send his artistic and musical conductor (at the Opera), M. Jahn, to Prague. It depends on the opinion of this person whether *Henry VIII.* is given at Vienna.

When you come again to Weimar you are sure to be received there with sympathy, gratitude and sincere admiration by your old attached friend,

F. LISZT.

WEIMAR, *May* 18*th*, 1884.

Thanks for the photograph. You will find it well placed here near a charming bust. The Court and town of Weimar keep their affectionate and kind sentiments towards you.

340. TO WALTER BACHE.

DEAR HONOURED FRIEND,

I am very gladly in accord with all your doings, and only protest against the sacrifice you have in the noblest manner made for my severely criticised works.

The English edition of the *Elizabeth Legend* with your sister's translation delights me.

Tell Mr. Alfred Littleton he can send me the proof-sheets (*bound*) of the piano edition, and the score, to Weimar.   Along with this the 4 four-hand pieces (published by Kahnt) might also be published. Would it be well perhaps to begin with these? Arrange about this as you like with Mr. Littleton. I have only to correct the proofs, which will quickly follow.

If you think it would do, I shall also add to the English edition a little Preface, in the form of a letter —addressed to Walter Bache.

By the same post to-day I send you the complete enormous programme of the *Tonkünstler-Versammlung* (going through 25 years). This evening they begin with the *acting* performance of the Elizabeth Legend.

Auf Wiedersehen! [To our next meeting!]

I shall stay at Bayreuth from July 5th till the middle of August, and then come back to Weimar.

Faithfully and gratefully,

WEIMAR, *May 23rd*, 1884.   F. LISZT.

I have told Kahnt all that concerns himself in your letter.

341. TO THE COMPOSER CARL NAVRÁTIL IN PRAGUE.
DEAR HERR NAVRÁTIL,

I write in haste to tell you that Smetana's [1] death has moved me deeply. He was a genius. More in my next. In haste.

F. LISZT.

WEIMAR, *May 30th*, 1884.

342. TO BARON FRIEDRICH PODMANICZKY, INTENDANT
    OF THE HUNGARIAN OPERA IN BUDAPEST.*
MONSIEUR LE BARON,   [1884.]

I have begged my friend M. de Mihalovich to lay before you a proposition, the fate of which depends

---

[1] Bohemian composer and pianist (1824-84).

* From a rough copy in Liszt's own handwriting in the possession of Abrányi.

on the committee that directs the orders for the sculptures of the new National Hungarian Theatre.

In my humble opinion it would be unjust, and even ungrateful, to exclude from them the likenesses of two composers of high distinction, the late Mosonyi and Franz Doppler.

A charming Opera of Mosonyi's of elevated taste, *Szép Ilonka*,[1] has been performed here some dozen times with success, and was then consigned to oblivion in the *oubliettes* of the administration. Another greater dramatic work by Mosonyi, *Almos*, has remained in manuscript, although Baron Orczy, your predecessor as Intendant, had some idea of producing it.

The whole of the brave musical activity of Mosonyi at Budapest is most honourable and meritorious, as much by his teaching as by his numerous compositions of Church music, orchestral music, and piano music. Many of his Hungarian pieces remain classical, as opposed to the current wares, supposed to be of this same kind, more frequently heard (at the present time in Vienna).

Franz Doppler has left the best possible remembrance of his rare talents and qualities at Budapest, where during many years he fulfilled the duties of conductor to the theatre, and shone by his virtuosity (very celebrated in Europe) as a flute player—an instrument which Frederick the Great condescended to use. Doppler's Operas *Beniowszky* and *Ilka* were favourably received ; and up to the present time *Ilka* is the only Hungarian opera admitted to the *répertoire* of

---

[1] "The fair Helen" : its subject, like that of his other Opera *Almos*, was taken from Hungarian history.

several theatres in Germany. Besides this Doppler has also written two acts of the *Elizabeth*,[1] by which Her Majesty the Queen of Hungary was entertained at the theatre of Budapest.

I venture then, Monsieur le Baron, to recommend you to see about the desirability of placing two fine reliefs of Mosonyi and Doppler[2] in a suitable position in the new theatre in the *Radialstrasse*, and beg you to accept the expression of my high esteem and sincere devotion.

F. LISZT.

343. TO FREIHERR HANS VON WOLZOGEN.

DEAR FREIHERR,

My admiration remains unlimited for the sublime genius of Wagner.

What blissful creative power and influence has he not, ever active from *Tannhäuser* to the *Ring des Nibelungen* and the marvellous *Parsifal.*—

The *Art* of our century finds its foundation and glory therein.

The little that I have written in letters about Wagner is at the service of the public.

With highest esteem yours most truly,

F. LISZT.

WEIMAR, *June 18th*, 1884.

To our friendly meeting in Bayreuth in the middle of July.

---

[1] The opera *Elizabeth*, composed by Franz Erkel and Doppler, was performed at the National Theatre in 1857.

[2] The reliefs adorn the vestibule of the opera house.

344. To the Concert-Singer Auguste Götze.[1]

Dear Friend,

In honour of you I will willingly endeavour to add the melodramatic accompaniment to Felix Dahn's poem.[2] This short work will only require a few hours ; but I can seldom get any free hours for working. . . . All sorts of interruptions keep me from writing.

Hearty greetings to your charming colleague, Fräulein von Kotzebue.

High esteem from your friendly

F. Liszt.

Weimar, *June 22nd*, 1884.

345. To Kornel von Abrányi.

Dear, excellent Friend,

The best person to make a suitable instrumentation of the "*Rheinweinliedes*" [Rhine-wine-song] for the Miskolcz Musical Festival will be our friend C. Huber.[3] This chorus for men's voices was written in Berlin in the year '42, and performed there several times, and afterwards in Leipzig also, about which a "*quèrelle d'Allemand*" [groundless quarrel] soon reached me in Paris.—

To bear and forbear is ever our life's task.

As I have marked on the accompanying copy, on

---

[1] Daughter of Professor Franz Götze, and—as one of the first singing mistresses of the present day—the inheritor of his school ; she is also a talented singer, reciter, and dramatic poetess. She lives at Leipzig.

[2] "Die Mette von Marienburg" [The Matins of Marienburg]. Liszt's intention remained, alas, unfulfilled.

[3] Carl Huber, conductor of the Hungarian Provincial Singers' Union, died 1885.

pages 3, 5, 7, instead of D♭, G♭ in the 2nd tenor, the C, F

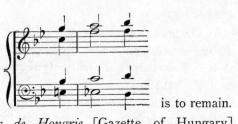

is to remain.

The *Gazette de Hongrie* [Gazette of Hungary], and still more the *Budapester Tageblatt* [Budapest daily paper], in which your son Kornel is a collaborator, gave me the tidings of the election doings in the *cara patria*.

Without in the least taking part in politics, yet I take that interest in them which it behoves every not uneducated man to do ; and I rejoice that Kornel Abrányi, junior, is taking his seat in Parliament.

Heartily, faithfully yours,

F. LISZT.

WEIMAR, *July 1st*, 1884.

From the 12th July till the middle of August I shall be at Bayreuth.

Tell Huber to do the instrumentation of the "*Rheinweinlied*" quite freely, according to his own will and what he thinks best, without a too careful attention to the printed piano accompaniment.

345A. To MADAME MALWINE TARDIEU.*

DEAR KIND FRIEND,

I have spoken to you several times of my excellent friend—of more than 20 years—Walter Bache.

* Autograph in possession of Constance Bache.

He maintains himself worthily in London as an artist of worth, intelligence, and noble character. His sister has made a remarkable translation of the *Elizabeth* into English.

Receive the Baches (who pass a day in Brussels) in a friendly manner.

Cordial devotion,

BAYREUTH, *August 9th*, 1884. F. LISZT.

To-morrow evening I shall be back at Weimar, and shall probably go to Munich for the second series of the *Nibelungen* performances (28th August).

Please give my cordial regards to Tardieu.

346. TO THE MUSIC PUBLISHER RAHTER IN HAMBURG.

DEAR HERR RAHTER,

Best thanks for kindly sending me the Russian *Fantasie* by Naprawnik—a brilliantly successful concert-piece—and the Slumber Songs by Rimsky-Korsakoff, which I prize extremely; his works are among the rare, the uncommon, the exquisite.—The piano edition of his Opera *Die Mainacht* [The May Night] has either not reached me or else has got lost.—Send it me to Weimar together with a second copy of Naprawnik's Russian *Fantasie*, which is necessary for performance.

Many of my young pianists will be glad to make this *Fantasie* known in drawing-rooms and concerts.—

With friendly thanks,

F. LISZT.

MUNICH, *August 28th*, 1884.

347. To Richard Pohl.*

My very dear Friend,

I have long wanted to repeat my hearty thanks to you for the faithful, noble devotion which you have always bravely and decidedly shown to the Weimar Period of Progression in the years 1849–58. The third volume of your collected writings "Hector Berlioz" affords another proof of this devotion, which is highly to be valued in contrast with the far too general wishy-washy absence of opinion.

After the unheard-of success of more than 20 performances of "The Damnation of Faust" by the concert societies of Lamoureux, Pasdeloup, Colonne, in the same season in Paris—*not counting* the *theatre*, for which this work is not suitable, the French Berlioz literature is increasing. You know Hippeau's octavo book "*Berlioz Intime*," which is shortly to be followed by a second, "*Berlioz Artiste.*" I wish this to profit by your work.

In reading the first volume I was painfully affected by several passages out of Berlioz's letters, in which the discord and broken-heartedness of his early years are only too apparent. He could not grasp the just idea that a genius cannot hope to exist with impunity, and that a *new thing* cannot at once expect to please the *ancient order of things*.

For the rest, there lies in his complaints against the Parisian "*gredins et crétins*" [fools and scoundrels], whom he might also find in other places, a large share

* Printed in the *Allgemeine Deutsche Musikzeitung* of 24th October, 1884.

of injustice. In spite of his exaggerated leniency in favour of a foreign country, the fact remains that up to the present time no European composer has received such distinctions from his own country as Berlioz did from France. Compare the position of Beethoven, Weber, Schubert, Schumann, with that of Berlioz. In the case of Beethoven the Archduke Rudolf alone bespoke the "Missa solemnis." The profit from his rarely given concerts was small, and at the last he turned to the London Philharmonic Society for support.

Weber acted as Court conductor in Dresden, and wrote his *Oberon* at the invitation of London.

Schubert's marvellous productiveness was badly paid by the publishers; other favourable conditions had he none.

Schumann's biography testifies no patriotic enthusiasm for his works during his lifetime. His position as musical conductor at Düsseldorf was by no means a brilliant one. . . .

It was otherwise with Mendelssohn, who had private means, and who, by his delicate and just eclecticism, clinging to Bach, Händel, and even Beethoven, obtained continual success in England and Germany. King William IV. called him to Berlin at the same time with Cornelius,* Kaulbach, Schelling, and Meyerbeer, which he did not enjoy any better than Leipzig.

I make no further mention of Meyerbeer here, because he owes his universal success chiefly to Paris. It was there that all his Operas, from *Robert* and *The Huguenots* to his posthumous *L'Africaine*, were *first*

---

* This means the *painter* Cornelius.—TRANS.

performed—with the exception of "*Das Feldlager in Schlesien*" [The Camp in Silesia], which also sparkled later in Paris as " *L'étoile du Nord.*"

Now let us see how things went with Berlioz in his native land.

Like Victor Hugo, he was, after three times becoming a candidate, elected a member of the " Institute of France,"—similarly (without any candidature) to be librarian of the Conservatoire; he was also a collaborator of the highly esteemed "*Journal des Débats*" and officer of the Legion of Honour.

Where do we find in Germany similar proofs of distinction? Why, therefore, the bitter insults of Berlioz against the Paris "*gredins*" and "*crétins*"? Unfortunately it certainly never brought Berlioz an out-and-out theatrical success, although his nature leaned that way.

I send you herewith Reyer's *feuilleton* (*Journal des Débats*, 14th September) regarding the latest *brochure* by Ernst "upon Berlioz."

With hearty thanks, yours most truly,

F. LISZT.

WEIMAR, *September 12th*, 1884.

348. To SOPHIE MENTER.

MY DEAR FRIEND,

My few days' stay at your *fairy-like* castle Itter[1] will remain a magic memory.

When you have signed the Petersburg Conservatorium contract let me know. You know, indeed, that I very much approve of this turn and fixing of

---

[1] In Tyrol.

your brilliant artistic career. It requires no excessive obligations, and will be an advantage to you.

Friendly greetings to the *New School* from your faithful admirer and friend,

F. LISZT.

WEIMAR, *September* 13*th*, 1884.

I am here ,till the end of October. Later on I shall visit my friends Geza Zichy and Sandor Teleky in Hungary.

349. TO BARON FRIEDRICH PODMANICZKY, INTENDANT OF THE ROYAL HUNGARIAN OPERA IN BUDAPEST.*

DEAR, HOCHGEBORENER † HERR BARON,

To your letter dated the 17th of this month I have the honour of replying as follows : that the song "Hahj, Rakóczy, Bercsényi" was not unknown to me is shown by the piano edition of my "Hungarian royal hymn" published by Taborsky and Parsch, on the title-page of which stand the words "After an old Hungarian air." I learned to know this song from Stefan Bartolus's Anthology, and it took hold of me with its decided, and expressive and artless character ; I at once provided it with a *finale* of victory, and without troubling my head further about its former

---

* Printed in the *Pester Lloyd* (evening paper of 27th September, 1884).—Liszt having sent Podmaniczky a Royal Hymn for the opening of the New Hungarian Opera House instead of a Festal Prelude, which the latter had requested, Podmaniczky wrote to the Master on the 17th September, 1884, that the motive of the hymn having been borrowed from a revolutionary song would prove an "unsurmountable obstacle" to its performance. The letter was also signed by Alexander Erkel as conductor. Whereupon Liszt wrote the above reply.

† Many of these titles have been left in their original language, being unused in England, and having no equivalent with us.—TRANS.

revolutionary words I begged Kornel Abrányi, jun., for a new, loyal text with the refrain " Éljen a király," so that my "Royal hymn" might attain its due expression both in words and music.

Transformations are nothing rare in Art any more than in life. From countless heathen temples Catholic churches were formed. In the classic epoch of Church music—in the 16th century—many secular melodies were accepted amongst devotional songs, and in later times the Catholic antiphones were heard as Protestant Chorales. And this went yet further, not excepting Opera, in which Meyerbeer utilised the Chorale "*Eine feste Burg*" for a stage effect, and in "*L'Étoile du Nord*" consecrated the "*Dessauer Marsch*" into the Russian National hymn. A revolutionary tendency is commonly ascribed to the universally known and favourite Rakoczy March, and its performance has been more than once forbidden.

Music remains ever music, without superfluous and injurious significations. For the rest, God forbid that I should anywhere push forward either myself or my humble compositions. I leave it entirely to your judgment, *hochgeborener* Herr Baron, to decide whether my "Royal hymn" shall be performed in the new Hungarian Opera House or not. The score, as also the many orchestral and vocal parts, are to be had at the publishers, Taborsky and Parsch.

I beg you, Sir, to accept the expression of my high esteem.

F. Liszt.[1]

WEIMAR, *September* 21*st*, 1884.

[1] To this Alex. Erkel made the proposal that Liszt's "*Königslied*"

350. TO WALTER BACHE.[1]

VERY HONOURED FRIEND,

For some twenty years past you have been employing your beautiful talent as a pianist, your care as a professor and as a conductor to make my works known and to spread them in England. The task seemed an ungrateful one, and its want of success menacing, but you are doing it nobly, with the most honourable and firm conviction of an artist. I renew my grateful thanks to you on the occasion of the present edition of the *Legend of St. Elizabeth*, published by the well-accredited house of Novello.[2]

This work, which was performed for the first time in 1865 at Budapest, has been reproduced successively in several countries and languages. Let us hope that it will also meet with some sympathy in England.

Your much attached

F. LISZT.

WEIMAR, *October* 18*th*, 1884.

351. TO THE COMPOSER MILI BALAKIREFF, CONDUCTOR OF THE IMPERIAL COURT CHOIR IN ST. PETERSBURG.

VERY HONOURED, DEAR CONFRÈRE,

My admiring sympathy for your works is well known. When my young disciples want to please me

(Royal Song), instead of being performed at the opening of the new theatre on the 27th September, should be given at an "Extra Opera performance." The Master consented, but did not appear at this first performance of his work, which took place on the 25th March, 1885, and met with tremendous applause.

[1] This letter is published, as a Preface, in the English edition of Liszt's *St. Elizabeth*.

[2] The translator of the English edition (Constance Bache) has also translated many of Liszt's songs into English.

they play me your compositions and those of your valiant friends. In this intrepid Russian musical phalanx I welcome from my heart masters endowed with a rare vital energy; they suffer in no wise from poverty of ideas—a malady which is widespread in many countries. More and more will their merits be recognised, and their names renowned. I accept with gratitude the honour of the dedication [to me] of your Symphonic Poem " *Thamar*," which I hope to hear next summer with a large orchestra. When the 4-hand edition comes out you will greatly oblige me by sending me a copy. From the middle of January until Easter I shall be at Budapest.

Please accept, dear *confrère*, the expression of my high esteem and cordial attachment.

F. Liszt.

Weimar, *October 21st*, 1884.

352. To Countess Louise de Mercy-Argenteau.[1]

October 24th, 1884.

Certainly, my very dear and kind friend, you have a hundredfold right to appreciate and to relish the present musical Russia. Rimski-Korsakoff, Cui, Borodine, Balakireff, are masters of striking originality and worth. Their works make up to me for the *ennui* caused to me by other works more widely spread and more talked about, works of which I should have some difficulty in saying what Léonard once wrote to you from Amsterdam after a song of Schumann's : " What

---

[1] Known through her zealous propaganda, in Belgium and France, of the music of the New Russian School. After the death of her husband (1888), Chamberlain of Napoleon III., she left her native land of Belgium and removed to St. Petersburg, where she died in November 1890.

soul, and also what success !"   Rarely is success in
a hurry to accompany *soul*.   In Russia the new composers, in spite of their remarkable talent and knowledge, have had as yet but a limited success.—The
high people of the Court wait for them to succeed
elsewhere before they applaud them at Petersburg.
A propos of this, I recollect a striking remark which
the late Grand Duke Michael made to me in '43:
"When I have to put my officers under arrest, I send
them to the performances of Glinka's operas."   Manners
are softening, and Messrs. Rimski, Cui, Borodine, have
themselves attained to the grade of colonel.

At the annual concerts of the German and Universal
Musical Association (*Allgemeiner Deutscher Musik-
Verein*) they have, for many years past, always given
some work of a Russian composer, at my suggestion.
Little by little a public will be formed.   Next year our
Festival will take place in June at Carlsruhe.   St.
Saëns is coming ; why not you, too, dear friend ?   You
would also hear something Russian there.

When you write to St. Saëns, please tell him of my
admiring and very constant friendship.   By the work
of translation which you have bravely undertaken, I
think that you are doing wisely and skilfully in freeing
yourself from the bondage of rhyme, and in keeping
to rhythmic prose.   The important point is to maintain
the lyric or dramatic accent, and to avoid the "*désast-
reuses salades de syllabes longues et brèves, des temps
forts et faibles*" [disastrous mess of long and short
syllables, and of the strong and weak time].   The
point is to make good prose without any other scruples
whatever.

It is said that M. Lamoureux is admitting the "Steppes" by Borodine into one of his programmes. We shall see what sort of a reception it will have. For the rest, I doubt Lamoureux's venturing so soon on the Russian propaganda. He has too much to do with Berlioz and Wagner.

Do not let yourself be disconcerted either by the "ineffable" carelessness, or by the square battalions of objections such as these: "It is confusion worse confounded; it is Abracadabra" *—etc.!

Without politeness or ceremony I tell you in perfect sincerity that your instinct did not lead you astray the day when this music so forcibly charmed you. Continue, then, your work with the firm conviction of being in the right path.

Above all I beg that you will not falsely imagine that I am taking hold of the thing wrong end foremost. When you knock I shall not merely say, Enter, but I myself will go before you. To return to Paris and show myself off there as a young composer or to continue the business of an old pianist in the *salons* does not attract me in the least. I have other things to do elsewhere.

Faithful homage.

F. LISZT.

P.S.—I do not know what date to put to these lines. I wrote the first page on the receipt of your bewitching letter. I meant to reply to it in full, but all sorts of pressing obligations and botherations intervened. . . . I have also been to the inauguration of the statue of Bach at Eisenach, illustrated by three concerts, composed

* Senseless jabber.

exclusively of numerous works of Bach's (the Mass in
B minor first and foremost) ; then I was present at
a more curious concert at Leipzig : on my return I
had a severe attack of illness, which prevented me
for several days from writing.   In short, this letter
ought to have reached you three weeks ago.   To-
morrow, 25th October, I leave Weimar, and shall not
return here till after Easter.   If you condescend to
continue writing to me, please address to Budapest
(Hungary) till the end of November.   A prompt
answer shall follow.

F. Liszt.

353. To Madame Malwine Tardieu.

Budapest, December 7th, 1884.

Dear kind Friend,

Really and truly when it sometimes happens
that I obtain success I rejoice less over that than over
the success of my friends.   Thank you for the pleasant
tidings of the brilliant success of Ossiana [1] at Godard's
concert. . — .

You do not tell me where the little notice appeared
(with my name at the heading) which you were so
good as to send me.[2]   One of my works is mentioned
in it with the greatest eulogy—the Gran Mass—which
was so unhappily performed at Paris in '66, and more
unhappily criticised then. . . . The mistake I made
was not to have forbidden a performance given under
such deplorable conditions.   A philanthropic reason,

---

[1] Madame Marie Jaell, the well-known artiste, a friend of Liszt's.

[2] In the *Gaulois*, from the pen of Fourcaud, and, later, in the
Album of the *Gaulois*, to which the most celebrated tone-poets had
contributed a piece of music as yet unpublished.

which is valueless in matters of Art, kept me from doing so. I did not wish to deprive the fund for the poor of the assured receipts of more than 40,000 francs. Pardon me for recalling this vexatious affair, which makes me all the more sensible of the flattering attention which the same work is receiving.

To my great regret the performances of *Henry VIII.* by our very valiant friend St. Saëns, which were to have taken place at Weimar and Budapest, are put off. *Mediocrity*, as Balzac said, governs even theatres. Anyhow its power must sometimes be intermittent. Please say many cordial things to your husband from your much attached F. Liszt.

On Wednesday I shall be in Rome, and back here towards the middle of January.

354. To Freiherr Hans von Wolzogen.

Dear Freiherr,

Hearty thanks for your kind letter. To include me in your noble, zealous, high-minded efforts in matters for the glorification of Wagner and according to the wishes of his widow, is to me ever a duty and an honour.

Faithfully yours,

Rome, *December 18th,* 1884. F. Liszt.

355. To Camille Saint-Saëns.

[*End of* 1884 *or beginning of* 1885.]

Very dear Friend and Companion in Arms,

Your sympathy for the " Salve, Polonia "[1] makes me quite happy. Still writing music, as I am, I some-

---

[1] Orchestral Interlude from the unfinished Oratorio *Stanislaus.* It was given at the *Tonkünstler-Versammlung* in Weimar in 1884, at which Saint-Saëns was present.

times ask myself at such and such a passage, "Would that please St. Saëns?" The affirmative encourages me to go on, in spite of the fatigue of age and other wearinesses.

If you do me the honour of playing one of my compositions at the Carlsruhe Festival please choose which it shall be : perhaps the *Danse macabre* [Dance of Death] with orchestra ; or—which I think would be better, for the public would rather hear you alone—the *Prédication aux oiseaux* [St. Francis preaching to the birds], followed by Scherzo and March.[1]

Cordial wishes for the year '85, and ever your admiringly attached

F. Liszt.

Give my best remembrances from Budapest to Delibes.

356. To Countess Mercy-Argenteau.

What wonders you have just accomplished with your Russian concert at Liége, dear admirable one! From the material point of view the Deaf and Dumb and Blind Institutions have benefited by it ; artistically, other deaf and dumb have heard and spoken ; the blind have seen, and, on beholding you, were enraptured.

I shall assuredly not cease from my propaganda of the remarkable compositions of the New Russian School, which I esteem and appreciate with lively sympathy. For 6 or 7 years past, at the Grand Annual Concerts of the Musical Association (" *Allgemeiner Deutscher Musik-Verein* "), over which I have the honour of presiding, the orchestral works of Rimsky-Korsakoff

---

[1] Saint-Saëns did not go to Carlsruhe.

and Borodine have figured on the programmes. Their success is making a *crescendo*, in spite of the sort of contumacy that is established against Russian music. It is not in the least any desire of being peculiar that leads me to spread it, but a simple feeling of justice, based on my conviction of the real worth of these works of high lineage. I do not know which ones Hans von Bülow, the Achilles of propagandists, chose for the Russian concert he gave lately with the Meiningen orchestra, of an unheard-of discipline and perfection.

I hope Bülow will continue concerts of the same quality in various towns of Germany.

The best among my disciples, brilliant *virtuosi*, play the most difficult piano compositions of Balakireff, etc., superbly. I shall recommend to them Cui's *Suite* (piano and violoncello).

Considering the rarity of singers gifted at once with voice, intelligence and good taste for things not hack-neyed,—there is some delay in regard to the vocal compositions of Cui, Borodine, etc. Nevertheless the right time for their production will come, and for making them succeed and be appreciated. In France your translation of the words will be a great help, and in Germany we must be provided with a suitable translation.

A portion of the articles which you kindly sent me upon your concert at Liége shall be inserted in the *Neue Zeitschrift für Musik*. I shall endeavour to find another paper also, although my relations with the Press are by no means intimate.

Rahter, the musical editor at Hamburg, and represen-

tative of Jürgenson in Moscow, will offer you in homage
three of my Russian transcriptions,—Tschaikowsky's
"Polonaise"; Dargomijsky's "Tarentelle" with the
continuous pedal bass of A, A; and a "Romance" of
Count Michel Wielhorsky. Let us add to these the
Marche tscherkesse of Glinka, and, above all, the prodigious *kaleidoscope* of variations and paraphrases on
the fixed theme

It is the most seriously entertaining thing I know;
it gives us a practical manual, *par excellence,* of all
musical knowledge; treatises on harmony and composition are summed up and blended in it in some thirty
pages, which teach the subject very fully—above and
beyond the usual instruction.

My very amiable hosts at Antwerp, the Lynens, have
invited me to return there this summer at the time of
the Exhibition, of which M. Lynen is the president.   I
am tempted to do so after the Carlsruhe Festival, as I
keep a charming remembrance of the kindness that was
shown to me in Brussels and Antwerp.

In about ten days I return to Budapest, whence you
shall receive a photograph of the old, sorry face of your
constant admirer and devoted servant,

F. LISZT.

ROME, *January 20th,* 1885.

A pertinacious editor keeps asking me for my transcription of Gounod's *Ste. Cécile.*   If amongst your old
papers you should find the manuscript of it, will you

lend it me for a fortnight, so that it may be copied, printed, and then restored to its very gracious owner ?

February and March my address—Budapest, Hungary.

357. To Camille Saint-Saëns.

VERY HONOURED, DEAR FRIEND,

In order not to become too monotonous I won't thank you any more. Nevertheless your transcription of my *Orpheus* for Piano, Violin and Violoncello charms me, and I beg that you will send it either to Härtel direct, so that he may publish it at once, or else to yours very gratefully, so that I may remit it to him, after having had the pleasure of reading and hearing it at Budapest, whither, by next Thursday, will have returned

Your much-attached fellow-disciple,

F. Liszt.

FLORENCE, *Tuesday, January 27th*, 1885.

Goodbye till we meet in May at Carlsruhe.

358. To Madame Malwine Tardieu.

I am writing to the director of our "*Musik-Verein*" to write to you, dear friend. You will tell Mademoiselle Kufferath, better than any one else can, how agreeable it will be to everybody, and to myself in particular, if she takes part in the concerts at Carlsruhe—in the last days of May.[1]

Our "*Musik-Verein*" has not the advantage of

---

[1] This did not come to anything. Saint-Saëns' "Deluge," in which she was to have sung, was not performed at Carlsruhe, and meanwhile Fräulein Kufferath married and gave up her artistic career.

material wealth ; nevertheless we have existed bravely for 25 years without getting into debt, and faithfully put in practice our principal rule, which is to perform every year in different towns the valid works of contemporary composers of any country whatsoever (exclusive of works for the theatre, with the exception of occasional vocal numbers). This rule, which is difficult to maintain, considering the expenses and the difficult preparations, distinguishes us from other musical societies and gives us the character of pioneers of progress. We have not been behindhand with the group of composers of young Musical Russia, Rimsky-Korsakoff, Borodine, Cui, etc., for we have been giving their works for four years past.

The very gracious Countess of Mercy-Argenteau has been making them known lately at Liége, with a brilliant success, quite justified by the qualities of the works and the charm of the patroness.

Will you, dear friend, be so kind as to express my acknowledgments to Mr. de Fourcaud,[1] and accept the expression of my cordial affection ?

F. LISZT.

BUDAPEST, *April 6th*, 1885.

In a few days I shall be back at Weimar.

359. To LINA RAMANN.

[WEIMAR,] *April 27th,* 1885.

I am sending you at once, my very dear friend, the volumes of scores which I have by me in Weimar.[2] The celebrated *Missa Papæ Marcelli* is not amongst

[1] Musical and Art Correspondent of the Paris *Gaulois*, with outspoken Wagner tendencies and opinions.

[2] Works of Palestrina's.

them, but can easily be found; the last edition of it by *Amelli*, Milan, the editor-in-chief of the Church-Music paper there. I got him to add a few indications of expression because, according to my opinion, without such indications any further editions of Palestrina and Lassus—the two great Cardinals of old Catholic Church-music—would serve only for reading, and *not* for actual performances. Of course no one can fix with absolute certainty the figures to the basses of Palestrina and Lassus; yet there are determining points from which one can steer.

The best model of all is and will continue to be—Wagner's arrangement of Palestrina's "Stabat Mater"—with marks of expression and plan of the division of the voices into semi-chorus, solos, and complete chorus.

Wagner made this *model* arrangement at the time when he was conductor in Dresden. It appeared 15 years later, published by Kahnt. It is to be hoped that people will gradually regulate themselves by this with judgment—and time.

Faithfully yours,

F. LISZT.

360. TO CAMILLE SAINT-SAËNS.

Thank you cordially, my very dear friend, for the concession you are willing to make to me.

The Society of Musicians, in which I have taken part for 25 years, holds to the principle of producing the works of *living* Symphonic composers of all countries. I claim then your superior and continued share in it, and remain your admiring and attached friend,

F. Liszt.

361. To Alexander Siloti.[1]

In Weimar it is wisest to keep oneself *negative* and *passive.*   Therefore, dear Siloti, attempt *no* " Liszt-Verein." [2]

With thanks, yours truly,

F. Liszt.

May, 1885.

362. To the Composer J. P. von Király in Eisenstadt.[*]

Dear Friend,

Ninety years ago my father was preparing for his duties as book-keeper to Prince Nikolaus Esterhazy in Eisenstadt.   At that time he often took part, as an amateur, among the violoncellos in the Prince's frequent Court concerts, under the conductorship of the happy great *master* Josef Haydn.   My father often told me about his intercourse with Haydn, and the daily parties he made up with him.   In 1848 I visited the dear, affectionate Father Albach at the Franciscan monastery of Eisenstadt, and dedicated to him my Mass

---

[1] Well known as one of the most gifted pupils of Liszt, and one of the first pianists of the present day.   Born 1863, and lives now in Paris.

[2] In consequence of the above letter the Liszt-Verein (Liszt Society) was not founded in Weimar, as Siloti intended, but in Leipzig in 1885, where it has flourished brilliantly under the direction of Professor Martin Krause.

[*] From a copy by Director Aug. Göllerich in Nuremberg.

for men's voices, which will be brilliantly performed
here very shortly. May the simple, artless genius of
Haydn ever rule over the Eisenstadt Kindergarten
conducted by your daughter.

"Joke and earnest!" Bravo, friend! The work
honours the master who knows so well the Muses.
In Oedenburg and Eisenstadt surely every one will
subscribe. At the beginning of July I shall send you
a small contribution for the Kindergarten. Perhaps
later on I shall be able to do more; unfortunately I
am anything but well off, and must content myself with
a small amount.

F. LISZT.

ANTWERP, *June 5th*, 1885.

363. To FERDINAND TABORSZKY, MUSIC PUBLISHER IN BUDAPEST.

ANTWERP, *June 8th*, 1885.

VERY DEAR FRIEND,

From Weimar, where I shall once more be in
ten days' time, you will receive at the beginning of
July some short Hungarian pianoforte pieces, which I
shall orchestrate later on, entitled

To the memory of

Stephan	Széchényi
Franz	Deak
Josef	Eötvös
Ladislas	Telek
Michael	Vörösmarti
Alexander	Petöfi.

The last piece has already been published by

Taborszky, but must have a few more concluding bars in the new edition.

Mosonyi's Trauerklänge (Mosonyi's funeral music), which you have already had by you for fifteen years, shall make No. 7. Our friend Mosonyi, so excellent and full of character, and so pre-eminent a musician, must also not be forgotten.

The seven numbers make altogether sixty pages of print. All the new pieces are perfectly ready, written out in manuscript, only requiring a copyist, whom I cannot find while I am on my journey.[1]

When I send you the manuscripts I will write all further particulars with regard to the publishing of them.

First of all, dear friend, will you be so kind as to go to my house with Frau von Fabry? I stupidly forgot there—in the bedroom, *not* in the *salon*—the beautiful and revised copy of a composition for piano and violin or violoncello, together with the transcription of the same for pianoforte alone. The title is "La lugubre Gondola" (the funeral gondola). As though it were a presentiment, I wrote this *élégie* in Venice six weeks before Wagner's death.

Now I should like it to be brought out by Fritzsch (Leipzig), Wagner's publisher, as soon as I receive it from you in Weimar.[2] Hearty greetings to your family.

Ever faithfully yours,

F. LISZT.

---

[1] Liszt's intention to orchestrate the pieces remained unfulfilled.

[2] Published by Fritzsch.

364. To Alfred Reisenauer.

DEAR FRIEND AND ART-COMRADE,

I beg you to send me here, in manuscript, your *capital* orchestration of the 3rd Mephisto-waltz. Don't take the trouble to alter anything in this manuscript or to write anything new; send it me *just as* I have seen it. When it has been copied the printed edition will follow, with the name of Reisenauer attached to it.

In all friendship,

F. LISZT.

WEIMAR, *September 1st*, 1885.

365. To the Editor of the " Allgemeine Musik-zeitung," Otto Lessmann, in Charlottenburg.*

DEAR MR. EDITOR,

With regret, and a firm conviction, I repeat to you in writing that Theodor Kullak's forgetfulness ought to be made good by his heirs. Otherwise it would be severely denounced as unfaithfulness to his position as an artist. A fortune of several millions gained by music-teaching ought not to remain buried without any regard to music students. Unless the heirs prefer to found a *Kullak-Scholarship*, I consider that they are in duty bound to endow the four existing musical scholarships—those in the names of Mozart, Mendelssohn, Meyerbeer, Beethoven—with 30,000 marks each: total 120,000 marks.

With well-known opinions, mindful of the *artist's standing*, I am yours truly,

F. LISZT.

WEIMAR, *September 5th*, 1885.

* Was published in the *Allgemeine Musikzeitung* of September 1885.

366. To Cäsar Cui.

VERY HONOURED FRIEND,

The very gracious propagandist, the Countess of Mercy-Argenteau, has already received a transcription of your brilliant *Tarentelle*. I will send a second copy of it to Bessel (Petersburg), and shall ask him to give it to you, trusting that you will not disapprove of the few liberties and amplifications that I have ventured to make in order to adapt this piece to the programmes of *virtuosi* pianists.

Sincere feelings of esteem and attachment.

F. LISZT.

MUNICH, *October 18th*, 1885.

367. To Countess Mercy-Argenteau.

DEAR ADMIRABLE PROPAGANDIST,

It is your habit to write the most charming letters in the world. Before receiving your last I had sent you from *Weimar* my transcription of Cui's *Tarentelle*. If you will condescend to illustrate it with your fingers it will receive its full meed of light.

I am sure you will be so kind as to send my note to Cui, who, I hope, will not be vexed with the varying readings and amplifications I have ventured to make, with a view of bringing the pianist still more forward. In this kind of transcription some sort of distinction is wanted.

To-morrow evening I shall be in Rome,—Hotel Alibert. Please send me word there of your safe receipt of the manuscript.

Constant homage, admiring and sincere.

F. LISZT.

INNSBRUCK, *October 24th*, 1885.

368. To Eduard Reuss in Carlsruhe.[1]

My dear Friend,

Thanks and praise for your *capital* orchestral arrangement of the "*Concerto pathétique*." It appears to me effective, well-proportioned, and done with a refined and due understanding of it. I had but little to alter in it; but some additions to the original are desirable, in order to allow full scope to the piano *virtuoso*.[2] Hence, in different places, there are altogether somewhere about fifty to sixty bars which I add to your manuscript. The beginning is also to be ten bars sooner, and the ending to conclude with twenty-two bars more.

I hear an orchestration of the same "*Concerto pathétique*" spoken of, as having been produced in Moscow. I do not know it myself, and after yours there is no use in it. I received in Weimar, almost simultaneously with yours, a letter from Joseffy in New York, begging me to instrumentate the piece. I shall answer him very soon that your score is already completed, and that he is to apply to my friend Eduard Reuss if he is disposed to perform the "Concerto" with orchestra in America.[3]

Enclosed is my recommendation to Härtel with regard to the publishing. Send it together with your manuscript, of which it is not necessary to make a

[1] Pianist, pupil of Liszt's.

[2] "This '*Concerto Pathétique*' seems to me a *murderous piece*, with which first-rate *virtuosi* can make an effect," writes Liszt, on the 10th November, to Reuss.

[3] Joseffy played the "*Concerto Pathétique*" in this form from a copy, in the spring of 1886, in New York.

copy—only my scribbling of the additions must be copied out clean and clearly on an extra sheet.—

Probably Härtels will not show themselves dis-obliging. If they undertake the publication I should still like to read through the last proof-sheets.

The most charming recollection remains to me of Carlsruhe.[1] The Grand Duke was so gracious and truly kind!—

Assure your wife of my sincere attachment.

Faithfully yours,

F. Liszt.

Hotel Alibert, Rome, *November 4th*, 1885.

369. To Breitkopf and Härtel.[2]

My dear Sirs,

Although your shop is already saddled with two editions of my "*Concerto pathétique*," I recommend you *most particularly* the excellent orchestral arrange-ment of the same piece,[3] to which I have added some bars for more completion, which should also be in-cluded in the possible (?) later piano editions.

The poet and the writer often make alterations. With the engraving of music this is more difficult, though not entirely to be put aside.

With esteem,

F. Liszt.

Rome, *November*, 1885.

[1] Namely, of the "*Tonkünstler-Versammlung*" of the "*Allgemeine Deutsche Musikverein*," from the 27th May to the 1st June, 1885.

[2] This is Liszt's last autograph letter to the Firm; a later one on the same subject (on the 16th June, 1886) is only signed by him.

[3] By Eduard Reuss. It was published by Breitkopf and Härtel.

370. To Walter Bache.

My very dear Friend,

Certainly your invitation takes precedence of all others. So choose the day that suits yourself and I will appear. Without Walter Bache and his long years of self-sacrificing efforts in the propaganda of my works my visit to London were indeed not to be thought of.

Do you know your namesake (without the final E), Herr Emil Bach, Prussian Court-pianist? I enclose herewith a second letter, which I have answered, as I did the first, that I must not be the occasion of expense and inconvenience to any one. Orchestral concerts are expensive everywhere, especially in London. Consequently I cannot encourage Emil Bach's project, and can only dissuade him from putting it into execution. Send me word about this.

Gratefully and faithfully yours,

F. Liszt.

Rome, Hotel Alibert, *November 17th*, 1885.

Mr. Stavenhagen,[1] a pianist and musician of real talent, wants to come out in London, and is writing to you on this subject.

370 A. To Walter Bache.

My very dear Friend,

It is fixed then: Thursday, 8th April, *Ricevimento* * at Walter Bache's house. Enclosed is the letter of the Philharmonic Society, together with the rough copy of my reply which I send off to-day.

[1] Now one of the most celebrated pianists.   * Reception.

Please observe the postscript :

" If, in the concert at which one of my Symphonic Poems will be performed, Mr. Walter Bache would play some Pianoforte composition of mine, that would give me great pleasure. I permit myself to give this simple hint without the slightest desire of influencing your programme, which it is for you to fix."—

I am quite of your opinion, dear friend. The *accented point* of my coming to London is to be present at the *Elizabeth* performance. It was this that decided my coming, and it is to be hoped it will be a success.[1]

I have answered Emil Bach's first and second letters to the effect that I should not wish to involve any one in expense, and that consequently I must dissuade him from giving an orchestral Liszt concert. Beg Littleton personally to make my wish quite clear to Herr Emil Bach, that his proposed concert should not be given.   . — .

Faithfully yours,

F. Liszt.

November 26th, 1885.

I have just received a second letter from the " Philharmonic Society."—To my answer to the first (sent yesterday) I have nothing to add.

370 B. To the Philharmonic Society.

Very honoured Directors,

Much flattered with your kind intention to admit one of my " Poèmes Symphoniques " on to the programme of the Philharmonic Society, during my

---

[1] It was given on the 6th April, 1886, under the conductorship of Mackenzie. Bache had already given it in London in 1876.

stay in London, I beg you to accept my sincere thanks.

Will you please choose, according to your own pleasure, the work which suits you best, and also ask your " conductor," Sir Arthur Sullivan, from me, to direct it ?

For twenty years past I have been quite outside of any work as orchestral conductor and pianist.

Distinguished consideration and loyal devotion.

F. Liszt.

Rome, *November 26th*, 1885.

P.S.— If, in the concert at which one of my Symphonic Poems will be performed, Mr. Walter Bache would [etc., see quotation in previous letter].

371. To Countess Mercy-Argenteau.

Dear admirable Propagandist,

Herewith is a different rendering of the shake, with an indication to the left hand of the motive which is then taken up again in full. This new *shake* is a little awkward to do, but not too troublesome. Will you be so kind as to send it to Cui, and beg him to be my emissary to the editor of the original of Cui's brilliant *Tarantelle*, for the publication of the transcription ? To my regret the smallness of my income obliges me to leave no stone unturned to make money out of my transcriptions,* for which I am now paid in

---

* La modicité de mon revenu m'oblige à faire flèche, non pas de tout bois, mais de fagots de mes transcriptions. The literal translation is, " Obliges me to utilise, not the wood, but the faggots of my transcriptions," the point of the sentence turning upon the French idiom "*faire flèche de tout bois*," which in English is rendered by a totally different idiom.—Trans.

Germany, Russia, France, at the rate of from twelve to 1500 marks apiece, for the copyright in all countries.

Observe that I choose works to be transcribed, and refuse myself to any other demands. This year, for instance, I have confined myself to the volume that you condescend to accept—and that you will, I hope, bring to the light by the diamonds and pearls of your fingers.

Mr. Bessel therefore only has either to send me 1200 marks in payment, or else to return me the manuscript without being ashamed.

Most humble and constant homage.

F. LISZT.

ROME, *November 21st*, 1885.

When you have sent me word of the result of the negotiation with Bessel, I will write my thanks and acknowledgments to Cui.

N.B.—The new shape should be printed as an *Ossia*, above the old one.

372. TO CAMILLE SAINT-SAËNS.

VERY HONOURED CONFRÈRE AND VERY DEAR FRIEND,

I shall certainly be in London the first week in April. With regard to my visit to Paris I am still very undecided, as I do not wish to expose myself to discomfiture like that which I had to go through in '66.[1]

Everywhere and always I shall be happy and proud

---

[1] Liszt's scruples were removed; as is well known, he went to Paris, and found himself indescribably fêted there. The triumphs of his youth were repeated once more in the evening of his life.

of your collaboration, and remain your sincere admirer
and devoted friend,

F. LISZT.

ROME (HOTEL ALIBERT), *November 28th,* 1885.

I shall remain here till the middle of January. This
summer Mme. Montigny [1] spoke to me of her marriage, which has now taken place. M. de Serres gave
me the impression of an honest man who adores his
wife. I have no news of the newly married couple.

There is nothing more witty than your remark on
the *perpetual* youth of composers in Paris. In your
company, dear friend, I would gladly be of the party,
in spite of my seventy-four years.

373. To EUGEN D'ALBERT. [2]

ADMIRED, DEAR " ALBERTUS MAGNUS,"

Thank you for the dedication of your worthy,
noble, effective Concerto, which I have again read
through with special pleasure, and heard played by
Stavenhagen.

Is no edition of it for two pianofortes come out ? I
think such editions are desirable—almost indispensable.
They are also much used now.

Congratulating you on your happiness in becoming a
father, with best regards to your wife,

Yours most truly,

F. LISZT.

ROME, *December 26th,* 1885.

[1] Mme. Montigny-Rémaury, an excellent pianist ; retired into private
life on her second marriage in Vienna.

[2] The most important and many-sided of the younger pupils of
Liszt.

374. To Sophie Menter.

KIND DIPLOMATIST AND VERY DEAR FRIEND,

I am writing my most humble thanks to the Grand Duke Constantine for his gracious invitation, together with the very kindly intentioned consideration of my age and failing eyesight—and especially my *unfitness* for pianoforte playing and orchestral conducting. This deters me from making any pretensions to a fee; but you know, dear friend, that my small income would not be sufficient to pay for lodging and a carriage in Petersburg. From the 1st to the 12th April I am detained in London. If it is *not too late* then, to Petersburg comes

Yours ever most faithfully,

F. LISZT.

ROME, *December 30th,* 1885.

In the middle of January I return to Budapest. Friendly greetings to the *New School,* whom I will beg to assist me as a veritable privy council in Petersburg. From the next letter of the Grand Duke Constantine I await the decision whether my journey to Petersburg *in the middle of April* is accepted or not.

375. To Eduard Reuss.

MY DEAR FRIEND,

Still some slight alterations and amplifications in the "*Concerto pathétique.*"

The drum rhythm

appears to me too risky; if the drummer comes down plump on it he will spoil the whole piece. Let us therefore put

This rhythm will serve us twice as a transition,—and at the end.

Before the end of this month I shall be in Budapest, and at the beginning of April in London, for the *Elizabeth* performance (St. James's Hall) under Mackenzie's conducting.

Faithfully yours,
F. LISZT.

ROME, *January* 10th, 1886.

376. TO WALTER BACHE.

MY VERY DEAR FRIEND,

They seem determined in London to push me to the Piano.

I cannot consent to this in public, as my seventy-five-year-old fingers are no longer suited to it, and Bülow, Saint-Saëns, Rubinstein, and you, dear Bache, play my compositions much better than what is left of my humble self.

Perhaps it would be opportune if friend Hueffer would have the kindness to let the public know, by a short announcement, that Liszt only ventures to appear as a grateful visitor, and neither in London nor anywhere else as a man with an interest in his fingers.

In all friendship yours,
F. LISZT.

BUDAPEST, *February* 11th, 1886.

377. To the Countess Mercy-Argenteau.

Very admirable and admired One,*

Your most amiable letter did not reach me without some delay, for I took about ten days to make the journey from Rome to Budapest.

Madame Falk writes to me also of the concert at Liège, but I fear I shall only have excuses to offer. On the 20th March I shall be in Paris, where the *Gran Mass*, too much criticised, and even hissed by some low fellows (at the Pasdeloup concert in '66), is to make its reappearance at St. Eustache on the 25th March. This time M. Colonne will conduct it, and I am assured that it will be *better understood* now. . . .

Invariable homage,

F. Liszt.

Budapest, *February 17th*, 1886.

Very affectionate thanks for the invitation of Argenteau. Whether I can avail myself of it must remain in abeyance for your very humble servant, old and enfeebled.

378. To Sophie Menter.

Dear and respected Diplomatist,

Eight days before the 19th April (Russian style) I will be in Petersburg. I entreat you to make *as little ceremony as possible* for my humble self. The two programmes appear to me all right ; I will tell you when I get to Petersburg what my small part in them will be. On the 19th April, then, *Elizabeth* ; on the

* Très admirable et admirée.

23rd a concert.—Tell the Committee to address their *invitation* to me, for the two performances, to "Novello and Co., Music Publishers, 1, Berners Street, London." From the 1st to the 12th April I am Novello's guest. How does it stand with regard to my lodging in Petersburg, for which my inadequate means will not suffice?—From you, dear friend, I shall expect to hear something definite in London.—However honourable for me were the invitation to Warsaw I could not comply with it now. My return to Weimar is requisite before the end of May, on account of the *Tonkünstler-Versammlung* at Sondershausen.

Heartily and truly yours,

F. LISZT.

ARGENTEAU [LIÉGE], *March 18th*, 1886.

Enclosed are some lines and the photographs that friend Zet wished for.—To write anything further under the photographs for the use of the newspaper I consider quite superfluous. Excess does not suit me at all.—

379. TO THE COUNTESS MERCY-ARGENTEAU.

WESTWOOD HOUSE, SYDENHAM (NEAR LONDON, WHERE EVERYTHING IS DISTANT).

Wednesday, April 14th, 1886.

VERY DEAR PRESIDENT AND BRAVE RUSSOPHILE PRO-PAGANDIST,—

The second performance of the *Elizabeth*, which is fixed for next Saturday, at the *Crystal Palace*, detains me here some days longer than I had anticipated.

From Tuesday next till Easter Tuesday I have asked for the kind hospitality of the Lynens (at Antwerp).

There is still some talk of the *Elizabeth* at the

Trocadéro on the 30th April.   If you were not to be there it would be an affront to your very humble and admiring old servant,

F. LISZT.

This time I shall stay at the Munkacsys' (Avenue Villiers, 53).

(In great haste.)

380. To ALEXANDER RITTER IN MEININGEN.

ANTWERP, April 24th, 1886.

MY VERY DEAR FRIEND,

Heartfelt thanks for the dedication.   Your "*fauler Hans*" has nothing lazy in it.   With its graceful, refined wit it is excellent company for our dear "Barber of Bagdad," which I shall shortly recommend Baron Loën (Weimar) to take up again in conjunction with the "*fauler Hans.*"[1]

Faithfully,
F. LISZT.

In the middle of May I shall be back in Weimar. Give my respectful greetings to your wife.

381. To FRAU AMALIE VON FABRY.

MY DEAR FRIEND,

I wish my rooms in Budapest to remain closed during my absence.[2]   For the rest, His Excellency Minister Trefort must give his own commands.   There is no risk of his meeting with any opposition from my humble self.

---

[1] Ritter's Opera, "*Der faule Hans*" (Lazy Hans).

[2] Many inquisitive people were fond of going and having a look round, so that Liszt was obliged to prohibit it.

I shall not pass this summer much quieter than the winter and the spring. Next week I shall be at the Musical Festival at Sondershausen ; then here again until the 30th June.

My granddaughter, Daniela von Bülow, is to be married on the 3rd July, at Bayreuth, to the highly esteemed Art-historian Thode. After that, I shall stay from the 5th to the 18th July with my dear, excellent friends the Munkacsys, at their castle of Colpach (Luxemburg). I shall be present at the entire cycle of the *Parsifal* and *Tristan* performances at Bayreuth, from the 20th July till the 23rd August.

I am already more than half blind ; perhaps I shall not have to wait long for the rest. . . .

Ever faithfully yours,

F. Liszt.

Weimar, *May 27th*, 1886.

382. To Madame Malwine Tardieu.

Weimar, *May 29th*, 1886.

My sight is going, dear friend, and I can no longer write without difficulty.

Cordial thanks for your letter, and farewell till we meet at Bayreuth, at the performances of *Parsifal* and *Tristan.*

Your very affectionate

F. Liszt.

I shall be at Bayreuth on the 3rd July—the wedding day of my granddaughter Daniela.

From the 4th to the 18th July my excellent friends the Munkacsys will be my hosts at their castle of Colpach (Luxemburg), whence I shall return to Bayreuth, to stay there till the last performance on the 23rd August.

Would you send me Victor Hugo's "*Le théâtre en liberté*"? We will settle our accounts at Bayreuth.

383. To Eduard Reuss.

My dear Friend,

The weakness in my eyes is increasing, and on that account I cannot write to you "*mano propria.*" I wish to bring good luck to *Wilhelm Franz*. Meanwhile I thank you heartily for making me godfather.

In sincere friendship yours most truly,

F. Liszt.

Sondershausen, *June 5th*, 1886.

384. To Frau Reuss-Belce, Opera-singer to the Court of Baden.

My dear Lady,

The thanks which I have just expressed to your husband I double to you, as you have played the principal part in the family-drama of *Wilhelm Franz*.

With the most heartful wishes for the continued prosperity of parents and child I remain

Yours most truly,

F. Liszt.

Sondershausen, *June 5th*, 1886.

385. To Eduard Reuss.

Very dear Friend,

I have just received the enclosed reply from Härtel. Send him, therefore, the score *with the Piano part*, and recommend him to print this *complete* score—not the orchestral score alone—if possible by next

October, that is to say, end of September. Then, for
the present, two copies of the complete score will be
wanted for performance—one for the conductor and one
for the soloist who has so long had to play the Piano
part out of the score, until you, perhaps with little delay,
arrange the orchestral part for a second Piano, and the
Concerto comes out in an edition like the E♭ Concerto.

Yours in all friendship,

F. LISZT.

WEIMAR, *June 22nd*, 1886.

N.B.—On the 1st July I am leaving here for a
couple of months.

386. TO SOPHIE MENTER.

BAYREUTH, *July 3rd*, 1886.

MY VERY DEAR FRIEND,

Tomorrow, after the religious marriage of my
granddaughter Daniela von Bülow to Professor Henry
Thode (Art-historian), I betake myself to my excellent
friends the Munkacsys, *Château Colpach, Grand Duchy
of Luxemburg*.

On the 20th July I shall be back here again for the
first 7-8 performances of the *Festspiel*: * then, alas!
I must put myself under the, to me, very disagreeable
cure at Kissingen, and in September an operation to
the eyes is impending for me with Gräfe at Halle.
For a month past I have been quite unable to read and
almost unable to write, with much labour, a couple of
lines. Two secretaries kindly help me by reading to
me and writing letters at my dictation.

How delightful it would be to me, dear friend, to

* Festival Play.

visit you at your fairy castle of Itter! But I do not see any opportunity of doing so at present.

Perhaps you will come to Bayreuth, where, from the 20th July to the 7th August, will be staying

Your heartily sincere

F. LISZT.

This was the very last letter written by the Master's hand. He returned in bad health from Colpach to Bayreuth. Yet once again he heard *Parsifal* and *Tristan* ;—then he lay down upon his death-bed, and at 11 o'clock on the night of the 31st July his great soul had passed away into everlasting peace.

SUPPLEMENT OF SOME LETTERS RECEIVED DURING THE PRINTING.

---

387. To Hofmarschall Freiherr von Spiegel in Weimar.*

Monsieur le Grand Maréchal,

I am very happy to learn through you that Her Imperial Highness the Grand Duchess has deigned to accept with kindness my *translation* of the beautiful work of Beethoven which I have permitted myself humbly to offer to her. For musicians, the original of this work marks the summit of perfection of the *classical* style (an extremely arbitrary designation, in my opinion) among non-symphonic instrumental compositions. Beethoven—as well as many great geniuses in the history of Art—is like the ancient Janus; one of his two faces is turned towards the past, the other towards the future. The Septet to a certain extent marks the point of intersection, and is thus unreservedly admired both by the devotees of the past and the believers in the future.

On this account I thought there was a suitability in paying my respectful homage to Her Imperial Highness by means of it, until such time as I should be

* Autograph in the Liszt-Museum at Weimar.

allowed to place a longer work at her feet, and one which will more particularly express my personal gratitude.

It is only yesterday that the very flattering lines of Your Excellency have reached me. It is therefore not my fault that I have not sooner replied to the gracious request which you are pleased to make me with reference to my journey to Weimar.

Without any doubt I eagerly accept Your Excellency's invitation for the month of October. Allow me only to beg you to be so good as to let me know whether you consider it will be best for me to arrive at the beginning or end of the month. Not being entirely master of my time, I should be particularly glad to know from you the most favourable week.

I have the honour, Monsieur le Grand Maréchal, to be, with respect, Your Excellency's very humble and obedient servant,

F. Liszt.

Paris, *September 30th*, 1841.

19, Rue Pigalle (Permanent Address).

388. To Eugenio Gomez, Organist of the Cathedral at Seville.*

You have been pleased, my dear Monsieur Gomez, to ask my *perfectly frank* opinion of your *Mélodies harmonisées*, and—quite frankly †—I am much embarrassed by it, for it is in vain I turn them over and over again ; on every side I find only compliments to make you about them. It is true that you could

* Autograph, without address, in the Liszt-Museum in Weimar. The addressee (born 1802) was both pianist and composer.

† Liszt uses the same expression—*tout franc*—in each case.

not doubt their sincerity any more than you could the real merit of your work. It is needless to speak of the modesty of true talent ; this modesty cannot go to the extent of foolishness, and the Artist and supreme Architect of the spheres gives us Himself the example of this legitimate satisfaction which the consciousness of having done *well* brings us, by rejoicing over His work each day of the Creation.

One defect, nevertheless, and a very grave defect, which I have discovered in your *Harmonies* by dint of searching, is, that there are only 12 instead of 24 or 48—as all true lovers will wish. Make haste, my dear Monsieur Gomez, set yourself to work, and repair as quickly as possible this unpardonable defect in your labour ; and, while extending it to the utmost, think sometimes of your most affectionate and devoted servant,

F. Liszt.

389. To Madame (?).*

[Sevilla, *end of December*, 1844.]

You have not told me too much of the wonders of Seville, Madame, and, nevertheless, you could hardly have told me beforehand of that which I have found the most charming—the letter from Mademoiselle Caroline. Thanks to her charming lines, I found myself in the best possible frame of mind for the enjoyment of all imaginable *chefs d'œuvre*, and I could not have been more disposed to admiration and wonderment !

* Autograph, without address, date, and conclusion, in the Liszt-Museum at Weimar.

During the ten days which I have just spent in Seville I have not allowed a single day to pass without going to pay my very humble court to the cathedral, that epic of granite, that architectural Symphony whose eternal harmonies vibrate in infinity !—

One cannot use any set phrases about such a monument. The best thing to do would be to kneel there with the faith of the charcoal-burner (if one could do so), or to soar in thought the length of these arches and vaulted roofs, for which it seems that there is even now "*no longer time*" !—As for me, not feeling myself enough of the charcoal-burner or of the eagle, I am constrained to stand with my nose in the air and mouth open. Nevertheless my prayer sometimes climbs up like useless ivy, lovingly embracing those knotted shafts which defy all the storms of the genius of Christianity.

Whatever you may think of my enthusiasm for *your* cathedral, it is a fact that I have been entirely absorbed by it during the ten days I have spent in Seville ; so much so, that it was only on the evening before my departure that I could prevail on myself to visit the Alcazar.

In truth, if one might wish for the re-introduction of the bastinado, it would be to apply it exclusively to those malicious wretches who have dared to besmear so many ravishing flights of fancy, so many fairy-like vagaries, with lime and plaster.

What adorable enchantment and what hideous devastation !

The heart expands—and then contracts at every step. Little do I care for the gardens (which, by the way, slightly resemble the ornamental gardens of a priest); little do I care even for the baths of Maria Padilla, which, in fact, have slightly the effect of an alkaline ; but what outlines, what harmonious profusion in these lines, what incredible voluptuousness in all this ornamentation ! Would that I could send them you in this envelope, such as I have felt and devoured them with my eyes !

Here are, indeed, many *marks of admiration*, and you will certainly smile at me, will you not, Madame ? But what can I do ? And how, after that, can I speak to you of myself and my paltry individuality ?

390. To Madame (?).*

[*Probably beginning of* 1845.]

What are your travelling plans for this winter, Madame ? Mine are quite unsettled. I did not succeed in leaving Spain, and the fact is that, being well, there is no sense in searching for better elsewhere. The only thing that provokes me is the necessity in which I am placed of having to give up the rest of my duties at Weymar for this winter. But I shall try to take a brilliant revenge in the course of this very year.

In spite of our agreement I have not sent you the *bulletin* of my peaceful victories in the arena of Madrid [1] (and elsewhere), because you know that there are certain things which are moreover very simple, but

---

* Autograph sketch of a letter, without address, date, and conclusion, in the Liszt-Museum at Weimar.

[1] Liszt gave concerts in the Teatro del Circo in Madrid from October till December 1844.

which I cannot do. More than once, nevertheless, I have regretted you in your founder's *loge*—the first in front—and I have turned to that side in expectancy of the inciting bravos which used to begin before all the others at the brilliant passages!

La Melinetti will doubtless have given you my ancient news from Pau! Poor woman, with her luxury of a husband (a superfluity which was not in the least a necessary thing for her), and her little impulsive ways, . . . she has really promised me to be at length reasonable, steady, and deliberate. I hope she will keep her word. With a little wit, behaviour, and tact, she could make herself a very good position in Pau. Mme. d'Artigaux,[1] who is the most ideally good woman I know, takes a real interest in her. Several other people sincerely wish her well—it only depends on herself to take a good position there—but unfortunately she is too outspoken, and inclined to play tricks.

What do you know of the elegiac and seraphic Chopin? I wrote a few lines from Pau to Mme. Sand, but my letter hardly asked for a reply, and she has, moreover, better things to do.

391. To Madame (?) in Milan.*

[1846.]

I am at your feet, Madame, and kiss your hands —but it is impossible not to quarrel with you, and that

[1] When unmarried, as Countess Caroline St. Criq, sixteen years before this time, she had possessed Liszt's whole heart, while hers belonged to him. But the command of her father, Minister St. Criq, separated their ways, because he—was only an artist. Liszt thought of her in his last Will, but she left this world before him, at the beginning of the seventies.

* Autograph in the Liszt-Museum in Weimar.

seriously, over the last lines of your letter! Through
what absence of mind, let me ask you, could you have
written to me, "I do not speak to you of our affairs
because *I remember* that your sympathies are not with
us"? Frankly, if you were to tell me that I have
never played any but false notes on the piano, and that
my calling was that of a retail grocer, this opinion
would offer, to my thinking, a greater degree of proba-
bility. Evidently, in my double character of citizen
and musician, I am not even to exonerate myself from
the fault you [ascribe] to me. Suffer me then not to
dwell longer upon it, and deign for the future to spare
me the pain which all suspicion of this kind would
cause me.

Otherwise your letter was a great joy to me; first,
as coming from you; and then, as announcing the
realization of a wish, an idea, to the postponement of
which I had resigned myself as well as I could, but
which I had hardly relinquished. Your Sardanapalus
comes in the nick of time, just as the 2000 francs will
be opportune to the poet. The mode of payment is
very simple. Belloni's sister being in Milan, she will
have the honour of calling upon you, and *in return for*
the restoration of the manuscript she will discharge the
total of my debt, viz., two thousand francs. Allow me
only a last request, which is that you will kindly take
the trouble to read the whole libretto through again,
and, if it should be expedient, to communicate to the
poet direct any observations which you consider
necessary. The notes and commentaries which you
have added on the margin of Rotondi's libretto (which
I keep very carefully) showed such a complete *virtuosity*

in this style of subject that one could not possibly do better than submit with confidence to your decision.[1]—

Thanks to God, and to this good star which has let me live many years pretty uprightly, "as if I were immortal," as you put it, behold me now since the end of September in last year entirely out of the circle of concerts—and it does not seem likely that I shall soon return to this drudgery.—I shall remain in Weymar till the 15th August; then I shall go and make a tour in the Crimea by way of the Danube, probably returning by Constantinople if I can manage it.—

Next spring Sardanapalus will be ready,—and I shall perhaps have to speak to you about another matter at the same time, a matter about which it is worth while speaking to you.—

Be good enough to acknowledge the receipt of these lines; but pray spare me abuse, and be pleased to do me the honour of believing without reserve or restriction in the upright sincerity of my *sympathies*, and in my frank and firm good-will to transform them into acts or deeds, according to circumstances, in the degree of which I am capable.

Yours ever, with admiration and friendship,

F. Liszt.

392. To Frau Charlotte Moscheles (?).*

I am most grateful to you, Madame, for wishing to keep me in remembrance on the occasion of the

[1] The plan of composing an opera "Sardanapalus" occupied Liszt for years.

* Draft of an undirected autograph letter in the Liszt-Museum at Weimar.—Presumably written to the wife of the distinguished piano-virtuoso and teacher Ignaz Moscheles.

publication of the Album of Workers, and I hasten to reply as quickly and as well as I can.

I must, nevertheless, confess to you in all sincerity that I am a little embarrassed as to the choice to be made among the number of useless and *unusable* manuscripts which I should be charmed to put at your kind disposal. After the *Arbeiter Chor* [workman's chorus] and the *Arbeiter Marsch* [workman's march] with which I have just gratified two Albums in Vienna, your gracious letter comes as a surprise rather short of *apropos*. How *malapropos*, is it not? But let us see how to remedy this.—

I thought first of a *Marche funèbre* for the use of the bankers; then of an *Elégie* dedicated to the idle; next of *Jérémiades Omnibus* [lamentations for all];— but nothing of that sort quite satisfies me.

In default of perfection, permit me to be satisfied with the relative best (which will be, it seems to me, a better choice): a Paraphrase—charitably adapted to the fingers of charitable pianists who will have the charity to buy and to play it—of Rossini's " *Charité*," which I shall have the honour of sending to you through Mr. Kistner early in July. An old saying of a very old Father of the Church would, if needful, justify this choice. " In things necessary, *Unity*; in matters doubtful, *Liberty*; in all things, *Charity*! "—

Will you have the goodness, Madame, to remember me very kindly to my excellent master and friend, Moscheles? and accept again, I beg you, the expression of my respect, and of my most affectionate sentiments.

F. Liszt.

Weymar, *June 22nd*, 1848.

393. To Heinrich Wilhelm Ernst.*

May 30th, 1849.

Dear Friend,

Weymar has not forgotten you, and I hope soon to be able, after the return of the Hereditary Prince whom we expect for the day of his *fête*, by the 24th of May at the very latest, to forward to you the token of the distinguished remembrance in which you are held. It pleases me to think that it will be agreeable to you, and that it will tend to attach you more in the sequel to people worthy to appreciate you.

I should have desired to tell you sooner of this, but the inevitable delays in present circumstances postpone more than one wish.

After the deplorable days in Dresden Wagner came here, and only departed again in order to escape from a warrant (*lettre de cachet*) with which the Saxon government is pursuing him. I hope that at the present moment he will have arrived safe and well in Paris, where his career of dramatic composer cannot fail to be extended, and in grand proportions. He is a man of evident genius, who must of necessity obtrude himself on the general admiration, and hold a high place in contemporary art. I regret that you have not had the opportunity of hearing his *Tannhäuser*, which is for me the most lyric of dramas, the most remarkable, the most harmonious, the most complete, the most original and *selbstwürdig* (the most worthy of its country), both in foundation and form, that Germany has pro-

* Portions of this, as of the previous letter, were printed in the "Voltaire."—Addressee the famous violin virtuoso and composer (1814—1865).

duced since Weber.   Belloni has, I believe, written to you on the subject of Wagner, to ask for information as to the actual state of the English Opera in London.

I make no doubt that if it were possible for Wagner to obtain from the directors a tour of performances in the course of the year for a new work (*Lohengrin*, the subject of which, having reference to the Knights of the Round Table who went to search for the Holy Grail, is of the most poetic interest) he would make a great sensation and large receipts by it.   As soon as he tells me the news of his arrival in Paris, allow me to induce him to write to you direct if his plans do not change in this matter.

394. To Joseph Dessauer.*

[Probably at the beginning of the fifties.]

Heartiest thanks for your Songs.   I rejoice that you consider me worthy of a dedication, and I promise you that if we meet again I will sing you the songs by heart.   Perhaps you will bring me again into such a mood for songs as will impel me to write something of that sort.   My earlier songs are mostly too ultra sentimental, and frequently too full in the accompaniment.

395. Testimonial for Joachim Raff.†

[Probably at the beginning of the fifties.]

The talents of M. Raff as composer and musician are a fact so evident and certain, his recent orchestral

---

* Draft of an autograph letter, without address, date, and conclusion, in the Liszt-Museum at Weimar.

† Draft of an autograph letter, without address and date, in the Liszt-Museum at Weimar.

compositions as well as his works for voice and piano furnish such forcible proofs of it, that I consider it superfluous to add to this evidence and to certify it further.

Having had more opportunity than others, during the few years of our intercourse, of appreciating his capacities (notably at the time of the Musical Festival at Bonn for the inauguration of Beethoven's monument in 1845,—and of those to Herder and Goethe at Weymar in 1850, etc.), knowing thoroughly both the score of his four-act Opera *King Alfred*, given many times with great success in Weymar under the author's conductorship, as well as many of his manuscript works, which I sincerely esteem, I shall always make it my duty seriously to recommend M. Raff to those of the Musical Institutes which attach a value to the possession of an intelligent director and one well acquainted with the exigencies and the progress of the art.

F. Liszt.

396. To Dr. Eduard Hanslick in Vienna.[1]

Sir,

The manner in which you have given an account in the *Presse* of the two concerts of Sunday and Monday, corresponds entirely with the opinion which I had of you—and you have proved yourself on this

---

[1] The renowned musical author and critic (born in Prague in 1825), professor of the history of music in the University of Vienna. —The letter refers to the Mozart Jubilee concert conducted by Liszt in Vienna, and to Hanslick's critique, in which he censured the want of courtesy with which Liszt, who had been invited to conduct this concert, was treated by the committee and the public.

occasion, according to your custom, an eminent critic and a perfect *gentleman*.*

Permit me to offer you my sincere thanks for the part you have been pleased to devote to me, and to hope that the coming years, in bringing us more together, will better enable me to prove the sincere sentiments of esteem and distinguished regard, the assurance of which I beg you to accept.

F. LISZT.

January 31st, 1856.

397. To the Austrian Minister of the Interior, Freiherr von Bach.†

YOUR EXCELLENCY,

The interest and protection which your Excellency extends to the spiritual interests of the empire permit me to bring forward the wish and the petition that the Mass which I composed by order of His Eminence the Prince Primate of Hungary for the Dedication-Festival of the Basilica at Gran, and performed there on the 31st August, may be printed and published in full score and piano score by the Royal Imperial State printing-press at the cost of the State.

Without improperly praising my own composition I venture humbly to express the confidence that the *Catholic* significance and spirit which form its ground-work and supplement its modest porportions would gradually be more propagated and comprehended by

---

* This word is in English in Liszt's letter.

† Autograph sketch of a letter in the Liszt-Museum at Weimar. The Gran Mass was in fact engraved and published by the State printing-press at Vienna.

the publication of the work, so that I might hope to have furnished a not unworthy contribution to Christian Art as well as to the great Church and Country's Festival of the 31st August.

In the expectation that my request will meet with that assisting favour which is indispensable to earnest and honest artistic effort, I have the honour to remain most obediently

Your Excellency's most humble and devoted servant,

F. LISZT.

VIENNA, *September 18th,* 1856.

398. To (?) IN LEIPZIG.*

[*Spring,* 1859.]

DEAR FRIEND,

At the same time with your letter I received from Brendel fuller information about the Leipzig preliminaries, to which he will also receive a fuller reply.

I am not of opinion that the Orchestral concert is to be given up immediately on account of the negative decision of Rietz. Very possibly *David* will undertake to conduct it, and I advise Brendel to come to a good understanding with him about it. On the other hand it might be expected, in a case of necessity, that the Weimar and Sondershausen orchestras would unite to carry out the *programme.* But this latter must be as strictly adhered to as was formerly determined, and

* Draft of an autograph letter, without address, date, and conclusion, in the Liszt-Museum at Weimar.—The contents refer to the Orchestral Concert of the *Tonkünstler-Versammlung,* planned and carried out at Leipzig in the beginning of June, 1859.

not lose its exclusive character as "*compositions* by *collaborators of the newspaper only*"—Schumann, Berlioz, Wagner, R. Franz, and lastly my humble self. I cannot therefore in any respect agree to the concession enjoined by Brendel, of admitting works of Haydn, Mozart, Beethoven, etc., nor do I see the motive of it. As far as the *musical* is concerned, I consider it impossible to give such an exceedingly rich programme on *one evening* without stupifying the public; that would go beyond the ill-famed London concerts which last six hours, not to speak of the fact that we should have to put the recognised classics far too much in the shade !—But, above all, such an over-loaded programme is thoroughly unsuitable to the Jubilee-celebration of the *Neue Zeitschrift*, which on this occasion [ought] especially to emphasize its just claims and the progress in Art which it aims at and supports. On this account it is necessary to adhere to the limits of the programme originally agreed upon.

Finally, in case insurmountable hindrances should arise to prevent the carrying out of this same, I have no inclination to substitute for the *Orchestral-concert one for Chamber-music*. But the word "*Evening entertainment*" must, as is self-evident, be entirely dispensed with. Our business is to raise, to educate the audience, not to amuse them ; and if indeed, as Goethe very pertinently says, " deep and earnest thinkers are in a bad position as regards the public," we will therefore not so much the less, but so much the more earnestly maintain this position. Meanwhile it is advisable to advertise the first evening's musical performance by the expression *Concert in the Gewandhaus*, until we have quite decided whether it shall be a *concert* with orchestra, or only with chamber-music.[1]

N.B.—Please *not to communicate* these remarks to *any one except perhaps Brendel*, as *the very outspoken opinions herein* about the Concert-programme must *absolutely be kept secret.*

399. To Dr. Eduard Hanslick.[2]

Sir,

Experience having taught me to regard as a fate attached to my name the impossibility of publishing anything which does not instantly gather round it opinions as contrary as they are forcibly enunciated, I am, although quite accustomed to these little storms, very sensitive to the kindly judgment of those who, not letting themselves be influenced by this transitory impulse, desire to take into consideration what I have written, with sobriety and composure, just as you have done in your account of my book " Des Bohémiens."— I am above all extremely obliged to you for having admitted that, if the requirements of my subject, and the opinion which after some twenty years of reflection I have formed of Bohemian music, compel me to attribute to a nomad people an art thoroughly imbued with a poetry which could only have been developed in a wandering nation, I have none the less endeavoured to bring into prominence everything for which this art is indebted to the comprehension and taste which the

---

[1] An orchestral concert took place in the theatre, when compositions by Mendelssohn, Schubert, and Chopin were, nevertheless, included among the others.

[2] The letter refers to Hanslick's notice of Liszt's book " Les Bohémiens et leur musique," in the Vienna *Presse* (the old one).

Hungarians have always had for the music of Bohemia. I desire in no way to diminish the merit of the works, while at the same time I see the impossibility of considering as emanating from them the expression of sentiments which could not in their nature belong to them, however sympathetically they were associated therewith. —

Still, the point which I notice first, in consequence of the very violent and premature attacks of which I have been the object, is not the one which I regard as the most important in my volume. As a matter of fact it would signify little to me as *artist* to know whether this music is originally from India or Tartary. That which has appeared to me worthy the study of an artist is this music itself, its meaning, and the feelings it is destined to reproduce.—It is in trying clearly to account for these latter that I have only found it possible to connect them with people placed in the exceptional conditions of the Bohemians; and it is through asking myself what the poetry of this wandering life would be (a question so often raised), that I have become convinced that it must be identical with that which breathes in the Art of the Bohemians. This identity once made evident to my mind, I have naturally sought to make it felt by and evident to my readers. The better to succeed in this I have corroborated my opinion by grouping together as a sort of complement various suppositions about the question of these sources. But the scientific side of this question has never been, in my eyes, anything but very accessory; I should probably not have taken up the pen to discuss it. If I have raised it, that has been the consequence, not the aim of my work. Artist, and poet if you like, I am only interested in seeing and describing the poetical and psychological side of my thesis. I have sought in speech the power of depicting, with less fire and allurement possibly, but with more precision than music has done, some impressions which are not derived from science or polemics—which come from the heart and appeal to the imagination.

Poetical and descriptive prose being little used in Germany, I can easily conceive that, on the announcement of the title of my book, a set of lectures, rather than a kind of poem in prose, will be expected. I own that I would never have attempted to lecture on a subject the materials of which did not appear to me sufficient for this purpose. How small a number of people, moreover, would have been interested in learning the *little* which it would be allowable to *affirm* in this case? Whilst the expression of the innermost and deep feelings, whatever they be, from the moment that they have been powerful enough to inspire an art, is never entirely unattractive, even to the more extended circle which includes not alone musicians, but all those who feel and wish to understand music.

Thanking you once more, Sir, for the perfect impartiality and clearness with which you have stated and criticised the compilation of my book, I beg you to accept this expression of my complete esteem and distinguished consideration.

F. LISZT.

September 24th, 1859.

INDEX OF NAMES.

The dark figures indicate the addressee of a letter, the light figures merely the mention of a name ; S. = Supplement.

FINIS.